SAINT FRANCIS OF ASSISI

A BIOGRAPHY

BY

JOHANNES JÖRGENSEN

TRANSLATED FROM THE DANISH WITH THE AUTHOR'S SANCTION
BY
T. O'CONOR SLOANE, Ph.D., LL.D.

TO
MY CHILDREN

TO
MY CHILDREN

as Vicar-General of the Order, made possible for me my Pilgrimage in 1903 through Franciscan Italy — next the historian of the Franciscan Order, Rev. Leonard Lemmens, and the Guardians and Fathers in the different convents which I visited on the above-named journey, especially Rev. Pacifico in Greccio, Rev. Giovanni da Greccio in Fonte Colombo, Rev. Teodoro da Carpineto in the convent of La Foresta, Rev. Vincenzo Stefano Jacopi in Cortona, Rev. Saturnino da Caprese, and Rev. Samuel Charon de Guersac at La Verna. I give hearty thanks again to Rev. Don Severino, pastor in Poggio Bustone, and to the learned engineer, Albert Provaroni, of the same place, to the Capuchins in Celle and to the Redemptorists in Cortona, under whose hospitable roof I found a refuge in the days I passed in the city of St. Margaret. With special recognition I give my thanks to the Brothers Matteuci, who gave me a home in Poggio Bustone and helped me in my work. I only wish that I could extend this list enough to include even a part of all who showed me friendship and hospitality in my wanderings. For those who know Italian people this seems very natural.

But the present book might never have been completed if I had not found a place of refuge in the Franciscan convent at Frauenberg, where next door to my room I had a rich library of Franciscan literature from the earliest to the most recent time. The second half (third and fourth books with the Conclusion of the Appendix) were written there. Should my work seem to have any worth, a due portion of the honor for its existence is due to Rev. Maximilian Brandys, Provincial of the Franciscan province of Thuringia, to which Frauenberg belongs, to Rev. Pacificus Wehner (now in Gorheim by Sigmaringen), as well as to the Guardian of Frauenberg, Rev. Saturnin Goer, who with such great hospitality and affection regarded me for six weeks as a member of his great convent family. I also thank the willing and friendly Fathers who tried to help in every way, and especially must I thank my tireless and devoted friend, Rev. Michael Bihl, by whose ever ready assistance so many stones were removed from my road. I shall never forget the summer evenings in the convent gardens of Frauenberg, when we walked up and down the long walk, as the sun, large and red, sank behind the trees, and I told him of my day's work and sought Pater Michael's practical opinion, sometimes on one, sometimes on another, difficult point.

And thus I take leave of this work which has so long been the centre of my labor and research. To write about St. Francis of Assisi should have been his own affair, for what does he himself say in the *Speculum perfectionis?* "The Emperor Charlemagne, Roland, Holger, and all the other Knights of the Round Table fought the heathen unto death and won the victory over them, and at the end became themselves holy martyrs and died in the battle for the faith of Christ. But now there are many who, by simply telling of their actions, hope to win honor and fame from mankind. Also there are now many who, by simply preaching on what the saints have done, wish to win honor and fame."

Deep and wise, therefore, was the saying of Francis: "Man has as much of knowledge as he executes," *tantum homo habet de scientia, quantum operatur.* The ultimate measure of wisdom is to serve and to properly conduct one's life; worth is only attained by putting into practice. Therefore there is a practical and moral design behind all the literary diligence of the old authors of legends. Thus also a modern biographer of St. Francis, who would really be inspired by the spirit of St. Francis of Assisi, like the old convent-brother writers, must utter the words: *Fac secundum exemplar.* "Learn from Francis, that ideals ought to be put into practice!"

J. J.

FRAUENBERG, Feast of St. Clara of Assisi, 1906.

CONTENTS

BOOK ONE

FRANCIS THE CHURCH BUILDER

CHAPTER		PAGE
I.	Francis' Sickness. 1204. Re-convalescence. The Vanity of All Things	3
II.	Francis' Ancestry. Birth, 1182. Name. Early youth. *La Gaya Sciensa*. Generosity to his friends and to the poor . . .	8
III.	Local History. War between Assisi and Perugia. Francis is taken prisoner at Ponte San Giovanni and is a prisoner 1202–1203	18
IV.	State of the Times. War between Emperor and Pope. Francis wants to enlist under Walter of Brienne, 1205. The Vision in Foligno. Francis returns home. New festivities. Francis thinks of taking a Bride	21
V.	Francis' frequent prayers in a cave outside the City. Goes to Rome and begs at the door of St. Peter's. Begins to take care of the Lepers	27
VI.	Francis prays in San Damiano. "Go hence and build up My House, for it is falling down!" Francis retires to a cave near San Damiano, 1207	36
VII.	Francis imprisoned by his Father is released by his Mother. He gives his clothes back to his Father and goes out into the world, April, 1207, as the Herald of God. He goes to Gubbio, takes care of the Lepers, returns to Assisi, begs from door to door. He rebuilds the churches of S. Damiano, S. Pietro, and Portiuncula. On February 24, 1209, he hears the priest in Portiuncula read Matth. x. 7–13, and decides to live by those Words.	43

BOOK TWO

FRANCIS THE EVANGELIST

I.	Francis preaches in Assisi. The first Disciples. Bernard of Quintavalle, Pietro dei Cattani, Giles. The first Mission Journeys. Bernard and Giles in Florence, Francis in Rieti. He hears in Poggio Bustone that his sins are forgiven	61

CONTENTS

II. The Shed at Rivo Torto. Francis writes a *forma vitæ* and goes, 1210, to Rome with eleven Brothers to have it ratified by Innocent III. He only obtains a verbal approval 76

III. Temptations to become a Hermit. The twelfth Disciple: the Priest, Silvester. New Missionary Activity. Preaching in the Cathedral of Assisi. Peace between the upper and lower classes in Assisi concluded, 1210. The Friars' life in Congregation. They leave Rivo Torto 96

IV. The Portiuncula Chapel. New disciples: Rufino, Masseo, Leo, Juniper. Brother Giles' Way of Life. Brother Masseo. Brother Rufino. Brother Juniper. Brother John the Simple. Brother Leo. Francis and Leo say the Breviary together. The Perfect Joy 105

V. St. Clara. Her family. Training. Hears Francis preach in Lent, 1212, in S. Giorgio's Church in Assisi. Leaves her home March 18, 1212, and takes convent vows in Portiuncula. Francis secures a shelter for her and the sisters, who have joined her in S. Damiano. She writes a *forma vivendi* for them. Clara's life. Her feast with Francis. She holds the Saracens back from S. Damiano. Her grief over Francis' death. Her contest for the right to be poor. She writes a Rule for her Sisters and dies, two days after getting it approved by Innocent IV, August 11, 1253 122

BOOK THREE
GOD'S SINGER

I. The Italian Mission of 1211–1212. Cortona, Arezzo, Florence. John Parenti. Francis tries to evade the homage of the people. Lent of 1211 on Lake Thrasimene, winter of same year in Hermitage of Sarteano. What is God's will? Francis asks the advice of Clara and Silvester, gets the answer that his call is to preach. He preaches to the birds 145

II. Francis wants to preach to the Heathen. He goes to Rome, meets Jacopa de Settesoli. On the way to the Holy Land is wrecked on the coast of Slavonia and goes thence as a stowaway to Ancona. In S. Severino converts the "Verse King," Guglielmo Divino. Francis' relations to the learned, to thieves, and robbers. He preaches, May 8, 1213, in Monte Feltro, converts Count Orlando dei Cattani and receives Mount Alverna as a gift. In the winter of 1213–1214 he visits Spain and is present at the Fourth Lateran Council. Jacques de Vitry's picture of the Order in 1216 151

CONTENTS

III. The Portiuncula Indulgence 166

IV. Constitution of the Franciscan Order. The Chapter-Assemblies. Francis' Admonitions at them.' The movement grows. Francis seeks help to direct it 175

V. Cardinal Hugolin. Pentecost Chapter of 1217. Missions are sent beyond the frontiers of Italy. Francis decides to go to France. On his way there visits Hugolin in Florence and is deterred from going. Hugolin organizes the Clares. The development of the Order of Clares up to 1253 181

VI. Missions in France, Germany, and Hungary not successful. Francis goes in the winter of 1217–1218 with Hugolin to Rome and has an audience with Honorius III. He meets St. Dominic. At the Pentecost Chapter of 1218 Hugolin is present for the first time as Protector of the Order. New missionaries sent out May 26, 1219. Honorius issues his Letters of Protection for the missionaries, June 11, 1219. Missions in Tunis and in Morocco. The first five martyrs 192

VII. Francis and Pietro dei Cattani start for the Holy Land, June 24, 1219, preach among the Crusaders in Egypt, and before the Sultan Malek el Kamel. Francis' two vicars, Gregory of Naples and Matthew of Narni, hold a Chapter, at which they try to change the Rule of the Order. Brother Stephen brings this news to Francis, and Francis returns. He goes at once to Rome and calls a Chapter for Pentecost, 1221. Honorius, in accordance with Francis, ordains a novitiate of the Order, September 22, 1220. Francis resigns his leadership and names Pietro dei Cattani as his vicar and after him Elias of Cortona. "The Chapter of Mats." The new German Mission. Anthony of Padua 202

VIII. Francis and Caesar of Speier work on a new Rule of the Order. Development of the Rule. Francis' *Admonitiones*. Rule for hermitages. Rule for Portiuncula. The original Rule and the "Rule of 1221" 213

IX. Disputes about the final Rule from May 30, 1221, to November 29, 1223. Opposition to Francis. Peter Stacia. Francis' contest for evangelical simplicity and evangelical poverty. Francis and Anthony of Padua. Francis in Bologna August, 15, 1222 226

X. The new movement and the older Franciscans. Brother Giles. The English Franciscans. The "Third Order." Contest between the Brothers of Penance and the authorities 236

CONTENTS

XI. Co-operation of Francis and Hugolin, and of Francis and Elias of Cortona. Francis' letter to Elias. The Rule is perfected. Francis at Fonte Colombo. The final Rule. 247

XII. Honorius approves the Rule, 1223. Francis and "Brother Jacoba." The Lambs and Francis. Francis with Cardinal Leo. He leaves Rome, celebrates Christmas, 1223, in Greccio. The first Christmas Crib 257

BOOK FOUR

FRANCIS THE HERMIT

I. Francis' Sickness. His literary activity. His five Circulars. Letter to Brother Leo 265

II. Francis Preaches by his example. His truthfulness. Zeal for Poverty. His Alms. Easter in Greccio. Francis and the Demons 273

III. Francis and his intimates. Brother Rufino's temptation. "The ideal Friar Minor." The Spanish Franciscans. Francis reads in the hearts of men. Francis and obedience. Francis and prayer. The Evangelic Joy. Francis' ecstasy 280

IV. Francis goes in the summer of 1224 to Mount Alverna. Francis and Brother Leo. The Stigmatization, September 14, 1224 . 291

V. Francis' Song of Praise in thanks for the Stigmatization. The Blessing for Brother Leo. He leaves Mount Alverna, passes through Borgo S. Sepolcro and Città di Castello to Portiuncula. Begins again to take care of the Lepers 301

VI. Francis' Blindness. Francis at San Damiano in the Summer of 1225. His love of nature. He composes the Sun Song . . 308

VII. Francis goes to Rieti. The vineyard in S. Fabiano. An angel plays for him at night in Rieti. He is treated by physicians for his eyes, goes to Siena, writes his first Testament to the Brothers. Brother Elias takes him to Celle, thence to Assisi. He lies sick in the Bishop's residence, makes peace between the Bishop and the Podestà. He sends his farewell to St. Clara, dictates his Testament. He lets himself be taken down to Portiuncula, blessing Assisi on the way. In Portiuncula he receives a visit from Jacopa de Settesoli, breaks bread with the Brothers. He dies October 3, 1226 316

VIII. The Funeral Procession. Jacopa de Settesoli 334

CONTENTS

APPENDIX

AUTHORITIES FOR THE BIOGRAPHY OF ST. FRANCIS OF ASSISI

I. His Writings 340
    Religious Poems 341
    Prose Writings 349

II. Biographers 351
    1. Thomas of Celano Group 352
    2. Brother Leo Group 356
        a. *Legenda trium sociorum* 356
        b. *Anonymus Perusinus* 367
        c. Thomas of Celano's *Vita secunda* 368
    3. St. Bonaventure Group 378
    4. Speculum Group 382
        a. *Speculum perfectionis* 384
        b. *Legenda antiqua* 391
        c. *Actus* (*Fioretti*) 393

III. Other Sources 395
        a. Histories of the Order 395
        b. Authorities outside of the Order 400
        c. Modern Works 401

INDEX 411

ILLUSTRATIONS

ST. FRANCIS OF ASSISI . . . . *Frontispiece*
    From the painting by Spagnoletto in the Palazzo Reale, Genoa.

CONTEMPORARY PORTRAIT OF ST. FRANCIS OF ASSISI AT
THE SACRO SPECO, SUBIACO . . . . *Facing page* 62
    (*From a photograph kindly lent by Perrin et Cie, Paris.*)

ST. CLARA OF ASSISI AND SCENES FROM HER LIFE . . . " " 122
    Attributed to Cimabue. Fresco in Church of Santa Chiara, Assisi.

ST. FRANCIS OF ASSISI . . . . " " 298
    From the fresco, attributed to Cimabue, at Assisi.

THE BLESSING OF BROTHER LEO . . . . " " 346
    Autograph of St. Francis.

BOOK ONE
FRANCIS THE CHURCH BUILDER

> Nunc latebat in eremis, nunc ecclesiarum reparationibus insistebat devotus.
>
> *Now he hid himself in hermitages, now he piously devoted himself to the restoration of churches.*
>
> ST. ANTONINUS OF FLORENCE

SAINT FRANCIS OF ASSISI

CHAPTER I

THE CONVALESCENT

THERE awoke one morning in Assisi a young man who was just recovering from a severe illness. It was seven hundred years ago. The hour was an early one. The window blinds were not yet opened. Out of doors the day's business was in full blast; the bells for mass had long ago rung out from St. Maria del Vescovado, which lay almost under the windows. The strong morning light streamed in through the crack where the window blinds met.

The young man knew it all so well — one morning after another the long weeks of his convalescence had passed thus. Soon his mother would come in and would draw the shutters aside, and the light would enter in dazzling brightness. Then he would get his morning draught, and his bed would be made over; he used to lie on one side of the wide bed while the other was made up for him. And so he would lie there, tired, but at peace, and look out on the blue cloudless autumn sky, listening to the splashing on the stones of the street as the people of the neighborhood threw their waste water out of the windows. As the forenoon advanced the rays of the sun began to come in — first along the high wall of the window alcove — then right across the brick floor of the room, and when they approached the bed, it was time to take the midday meal. After midday the blinds were again closed, and he took his siesta in the quiet comfortable obscurity of the room. Then he awoke and the blinds were again thrown open to admit the light; the sun had left the window — but if he raised himself up in the bed, he could see the mountains under a blue veil on the other side of the plain, and soon the crimson evening red of the late autumn day burned in the western sky. As the darkness quickly fell, he heard the noise of sheep, which were driven bleating into the stable, and of peasants and peasant girls, who sang on their way home from the fields. They were the wonderful heart-gripping folk-songs of Umbria which the invalid heard — the songs which even to-day are in the people's mouths and whose slow, wonderfully melancholy tones fill the soul with sadness till it is ready to burst with helpless longing and melancholy.

At last the songs ceased and it was night. Over the distant mountains gleamed a single bright star. When that showed itself, it was time to close the shutters and to light the night-lamp — the lamp which in the long nights of fever had constantly burned through the long hours of his uneasy dreams.

To-day there was to be a change — to-day at last he was to have permission to leave his bed. How glad he was to go into the other rooms, to see and touch all the things he had so long missed, and had been so near losing for ever. He must even venture down into the business offices — see the people come and do business, see the clerks measure the good Tuscan cloth with their yardsticks, and draw in the bright ringing coins.

Just as the young man was busy with these dreams the door opened. As on every morning of his illness, it was his mother who entered. As she threw the shutters aside he saw that she carried, as she brought his morning meal, a suit of man's clothes over her arm.

"I have had a new suit of clothes made for you, my Francis," said she as she laid them down at the foot of the bed.

And as he finished his meal she sat down by the window while he dressed himself.

"What a lovely morning it is," said she, almost as if she were talking to herself. "How brightly the sun shines! I see all the houses over in Bettona so clearly, although there is the whole extent of the broad plain between us, and out in the middle of the green vineyards, Isola Romanesca lies like an island in a lake. And smoke is rising straight up from all the chimneys — as if from a censer in a church. Ah, it seems to me, my Francis, that on such a morning as this, heaven and earth are as beautiful as a church on a feast-day, and that all creatures praise, love and thank God."

To these words Francis gave no answer but silence.

But a moment later he broke out, as he ceased his dressing: "How weak I am!"

His mother changed the current of her remarks and their tone.

"It is always so, when one has been sick," she said brightly. "As long as you lie in bed you think that you can do anything, but as soon as you get your feet from under the covers you find that it is different. I know this from my own experience, and therefore I had the foresight to bring a stick for you."

And she went to the door and brought in a beautiful polished stick with an ivory handle. Soon after the mother and son together left the sick-room.

. . . .

Some time passed before Francis could venture to go out of his home alone. He and his mother had visited all the rooms. They had been down in the shop, where the clerks had greeted them with a hearty and delighted "Good morning, Madonna Pica! Good morning and welcome back, Signorino Francesco!" But Francis had to go further than through rooms and shop, further than through the house — he must go out and greet the fields and vineyards, greet the open heaven and look far over the wide fertile plain.

And now he stood outside the city gate on the road which goes to Foligno along the foot of Monte Subasio. Here he stood, supported by his stick, and looked out. Directly in front of him was a vineyard; the vines were festooned from tree to tree; heavy blue bunches hung under the broad leaves; soon it will be the grape harvest and the beautiful time of wine-pressing. Further down the slope were the olive groves that extended over the plain and covered it with a silver-grey veil. Here and there appeared the white buildings and farmhouses under a veil of mist which now towards midday began to rise out of the earth — the most distant buildings seemed hardly larger than little white stones.

Francis saw it all, yet not as he should have seen it. That excess of delight, with which the sight of the landscape's bright colors and of the mountain's fine outline against the clear sky formerly affected him, was missing. It was as if the heart which formerly had beaten so young and strongly in his breast had suddenly grown old — it seemed to him as if he never again could enjoy anything. He felt too hot in the sun, and retreated to the shadow of a wall. His knees were too weak to let him go down the hill; he also was hungry and caught himself dreaming of a good dinner and of a glass of wine. And like a shudder the sensation went through him that his youth was gone — that the things which he had believed would constantly give him peace would now give him no joy — that all that he had thought to be a treasure which never could be taken from him: the sunshine, the blue heaven, the green fields — all that he in his convalescence's weary days had so bitterly longed for like an exiled king for his kingdom — that all this in his hands was now worthless, smouldering and going to ashes, like the palms of Palm-Sunday burned and reduced to the ashes which the priest on Ash-Wednesday puts upon the heads of the faithful, with the sad and truthful words, "Remember, man, of dust thou art, and unto dust thou shalt return."

It was all dust, dust and nothing but dust — and ashes, death and judgment, mortality and vanity — all was vanity!

Francis stood there a long time and looked into space — it was as though he saw the future blossoming before his eyes. Slowly he turned away, and, leaning heavily on his stick, went back to Assisi.

For him the day was come of which the Lord spoke to the prophet: "I will spread thy path with thorns" — the day when a mysterious hand writes words of death and corruption on the walls of the feast chamber.

But, like all who are in the first steps of their conversion, the young man immediately thought as much of the failings of others as of his own. For as he saw the change that had taken place in himself, his thoughts were directed to his friends with whom he had so often stood there and admired the beautiful view. "How foolish they are that they love perishable things," he thought within himself with a sort of feeling of superiority as he went back to the city gate.[1]

[1] The material for this sketch is found undeveloped, but clearly enough expressed, in the first and second chapters of Thomas of Celano's *Vita prima* — and the stick on which Francis rests himself is even included — also in Bonaventure (*Legenda major*, cap. I, n. 2) and Julian of Speier (*Acta Sanctorum*, Oct. II, p. 563).

CHAPTER II

INFANCY AND YOUTH

FRANCESCO — or as we say in our language, Francis — had that morning just completed his twenty-second year and was the eldest son of one of the richest men of Assisi, the great cloth-merchant Pietro de Bernardone.

The family was not indigenous to Assisi — Pietro's father Bernardone or "great Bernhard" had come from Lucca, and belonged to the renowned Luccan family of weavers and merchants, the Moriconi. Francis' mother, Lady Pica, was of still more distant origin; Ser Pietro had made her acquaintance on one of his business trips in beautiful legendary Provence, and took her home as his bride to the little Italian village under the mountain declivity of Subasio.[1]

Assisi is one of the oldest cities of Italy. Even in the books of Ptolemy it is called Aisision; and in the year 46 B.C. the Latin poet Propertius was born there. Christianity was

---

[1] Ottavio, Bishop of Assisi, tells in his book, published in 1689, *Lumi sulla Portiuncula*, that he, during a visit to Lucca, had seen an old manuscript, whence he copied the following, word for word: "There were in Lucca two brothers who were merchants named Moriconi. One remained in the region, while the other with the surname, Bernardone, went to Umbria and settled in Assisi, married there and had a son whom he named Pietro. Pietro, who was heir to a considerable fortune, courted a young girl of noble family, named Pica, and was St. Francis' father." For Pica's Provençal extraction see *Règle du Tiers Ordre de la Pénitence* . . . explained by R. P. Claude Frassen, Paris, 1752, and *Annales Franciscaines*, Oct., 1890. Wadding (*Annales*, I, p. 17) gives a family tree of the Moriconi, coming within the fourth degree of consanguinity of St. Francis. Also according to Wadding (ditto, p. 18) the priors in Assisi, February 3, 1534, testify that there lived two descendants of Pietro di Bernardone in the city, namely the brothers Antonio and Bernardone, both of whom supported themselves as beggars. See also *A. SS.*, Oct. II, pp. 556-557, Cristofani: *Storie d'Assisi*, I, pp. 78 et seq. Sabatier: *Vie de St. F.* (1905), p. 2, n. 2, le Monnier: *Hist. de St. F.*, I (1891), pp. 1-6, Cherancé: *St. F. d'A.* (1900), pp. 2-3.

brought to this region by St. Crispolitus or Crispoldo — according to the legend a disciple of St. Peter as well as of St. Britius, Bishop of Spoleto, who at the command of the prince of the Apostles, in the year 58, is said to have consecrated St. Crispoldo as bishop in Vettona, now Bettona, and to have assigned him the charge over the whole district from Foligno in the south to Nocera in the north. Under the persecutions of Domitian, St. Crispoldo suffered martyrdom; the same fate overtook later three of Umbria's bishops — St. Victorinus (about 240), St. Sabinus (303), and St. Rufinus who was the apostle of Assisi.[1]

In honor of the last named there was erected in Assisi, in the middle of the twelfth century, the beautiful romanesque basilica of San Rufino, after the designs of John of Gubbio, and when it was completed it became the cathedral of the place, replacing the very old church by the Bishop's palace — Santa Maria del Vescovado.

And in this church of San Rufino still stands the romanesque baptismal font in which the first-born of Ser Pietro and Madonna Pica received the water of holy baptism one day in September, 1182 (it is said to have been the 26th).

A legend which is not older than the fifteenth century says that while Madonna Pica's hour with Francis was come the child could not be born. Then a pilgrim knocked at the door, and, when it was opened, said that the child would not be born until the mother left the beautiful bedroom, went into the stable, and there lay upon straw in one of the stalls. This was done, and hardly was the change effected when the heartrending cries of the mother ceased, and she bore a son, whose first cradle, like that of the Saviour, was a manger full of straw in a stable.

Bartholomew of Pisa, who wrote in the end of the fourteenth century, and who in his work *Liber Conformitatum* goes very far in drawing analogies between Jesus Christ and Saint Francis, knew nothing of this story; yet it would have exactly suited the scope of his book. On the other hand, Benozzo Gozzoli in the year 1452 painted the birth in the

---

[1] Ughelli: *Italia sacra* (1717), vol. I, col. 680; *A. SS.*, 12. May: *Analecta Franciscana*, III (Quaracchi, 1897), p. 226, n. 1.

stable upon the walls of the church of St. Francis in Montefalco, and Sedulius, whose *Historia Seraphica* appeared in Antwerp in the year 1613, says that he saw the stable in Assisi converted into a chapel.

Even to-day this chapel can be found in Assisi. It is called S. Francesco il piccolo (St. Francis the little), and over the door can be read the following inscription:

Hoc oratorium fuit bovis et asini stabulum
In quo natus est Franciscus mundi speculum.

"This oratory was the stable of ox and ass in which Francis the mirror of the world was born."

The chapel is not far from the place where now the house of the father of St. Francis is shown, and where since the seventeenth century the *chiesa nuova* (new church) lifts its barocque walls. The Bollandists have propounded the theory that the chapel may be a part of Pietro di Bernardone's original house, which the family later moved out of while Francis was still a child. Perhaps the name of the chapel, "Little Francis," led to the development of the legend.[1]

Of the same legendary quality as that of the birth in the stable is another tradition that is first given by Wadding. This tells us that the same pilgrim who had given the good advice about the flight to the stable was also in the church at the time of the child's baptism immediately after the birth, and held the child over the font. There is still shown in San Rufino's church a stone on which are what resemble footprints. It is told by the guide who shows the stone that the pilgrim — or the angel in guise of a pilgrim — stood upon this stone when St. Francis was baptized.

The seed from which this legend has sprung is undoubtedly a tale, which still exists in a manuscript of the so-called Legend of the Three Brothers.

It is told in it that while the new-born Francis was being baptized, a pilgrim came and knocked at the door and asked to see the child. The maid who opened the door naturally refused this request, but the stranger declared that he would not go until he obtained his wish. Ser Pietro was not at

[1] *Acta sanctorum*, Oct. II., pp. 556-558.

home, and they told the lady of the house what was going on. To the astonishment of all, she ordered them to do what the pilgrim asked. The child was taken out, and as soon as the stranger saw the child he took it in his arms just as Simeon had taken the Divine Infant, and said: "To-day there have been born in this street two children, and one of them, namely this very child, shall be one of the best men in the world, but the other shall be one of the worst."[1]

Bartholomew of Pisa adds that the pilgrim made the sign of a cross upon the right shoulder of the little one, warning the nurse to look well after the child, for the devil strove after its life. And when the stranger had said this, he disappeared before the eyes of all.

In baptism the son of Ser Pietro had received the name of John. The father was absent on a journey to France when the child was born, and one of the first things he undertook after his return was to change his first-born's name from John to Francis. This name was then rare, although not entirely new. It was in use in the immediate neighborhood of Assisi, as the name of the road (via Francesca) which then ran along the west side of the town from S. Salvatore degli Pareti (now Casa Gualdi) and ended at S. Damiano. This road is referred to by name in a bull of Pope Innocent III, published May 26, 1198, when Francis was only fifteen years old, and not yet famous enough to have a road called after him. Many surmises have been made as to why Pietro di Bernardone changed his son's name. The love of the merchant just returning from Provence for France must have been a principal motive; he wished his son to be a real Frenchman in nature and ways. A certain protest against the name-giving by the woman of the house may also have played its part. St. Bonaventure says explicitly that the name John was given him by his mother. "I wish no camel's-hair John the Baptist, but a Frenchman with fine nature," is what the father's changing of the name may be thought to have meant.

[1] *Tres Socii*, cap. I, n. 2, in the Vatican MS. 7339, published in Pesaro, 1831. Barth. of Pisa's *Conformitates* (Milano, 1513), fol. 12v, 13r, and 25r. Wadding, I, (Romae, 1731), pp. 20–21.

Others hold that the name "the Frenchman" was first bestowed upon the youth as he grew up because of his skill in the French language — a skill which certainly was not very great, as he never could speak the language perfectly.

In any case, the youth became familiar from youth with the French tongue. He also learned Latin; this part of his education was undertaken by priests of the neighboring church of St. George.[1]

St. Francis' first biographer, Thomas of Celano, gives us an unpleasant picture of the education of the period. He tells us that children were scarcely weaned before they were taught by their elders to both say and do improper things, and that from false human respect no one dared to behave honorably. And from so bad a twig no good and healthy tree naturally could spring. A wasted childhood was followed by a riotous youth. Christianity was only a name with the young, and all their ambition was simply in the direction of seeming worse than they were.[2]

Thomas of Celano was a poet and a rhetorician, and it is not easy to know how much weight should be attached to his assertions. Perhaps he thought of the conditions in his own childhood's home, Celano in the Abruzzi. Of the other biographers, only Julian of Speier has anything of the same sort to say, and he copies it all from brother Thomas.

At an early age, in accordance with a custom still obtaining in Italy, Francis began to assist his father in the shop. He soon showed himself adapted for business — "even more forward than his forbears," Julian of Speier, referred to above, says of him in this respect.[3] He was a skilful and active business man, and lacked only one business trait — but this was also very essential — he was not economical, rather was he absolutely wasteful.

To understand the cause of this wastefulness it is necessary to take a look at the period in which the young merchant grew up.

---

[1] St. George's church was situated where now is Santa Chiara. The distance thence to the new church, built on the site of St. Francis' paternal home, is not great.
[2] *Vita prima*, I, cap. I.   [3] *A. SS.*, Oct. II, p. 560.

It was the end of the twelfth century and beginning of the thirteenth — in other words, it was the flowery time of knighthood and chivalry. Europe's ideal was the knight and the life of chivalry, as it developed in the courts of love in Provence and with the Norman kings in Sicily. In Italy the minor courts of Este, Verona, and Monteferrato contended with the great republics of Florence and Milan to see who could give the most magnificent tournaments and tilting matches. The most celebrated troubadours of France, Rambaud de Vaqueiras, Pierre Vidal, Bernard de Ventadour, Peirol d'Auvergne, wandered over the peninsula on endless journeys from court to court, and from festival to festival. Everywhere were to be heard the *Chansons de Geste* of Provence, fables and ballades, everywhere were to be heard songs of King Arthur and the Knights of the Round Table. Even in the smallest cities the courts of love were established, devoted to the "Gay Science," *la gaya scienza*.[1]

Pietro di Bernardone's "French" son was, as it were, destined to be caught in this movement. He was not like his father — only the saving, easily contented Italian, to whom it was enough to accumulate money. There flowed through his veins also the sparkling blood of Provence — he must have enjoyment by means of his money, he wanted to change gold into splendor and joy.

Thus Francis, the richest young man of the place, very naturally became what in our days would be called the leading society man of the town. He was skilled in earning money, but very frivolous in giving it away again, says Thomas of Celano. No wonder that he soon gathered a circle of friends about him, not only from Assisi, but also from the neighboring villages; we even find him seeking a friend in the somewhat distant town of Gubbio.

How did these young men spend their time when they were together? Like all young men up to the present day — in taking their meals together, eating well, drinking better, and finally in high spirits going through the streets of the city arm in arm, singing at the top of their voices, and disturbing

[1] Le Monnier: *Histoire de St. François*, Paris, 1891, I, pp. 11–16. Paul Sabatier: *Vie de S. François d'Assise* (32d ed., Paris, 1905), p. 10, n. 2.

the slumbers of the citizens. The austere Friar Minor from Celano enumerates for us the sins of these wild young men — they joked, he says, were witty, said foolish things, and wore soft, effeminate clothes.

I remember a day in May a few years ago, a day in May in Subiaco in the Sabine hills. I had visited Sagro Speco, St. Benedict's celebrated hermitage cave and St. Scolastica's convent. I had gone into an inn by the wayside to get a light meal, until I could take the train back to Rome via Mandela. I had my meal served in a pleasure house situated on a projecting point of rock, so that I looked down between the openings of a screen into a fig orchard's broad-leaved tops, lighted by the sun. Over the fig trees I had a view into the valley, where the Anio shining like silver rushed down between blue-grey cliffs, and far away the village of Subiaco with proud towers and spires lifted itself up like a castle on a mountain top.

In these cheerful, exalting, and sunny surroundings was a company of youths who were taking their dinner in the same inn with me. Out in an open veranda, which gave a most beautiful view in among the wild mountains, they had had a long table set — I saw the bright white cloth, the mighty flasks, the glasses with the red wine, and the waiters who ran back and forth with great dishes of macaroni. And laughter and song arose, but never became ungoverned riot, and they stood up in their places and made speeches, and after the speaking there was a little cornet-playing.

Such, thought I to myself, were the festivals, filled with Italian enjoyment and at the same time with Italian politeness, at which Pietro di Bernardone's son bore the sceptre as *rex*, as king of the festive party, king for a day and an evening. And if the old Franciscan from Celano had been familiar with the wild inspired drinking songs of the youth of the north or with the "Salamanderreiben" of the German sons of the Muse, then he would have been milder in passing judgment on these festivals, whose delights were as mild and clear as the yellow wine that ripens on the Umbrian hillsides.

But he knew them not, and therefore tells us that Francis

was the worst of all the brawling youths — the one who led and misled the others. The "gilded youth" of Assisi went from feast to feast, and at night they could be heard going through the streets, singing to the accompaniment of the lute or violin, as if they were a wandering band of Troubadours or "jongleurs." Indeed so far did Francis go in his admiration for the "joyful science" of Provence, that he had a parti-colored minstrel's suit made for himself, which he wore when among his friends.[1]

Even at this early time Francis' father had most probably taken his son as associate in his business; at any rate, the young man had control over considerable sums of money. Everything that he earned went for pleasure; now and then the father could hardly withhold the remark: "Anyone would think you were a nobleman's son, and not the son of a simple merchant." Yet none of his elders cared to restrain Francis in the life he led, and when well-meaning neighbors complained to Madonna Pica of the wild son she had, she used only to answer: "I have the hope that he too some day will be a son of God."

It was impossible to say anything really bad about him. In all that related to his intercourse with the other sex he was a model: it was known among his friends that no one dared say an evil word in his hearing. If it happened, at once his face assumed a serious, almost harsh, expression, and he did not answer. Like all the pure of heart, Francis had great reverence for the mysteries of life.[2]

He was, on the whole, decorous in his life, and there was only one thing that really offended his family — it was that he clung so to his friends that, as he sat at the table in his home, if a message came from them, he would jump up, leave his meal, and, going out, would not return to finish his repast.

In one respect he was worthy of admiration — this was his regard for the poor. His extravagance extended even to them; he was not one of those typical society men who

---

[1] "In curiositate tantum erat vanus, quod aliquando in eodem indumento pannum valde carum panno vilissimo consui faciebat." *Tres Socii*, cap. I, n. 2.
[2] *Tres Socii*, cap. I, n. 3.

hardly have a penny to give a beggar, but willingly spend their hundreds on a champagne feast. His way of thinking was the following: "If I am generous, yes, even extravagant with my friends who at the best only say 'thanks' to me for them, or repay me with another invitation, how much greater grounds have I for almsgiving which God himself has promised to repay a hundredfold?" This was the inspiring lifethought of the Middle Ages, which here carried out the genially literal and genially naïve translation of the words of the gospel: "As long as you did it to one of these my least brethren, you did it to me." Francis knew — as the whole Middle Ages knew it — that not even a glass of cold water, given by the disciples, would remain unpaid and unrewarded by the Master.

Therefore a pang went through his heart when, one day as there was a crowd in the shop, and he was in a hurry to get through, he had sent a beggar away. "If this man had come from one of my friends," said he to himself, "from Count this or Baron that, he would have got what he asked for.[1] Now he comes from the King of kings and from the Lord of lords, and I let him go away empty-handed. I even gave him a repelling word." And he determined from that day on to give to every one who asked him in God's name — *per amor di Dio*, as the Italian beggars still are wont to say.[2]

One effect of his kindness to the poor was, perhaps, this — as Bonaventure tells it. One of the original characters of the village, a half-witted or entire simpleton, who travelled around the streets and by-ways, every time he met Francis, took off his cloak and spread it out on the ground, and asked the young man to step upon it. Perhaps it was the same queer fellow, perhaps another of the wandering weaklings of the Middle Ages, who used to wander through the streets of Assisi, calling out ceaselessly: *Pax et bonum!* ("Peace and Good!") After Francis' conversion this warning voice ceased,

---

[1] This reflection of Francis gives us a new little insight into the position the young man held in his circle — they used to borrow money from him.

[2] Two of his biographers — the Anonymous of Perugia and St. Bonaventure — assert that Francis ran after the beggar, found him and gave him the alms he had denied him (*A. SS.*, Oct. II, p. 562. Bonav., *Leg. Maj.*, cap. I, n. 1. *Tres Socii*, cap. I, n. 3. Celano, *Vita prima*, I, cap. VII).

which is treated in the legend as a kind of precursor of the great saint's coming.[1]

Finally Francis was endowed with a vivid feeling for nature. For it was in Provence that this sentiment, now so spontaneous in life as in literature, found, a century later, in the works of Petrarch, its first literary expression since the days of antiquity. But already in the half-Provençal Francis it is found fully developed — "The beauty of the country, the charm of the vineyards, all that was pleasing to the eye" rejoiced him, says Thomas of Celano,[2] and we will not go wrong if we regard this feeling as a part of Francis' inheritance from his mother. This was then a notable element of his personality and was temporarily only obscured by the spiritual crisis which preceded his conversion. As all good which is to grow, so must this side of his nature be pruned down even to the very roots — but only to bear a still richer crown. For as a German mystic has said: "No one has a true love for created things unless he has first forsaken it for love of God, so that it has been dead for him and he dead for it."

[1] Bonav., cap. I, n. 2. *Tres Socii*, VIII, 26.
[2] *Vita prima*, I, cap. II.

CHAPTER III

HISTORY OF THE EPOCH

FRANCIS grew up in warlike times. Emperor was opposed to pope, prince to king, village was against village and burgher against noble. Francis was but a child when Frederick Barbarossa at the peace of Constance (June 25, 1183-1196) had to grant the Lombardy States all the privileges which they, supported by the power of the Papacy, had conquered for themselves in the battle of Legnano (1176). Barbarossa's successor, Henry VI (1183-1196), meanwhile made the imperial power firm once more in Italy, and Assisi, which already in 1174 had been taken by the German Royal Chancellor, Archbishop Christian of Mayence, but which in 1177 had won its communal freedom with its own consuls, had to waive its municipal privileges, and bow down under the imperial Duke of Spoleto and Count of Assisi, Conrad of Irslingen.

A year after the death of King Henry, Innocent III ascended the Papal throne, and this powerful Prince of the Church immediately took the affairs of the Italian states into his own strong hand. Duke Conrad had to go to Narni and submit himself to the Pope, and his absence was at once utilized by the citizens for an assault by storm on the "Zwingburg" (Guarding Castle), which, threatening the city, was enthroned on the top of Santo Rosso. The castle was taken and so thoroughly laid waste that, when the Papal emissary came to take possession of it, as property of Peter, there was only a ruin left, the same which still looks down upon Assisi. And to be prepared to take the consequences of this daring act, the citizens determined to erect a wall around their city; with spirit all went to work, and in the course of an incredibly short time the people of Assisi built the city wall with towers, which even to-day has an imposing effect upon the visitor.

At this time Francis was about seventeen years old, and, as Sabatier says, it is not unreasonable to suppose that on this occasion he acquired that ability in handling stone and mortar which later stood him in good stead at San Damiano and Portiuncula.

Naturally the greatest part of the work, both of tearing down and building up, was done by the lower people — *minores*, as it was the universal custom to call them. The common people thus realized their power, and after overcoming the foreign foe, the tyrannical German, they turned their attention to the foe at home, the minor tyrants, the noble lords, whose fortified residences — as later the *Steens* in the Flemish cities — stood here and there in the village. A real civil war broke out; the nobles' houses were besieged, many of them were burned, and the fall of the nobility seemed inevitable.

Then the nobles of Assisi turned in their need to Assisi's former enemy — the neighboring and powerful Perugia. Ambassadors from Assisi's nobility promised to recognize Perugia's supremacy over the city whenever she could come to their assistance.

The republic of Perugia then stood at the summit of its power and greatness and eagerly seized the opportunity to reduce Assisi to subjection. Its army advanced into the field to the relief of the besieged nobility. The citizens of Assisi did not lose courage; together with such of the nobility as had remained true to their ancestral city, they met the troops of Perugia at the bridge of San Giovanni, on the plain between the two cities. Victory fell to the Perugians and a quantity of the combatants of Assisi were taken prisoners — among them also Francis. On account of his noble appearance the young merchant's son was not put in prison with the rest of the citizens, but, just as the laws of many old French cities provide for *les bourgeois honorables*, he received permission to share the lot of the nobility.[1]

The defeat at Ponte San Giovanni took place in the year

[1] Cristofani: *Storie d'Assisi*, I, Assisi, 1875, pp. 83–96; Le Monnier: *Histoire de St. François d'Assise*, I, pp. 24–26; P. Sabatier: *Vie de S. François d'Assise*, pp. 12–15. — The place where the battle between the two cities was fought is given in *Vita B. Columbae Reatinae* (A. SS., May 20), where it is told how Columba with her father and others accompanying her were captured by ruffians

1202, the imprisonment in Perugia lasted a year, and, during it, Francis astounded his fellow-prisoners by his constant cheerfulness. Although there seemed little reason to be contented he was always to be heard singing and joking, and when the others peevishly or angrily rebuked him, he answered only: "Do you not know that a great future awaits me, and that all the world shall then fall down and pray to me?" This is the first expression of his firm conviction of his future, the definite certainty that a great future belonged to him, which is so remarkable in St. Francis in these years of his youth.

In November, 1203 peace was declared between the two contending powers. The conditions were that the citizens of Assisi should repair the damage they had done to the property of the nobles, and that the nobles should on their part not be free to enter into any alliance without permission of the city. Francis was now liberated with the other prisoners, among whom he who had formerly been an apostle of happiness now assumed the rôle of peacemaker. For there was among the prisoner-warriors one who, on account of his pride and unreasonableness, was very unpopular with all. Instead of avoiding this difficult character, Francis undertook to be in his company, and went so far in this direction, during the time of captivity, that the ill-humored unreasonable prisoner changed, and was received into the circle of his companions, whence he had exiled himself.

The long intercourse with the noble prisoners seems to have affected the young merchant's heart with a greater attachment to the ways of life of the nobility than ever, which in the years following the imprisonment (1203–1206) became very evident in him. It was now that he became a disciple of the "gay science" of Provence; it was now that he submerged himself in the whirl of festivities and enjoyments, out of which his sickness, which in his twenty-third year brought him so near to the portals of death, was first to rescue him — and even at that not too securely.

on the bridge of S. Giovanni. The author of the biography adds to the above: "Memini, me legisse, hoc eodem loco, B. Franciscum, tunc juvenem, cum pluribus sodalibus carceri mancipatum" (ditto, n. 74). — The bridge of S. Giovanni crosses the Tiber a little north of Perugia.

CHAPTER IV

FRANCIS BECOMES A SOLDIER

FOR even now he was a long way from conversion. He had realized his soul's barrenness, but he had found nothing with which to fill it. As his convalescence progressed and his strength returned, in such measure did he return to his worldly life, and trod again the same paths as before his sickness. The only difference was that he had no enjoyment now in the life he led. There was a sort of unrest in him, that gave him no peace; there was a thorn in his soul that ceaselessly irritated him. More than ever he dreamed of great deeds, of strange adventures and of achievements in strange and distant lands.

And again the life of chivalry presented itself to him as the only one which would assuage his soul's indefinable longing to attain the highest. From his youth he had been intimate with the romances of King Arthur and the Knights of the Round Table. He too would be a Knight of the Holy Grail, he too would go out into the world, offer his blood for the cause of the Greatest and Highest, and — for this was not excluded from his thoughts — he could return home crowned with undying laurels.

Just at this time the Middle-Ages' long-standing dispute between emperor and pope had entered on a new phase. Henry VI's widow had invoked the guardianship of Innocent III for the heir to the throne, afterwards the Emperor Frederick II. One of the oldest of the Emperor's generals, named Markwald, made the claim that it was he who, in virtue of the will, should properly be regent for king and kingdom.[1] But

---
[1] "*Balius regius et regni*," *Vita Innocentii III*, quoted by Le Monnier, I, p. 34, n. I.

Innocent had no idea of giving up what he had undertaken, and was prepared to defend his cause with arms. The war was carried on in Southern Italy, because the widow-queen, Constance, being heir to the Norman kings, was also queen of Sicily. Innocent suffered for a long time one defeat after another, until he entrusted his army to Duke Walter III of Brienne, who in the name of his Norman wife, Albinia, laid claim to Tarentum. This illustrious leader overcame the Germans in a series of defeats — at Capua, at Lecce, at Barletta — and his fame spread over all Italy, and inspired all the land. The Germans were hated everywhere; in Sicily the word "German" signified coarse, impolite, unjust. The French troubadour, Pierre Vidal, wandered through Lombardy and sang sarcastic songs about the Germans — "I would not be a nobleman in Friesland," he sang, "if I had to hear the language they speak there; it sounds like geese, not like the language of men."[1] All that was young, proud and noble in Italy rose against the foreign dominion, and Walter of Brienne's name seemed to wave over inspired ranks like a banner blessed by the Pope.

The national inspiration reached even Assisi; one of the nobles of the place armed himself to go with a little troop to the aid of Walter's army in Apulia.[2] As soon as Francis heard this, a feverish longing took possession of him. Here was the chance he so long had wished for, here was the moment which must not be allowed to escape; now or never was the time — the nobleman from Assisi should take Francis with him in his troop, and Duke Walter should knight him!

With all his zeal Francis pondered over the means of carrying this plan into effect. He was seized by wild joy, such as one feels when preparing for a new and, as one may hope, an entrancing epoch of life. A sort of "wanderlust" mastered him; he ran rather than walked through the streets. His friends found that his usual good humor had risen to an excessive height, and asked him the reason therefor, when he

---

[1] Le Monnier, p. 35, n. 1.
[2] The biographers of Francis did not know the name of Walter of Brienne; they allude to him only vaguely under the title *gentilis* (*Tres Socii*) or *liberalis* (Bonaventure). In June, 1205 Walter fell at the siege of Sarno, but his army prosecuted the contest.

FRANCIS BECOMES A SOLDIER

would answer with glittering eyes: "I know that I am now going to be a great prince."[1]

It goes without saying that nothing was spared in equipping the young merchant's son for war. One of his biographers says that all of his clothes were "individual and costly."[2] This was what was to be expected in the extravagant and luxurious rich young man. But what is also completely characteristic of him is that when, just before starting, he met one of his fellow-travellers, a nobleman, and saw that he on account of his poverty could not clothe and arm himself properly, Francis gave all his costly equipment to him, and took the nobleman's poor things in exchange.

Engrossed as he was in the new life, he naturally dreamt every night of war and weapons. The very night after he had been so generous to the poor knight, such a dream came to him, and it seemed to him more pregnant with meaning than any of the others. It seemed to him that he — perhaps to bid farewell — stood in his father's shop. But instead of the rolls of goods which usually filled the shelves from floor to ceiling, he saw now on all sides shining shields, bright spears, shining armor. And as he wondered he heard a voice which said: "All this shall belong to you and to your warriors."[3]

It was only natural that Francis should take this dream for a good omen. And one bright morning he sprang upon his horse to go with the rest of the little troop to Apulia. Their road led them through the present Porta Nuova to Foligno and from Foligno to Spoleto. Here they approached the Flaminian Way — the road to Rome and south Italy. And here Francis had nearly reached the goal of his warlike journey.

---

[1] *"Scio me magnum principem affuturum"* (*Tres Socii*, cap. II, n. 5). In the same strain in the prison in Perugia: *"Adhuc adorabor per totum mundum"* (*Tr. Soc.*, II, 4, and Celano, *Vita secunda*, I, 1).

[2] *"curiosa et cara"* (*Tres Socii*, cap. II, n. 6).

[3] The dream is thus told by Thomas of Celano (*Vita prima*, I, cap. II) and Julian of Speier (*A. SS.*, Oct. II, p. 564). In the *Tres Socii* (cap. II, n. 5) the locality is no longer his home but is a palace, as also in Thomas of Celano's second Biography (I, 2) and in St. Bonaventure (I, 3), and the apparition is otherwise enlarged upon (the weapons are marked with crosses, a beautiful bride awaits Francis in the palace hall, etc.).

For the same hand which had formerly cast him upon a sick-bed to bring him to reflection and realization, again grasped him in Spoleto. An attack of fever forced him to take to his bed, and as he lay there between sleeping and waking, it happened that he heard a voice asking him where he wanted to go. "To Apulia to be a knight," was the invalid's answer. "Tell me, Francis, who can benefit you most: the Lord or the servant?" "The Lord," answered Francis in astonishment. "Then why do you desert the Lord," repeated the voice, "for the servant, and the Prince for his vassal?"

Then Francis knew who it was who spoke to him, and in the words of Paul cried out: "Lord, what do you wish me to do?"

But the voice answered: "Go back to your home; there it shall be told you what you are to do. For the vision you saw must be understood in another way!"

The voice ceased and Francis awoke. The rest of the night he lay awake. But when morning came he silently arose, saddled his horse and rode back to Assisi in all his warlike equipment, which now suddenly seemed to him so vain.[1]

We do not know what reception awaited him at home, but we can imagine it. This, like all his other eccentricities, was undoubtedly soon forgiven him, and for a good while he was again the centre of his friends' joyous circle. Soon the old life with feasting and enjoyment was in full swing; again was Francis the one who in spite of all had to be acknowledged as the leader of his circle of young men — *flos Juvenum*.[2] If his futile trip towards Apulia was referred to, he replied very definitely that he certainly had given it up, but only to do great things in his own land.[3]

[1] *Tres Socii*, cap. II, n. 5, and Celano, *Vita secunda*, I, 2. Thomas of Celano in his first life of St. Francis knew nothing of this second dream, he only says: "immutatus ... mente ... ire in Apuliam se recusat"; first through the *Tres Socii* he learned about the strange motive for so unexpected a determination.

For the connection between the two biographers of Francis and the *Tres Socii* legend, consult the appendix. One of the biographers would have us believe that, as Francis on his return home passed through Foligno, he sold horse and arms there and bought himself other clothes. (Anonymus Perusinus in *Acta SS.*, Oct. II, p. 565.)

[2] Wadding (*Annales*, vol. I, p. 23).

[3] Julian of Speier (*A. SS.*, Oct. II, p. 566, n. 109). Celano, *Vita prima*, I, cap. III. *Tres Socii*, cap. V, n. 13.

He really had less confidence than he assumed. Opposing emotions contended in his soul — now he listened to the voice of the world only, now he longed to serve the Lord whose inspiring voice had spoken so pleadingly to him that night in Spoleto. Stronger and stronger the feeling arose in him to withdraw from all and in loneliness to become sure of his calling. But if he sought his friends no more they sought him, and, to avoid all appearance of parsimony, he was the same luxurious host as before.

And thus it happened that one evening — it was in the summer of 1205 — invitations were sent out in his usual way for a festival which was to be richer and more sumptuous than ever. He was to be the king of the feast, and, when the table was cleared, all joined in overwhelming him with praise and thanks. After the dinner the company as usual went singing through the streets, but Francis, who kept a little behind the others, did not sing. Little by little he dropped behind his friends; soon he was alone in the quiet night in some one of Assisi's small steep streets, or in one of its small open squares, from which one looks out so far over the lansdcape.

And there it came to pass that the Lord again visited him. The heart of Francis, which was weary of the world and of its vanities, was filled with such a sweetness that there was room for no other feeling. He lost all consciousness of himself, and if he had been cut to pieces limb by limb — as he himself later told of it — he would not have known of it, would never have tried by a movement to escape it.

How long he stood there, overcome by the heavenly sweetness, he never knew. He first came back to himself when one of his friends, who had gone back in search of him, called out:

"Hello, Francis, are you thinking of your honeymoon?"

And looking up to heaven where the stars were shining, then as now in the serene August night, the young man answered:

"Yes, I am thinking of marrying! But the bride I am going to woo is nobler, richer and fairer than any woman you know."

Then his friends laughed — for a number had approached — and the wine had made them loquacious. "Then the tailor will again have a job, just as when you started to Apulia," we may think some of them said with a sneer.

Francis heard their laughter and was angry, but not with them. For in sudden light the whole of his former life was before him, in its folly, its lack of object, its childish vanity. He saw himself in all his pitiful reality — and in front of him stood in shining beauty the life he hitherto had *not* led — the true life, the just life, the beautiful, noble, rich life — life in Jesus Christ.

In this aspect Francis could be angry at no one but himself, and therefore the old legend says also that from that hour he began to value himself little.[1]

[1] "ab illa hora coepit sibi vilescere." (*Tres Socii*, cap. III, whence the above particulars are essentially taken. Compare Celano, *Vita sec.*, I, 3.)

CHAPTER V

THE CONVERSION

AN author of the fifteenth century, St. Antonin of Florence (1389-1459) in his Chronicles of the Church has put the summary of Francis' activities in the first year which followed his parting from his friends and the joyous life into two lines: "He now kept in hiding in hermit caves, and now piously built up ruined churches."[1] Solitary prayer and personal work for the kingdom of God were the two means by which the rich man's son, young, spoiled and worldly, sought to ascertain the will of God as applied to his own case.

A little way outside of the city there was a cave in the cliff, where he liked to go to pray, sometimes alone, but oftener with one of his friends — the only one who seems to have remained true to him after his change of mind. None of his biographers has preserved for us this man's name — Thomas of Celano only says that he was a distinguished person.[2]

Francis had by nature a strong inclination to speak of his experiences. His biographers say of him, that even against his will he would speak of things which occupied him.[3] It is no wonder that he confided in a friend, and in the metaphor of the Bible told of the costly treasure which he had found in the cave outside the city, and which only needed to be dug out of the soil. But he had to be alone to raise the treasure —

---

[1] nunc latebat in eremis, nunc ecclesiarum reparationibus insistebat devotus. (S. Ant. *Chronicon*, pars III, tit. 24, cap. 7.)

[2] "magnus inter ceteros" (Cel., *V. pr.*, I, cap. III). Sabatier (*Vie*, pp. 22-23) would identify this associate of the earliest times with Elias of Cortona. This is not very logical. Elias, who, according to Salimbene (*Chron.*, ed. Parm., p. 402), was by profession a saddlemaker and school-teacher, hardly belonged to Francis' circle of acquaintances, much less could be called "magnus inter ceteros."

[3] "Jam se continere non valens, quaedam etiam nolens in publicum verbotenus depromeret" (Julian of Speier in *Anal. Boll.*, t. XXI, p. 163).

therefore he left his friend outside while he went in by himself.

And there apart, in the dark cave, Francis found the secret chamber where he could pray to his Heavenly Father. Day by day the desire to do the will of God increased until he had no peace, until he had clearly determined what it was that God asked of him. Again and again were the words of the psalmist on his lips, the words which are the foundation of all true worship of God: "Shew, O Lord, thy ways to me, and teach me thy paths" (Ps. xxiv. 4).

And against this pure ideal his past life stood out dark and repulsive. With increasing bitterness he thought of his past youth, and it delighted him no longer to think over its delights and extravagances. But what was to be done not to fall back again?—had he not time and again been warned, and had he not time and again despised the warning and again followed his inclinations? When friends again called on him, when the wine once more seduced him, when the smell of the feasts again reached him, and the sounds of violin and lute rang in his ears — would he then have power to resist, would he not as before immerse himself in the glad world of festivity and drinking, which hovered like a golden heaven over the dark everyday world?

Francis did not depend upon himself, and God seemed unwilling to give him the desired word of help which he asked for. In agony of mind and desolation of soul, Francis fought the battle of his salvation in the loneliness and darkness of the cave, and when he finally, torn and tortured, again appeared in the light of day, his friends hardly recognized him, his face seemed so haggard.[1]

Thus Francis became a man of prayer. He had begun to taste the sweetness of prayer and prayed continually. It often happened that, as he would be going through the streets or about his home, he would stop everything to go off into a church to pray.[2]

Francis' father seems to have been away from home a great

---

[1] Celano, *V. pr.*, I, cap. III. Cel., *V. sec.*, I, cap. V.
[2] "ipsum ad orationem de platea et aliis locis impellabat" (*Tres Socii*, cap. III, n. 8).

THE CONVERSION

deal during this period of change in his son's nature. The mother, who, according to the authorities, loved Francis more than her other children, let him do just what he wished. In one sense he led the same life as before — only that the poor had taken the place of his friends. It was they he sought, it was to them he gave feasts. One day when his mother and he were to sit at table together, he laid out such a quantity of bread that there was enough for a large family. When his mother asked the reason for such profusion, he answered that he had intended it all for the poor. If he met a beggar in the street who asked for alms, he gave him all the money he had with him. But if his money was all gone, he would give him his hat or his belt; sometimes when he had nothing else, he would take the poor man with him to a secluded place, take off his shirt and give it to him.[1] He also began to think about poor priests and poor churches; he bought church goods and sent them secretly to places where they were wanting. This is the first indication we have of Francis' vivid interest, manifest in his after life for everything relating to churches, and which, among others, found expression in his sending "to all provinces good and fine irons to make fine and white altar-bread with."[2]

Design in Host Mould; in Convent at Greccio

But first of all the poor were in his thoughts. To see them, to hear their troubles, to help them in their necessities — these were hereafter his principal concerns. And little by little the desire was firmly established within his heart: "If I could only find by personal experience how it felt to be poor — how it is to be, not one of those who go by and throw down a shilling, but to be the one who stands in rags and dirt, and humbly bowing, stretches out his faded hat for alms!" Many a time, we may think, he stood among the beggars at some church door — stood among them while they pitifully asked for a mite. But it was not like him to do only this. He himself must do the begging in order to understand poverty, and this could not be done in Assisi where every one knew him.

[1] *Tres Socii*, cap. III, nn. 8–9. [2] *Speculum perfectionis*, ed. Sab., cap. LXV.

It was this which inspired him with the idea of going on a pilgrimage to Rome. There in the great city no one knew him, there he could put his plan into execution.

Perhaps there were some particular circumstances which brought near to him this idea of a pilgrimage to the Apostle's grave. From September 14, 1204, until March 25, 1206, and again from April 4 until May 11, 1206, Innocent III had transferred the Papal residence to the bishopric of St. Peter.[1] So long a stay by the unhealthy waters of the Tiber may have had some connection with special church-functions in St. Peter's — perhaps the granting of some indulgence. The Bishop of Assisi at this time was also going on a journey to Rome.[2]

However all this may be, Francis went to Rome. We know only a little of his first visit to the Eternal City. He approached by the Flaminian Way and apparently at once went to St. Peter's. Here he met many other pilgrims and saw that they — as was the custom in the Middle Ages — threw coins as offerings through the *fenestrella* or grated window of the Apostle's tomb. The majority of the gifts were only small pieces. Francis stood a while and watched — then the last sign of his old desire to show off appeared, he pulled out his well-filled purse and threw a whole handful of coins in through the grating, so that the money flew about and rang as it fell, and all the people were astonished and looked at him.

The next minute Francis had left the church and called one of the beggars aside, and a moment after he had at last fulfilled the purpose of the whole journey — as a real beggar clothed in real rags he stood among the other beggars on the steps which led up to the church.[3] Of his sensations at this moment we know enough when we read in one of his biographers that he begged in French, "which he liked to talk, although he never could do it perfectly." For him French was the language of poetry, the language of religion, the language of his happiest memories and of his most solemn

---

[1] Potthast: *Regesta*, nn. 2280-2727 and 2736-2778.
[2] Ughelli: *Italia sacra*, I, col. 419.
[3] "in gradibus ecclesiae" (*Tres Socii*, cap. III, n. 10) "in paradiso ante ecclesiam Sancti Petri," says Thomas of Celano (*Vita sec.*, I, 4), using for the area in front of the church the technical expression "the paradise."

hours, the language he spoke when his heart was too full to find expression in everyday Italian, and therefore his soul's mother-speech. When Francis talked French, those who knew him knew that he was happy.

How long Francis stayed in Rome is unknown to us. He may have started back the day after his arrival. The authorities only say that after he had shared the beggars' meal he took off the borrowed clothes, put on his own and went home to Assisi. He had now had the great experience of what it was to be poor — he had worn rags and eaten the bread of necessity — and although it must have been a happiness to be in his own good clothes again, and to sit at home at his mother's profuse table, yet he also felt the spiritual fascination which contentment and poverty can inspire — what a delight it can be to own nothing on this earth except a drink of water from the spring, a crust of bread from the hand of a merciful man, and a night's lodging under the blue heavens with its shining stars. Why should he be troubled about so many things, about goods and money, house and garden, people and flocks, when so little is enough? Does not the Gospel say, "Blessed are the poor," and "It is easier for a camel to pass through the eye of a needle than for a rich man to enter the kingdom of Heaven"?

Questions of this sort certainly troubled Francis after his return from Rome. With greater zeal than ever he called out to God for guidance and light. The friend who used to accompany him to the cave seems now to have wearied of going on this search for treasures, that was always fruitless. The only man to whom Francis now and then revealed himself was Bishop Guido of Assisi, who probably was his confessor.[1]

[1] *Tres Socii*, cap. III, n. 10. Compare the words which St. Francis, according to the *Speculum perfectionis*, said shortly before his death to a certain Dominus Bonaventura in Sienna: "ab initio meae conversionis posuit Dominus in ore episcopi Assisii verbum suum, ut mihi consuleret et bene confortaret in servitio Christi" (ed Sab., cap. X, p. 24). See also the Anonymous of Perugia: "parvi et magni, masculi et feminae despiciebant et deridebant eos . . . nisi solus episcopus civitatis, ad quem ibat frequenter beatus Franciscus ad consilium postulandum." *A. SS.*, Oct. II, p. 584, n. 207. In the same, n. 208: "Quadam vero die cum adiisset beatus Franciscus dominum episcopum." See also Cel., *V. pr.*, n. 15; *Tres Socii*, nn. 20, 35, 47. It follows from all these citations that the relations between Francis and the authorities of the Church had from the start been of the best.

The light cast upon this period by the Testament which Francis has left us has therefore a special value for us. In this document, which was written the year before the Saint's death, we are told:

"The Lord granted me to begin my conversion, so that as long as I lived in my sins, I felt it very bitter to see the lepers. But the Lord took me among them and I exercised mercy towards them."[1]

For the lepers occupied a very particular position among the sick and poor of the Middle Ages. Based on a passage in the Prophet Isaiah (liii. 4) the lepers were looked upon as an image of the Redeemer, more than all other sufferers. As early as the days of Gregory the Great we find the story of the monk, Martyrius, who met a leper by the wayside, who from pain and weariness was fallen to the ground and could drag himself no further. Martyrius wrapped the sick man in his cloak and carried him to his convent. But the leper changed in his arms to Jesus himself, who rose to heaven as he blessed the monk, and said to him: "Martyrius, thou wert not ashamed of me on earth; I will not be ashamed of thee in heaven!" A similar legend is told of St. Julian, of St. Leo IX, and of the Blessed Colombini.

And so the lepers were more than any others an object for pious care during the Middle Ages. For them was founded a special order of knights — Knights of Lazarus — whose whole office was to take care of the lepers. So too there were erected all over Europe the numerous houses of St. George, where the lepers were taken care of in a sort of cloistered life. Of these lepers' homes there were 19,000 in the thirteenth century. But in spite of everything the life of the leper was sad enough, they were repulsed by the rest of humanity, and they were hedged in by severe laws isolating them and hemming them in on all sides.[2]

As with all other cities, there was also in the vicinity of Assisi a lepers' hospital — the lepers were in fact the first real hospital patients and in some languages their name expresses

---

[1] *Opuscula S. Francisci* (Quaracchi, 1904), p. 77.
[2] Chavin de Malan has in his book on St. Francis treated this subject thoroughly. See Guasti's Italian translation of the book (Prato, 1879), pp. 48–60.

this fact. The hospital lay midway between Assisi and Portiuncula, near where the words *Casa Gualdi* appear over the entrance to a large estate. It was called San Salvatore delle Pareti, and was owned by an order of Crucigers, founded under Alexander III for the care of the lepers.[1]

On his walks in this place, Francis now and then passed by the hospital, but the mere sight of it had filled him with horror. He would not even give an alms to a leper unless some one else would take it for him. Especially when the wind blew from the hospital, and the weak, nauseating odor, peculiar to the leper, came across the road, he would hurry past with averted face and fingers in his nostrils.[2]

It was in this that he felt his greatest weakness, and in it he was to win his greatest victory.

For one day, as he was as usual calling upon God, it happened that the answer came. And the answer was this: "Francis! Everything which you have loved and desired in the flesh it is your duty to despise and hate, if you wish to know my will. And when you have begun thus, all that which now seems to you sweet and lovely will become intolerable and bitter, but all which you used to avoid will turn itself to great sweetness and exceeding joy."

These were the words which at last gave Francis a definite programme, which showed him the way he was to follow. He certainly pondered over these words in his lonely rides over the Umbrian plain and, just as he one day woke out of reverie, he found the horse making a sudden movement, and saw on the road before him, only a few steps distant, *a leper*, in his familiar uniform.

Francis started, and even his horse shared in the movement, and his first impulse was to turn and flee as fast as he could. But there were the words he had heard within himself, so clearly before him — "what you used to abhor shall be to you joy and sweetness." . . . And *what* had he hated more than the lepers? Here was the time to take the Lord at His word — to show his good will. . . .

---

[1] Sabatier: *Vie*, p. 123, n. 1.

[2] "vultum suum semper avertens, nares suas propriis manibus obturabat" (*Tres Socii*, cap. IV, n. 11).

And with a mighty victory over himself, Francis sprang from his horse, approached the leper, from whose deformed countenance the awful odor of corruption issued forth, placed his alms in the outstretched wasted hand — bent down quickly and kissed the fingers of the sick man, covered with the awful disease, whilst his system was nauseated with the action. . . .

When he again sat upon his horse, he hardly knew how he had got there. He was overcome by excitement, his heart beat, he knew not whither he rode. But the Lord had kept his word. Sweetness, happiness, and joy streamed into his soul — flowed and kept flowing, although his soul seemed full and more full — like the clear stream which, filling an earthen vessel, keeps on pouring and flows over its rim, with an ever clearer, purer stream. . . .

The next day Francis voluntarily wandered down the road he had hitherto always avoided — the road to San Salvatore delle Pareti. And when he reached the gate he knocked, and when it was opened to him he entered. From all the cells the sick came swarming out — came with their half-destroyed faces, blind inflamed eyes, with club-feet, with swollen, corrupted arms and fingerless hands. And all this dreadful crowd gathered around the young merchant, and the odor from their unclean swellings was so strong that Francis against his will for a moment had to hold his breath to save himself from sickness. But he soon recovered control of himself, he drew out the well-filled purse he had brought with him, and began to deal out his alms. And on every one of the dreadful hands that were reached out to take his gifts he imprinted a kiss, as he had done the day before.

Thus it was that Francis won the greatest victory man can win — the victory over oneself. From now on he was master of himself, and not like the most of us — his own slave.

But even the greatest victor in the spiritual field must be ever on the watch for his always vigilant enemy. Francis had conquered in great things — the tempter tried now to bring him to defeat in small things.

Francis continued as before to go every day to his oratory

in the cave outside the city to pray there. Now it often happened that on the way there he met a humpbacked old woman — one of the common deformed creatures who, in the south, so willingly betake themselves to the sheltering obscurity of the churches. They can be seen there all day long, rattling their rosaries, or dozing in a corner, but the instant a stranger approaches, they draw the kerchief around their heads, limp out from their corner, and mutter piteously with outstretched hand: "*Un soldo, signore! Un soldo, signorino mio!*" (A penny, sir! A penny, sir!)

Such a pitiful old beggar was it who now every day limped across the young man's path. And it happened that in the newly converted young soul there rose a repugnance and a resistance — a repugnance to the dirt and misery of the old woman, a resistance to her troublesome ways and to her persistency. And as he went on his way, and the sun shone, and the fields were green, and the distant mountains showed grey-blue, a voice whispered within him: "And are you willing to give up all this — are you willing to abandon it all? You will give up light and sun, life and joy, the cheerful open-air feasts — and will shut yourself up in a cave and waste your best years in useless prayers, and finally become an old fool, shaking with the palsy, who pitifully wanders about from church to church, and, perhaps in secret, sighs and mourns over his wasted life?"

Thus the wicked enemy whispered into the young man's soul, and this was the moment when Francis' youth and light-loving eyes and knightly soul weakened. But as he reached his cave he always succeeded in conquering himself — and the harder the struggle had been, the deeper was the peace which followed — the joy and the hope — all in converse with God.[1]

[1] I believe that in this description I have given the right interpretation of the episode, which in the *Tres Socii* is only told in the following words: "Quaedam mulier erat Assisii gibbosa deformiter, quam daemon viro Dei apparens sibi ad memoriam reducebat, et comminibatur eidem, quod gibbositatem illius mulieris iactaret in ipsum, concepto nisi a proposito resiliret. Sed Christi miles fortissimus, minas diaboli vilipendens, intra (intrans?) criptam orabat." (Cap. IV, n. 12.)

CHAPTER VI

THE MESSAGE IN SAN DAMIANO

"GOD gave me also," thus St. Francis speaks, where in his testament he speaks of his youth, "God gave me also so great a confidence in the churches that I simply prayed and said this: 'We pray to thee, Lord Jesus Christ, here and in all thy churches, all over the whole world, and we bless thee because with thy Holy Cross thou hast redeemed the world!'"

"And then the Lord gave me and still gives me so great a confidence in priests, who live by the rite of the Holy Roman Church, that if they even persecuted me, I would for the sake of their consecration say nothing about it. And if I had the wisdom of Solomon and travelled in the parishes of poor priests, yet I would not preach without their permission. And them and all other priests I will fear, love, and honor as my superiors, and I will not look on their faults, for I see God's Son in them, and they are my superiors. And I do this because, here on earth, I see nothing of the Son of the Highest God, except his most holy body and blood, which the priests receive and which only they give to others. And these solemn secrets I will honor and venerate above everything and keep them in the most sacred places."[1]

We have here from the last year of Francis' life the most authentic testimony as to his feeling all through his life towards the Church and the clergy. And this testimony coming from himself accords exactly with all that his biographers tell us about the same phase of his character.

---

[1] "in locis preciosis." This referred both to the churches and to the tabernacles in which the Blessed Sacrament is kept, and finally to the vessels of the altar (ciborium, pyx). *Opuscula S. P. Francisci* (Quaracchi, 1904), pp. 77-78. Compare Celano, *V. pr.*, n. 45; *Tres Socii*, n. 37; Anon. Perus. (*A. SS.*, Oct. II), p. 584, n. 210; Bonav., n. 42.

It has already been told how Francis showed his interest in church affairs in supplying poor churches with proper vestments and the like. The environs of Assisi even to-day contain enough of such small churches, road- and field-chapels, often half in ruin. Their doors are frequently locked, so seldom are they used; one can look into them through low windows, outside of which kneeling benches are often placed, and on the altar there will be seen a torn cloth, laid awry, wooden vases with dusty paper flowers, and wooden candlesticks which were once gilded but are now cracked and grey.

Nevertheless there can be something very devotional in such lonely deserted churches. If they are open so that one can enter, perhaps on the walls will be found half-obliterated old frescoes, painted by those disciples of Giotto or Simone Martini who, in the fourteenth century, seem to have personally visited the most remote of the smaller cities and villages of the Apennines. The holy-water font is long empty and full of dust, but as one kneels in prayer, the wind is heard sighing through the chestnut groves or a mountain stream foams in the solemn loneliness.

The old church of San Damiano, a little outside of and below the city, was such a half-ruined chapel in the time of Francis' youth.[1] The road to it has not changed much in the seven centuries which have passed; it slopes rather steeply and passes by a broad whitewashed house, with large, yellow grain-houses of the shape of beehives around it, and among the olive groves, where the corn grows luxuriantly under the gnarled olive trees' fine silver-grey web of branches and leaves. In fifteen minutes' walking San Damiano is reached, which now is a convent, occupied by brown Franciscans.

In the days of Francis' youth, San Damiano was only a little tottering field-chapel, whose material adornment consisted of a large Byzantine crucifix over the high altar. In front of this crucifix Francis was often wont to pray, and thus it happened to him that once, a little while after his visit to the lepers, he knelt one day in prayer before the image of the

[1] This was mentioned in 1030. Henry Thode: *Frans v. Assisi und die Anfänge der Kunst* (Berlin, 1885), p. 298.

Crucified One within the church of San Damiano. After he had placed himself in thought upon the Cross for the first time, this spiritual crucifixion became a favorite exercise for his meditations. With an imploring gaze fixed upon the hallowed countenance of Jesus, he uttered the following prayer, which tradition has preserved for us:

"Great and glorious God, my Lord Jesus Christ! I implore thee to enlighten me and to disperse the darkness of my soul! Give me true faith and firm hope and a perfect charity! Grant me, O Lord, to know thee so well that in all things I may act by thy light, and in accordance with thy holy will!"[1]

The whole of the young man's striving in the year that had passed since he had stood on the roadside not far from San Damiano, and had found the world empty and his soul a waste, are gathered together and framed in this simple and profound prayer. This it was that he had always sought for and wished for, through all his errors and weakness — light to see the will of God and to act in accordance therewith. The whole of his life from that time up to this moment had been one repetition in many forms, but with increasing fervor, of the words: "Speak, Lord, for thy servant heareth!"

And so it came to pass that God deigned to speak to his servant, Francis. From the crucifix came a voice that could only be heard within the heart, and what the voice said was this: "Now go hence, Francis, and build up my house, for it is nearly falling down!"

And just as that time in Spoleto, when he was commanded to abandon his journey to Aquila, Francis was at once ready to obey the divine message. Simple and literal as he was, he looked about him in the old chapel and saw that it was nearly falling down. And trembling under the solemnity of the moment, he answered the Crucified One who had vouchsafed to speak to him: "Lord, with joy will I do what thou wishest."

At last God had heard his prayer! at last God had set him to work! And quick in his movements as Francis was, he at once set to work to carry out the Lord's directions. Out-

[1] Wadding: *Annales Minorum*, I (Romae, 1731), p. 31.

side the door he found the priest of the place, a poor old Father, sitting in the sun on a stone bench. The young man approached him deferentially, kissed his hand in greeting, took out his purse, and gave to the astonished priest a considerable sum of money, saying: "I beg you to buy oil with this money so that there shall always be a lamp burning before the crucifix within, and you may let me know when there is no more and I will supply it again."

Before the old priest could recover from his astonishment Francis was gone. His heart was overflowing, his soul was trembling with the great event that had happened to him. As he went along, he made now and then the sign of the Cross, and it seemed as if he each time imprinted deeper and deeper the image of the Crucified One upon his heart. Unsurpassably true and incomparably beautiful, the old legend goes on to say that from that hour the thought of the sufferings of our Lord made Francis' heart melt, so that he from now on as long as he lived bore in his heart the wounds of our Lord Jesus.[1]

But more money was needed to build up San Damiano's church than what Francis had with him at the moment. But in the interim he had not the least doubt as to how he should get the necessary means. As fast as his feet could carry him he hurried home, took some rolls of fine cloth out of the shop, loaded a pack-horse with it, and took the road to Foligno, to bring his goods to the market in this large neighboring city as he had been wont to do. In the course of a short time he had sold both goods and horse, and was back with the money to San Damiano — the distance between the two places is a small number of miles, and Francis rode on the outward trip.

Perhaps he found the priest still on the stone bench, sunning himself as he returned. In any case, the young man found him, and as he again greeted him reverentially, he put the whole sum of money, no inconsiderable one, which his

[1] "Ab illa itaque hora ita vulneratum et liquefactum est cor ejus ad memoriam Dominicae passionis, quod semper dum vixit, stigmata Domini Jesu Christi in corde suo portavit" (*Tres Socii*, cap. V, n. 14. Compare Bonav., *Leg. Major*, I, n. 5, II, n. 1).

transaction had brought him, into the priest's lap, with the words that it was for the restoration of the church.[1]

The priest had accepted the former and less considerable alms, but when Francis now came with all this sum of money, and wished to give it to him, he feared that something was wrong, and said no. Perhaps he thought that it was one of the young society man's wild impulses, and that the gift was not seriously meant. In any case, he wanted to stand well with Pietro di Bernardone, and was therefore determined to have nothing more to do with the affair. In vain did Francis sit down by the side of the old priest and use all his powers of persuasion to weaken his determination. All was futile; Francis only obtained this much: the priest would permit him to live at San Damiano for a while, to devote himself without interruption to prayer and works of piety.

From now on, Francis was virtually ordained to lead what was called in the Middle Ages "a religious life," that is to say, the life of a monk or hermit. He did not think of entering a convent, — in his Testament he says himself that no one showed him the way to his *vita religiosa*, but that the Almighty taught it to him. But in referring to the change that came to him at this time, he uses the exact classical expression in the same place, which designates the entering an order: "to leave the world." *Exivi de saeculo*, he says, "I abandoned the world."[2] The time he was now to spend with the priest in San Damiano can be properly regarded as his novitiate — but a novitiate in which the spirit of God alone was his teacher, director and taskmaster.

Near the priest's house there was a cave, and, true to his custom, Francis had chosen this as his prayer chamber. Here he spent nights and days in prayer and fasting, with tears and "unspeakable groanings."[3]

While these things were occurring, Pietro di Bernardone had been on one of his business trips. Now he returned home and did not find his son. Pica did not know what had become of him, or, if she did know, would not tell. But, however this may be, the old merchant soon found his son's

[1] *Tres Socii*, cap. VI, n. 16. Thomas of Celano, *Vita prima*, I, cap. IV.
[2] *Opuscula* (Quar., 1904), pp. 79, 77.   [3] Rom. viii., 26.

hiding place, and betook himself thither, but did not find Francis, who was hidden in his cave. Meanwhile, the priest seems to have utilized the opportunity to give Pietro di Bernardone the money from his son's business transaction; Francis had laid it aside in a window recess in the church. The disappearance of the cloth and of the horse had naturally been one of the causes of the coming of Pietro di Bernardone; after he had recovered the money, he went home much quieted, and spent a whole month without making any new attempt to find or to speak to his first-born. Food was meanwhile brought to him in the cave from his home — probably by his mother's contrivance.[1]

It is fair to say that Francis employed this month to imbue himself in the great thought which, from now on, presented itself to him as the essence of Christianity — *the life of Christ the Crucified in every one of the faithful.* The Epistle of Paul to the Romans is one of the Biblical writings Francis most frequently quotes.[2] And it is precisely in this book that Paul appears more strongly than elsewhere to be not only the great Christian dogmatic, but also the great Christian mystic. This is neither scientific hypothesis nor flower of literature, but is in accordance with the facts, when I find the emotions of the young son of the Italian merchant, in this

[1] Celano, *Vita prima*, I, cap. V. *Tres Socii*, cap. VI, n. 16. — According to a later tradition Francis, on his father's return, found refuge in an opening which miraculously appeared in the road, and into which he disappeared, while his father walked past it. Wadding (I, p. 31) is the first who refers to this "concavitas . . . cui ego, quo potui affectu et reverentia memet immersi." The hole, upon whose rear wall is a life-size painting of St. Francis, is still shown to those who visit S. Damiano — as a rule with the above explanation. So far from having any miraculous origin, the said excavation has its origin in the desire men, in old as well as recent times, have had to perpetuate the height of celebrated persons (compare the gate in the Lateran church in Rome, said to be of the height of Our Lord — the historic column in the cathedral in Roskilde, etc.). In his *Annales* (1226, n. 42) Wadding for instance tells the following of St. Clara, the friend of St. Francis, into whose possession, as is known, San Damiano eventually passed: "mensa est sancti patris corpus, ad cujus staturam postea curavit fieri quoddam receptaculum ad tribunae dorsum, ubi et ejus imaginem fecit depingi." This explains the existence of the recess or excavation as well as of the painting.

[2] Thus in the *Admonitiones*, cap. VI: Rom. viii. 35; cap. XI: Rom. ii. 5; in the first Rule, cap. IX: Rom. xiv. 3; cap. XI: Rom. i. 29–30; in the second Rule, cap. IX: Rom. ix. 28.

time of proof and probation at San Damiano, expressed in these words of the eighth chapter of the Epistle to the Romans:

"There is now, therefore, no condemnation to them that are in Christ Jesus, who walk not according to the flesh. For the law of the spirit of life, in Christ Jesus, hath delivered me from the law of sin and of death . . . that the justification of the law might be fulfilled in us, who walk not according to the flesh, but according to the spirit. . . . For if you live according to the flesh, you shall die: but if by the spirit you mortify the deeds of the flesh, you shall live. For whosoever are led by the Spirit of God, they are the sons of God. . . . For the Spirit himself giveth testimony to our spirit, that we are the sons of God. And if sons, heirs also: heirs, indeed of God, and joint heirs with Christ: yet so if we suffer with him, that we may be also glorified with him. . . . For whom he foreknew, he also predestinated to be made conformable to the image of his Son: . . ."

It is probable that to this month at San Damiano we may assign an occurrence, preserved for us in the legends without any more exact chronology. Francis was seen one day wandering around on the plain below Assisi in the vicinity of a little old chapel which was called *Portiuncula* or *S. Maria degli Angeli*, "Our Lady of the Angels." He wandered around the chapel sighing and weeping as if overcome by a great sorrow. A passer-by approached him and asked in sympathy what had gone wrong with him, and why he wept. Then Francis answered: "I am weeping over the sufferings of my Lord Jesus Christ, and I will not be ashamed to wander around the whole world and weep over them." This so affected the stranger that he too began to shed tears, and they wept together.[1]

Thus for Francis of Assisi the life began, not after the flesh but after the spirit, which was to lead him ever higher, until he approached as near as man can attain to the image of Jesus Christ, the Crucified.

[1] *Tres Socii*, cap. V, n. 14. Celano, *Vita secunda*, I, cap. VI.

CHAPTER VII

THE ABANDONMENT OF HIS HOME AND FATHER

ONE April day in the year 1207, Pietro di Bernardone stood behind the counter in his shop, when he heard a great noise in the street — the sound of many voices, shouting, screaming, and laughter. The noise approached nearer and nearer; now it seemed to be at the nearest corner. The old merchant signed to one of his clerks to run out and see what was going on.

"*Un pazzo, Messer Pietro!*" was the clerk's contemptuous report. "It is a crazy man, whom the boys are chasing!"

The clerk stood yet a moment and turned around white in the face. He had seen who the crazy man was. . . .

And a moment after, Pietro di Bernardone stood in the doorway, and saw in the midst of the howling crowd who now were close to the house, *his son*, his Francis, his firstborn, for whom he had dreamt such great things, and for whom he had nourished such bright hopes. . . . There he came now home at last, in a disgraceful company, pale and emaciated to the eye, with dishevelled hair and dark rings under his eyes, bleeding from the stones thrown at him, covered with the dirt of the street, which the boys had cast upon him. . . . This was his Francis, the pride of his eyes, the support of his age, the joy of his life and his comfort — it had come to this, to this had all these crazy, cursed ideas brought him. . . .

Sorrow, shame, and anger almost overcame Pietro di Bernardone. Nearer and nearer came the shouting and howling throng — mercilessly grinning they called to him where he stood upon his steps: "See here, Pietro di Bernardone, we bring you your pretty son, your proud knight —

now he is coming home from the war in Aquila, and has won the princess and half the kingdom!"

The old merchant could control himself no longer. He had to give way to rage to avoid weeping. Like a wild beast he ran down into the mob, striking and kicking to right and left, until the crowd, fairly frightened, opened and dispersed. Without a word, he seized his son and took him up into his arms. His rage gave the old man a giant's strength: raging and gritting his teeth he bore Francis through the house and finally threw him, almost exhausted and out of his senses, down upon the floor in a dark cellar, where he locked him in. With trembling hands he stuck the keys in his belt and returned to his work.[1]

Pietro di Bernardone's hope was to overcome his son's last madness with a good term of *carcer* — to use the German students' expression. To the dark prison he added therefore in addition a diet of bread and water, thinking that he would thus reach his son's weak point, whose sweet tooth he had known since his early days.[2]

But the old days were gone, and Francis had changed — he was approaching the times when he would sprinkle ashes on his food, if it tasted too good, saying to his brothers that "Brother Ashes" was chaste.[3] And when Messer Pietro after the lapse of a few days had to go out again, and Fru Pica opened the door of the prison, hoping to do with her tears and prayers that which imprisonment and hunger had not accomplished, she found her son uncowed and unsubdued, yes, glad to have suffered something for his convictions.

After she realized that Francis would not give up his new mode of life, she took advantage of the absence of her husband

[1] I have here attempted, as I have done in the first chapter and in the end of chapter V, a fuller psychological description of that which biographers have only given a few words to. But no fault can be found with the description of Pietro di Bernardone in the *Tres Socii* ("torvo oculo," "hirsuta facie," etc.). Like all who, as opposed to an absolute ideal, represent the more limited scope of the practical, Pietro di Bernardone has often been unjustly condemned. See Celano, *Vita prima*, cap. V, n. 15.

[2] "ut ipse vir Dei confessus postea est frequenter, electuariis et confectionibus utebatur et a cibis contrariis abstinebat." *Tres Socii*, cap. VII, n. 22.

[3] "in cibis, quos edebat, saepe ponebat cinerem, dicens fratribus in abstinentiae suae velamen, fratrem cinerem esse castum." *Tres Socii*, cap. V, n. 15.

and set the prisoner at liberty. And as a bird flies to its nest, Francis at once returned to his refuge by San Damiano.

Pietro di Bernardone soon returned from his trip and found the cage empty. Instead of again seeking his son in San Damiano, he tried the law. He turned to the lawyers of the city for the purpose of disinheriting his erring son, or at any rate of banishing him from the locality.[1] Furthermore, he wanted to get back all the money that Francis was in possession of. Apparently the mother had not let her son go away from home empty-handed; perhaps all the money of the Foligno transaction was not yet spent.

In the words of the chronicler, Mariano, Pietro di Bernardone was "Reipublicae benefactor et provisor" (a benefactor and guardian of the republic) — one of the city's greatest benefactors.[2] Nothing was more likely than that the authorities would seek to accede to his request, and the herald of the state was sent down to arrest Francis. On his part he refused to obey the summons, answering: "By the grace of God I am now a free man and not obliged to appear before the court, because I am only the servant of the Highest God." As Sabatier has remarked, this answer can only be taken in the sense that Francis had now received the lower orders and so came under the jurisdiction of the Church. The intimate relations between him and the Bishop of Assisi give this supposition great probability.[3]

The father seems to have awaited the return of the herald in the City Hall. In any case, the lawyers let him know at once that they to their sorrow had to let the case go. Pietro di Bernardone, however, would not let the legal prosecution thus begun cease, and shortly brought his complaint into the episcopal palace on the *Piazza del Vescovado* before the representatives of the Church. The affair was here taken up, and at an appointed time father and son met before the Bishop.[4]

From the first it was evident on whose side his sympathies

[1] Julian of Speier (*A. SS.*, Oct. II, p. 568, n. 124).
[2] Quoted in Wadding (I, p. 17).
[3] Sabatier: *Vie*, p. 68, n. 2.
[4] Guido II had occupied the Bishop's throne in Assisi since 1204. Cristofani: *Storie*, I, 169 et seq.; Sabatier: *Vie*, p. 69, n. 2.

were. The motive, which he adduced to persuade Francis to return all the money he might have received from his father, was anything but acceptable to Pietro di Bernardone. "If it is your desire to serve God," said he to the young man, "then give his mammon back to your father, which perhaps has been obtained by unjust methods, and therefore should not be used for the benefit of the Church."[1]

These words, said in the presence of the numerous hearers who had come to the place to hear the celebrated suit between one of the city's most distinguished men and his crazy son, were not adapted to pacify the old merchant. All eyes turned from him to his son, who sat on the other side of the Bishop, still clothed in his costly scarlet clothes. And now something wonderful happened — something that never before had happened in the world's history, and never will happen again — something which the painters of succeeding centuries should immortalize, which poets should sing of, and priests preach about. Francis stood up in silence with streaming eyes. "My Lord," said he, turning towards the Bishop, "I will not only give him the money cheerfully, but also the clothes I have received from him." And before anyone had time to think what he intended to do, he had disappeared into an adjoining room, back of the courtroom, a moment later to reappear, *naked*, except for a girdle of haircloth about his loins, and with his clothes on his arm. All involuntarily stood up — Pietro di Bernardone and his son Francis were face to face. And with a voice that trembled with emotion, the young man said, as he looked over the heads of the audience, as if he saw some one or something in the distance:

"Listen, all of you, to what I have to say! Hitherto I have called Pietro di Bernardone father. Now I return to him his money and all the clothes I got from him, so that hereafter I shall not say: Father Pietro di Bernardone, but Our Father who art in heaven!"

And Francis bent down and laid his clothes of scarlet and fine linen at his father's feet, with a quantity of money. A mighty movement ran through the audience. Many began

[1] *Tres Socii*, cap. VI, n. 19.

to weep; even the Bishop had tears in his eyes. Only Pietro di Bernardone wàs unmoved. With a face of stone, he stooped down, white with rage but without uttering a word, and took up the clothes and money. Then the Bishop stepped over to Francis, spread his cape over him, and clothed the naked young man in its white folds as he pressed him to his heart. From now on Francis was what he so long had wished to be — the servant of God only and a man of the Church.

When the first strong emotion was over, and Francis was alone with the Bishop, he began to think of clothing for the young man. In the Bishop's residence there was found an old cloak which had been the property of the gardener; Francis took this with delight and, as he left the Bishop's palace, drew with a bit of chalk he had found a cross on the back of the poor garment.[1]

It was in April, 1207,[2] that Pietro di Bernardone's son thus literally complied with the words of the gospel, to forsake everything and, taking up the Cross, to follow Jesus. The Umbrian April is equivalent in point of view of the season to May, or better, June, in Denmark. The clear sun shines day after day brightly from a clear sky. The air is fresh and healthy, purified by the many downpours of the winter's rain. The roads are not yet dusty, but firm and good to travel over, and the corn is growing under the olive trees, bright green and of half its final height, sprinkled with quantities of bright red poppies. It is the most beautiful of the Italian seasons, far better than the unhealthy, torrid, fever-bearing autumn.

It was on such a sunny April morning that Pietro di Bernardone's son, clothed in the old gardener's cloak, left the Bishop's palace in Assisi to go out into the world, like one of those

[1] The only one who tells of this is St. Bonaventure (*Leg. maj.*, II, 4), who apparently got it from Brother Illuminato of Rieti, who is responsible for many other minor traits (See Appendix).

[2] This date seems to follow from the following place in Anon. Perus. (*A. SS.*, Oct. II, p. 572, n. 141): "Postquam impleti sunt anni ab incarnatione Domini MCCVII mens Aprilis, XVI kalendas Maii, videns populum suum Dominus . . mandatorum ejus oblitum . . . sua benignissimâ misericordiâ motus voluit operarios mittere in messem suam et illuminavit virum qui erat in civitate Assisii, nomine Franciscum." XVI kalendas Maii is April 16.

evangelic "Strangers and Pilgrims" the Scripture tells of. Every man's life is the fruit of his innermost will, and therefore Francis had attained that which he so long had striven for — that which he had put to the proof in Rome, what he had prayed for in the solitude of the Umbrian cave — to be allowed to follow the naked and suffering Saviour, himself naked and suffering.

Francis wandered forth from the home of his youth and from the city of his early days, from father and mother, from family and friends, from all his past and all his memories. He went neither out to San Damiano, nor down the plain to Portiuncula's little chapel. There are moments in the life of man when the soul is drawn to the greatest things in nature's gift — to the mountains or to the sea. Francis wandered forth from Assisi by the gate in the direction of Monte Subasio, on the road which takes one up the mountain. And remembering the words of the gospel, about him who lays his hand to the plough, he certainly never looked back until the towers and roofs of Assisi were long out of sight beneath him and he found himself alone on the heights of Monte Subasio, — in a young oak-woods or among great barren fields of stone. Hence his glance wandered far over the world; the valley of Spoleto lay under his feet, as if seen from an air-balloon, with its white roads, bright rivers, fields, with olive trees in regular order, and houses and churches like toys. The mountains, which below Assisi hem in the horizon, seem sunken down and low, and behind them, higher ones of paler blue lift up their summits — the far-distant Apennines.

Francis had started off in the direction of Gubbio. In this village, which in a straight line is not very many miles from Assisi, lived one of the friends of his earliest youth — perhaps the same friend who used to go with him to discover the treasure in the cave. It inevitably takes time to wander about the mountains; day was already waning and Francis had not yet crossed the wild wood-grown mountain side that separates Assisi from Valfabbrica. Still he wandered along confidently and sang in French the praises of God, as he was wont to do in the happiest moments of his life. Then there was a rustling among the dry leaves that spread the ground, the branches and twigs were disturbed, and a robber band broke out from concealment with a threatening "Who is there?" Undisturbed Francis answered: "I am the herald of the great King. But what is it that you desire?" The highwaymen looked for a moment at the wonderful apparition in the shabby cloak with the chalk-drawn cross on the back. Then they determined to let him go without further molestation, but so as to let him know what he had escaped, they took him by the arms and legs and flung him into a cleft, where the snow, in spite of the April sun, was still deep. "Lie there, you peasant, who wants to play at being a herald!" they said to him, and departed. It was only with difficulty that Francis managed to work his way out of the drift in the cleft; singing the praises of God as before, he wandered on over the mountain.[1] After a little space of time he drew near to a little Benedictine convent, where he received shelter in exchange for serving in the kitchen. Here he stayed several days in the hope that he would be able to supplement his scanty garments by a cast-off monk's costume. They gave him while there hardly enough food, and, as his first biographer says, "not actuated by anger, but driven by necessity," he went on to Gubbio. It is easy to believe that the prior of the convent came to give excuses after Francis had become a celebrity. But at this time Francis was not celebrated, and it is also credible that the good prior never gave a thought to his hard-hearted inhospitality. And yet St. Benedict in the Rule of his Order commands: "The strangers shall be received as Christ."[2]

At last Francis reached Gubbio, and there found a friend, from whom he received the clothing he had wished for and which was the same that hermits used to wear, with a girdle

---

[1] Celano, *Vita prima*, I, cap. VII. Julian, *A. SS.*, Oct. II, p. 575, nn. 160-161. Bonav., II, 5. According to Lucarelli (*Memoria e guida storica di Gubbio*, Citta di Castello, 1888, p. 583) the meeting of Francis and the robbers occurred near Caprignone, where are still be to seen frescoes of the fourteenth to the fifteenth centuries in an old convent church. One of these shows Francis clothing himself in a ragged garment.

[2] *Reg. S. Benedicti*, cap. LIII: "Omnes supervenientes hospites tanquam Christus suscipiantur." — A local tradition, which is not incredible, places this scene at the cloister of Sta. Maria della Rocca (la Rocchiciuola), between Assisi and Valfabbrica. See my book "Reisebogen" (2d ed., 1905), pp. 122-123.

around the body and shoes and staff.[1] Other friendly services he did not accept, and the biographers tell how Francis lived in the hospital of Gubbio, how he washed the lepers' feet, bound up their sores, treated their boils, dried up the matter, and often kissed the suppurating sores.[2]

But meanwhile Francis' own particular work awaited him in San Damiano near Assisi, and one day he found himself there again, to begin the work God had given him to do — to restore the church edifice. During his absence rumors seem to have flown fast, for the priest was, it appears, anything but glad to see him again, and Francis had to appeal to the word of the Bishop, which affirmed that he had the approval of the authorities of the Church.[3]

A question, which never before had occupied Francis, now presented itself to him in all its prosaic obtrusiveness — the question of money. Where would the money come from with which to restore San Damiano? If necessary Francis could handle the trowel, but stone and mortar could not be had for nothing.

And this last was the very thing Francis undertook to provide for — to procure for nothing the required stone and lime. Now he could avail himself of what he had learned in his troubadour and jongleur days. One day men saw Francis in his hermit robes in the market-place in Assisi, singing in public like another wandering minstrel. And when

---

[1] "quasi heremiticum ferens habitum, accinctus corrigia et baculum manu gestans calceatis pedibus incedebat." Celano, *Vita prima*, I, cap. IX, and *Tres Socii*, VIII, 25. Giuseppe Mazzatinti has in *Miscellanea Francescana* (vol. V, pp. 76–78) maintained that the friend in Gubbio was Frederico Spadalunga, the oldest of three brothers, himself, Giacomello and Antonio. In the time of Aroldi there were still to be seen in the Palazzo dei Consoli in Gubbio, frescoes, whose subject was the kindness of Spadalunga to Francis. In the first of these "si representa S. Francesco nudo e havendo in terra dietro a se alcuni stracci, riceve una veste in atto di ricuoprirsi da un huomo il quale mostra di essere giovanetto" (F. Haroldus: *Epitome Annalium Ord. Min.*, Roma, 1662, vol. I, p. 29, quoted by Mazzatinti, loc. cit.). I avail myself of this opportunity to refer to the remarkable Journal, named above, *Miscellanea Francescana*, which now for a number of years has been published in Foligno by the learned canon, Mgr. Mich. Faloci-Puligani. (Unfortunately this journal, which is a real gold-mine for those interested in our subject, is not easily to be found in public libraries.)

[2] Bonav., *Leg. major*, cap. II, n. 6.

[3] *Tres Socii*, VII, 21.

he had ended his song, he went around among his auditors and begged. "He who gives me a stone will have his reward in heaven," said he; "he who gives me two stones will have two rewards; he who gives three stones will receive three rewards." Many laughed at him, but Francis only laughed back. Others, the legend tells us, "were moved to tears to see him converted from such great worldliness and vanity to such an intoxication of love to God." Francis actually succeeded in getting together a quantity of stone, which he carried away on his own shoulders. He also did the masonry work, and people who went by used to hear him singing in French as he worked. If anyone stopped to look at him, he would call out to them: "You had better come and help me to build up St. Damian's church again."[1]

Such zeal and self-sacrifice could not fail to affect the old priest of San Damiano's, and to show Francis his appreciation he used every evening to wait upon him with one or another selected dish, according to his limited means. This went on very well for a time, until one fine day it occurred to Francis to ask himself if he ever would be able on his return to the world to be certain of finding so attentive a host as here. What I am doing, said he to himself, is not living the life of a poor man, as I have wished to do. No, a real pauper goes from door to door with his bowl in his hand and takes everything that good men will give him. And this is what I must do from now on!

Scarcely had the midday bell rung in Assisi the next day, and the people were sitting at their tables, when Francis with his bowl in hand went on his circuit through the city. He knocked at all doors and got something at many of them — here a sup of soup, a bone with a little meat on it, a crust of bread, some leaves of salad, all sorts of things mixed together. When Francis had ended his begging trip his bowl was full, but of the most unappetizing mixture one could think of. Lost in thought, the young man sat on a stoop and stared down into the bowl, which seemed most like a trough filled

[1] *Tres Socii*, VII, 24. Th. of Celano, *Vita prima*, I, cap. VIII. By the first named of these two biographers this invitation is made into a prophecy referring to St. Clara and her nuns, who were to build there later.

with dog's meat. Nearly vomiting with nausea, he put the first bit to his lips.

And behold! — it was just as when he kissed the leper in other times. His heart was filled with the sweetness of the Holy Ghost, and it seemed to him as if he never had tasted such exquisite food. Entranced, he rushed home and said to the priest that for the future he should do his own providing well enough.

Thus was the son of Pietro di Bernardone become a public beggar, and it is easy to understand that the old, purse-proud merchant, so jealous of his honor, felt the blow even heavier than any of the preceding ones. From now on he could not bear to see his son, but burst out into wild curses when he met him. Francis was perhaps not altogether insensitive to this outburst of wrath; in any case, from this time Francis used to take with him an old beggar named Albert on these peregrinations, and when they would meet Pietro di Bernardone, Francis would kneel down in front of his companion and would say: "Bless me, father!" "See now," he would say, turning to the old merchant, "God has given me a father who blesses me, in your place, who curse me!"[1]

Francis' younger brother, Angelo,[2] also shared in the persecution of the voluntary beggar and church builder. One cool morning he saw Francis, who in his humble clothes was hearing mass, in one of the churches of Assisi. Then Angelo said to his companion, and so loud that his brother could hear him: "Go there and ask Francis if he will not sell you a shilling's worth of sweat!" Francis heard it and answered back in French: "I have already sold it at a good price to my Lord and Saviour!"

Meanwhile the work at San Damiano progressed rapidly. It was more a putting to rights than a rebuilding.[3] As a sort

[1] *Tres Socii,* cap. VII, n. 23. Anon. Perus., *A. SS.,* Oct. II, p. 577, n. 167.

[2] The name is preserved in old documents, printed in Cristofani's *Storia d'Assisi,* I, pp. 78 et seq. See Sabatier, *Vie,* p. 2, n. 2, together with the family tree copied from a manuscript of 1381, which the Bollandist Suysken gives in the *Acta Sanctorum,* Oct. II, p. 556, and Wadding in the *Annales,* I, p. 17.

[3] According to Cristofani (*Storia di S. Damiano,* Assisi, 1882, pp. 50 et seq.), Francis can hardly have made any new additions to the church. Henry Thode, on the other hand ("*Frans v. Assisi und die Anfänge der Kunst der Renaissance,*" Berlin, 1885, p. 298), thinks that Francis was the builder of the front pointed

of conclusion to the work Francis wished to leave the priest a good supply of oil for the altar lamps, especially for the perpetual lamp before the Blessed Sacrament. For this purpose he went on a round through Assisi to beg for oil, and it so happened that on this occasion he came to the house of an old-time friend, just at the height of a festival. Now at last his courage weakened. He who had defied his father and had not feared the robbers on Monte Subasio was ashamed to be seen by his old companions. Perhaps he had one of those indescribable, depressing moments, experienced by all converts, when that which has been left behind appears with perfect clearness to be one of the natural, right and reasonable things, while the new thoughts and the new life suddenly present themselves to one as something artificial, acquired, stilted—something one would give anything to attain, but which it seems useless to strive after. Perhaps the hermit's costume, which Francis in general so willingly wore, suddenly seemed to him a laughable mummery, and perhaps he seemed to himself less of a man than in those days of joy, long passed, when he wore the parti-colored costume of the jester.

If he had been fighting his own fight at this time, it would have lasted but a short time. The legend tells us that he walked a few steps beyond the house of festivity, but that he despised his weakness, turned around and told his friends how weak he had been, as he at the same time begged them for charity's sake to give him an alms for oil for the lamps of St. Damian.

After he had finished this work, Francis — so as not to be idle — undertook a similar one, in repairing the old Benedictine church of St. Peter, which is now in Assisi, but then was outside the walls.[1] And finally he began the restoration

Gothic portion of the building, while the rear vaulted portion with the apse is older. Thode calls attention to the curious kind of pointed vaulting which Francis used not only here in S. Damiano, but also in Portiuncula, in *la Chiesina* in La Verna and in one of the Franciscan retreats near Cortona, and which elsewehere is only found in the south of France (ditto, p. 296).

[1] "longius a civitate distantem," says Bonaventure (II, 7), who, however, only knew Assisi from a short visit there. In reality S. Pietro was very near the city. It is first mentioned, according to Thode (ditto, p. 300), in the year 1029. The façade dates back to 1268. From 1250 to 1577 it was in the hands of the Cistercians, now it is in the hands of the Benedictines again.

of the little old field-chapel, before which he was one day found weeping over the sufferings of Christ — Portiuncula, also called *Santa Maria degli Angeli,* "Our Lady of the Angels." Francis chose as his abode for a longer time a spot in the vicinity of this little church, which, like San Damiano, belonged to the Benedictine convent on Monte Subasio, and was said to have been built by pilgrims returning from the Holy Land in the year 352.

There is no doubt that he constantly regarded the restoration of churches as his real vocation in life. Even so late as 1213 he founded a church in honor of the Blessed Virgin,[1] and in 1216 he filled a not inconsiderable rôle in the renovating of Santa Maria del Vescovado in Assisi.[2] Like all humble souls, he knew that it is of less importance what one does than how one does it, and he felt the call to what Verlaine many years after called *la vie humble aux travaux ennuyeux et faciles* — the humble life of tiresome and easy achievements; this life which, precisely on account of monotony and lack of great things to be done, exacts so much charity, so great a power of seeing God's eternal will back of the whole mass of small endless affairs, so as every day to live in the Sunday's spirit.

rester gai quand le jour, triste, succède au jour,
être fort, et s'user en circonstances viles. . . .

Francis belonged to the strong and cheerful souls who can do this. He saw laid out before him a vista of his future life, to be spent in the work of a day-laborer for little or no coarse bread; he saw evenings of lonely prayer, the lonely hearing of mass in the mornings, and visits to the altar in chapels and churches by the wayside and among the mountains.

For the mass, the liturgical sacrifice in memory of the sufferings and death of Jesus, was already the central point in Francis' religious life. He writes of this, the first year of his conversion, in his Testament: "Here in the world I see nothing of the Son of the Highest God but his most holy Body

---

[1] Wadding in the *Annales,* 1213, n. 17.
[2] Lipsin, *Compendiosa Historia,* Assisi, 1756, p. 19, and Faloci's studies of the ancient inscription on the outside of the choir of the same church, in *Misc. Franc.,* II, pp. 33–37.

and Blood, and these most sacred Mysteries I will venerate and honor above all things."[1] And in one of the oldest of his *Admonitiones*, his "Admonitions" to Brothers in his Order, an accordance is found with the above: "All, who have seen Jesus Christ in the flesh, but have not seen him after the Spirit and in his Divinity and have not believed that he was really the Son of God, are doomed. Also all those are doomed who see the sacrament of the Body of Christ, which is consecrated with the words of the Lord on the altar, and by the hand of the priest, in the form of bread and wine, but do not see it in the Spirit and Divinity and do not believe that it really is Our Lord Jesus Christ's most holy Body and Blood."[2]

It was not the general custom in the beginning of the thirteenth century for every Catholic priest to say mass daily. Only on Sundays or else after a special request and on important holidays was mass celebrated. On all such occasions Francis was invariably there at the place, and to please him the priest from San Damiano used often in the mornings to go down to Portiuncula and hold the divine service in the newly restored chapel.

All who have lived in Italy and have participated in the spiritual life of the people can tell by experience of the singularly impressive power of these very early divine services. Out of the morning's darkness, which perhaps is lessened by the light of the setting half-moon, or by that of a solitary great star, shining far away over the mountains, one walks into the church, where the lights cast their ruddy glow over the altar table and the priest in his bright vestments stands at the foot of the altar steps, makes the full sign of the Cross and solemnly with a low voice begins the prayers of the mass with David's wonderful forty-second Psalm. And the responses of the acolyte are heard; the holy service goes along rapidly; in the deep silence and morning peace of the church

---

[1] *Opuscula* (Quaracchi, 1904), p. 78.
[2] *Admonitio Prima, De Corpore Christi* (Quaracchi edition, p. 4). Also in *Epistola prima* (ditto, p. 91): "We may all truly know that no one can be saved except by the blood of Our Lord Jesus Christ and by the sacred words of the Lord which the clerk says," i.e., the words of consecration in the mass. See also the same letter, p. 95, where the faith in and the reception of the sacrament of the altar is simply adduced as characteristic of all the good.

are heard distinctly the whispered words from the priest's lips: "*Hoc est enim corpus meum. . . . Hic est enim calix sanguinis mei.*" . . . And while the altar bell rings over and over again there is raised high over the bowed heads of the kneeling congregation the white Host, the shining Chalice — the Body and Blood of Christ offered by the hands of the priest as the Lamb of God who bears all the sins of the world. In such moments one is lifted on mighty wings above oneself, and one's misery and faith make themselves felt, one cares to hope, one desires to love God always, to do his will and serve him only, and never more to bow down to false gods.

On such a morning in the little chapel of Portiuncula, one day in February, 1209, Francis heard the passage in the gospel, which seemed to him a new and clearer message from the Lord, still clearer than the words he had heard two years before in San Damiano, and which therefore remained effective for the rest of his life. It was the feast of the Apostle St. Matthias, February 24, on which Francis heard the priest read the following passage from the Gospel of St. Matthew (x. 7-13): "At that time Jesus said to his disciples. And going, preach, saying: The kingdom of heaven is at hand. Heal the sick, raise the dead, cleanse the lepers, cast out devils: freely have you received, freely give. Do not possess gold, nor silver, nor money, in your purses: nor scrip for your journey, nor two coats, nor shoes, nor a staff; for the laborer is worthy of his meat. And into whatsoever city or town you shall enter, inquire who in it is worthy, and there abide till you go thence. And when you come into the house, salute it, saying: Peace be to this house. And if that house be worthy, your peace shall come upon it; but if it be not worthy, your peace shall return to you." [1]

When Francis went back in thought to that mass of St. Matthew in Portiuncula, he regarded the mere reading of the gospel of the day as a divine revelation. We read in his Testament: "The Highest One himself revealed to me that I should

[1] The Gospel of St. Matthias' feast has since been changed. In the thirteenth century and as late as the fifteenth the gospel cited in the text was still read. See *Analecta Franciscana*, vol. III (Quaracchi, 1897), p. 2, n. 5. It is Wadding who follows Mariano of Florence in telling that the priest from S. Damiano went to Portiuncula and read mass for Francis.

live in accordance with the holy gospel." And again, "The Lord revealed to me a salutation that we were to say: The Lord give thee peace."[1]

The biographers tell us that after he had listened to these words and heard them exhaustively explained by the priest he was inspired and exclaimed, "This is what I want, this is what I with all my soul want to follow in my life!"[2] As if in a vision he had understood what the Lord asked of those who aspire to be his disciples, who would belong to him completely, who would sacrifice themselves for him and serve him alone — that they should be *Apostles*, that free from all superfluity, and without the troubles of the world, they were to go out into the world, rejoicing in spirit, bearing the old, serious, joyful message, "Be you converted, for the kingdom of heaven is near!"[3]

Francis the church builder and hermit was now to become Francis the apostle and evangelist — the announcer of the gospel of conversion and peace. He had scarcely left the church before he took off his shoes, threw away his staff, cast off his outer garment, which he wore against the cold. In place of his belt he tied a rope around his waist, and clothed in a long brown-grey blouse of the kind the peasants of the region wore, with a hood attached to go over his head, he was prepared to wander through the world on his naked feet, as the Apostles had gone, and bring it his Master's peace, if they wished to receive it.

[1] *Opuscula*, pp. 79, 80.
[2] Cel., *V. pr.*, I, cap. IX: *Tres Socii*, VIII, 25; Bonav., III, 1.
[3] "regnum Dei et poenitentiam praedicare, continuo exultans in spiritu Dei." Celano ditto. "pacis et poenitentiae legationem amplectens." *Tres Socii*, cap. X, n. 39 (in Boll.), n. 40 (Foligno edition).

BOOK TWO
FRANCIS THE EVANGELIST

> Pacis et poenitentiae legationem amplectens.
>
> *Embracing the embassy of peace and penitence.*
>
> LEGENDA TRIUM SOCIORUM

CHAPTER I

THE FIRST DISCIPLES

*P**RAECO sum magni regis*, "I am the great King's herald!" Thus had Francis that April day, in 1207, answered the robbers in the woods of Monte Subasio, and he had in that ejaculation given the war-cry and motto for all of his future life.

It was after the mass of St. Matthias in Portiuncula that it became clear to him how this career of herald should be carried to a conclusion, and now he wasted no time in beginning it.

From that day on a remarkable sight was to be seen in Assisi. Now here, now there in the streets and squares of the city a figure showed itself, clad in a peasant's grey cloak of undyed wool, with the hood drawn over the head and a rope around the waist. He greeted all whom he met as he went along with the words, "The Lord give you peace!" and where he saw a larger crowd assemble, he went to them, stood barefoot upon a flight of steps or on a stone and began to pray.

This remarkable man was the son of Pietro di Bernardone, who thus began his work as an evangelist. What he said was very simple and without art, — it only concerned one thing, namely, peace as the greatest good for man, peace with God by keeping his commandments, peace with man by a righteous conduct, peace with oneself by the testimony of a good conscience.[1]

The laughter which a year before had greeted Francis, when he made public entrance into his native city, was evidently

[1] *Tres Socii*, VIII, 25-26. Cel., *V. pr.*, I, cap. X. Bonav., III, 2. Julian, *A. SS.*, Oct. II, p. 579, n. 182. *Test. S. Fr.* (Op., p. 80). Compare P. Hilarin Felder: *Geschichte der wissensch. Studien im Franziskanerorden,*" Freib. in Br., 1904, p. 8, and pp. 33-37.

stilled after the scene in the Bishop's palace. They listened to him with attention, even with reverence. And the words which he said were not forgotten; they fell like living seed into many a receptive mind, into many a heart which without knowing it longed greatly to live its life nearer to God.

Thus it was that Francis in a little while found disciples. As the first we are told of [1] "a pious and simple man from Assisi," whose name has not been preserved for us, and of whom history knows no more. The first disciple known to history is therefore Bernard of Quintavalle.[2]

Bernard was a merchant like Francis and apparently not much older than he. He did not belong to Francis' circle, but followed his wonderful career only at a distance. At the outset — like so many — he had only taken Francis' conversion and church building as a new craze with him. But as time went on and Francis continued to persevere in his way of life, Bernard's doubt turned into regard and his wondering became admiration.

Bernard certainly had led hitherto a perfectly regular and good civic life. What seized him now was the feeling which Sabatier has in one place so beautifully called *la nostalgie de la sainteté* — homesickness for holiness. The sacred fire burst out within his soul — the desire for over-sanctification which is the innermost kernel of Christianity, the longing to give up the thousand things with which the soul vainly creates unrest and perturbation for itself, and to seek the one thing which satisfies. There ripened in him the determination to follow Francis — to be poor like him, wear his habit and live his life. The desire to be satisfied with little, a deep, supernatural longing, as well as an insatiability that never can get enough, waxed stronger and stronger within him. But hitherto he had never talked with Francis on the subject; on the contrary, he found a kindred soul and a confidant in one of the canons of the cathedral church of S. Rufino,

---

[1] Celano, *V. pr.*, I, cap. X.
[2] Celano, ditto, *Tres Socii*, VIII, 27-29. Bonav., III, 3. Anon. Perus., in *A. SS.*, Oct. II, pp. 580-581, nn. 187-190.
Bernard of Bessa is the first, who in his *De Laudibus b. Francisci* employs Bernard's title "of Quintavalle." See the above work in *Analecta Franciscana*, III (Quar., 1897), p. 667.

CONTEMPORARY PORTRAIT OF
ST. FRANCIS OF ASSISI
At the Sacro Speco, Subiaco

Pietro dei Cattani, a layman who, in his position of law-counsel of the church, enjoyed one of its prebendships.[1]

In later legends it is told how Bernard, before he finally enrolled himself under Francis, tried to find out by a trick if Francis' piety was true or assumed. He asked Francis a number of times to spend the night with him — an invitation which he, who at this time could hardly be said to have any fixed abode, gladly accepted. One evening, therefore, he asked his guest into his own sleeping chamber, where, after the custom in the better class of houses, a light was kept burning all night.[2]

"But to hide his holiness," thus it is told in the *Chronica XXIV generalium* and in the *Fioretti*, "St. Francis cast himself on the bed, as soon as he came into the room, and acted as if he slept, and after a while Bernard did the same, beginning to snore strongly, as if in deep slumber. And St. Francis, who believed that Bernard really slept, arose from his bed and started to pray, while with eyes and hands raised towards heaven, and with great devotion and fervor, he cried out: 'My God and my All!' And thus he remained praying and weeping greatly until morning, and repeated constantly: 'My God and my All!' and said nothing more."[3]

That back of this tale there is concealed a real occurrence is clear from Thomas of Celano's briefer description: "[Bernard] saw Francis praying at night, sleeping little, praising God and his Mother, the Blessed Virgin."[4] As day dawned Bernard determined to follow Francis therefore irrevocably. He laid before him his wish in the form of a question for solution in a case of conscience.

---

[1] Silvester, the eleventh or twelfth disciple, was the first priest of the order. In Glasberger is found the comment, that Peter of Cattani was "jurisperitus et canonicus ecclesiae S. Rufini" (*Anal. Franc.*, II, p. 6).

[2] Cel., *V. pr.*, I, X. *Vita fr. Bernardi* in *Anal. Franc.*, III, pp. 35 et seq. It says that Francis for two years was regarded as "stultus et phantasticus," and that Bernard invited him to visit him "ut ejus fatuitatem vel sanctitatem posset melius explorare."

Bernard of Quintavalle's house is the present Palazzo Sbaraglini on the Piazza del Vescovado (or of S. Maria Maggiore) in Assisi.

[3] *Fioretti*, cap. II. *Chronica XXIV generalium* in *Anal. Franc.*, III, p. 36. *Actus beati Francisci*, ed. Sabatier (Paris, 1902), cap. I.

[4] *Vita prima*, I, cap. X.

"If some one," he said, "had received from his master property entrusted to his care, be it much or little, and had had possession of it for many years, and now wanted to keep it no longer, what would be the best way to act in such a case?"

"Give it back to him of whom he had received it," was Francis' obvious answer.

"But, my Brother, the case is this, that all that I own of earthly property I have received from my God and Lord Jesus Christ, and now I want to give it back again, as it may seem best to you to perform it."

Then Francis said:

"What you tell me of, Lord Bernard, is so great and difficult a work that we will ask Our Lord Jesus Christ for advice about it, and pray him to let us know his will and to teach us how we shall bring this intention to execution. We therefore next morning will go into the church and read in the Book of Gospels, what the Lord told his disciples to do."

When the time came Pietro dei Cattani seems to have reached his decision; in any case the three men went together the few paces across the Assisi market-place to the church of S. Niccolo, which occupied what is now the site of a barracks of carabineers. Here they entered and prayed together, whereupon Francis went up to the altar and took the massbook, opened it and found the following words: "If thou wilt be perfect, go sell what thou hast, and give to the poor, and thou shalt have treasure in heaven."[1] Twice more he opened the book, and found the first time: "If any man will come after me, let him deny himself, and take up his cross, and follow me," and the next time: "And he commanded them that they should take nothing for the way."

As Francis closed the book, he turned himself towards the two men, and said:

"Brothers, this is your life and our rule, and not only ours, but all theirs who wish to live with us. Go away therefore and do that which you have heard!"

But Bernard of Quintavalle arrested his steps on the square of the church of San Giorgio — now the Piazza S. Chiara —

[1] Matth. xix. 21. The two next quotations are from Matth. xvi. 24, and Mark vi. 8.

and began to distribute all his property to the poor. And Francis stood by his side and praised God in his heart. In place of Pietro di Bernardone he had chosen a beggar for a father, and now God sent him a far better brother than Angelo.

While Bernard and Francis thus stood together, and Pietro dei Cattani had also gone in search of his possessions, it happened that a priest came by, from whom Francis had bought stone for the restoration of San Damiano. This priest, whose name was Silvester, had sold the stone cheap—perhaps on account of the good object it was to be devoted to. When he now saw so much money given away, he approached and said to Francis: "The stone which you in your time bought from me, you paid for only poorly." Incensed at the covetousness of the priest, Francis suddenly reached down into the money, which Bernard had in the lap of his cloak, and without counting the amount, poured it out into the priest's hand as he asked: "I wonder if you are now satisfied, Sir priest?" But Silvester thanked him coldly and went away.

As the legends tell, this occurrence was none the less the beginning of a new life for the avaricious priest. He began to draw comparisons between his own avarice and the contempt for property and gold shown by these two young laymen, and the words "No one can serve two masters" began to ring like a judgment in his soul over the life he had hitherto led; after a further delay he too had to come to Francis, and beg him to receive him among the Brethren.[1]

The three brothers and followers of Christ, after all was arranged, left Assisi together and spent the night in Portiuncula. Near this church they next erected a hut of boughs plastered with mud, where they could find a refuge for the night and pray in the daytime.

It was down here also that a young man from Assisi named Giles (in Latin *Ægidius*, in Italian Egidio), eight days after Bernard's conversion, sought to join them. Naturally the treatment awarded to their possessions by the rich Bernard and the accomplished lawyer Pietro had excited the greatest attention in the city and was the inexhaustible source of

[1] *Tres Socii*, VIII, 28-IX, 31. *Fioretti*, cap. II. Glassberger, *Anal. Franc.*, II, p. 6, in which Bernard's conversion is dated April 16, 1209.

conversation, as well by day on the market-place as by night at the fires, where were held *veglia*. On such an evening of gossip before the sparkling fire of juniper branches and chestnut embers, which in the cold April evenings were necessary in Assisi, Giles heard his family talk about Francis and his friends.[1]

Next morning Giles rose early, "troubled about his salvation" as the old legends say. It was April 23, the feast of the martyr St. George, and the young man betook himself to St. George's church to hear mass. Thence he took the direct road down to Portiuncula, where he knew that St. Francis would keep himself. At the hospital of S. Salvatore degli Pareti the road forks, and Giles prayed God that he might select the right one. His prayer was heard, for after wandering about a while he approached a wood and saw Francis coming out of it. Giles at once cast himself at the feet of Francis and begged to be received into the Brotherhood. But Francis looked at Giles' pious young face, raised him up and said:

"Dearest brother, God has shown you a wonderful favor! For if the Emperor were to come to Assisi and wished to make one of the citizens his knight or his chamberlain, then would the citizen be greatly rejoiced. How much more should you rejoice, whom God has chosen as his true knight and servant and to maintain the holy evangelical perfection."

And he took him to the place where the other Brothers were keeping themselves and presented him to them with these words: "The Lord our God has sent us a new good Brother. Let us therefore rejoice in the Lord and eat together in charity."

But after the meal was ended, Francis and Giles went up to Assisi to obtain cloth for the new Brother's habit. On the way an old woman met them and asked for alms. Then Francis turned around towards Brother Giles and said to him, as he looked at him "with an angel's expression":

"My dearest brother, let us for God's sake give your cloak to this poor woman!"

---

[1] Cum vero fr. Aegidius, adhuc saecularis existens, post VII dies, hoc cognatis suis narrantibus audivisset. *Vita fr. Aegidii, Anal. Franc.*, III, p. 75.

And Brother Giles at once took off his beautiful cloak and gave it to the woman, and it seemed to him — thus he told it afterwards — that this alms seemed to ascend to heaven. But he himself felt in his heart an inexpressible joy.[1]

There were now four living together in the hut at Portiuncula. In this first year they had little need for a house and home, for they spent most of their time in missionary trips. What Francis had up to this time done alone, the four did together or in couples. Thus Francis associated himself with Giles, whom he had quickly learned to love, and whom, with an expression borrowed from his reading of romance, he called his "Knight of the Round Table,"[2] and with him started on a trip through the near environs—to the Mark of Ancona, the region between the Apennines and the Adriatic Sea. On his return, Francis had the happiness to receive three new disciples, Sabbatino, Morico, and John — the last named acquired the title of Capella, "of the hat," because he was the first to wear a hat in violation of the rule of the order. All seven started out again, and Francis now chose Rieti in the Sabine Mountains as the goal for his mission.

In contrast to the regular ecclesiastical eloquence, Francis and his friends were to the last degree simple in their preaching. His sermons had more of the flavor of exhortations than of elaborated discourses — they were artless words, which came from the heart and went to the heart. His preaching always came back to three points: fear God, love God, convert yourself from bad to good. And when Francis was through, Brother Giles would add: "What he says is true! Listen to him and do as he says!"

---

[1] *Vita fr. Aegidii, Anal. Fr.*, III, pp. 74 et seq. *Vita di frate Egidio* in most editions of the *Fioretti*. *Vita beati fratris Aegidii* in Doc. Antiq. Franc., pars I: *Scripta fratis Leonis*, ed. Leonardus Lemmens (Quaracchi, 1901). *Tres Socii*, cap. IX, n. 32; XI, 44 in fine. *Speculum perfectionis*, ed. Sabatier, cap. XXXVI. Celano, *Vita prima*, I, cap. X. Bonaventure, III, 4. *Vita Aegidii* in *A. SS.* for April 23;—The date of Giles' (Latin Ægidius) conversion is given by most authorities and is one of the surest data in Franciscan chronology. See the Bollandists as above in the introduction § 2 and *Analec. Franc.*, III, p. 75, n. 3. Concerning Brother Giles' Biography as a work of Brother Leo, see Salimbene: *Chronica* (Parma edition), p. 323, "cujus vitam fr. Leo, qui fuit unus de tribus specialibus sociis beati Francisci, sufficienter descripsit."

[2] *Anal. Franc.*, III, p. 78: "Iste est miles meus tabulæ rotundæ."

Wherever they went, their sermons excited the greatest attention in peasant circles. To some they looked like wild animals.[1] Women ran away when they saw them coming. Others would speak to them, asking what order they belonged to and whence they came. They answered that they were of no order, but were only "men from Assisi, who lived a life of penance."[2] But if they were penitents, they were not for that reason shamefaced — with Francis at their head, who sang in French, praised and glorified God for his untiring goodness to them. "They were able to rejoice so much," says one of the biographers, "because they had abandoned so much." When they wandered in the spring sunshine, free as the birds in the sky, through the vineyards of the Mark of Ancona, they could only thank the Almighty who had freed them from all the snares and deceits which those who love the world are subject to and suffer from so sadly.[3]

Before sending out his six disciples, Francis had assembled them in the forest about him, near Portiuncula, where they were wont often to pray.[4] In his own cheerful yet impressive manner he addressed them on the subject of the kingdom of God, as they were going out to induce men to despise the world, to subdue their self-will, to discipline the body. "Go out, my beloved ones, and announce the gospel of peace and conversion! Be patient in trouble, give to all who insult you an humble answer, bless them who persecute you, thank those who do you wrong and slander you, because for all this your reward shall be great in heaven! And fear not because you are unlearned men, for you do not speak by yourselves, but the Spirit of your Heavenly Father will speak through you! You will find some men who are true, good and peaceful — they will receive you and your word with gladness! Others, and these in great number, you will on the other hand find to be revilers of God — they will oppose you and speak against you! Be therefore prepared to endure all things patiently!"

[1] *Sylvestres homines.* Tres Socii, IX, n. 37. Anon. Perus., p. 585a, n. 211.
[2] "Viri poenitentiales de civitate Assisii oriundi." Tres Socii, IX, n. 37.
[3] Anon. Perus., p. 582, n. 198. *Vita fr. Aegidii, Anal. Franc.*, III, p. 76. Bernard a Bessa, ditto, p. 671.
[4] Anon. Perus., p. 584b, n. 208. Compare *Anal. Franc.*, I, p. 418.

After these words, Francis embraced them one by one, "as a mother her children," blessed them, and gave them as a last aliment for the road this extract from the Bible: "Cast thy care upon the Lord, and he shall sustain thee!"[1]

Thus the disciples went out into the world, travelling in pairs. And when they came to a church or a cross, or merely saw a church-tower in the distance, they bowed down in the dust and uttered the little prayer which Francis had taught them: "We adore thee, O Christ, here and in all thy churches over the whole world, and we bless thee because by thy holy Cross thou hast redeemed us!" But if they approached one of the small towns, which then as now stood upon the mountain-tops with circling wall and towers, they directed their steps in through the city gates, and when they were come to the market-place they stopped and began to sing the song of praise which Francis had taught them, and which ran thus:

"Fear and honor, praise and bless, give thanks and adore the Lord God omnipotent in trinity and unity, Father and Son and Holy Ghost, Creator of all things. Do penance, make fruits worthy of penance, for know that you soon will die. Give, and it will be given unto you. Forgive, and it will be forgiven unto you. And if you will not have forgiven men their sins, the Lord will not forgive you your sins. Confess all your sins. Blessed those who die in penance, for they will be in the kingdom of heaven. Woe to those who do not die in penance, for they will be the sons of the Devil, whose works they do, and will go into eternal fire. Beware and abstain from all evil and persevere up to the end in good."[2]

The Brothers soon had need of the warning to be patient, which Francis had given them for use on their journeyings. Many regarded them as weak-minded, and in the heartless way of the times derided them and threw the dirt of the street upon them. Others robbed them of their clothing, and like good men of the gospel the Brothers made no resistance, but went their way half-naked. Others seized the

---

[1] Celano, *V., pr.* I, XII. *Tres Socii* X, 36. Julian, p. 583, n. 204. Bonav., III, 7. — Psalms, liv. 23.
[2] Reg. I, cap. XXI. "De laude et exhortatione, quam possunt facere fratres." (*Opuscula*, pp. 50–51.)

Brothers by the cowls and carried them on their backs as if they were meal-sacks. Others came to them with dice, stuck them in their hands, and asked them to gamble. Some others took them for thieves and wanted to refuse them shelter for the night, so that the Brothers often had to sleep in caves, cellars or porches of houses or churches.[1]

Together with an associate — the latter, according to Thomas of Celano, was Brother Giles — Bernard of Quintavalle went northwards and reached Florence. Here they for a long time travelled about the city, vainly seeking refuge for the night; at last they found a porch outside of a house, and now they thought that they might rest at last. They knocked and got permission from the woman of the house to spend the night in the shelter of some wood-sheds that stood there.

Scarcely had this been arranged for, when the master of the house came home, and started to quarrel with his wife about her rather moderate hospitality. She managed to pacify him to such an extent that they got permission to stay — "they can steal nothing but a little of the firewood down there," she remonstrated with him. But a rug she had intended to lend the two wanderers she was not allowed to give them, although it was winter time and the night was cold.

After but a poor sleep, Bernard and his companion left their inhospitable host early in the morning, overcome by cold and hunger, and betook themselves to the nearest church as soon as the bell rang for eight o'clock service.

Their hostess found herself soon after in the same church, and as she saw the Brothers praying so piously, she thought to herself: "If these men had been thieves or robbers they would not have been here now and taken so devout a part in the divine service." While the woman was occupied with

---

[1] *Tres Socii*, n. 37–39. Celano, *V. pr.*, I, XV. *Vita di frate Egidio*, cap. II: "fu chiamato da uno uomo a cui egli andò pure assai volentieri, credendo avere da lui qualche limosina: e distendendo la mano, gli puose in mano un paio di dadi, invitandolo se volea giucare. Frate Egidio rispuose molto umilmente: Iddio te lo perdoni, figliuolo." *Actus*, cap. IV: "Et quidam trahebant caputium retro, quidam ante, quidam vero pulverem, quidam vero lapides jactabant in eum. . . . Ad cuncta vero opprobria frater Bernardus gaudens et patiens permanebat."
Sometimes they slept in deserted churches (Anon. Perus., 584, n. 210).

these thoughts, she saw a man named Guido enter, who every morning went to the church to give alms to the poor beggars who gathered together there. On his rounds he came to Bernard and his companion, but they refused to take anything. Guido, astonished, asked: "Are you not paupers like the others, that you will take nothing?" Bernard answered: "Certainly we are paupers, but poverty is no burden to us, for in our case it is voluntary, and it is in obedience to the will of God that we are poor." Still more astonished, Guido asked them other questions, and ascertained that Bernard had been a very wealthy man, but had given everything away so as to be able without disturbance to preach the gospel of peace and conversion.

At this moment the woman, in front of whose house the Brothers had spent the night, joined in the conversation. Bernard's refusal of money from Guido had convinced her of the utter injustice she had done the two strangers. "*Christiani!*" she now said, using a mode of address still common in Italy. "You Christian men, if you will return to my house, I will gladly receive you under my roof!" But when Guido now heard how no one the night before had been willing to receive them, he at once offered them hospitality, and thanking the woman who had come to a better state of mind, the Brothers accepted the last offer.[1]

As before mentioned, Francis had chosen Rieti as his own mission district for this time. From Terni he followed the course of the river Velino, which brought him through a whole series of larger or smaller towns — Stroncone, Cantalice, Poggio Bustone, Greccio. Everywhere he found — as the legends tell us — the fear of God and the love of God almost vanished, and the way of penitence untrod and despised.[2] The broad way, the way of the world, the way the three evil lusts urge men along, were thickly frequented — the lust of the flesh, the lust of the eyes, and the pride of the world had almost unlimited sway. To "block the wrong and endless

---

[1] *Tres Socii*, cap. X. Anon. Perus., p. 585, nn. 212–213. There is reason to believe that the two Brothers on this trip got as far as the celebrated place of pilgrimage S. Jago di Compostella. Celano, *V. pr.*, I, XII. Vita Egidii, *A.SS.*, April 23, p. 222. *Fioretti*, cap. IV.

[2] *Tres Socii*, n. 34.

way of lust"[1] was therefore everywhere the principal task for Francis. At the present time, in the valley of Rieti, the great saint's preaching in those early days is regarded as an evangelization in the proper signification of this word — a conversion from heathenism to Christianity.[2]

It was while engaged in this work that Francis, according to his biographers, was made certain of the forgiveness of his sins, the certainty of which may be said to have been absolutely necessary to carry out the work which he was to do.

Five hundred metres high in the mountain above the town of Poggio Bustone and a thousand metres above the plain, there is a cave, to which Francis, true to his Assisi habits, was wont to betake himself for prayer. Here in the great loneliness and dead silence, where only a single bird twittered, and a mountain brook gurgled, Francis knelt long hours together on the hard stone under the naked cliff. And if we wish to really understand Francis, we must follow him to this mountain cave.

There had been, and was still, the hermit as well as evangelist and missionary in his make-up, and wherever he has set his feet are found these grottoes and caves, these *eremi* and *ritiri*, to which he was accustomed from time to time to withdraw himself. Carceri at Assisi, St. Urbano at Narni, Fonte Colombo at Rieti, Monte Casale at Borgo San Sepolcro, Celle at Cortona, le Coste at Nottiano, Soteano at Chiusi, La Verna in the valley of Casentino, give widespread testimony that the spirit which inspired Francis of Assisi was none other than that which, in the latest of the olden days, had inspired Benedict of Nurcia, and the same which later, in the first of the modern days, was to inspire Ignatius of Loyola. Francis in Poggio Bustone or by Fonte Colombo is a side piece to Benedict in Sagro Speco by Subiaco, to Ignatius Loyola in the cave at Manresa. To all of them applies the same twofold exhortation: "Pray and work," *ora et labora* — all three strove in the midst of the industry of Martha to have the devotion of Mary.

---

[1] "erroneam et interminam cupiditatis viam." Julian Speier, *A. SS.*, Oct. II, p. 583, n. 204.

[2] Johannes Jörgensen: "*Pilgrimsbogen*," p. 141.

And in the cave at Poggio Bustone, Francis tried to have such an hour as that of Mary at the feet of the Crucified One. Perhaps he had already uttered the prayer which is first revealed to us in the later hours of his life, and which in all its comprehensive conciseness is given here: "Who art thou, my dear Lord and God, and who am I, thy miserable worm of a servant? My dearest Lord, I want to love thee! My Lord and my God, I give thee my heart and my body, and would wish, if I only knew how, to do still more for the love of thee!"

In any case there was a double abyss (as Angela of Foligno has called it) which in these hours of lonely prayer yawned in front of Francis — the Divine Being's abyss of goodness and light, and opposed to it his own abyss of sin and darkness. For who was he that he dared to be the finger-post for mankind and the master of disciples, he who only a few years ago had been a child of the world among children of the world, a sinner among sinners? Who was he who dared to preach to others, to warn others, to guide others — he who was not worthy to take the holy and pure name of Jesus Christ into his impure mortal mouth? Then he thought of what he had been, of what he yet might be if God did not stand by him, for that danger was always within his nature — when he thought next of what others thought of him, some who honored him, some who followed him, some who hated him, it was then he knew not where to hide himself for very shame, and the words of the Apostle rang in his ears: "Lest perhaps, when I have preached to others, I myself should become a castaway."

Thus humility raged in his soul like a lion that leaves nothing of his prey, but grinds the bones for the marrow. And all torn asunder, all annihilated, Francis cast himself on his face before God, the God who had made heaven and earth, the God who is all truth and all holiness, and before whose omnipotence nothing can stand without complete truth, complete holiness. Francis looked into the depths of his being, and he saw that on the whole earth there was not to be found a more useless creature, a greater sinner, a soul more lost and fallen to the bad than himself, and from the depths of his need he groaned before God: "Lord, be merciful to me a poor sinner!"

And it came to pass that the empty cave over Poggio Bustone beheld a miracle, one that always happens when a soul in complete distrust of itself calls out to its God in confidence and hope and charity — then there comes to pass the great miracle of *justification*. "I fear everything from my badness, but from thy goodness I also hope for all," this was the innermost meaning of the prayer Francis sent up to God. And the answer came, as it always comes — "Fear not, my son, thy sins are forgiven thee!"

From this hour Francis was fully armed for the things that awaited him — he was drawn into the heart of Christianity. Because he had abandoned everything, he was to win everything. For not only had he given up father and mother, house and home, property and money, but what means more than all else, if God was to belong to him and he to God — he had given up *himself*. All his righteousness from now on was that which the Apostle says is given by Christ to the faithful — and his life in holiness breathed out this righteousness. Therefore it is true, with a deeper truth than that of history, what the *Fioretti* relates in the tenth chapter:

"But one day Brother Masseo from Marignano said to St. Francis: 'I wonder why the whole world runs after thee more than after others, and all men want to see thee and hear thee and obey thee? Thou art not fair of body, thou art not deeply learned, thou art not of noble birth — why does the whole world run after thee?'

"When St. Francis heard this he rejoiced in his soul and turned his eyes to heaven, and stood a long time thus, with soul lifted up to God; and when he came to himself he kneeled down and gave thanks and praise to God, and turned to Brother Masseo and said to him with great spiritual power: 'Do you wish to know why this happens to me? Do you wish to know why the whole world runs after me? For I knew that thing from the all-seeing God, whose eyes see the good and the bad over all the earth. For these most holy eyes have nowhere seen a greater, more miserable, poorer sinner than I; because in all the earth he has found no more wretched being to do his wonderful work, which he wishes to have done, therefore he has chosen me, so as thus to put to shame the noble, the great, strength and beauty, worldly wisdom, that all may know that all power and all virtue come from him and not from creatures, and that no one can exalt himself before his face; but he who praises himself, let him praise himself in the Lord, for his is the honor and the power for ever and ever." [1]

[1] *Fioretti*, cap. X. *Actus b. Francisci* capp. IX–X. Celano, *Vita prima*, I, cap. XI. Julian, *A. SS.*, Oct. II, p. 583, n. 203: ("usque ad quadrantem novissimum remissionis debiti culparum certitudo," — a version not found in the other biographies. Bonaventure, III, 6. Wadding, 1209, n. 24, with the following parallel from St. Bridget's *Revelationes* (VII, 20): [Franciscus] "obtinuit veram contritionem omnium peccatorum suorum et perfectam voluntatem se emendandi dicens: Nihil est in hoc mundo, quod non volo libenter dimittere propter amorem et honorem Domini mei Jesu Christi; nihil est etiam tam durum in hac vita, quod non volo gratanter sustinere propter ejus caritatem, faciendo propter ejus honorem omnia quae ego potero juxta meas vires corporis et animae; et omnes alios quoscumque potero, volo ad hoc inducere et roborare, ut Deum super omnia diligant toto corde."

We see with what clearness the forgiveness of sins is defined by the Swedish saint as synonymous with the beginning of a new life, the acceptation of a perfect will to do good, *Inspiratio amoris*. A complete description of Poggio Bustone is given in my (the author's) *Pilgrimsbogen*, cap. XIII.

CHAPTER II

THE FOUNDATIONS OF THE ORDER

FRANCIS found himself one day in Bishop Guido's private room. As was customary with him, he had gone to the man he regarded as "the father of souls"[1] to get advice — perhaps also to pray for alms. It was a period of hard times for the Brotherhood. After the return from the mission journeys, four new Brothers had joined the ranks — Philipp Lungo, John of San Costanzo, Barbarus, and Bernard of Vigilanzio. Francis himself had brought a fifth new Brother with him from Rieti — Angelo Tancredi, a young knight whom Francis had met in the streets of Rieti, and whom he had won by suddenly calling out to him: "Long enough hast thou borne the belt, the sword and the spurs! The time has now come for you to change the belt for a rope, the sword for the Cross of Jesus Christ, the spurs for the dust and dirt of the road! Follow me and I will make you a knight in the army of Christ!"[2]

Thus it was that there were no longer so few men to have food daily. In the beginning the people of Assisi had been seized with a kind of wonder, and the Brothers had got considerable alms as they went from door to door. Now people began to grow weary of them; now the relatives of the Brothers were ready to persecute them. "You have given away what you had, and now you come and want to eat up other people's things!"

As their number increased they went from the hut at Portiuncula to a tumble-down outhouse or shed some twenty

---

[1] *Tres Socii*, VI, 19: "pater et dominus animarum."
[2] Wadding, *Annales*, T. I., p. 80 (1210). The narration was first found in the rather unreliable work, *Actus b. Francisci in valle Reatina*. Compare *A. SS.*, Oct. II, p. 589, n. 231.

minutes distant, in a place which because of its vicinity to a bend in a little stream was called *Rivo Torto* (crooked stream). Here the Crucigers from S. Salvatore delle Pareti owned a few small buildings, and as one of the newly accepted Franciscans had been a member of this order, it is reasonable to suppose that Francis by his intercession had obtained the right to use this new abode.[1]

This shed or *tigurium* at Rivo Torto was so small that Francis had to write on the beams the name of each Brother over his place, so as to avoid all disorder or confusion.[2] There was no church or chapel there; the Brothers prayed before a large wooden cross which was erected in front of the shed.[3] Francis for his part had nothing against so great poverty. He really liked Rivo Torto, because by following the course of the river he could easily reach some caves on Monte Subasio, where it was good to pray, and which Francis because of their narrowness called his "prisons" (*carceri*).

All this excited much talk in Assisi, as was to be expected, and the Bishop showed good judgment. He tried by gentleness to draw Francis away from the ideas which to the prelate of the church seemed extravagant. Little was the amount which the Brothers permitted themselves to own, but he only allowed himself so much as was needed to ensure his daily bread. To the Bishop, as to all men living an ordinary life, the begging was particularly repulsive.

But Francis was immovable in this point. Just as Tolstoy has clearly seen it in the nineteenth century, so he saw what a hindrance is removed from the way when money and possessions are given up. "Lord Bishop," he therefore replied,

---

[1] Bonaventure tells (IV, 8) that Morico had long lain dangerously sick in S. Salvatore delle Pareti, and that Francis healed him by sending him a piece of bread dipped in oil of the lamp which burned before the altar of Our Lady in Portiuncula. From gratitude Morico followed Francis thereafter and distinguished himself by extreme penances (he lived on raw green vegetables for years, never tasted bread nor wine, etc.). — There are still two small chapels remaining of the original Rivo Torto: S. Rufino d'Arce and S. Maria Maddalena, nearer to Portiuncula than the large Franciscan church erected later, which now has the old name. See *Lo Specchio di perfezione* (Assisi, 1889), p. 39, n. 9.

[2] *Tres Socii*, XIII, 53. Celano, *V. pr.*, I, cap. XVI.

[3] Bonav., IV, 3.

"if we had possessions we should have to have weapons with which to defend them. For from property comes strife with our neighbors and relatives, so that charity to God and to men suffers many a scar, and in order to preserve it whole and unimpaired, it is our firm determination to own nothing in this world."[1]

The Bishop, who himself was not clear of property disputes, for he was involved in a suit with both the Crucigers and with the Benedictines on Monte Subasio,[2] bowed his head and was silent. Even if he could not mount to the height of such an ideal, he did not dare to hinder or restrain them in carrying it out.

Moreover, begging was not the only or even principal resource of the Brothers. Francis himself says in his Testament about these early times:

"And after the Lord had given me Brothers, no one showed me what I was to do. But the Highest revealed to me that I was to live after the holy gospel. . . . And they who came to me and accepted this way of life gave all they possessed to the poor, and were satisfied with a tunic, patched both inside and outside if they wished it, and a rope and breeches. And we wanted nothing more.

"We said the Office, those of us who were clerks, like other clerks, but the lay-people said the 'Our Father,' and we liked to be in the churches. And we were simple (*idiotae*) and subject to all men. And I worked with my hands, and moreover wanted to work, and I desired that all the other Brothers should be occupied with honorable work. And those who could do no work must learn it, not for the desire of remuneration, but to give good example and not to be lazy. And if they will not give us pay for our work, we must have recourse to the table which the Lord has spread, as we go from door to door and beg for alms."[3]

We have in these few words from Francis' own hand the entire programme of the life they led at Portiuncula and in

---

[1] *Tres Socii*, IX, 35.
[2] See *Opera Honorii III*, ed. Horoy, t. I, col. 200 and col. 163, and Potthast's *Regesta*, Nr. 7746 and Nr. 7728. Sabatier, *Vie*, p. 92, n. 1.
[3] *Opuscula*, p. 79.

the shed at Rivo Torto. What Francis desired was what Jesus of Nazareth desired — that men should own as little as possible, that they should work with their hands for their food, and ask others for help when work failed them, that they should not give themselves unnecessary troubles and lay up superfluous possessions, that they should keep themselves free as birds and not let themselves be caught in the snares of the world, that they should go through life with thanks to God for his gifts and with songs of praise for the beauty of his works. "Like strangers and like pilgrims," these words of an Apostle return over and over again to the mouth of Francis, when he wants to express his ideal. "He wished," says one of his biographers, "that all things should *sing pilgrimage and exile*."[1]

The following by-laws and admonitions in the first Rule which Francis wrote for the Brothers are in accord with this:

"No Brother who works or serves in another's house can be treasurer or secretary or have any authoritative position ... but they must be lowly (*sint minores*) and subject to all in the house. And the Brothers who can do one kind of work should work and practise the art they have learnt, if it does not interfere with their soul's salvation or is not dishonorable. ... For the Apostle says: 'If any man will not work, neither let him eat!' and: 'Let every man abide in the same calling in which he was called!'

"And they can receive for their work whatever is necessary, but not money. And should that be needed, they must go out begging like the other Brothers. And they have permission to own tools and utensils which they need ... (cap. VII).

"The Lord teaches us in the gospel: 'Watch ye, that your hearts be not troubled with avarice and with care for your nourishment!' Therefore none of the Brothers, wherever he may go, and wherever he may be, may receive in any way or permit money to be received, either for clothing or for

---

[1] "Non solum domorum arrogantiam odiebat homo iste, verum domorum utensilia multa et exquisita plurimum perhorrebat. Nihil in mensis, nihil in vasis, quo mundi recordaretur, amabat, ut omnia peregrinationem, omnia cantarent exilium." Thomas of Celano, *Vita secunda*, p. III, cap. VI.

books or as wages for work, or for any other reason, except when a Brother is sick and calls for help. For we ought not to care for or to look on money as of more worth than a stone. . . . Let us therefore beware lest we, who have abandoned all, shall lose heaven for so small a thing. And if we find money anywhere, let us not then be more concerned about it than if it was dust that we tread in. . . . Yet the Brothers if the lepers are in need can collect money for them, but must be greatly on their guard against money (cap. VIII).

"All Brothers must try to follow our Lord Jesus Christ's humility and poverty, and remember the Apostle's words, that, when we have food and clothes, we should be content with them. And the Brothers should rejoice when they are among humble and despised people, among poor and weaklings, sick and lepers and beggars on the road. And if it is necessary, they may go and beg for alms. And they should not be ashamed, but remember that Our Lord Jesus Christ, the Son of the living Almighty God, made his face as hard as stone and was not ashamed; and he was poor and a stranger and lived on alms, both he and the Blessed Virgin and his disciples. And when men cause shame to the Brothers and will not give them alms, then they shall thank God therefor . . . and they shall know that the shame is not counted against them who suffer it, but against them who inflict it. For alms are an inheritance and a piece of justice which is due to the poor, and which Our Lord Jesus Christ has levied upon us"[1] (cap. X).

With these and similar words Francis has certainly often enough inspired his friends to persevere in the severe life of poverty. Soon they were giving their services in the hospitals, soon helping the peasants with the harvest in the fields, and never was their recompense other than their daily bread and a drink of water with it from the spring.[2]

---

[1] *Opuscula*, pp. 33-39.

[2] "Diebus vero manibus propriis quod noverant laborabant, existentes in domibus leprosorum, vel in aliis lociis honestis, servientes omnibus humiliter et devote. Nullum officium exercere volebant, de quo posset scandalum exoriri, sed semper sancta et juxta opera honesta et utilia." These words of Celano (*V. pr.*, I, XV) depict the activities corresponding to the Rule. Compare Barth. of Pisa's *Conformitates* (Milan, 1513), f. 25b: "ut serviant summa cum

It often happened that there was no work to be had, and in Assisi, as we have said, all doors were closed in the faces of the Brothers. Then it was that hope could hardly be sustained, and it may well be believed that discontent and despair were sometimes on the point of overcoming the poor "Penitents from Assisi" in their shed at Rivo Torto. On dark and rainy days, when the water drove in through the leaky roof of the building and the earth was black and miry and cold for the bare feet to tread upon, and they sat there in their coarse, ragged gowns, seven or eight in number, and had got nothing to eat all day, and did not know if the Brothers who had gone out to beg would bring anything home, and there was no fire to warm them, and no books to read. . . . In those days of rain, in those dark, cold hours, during the short but raw and uncomfortable winter of Umbria, did it not perforce occur to one or another of them that it was all foolishness, and that the best thing to do was to turn the back on the dark hole and its crazy inhabitants, to go back to the city — to the city where one had, alas! once owned a house and garden, money and goods, which foolishly had been cast aside and given to the poor? There must surely have been some such moments, when more than one of the Brothers felt the spirit of penance weaken. And yet we hear of only one falling away among the first disciples — John of Capella. All the others held fast and persevered, even if they, as the legends tell us, often had to eat roots instead of bread.[1] They persevered and they conquered.

For the public opinion which had long been opposed to them began to reverse itself, little by little. The inflexible

diligentia suo exemplo leprosis et horribilibus. Et sic fratribus mandabat statim ordinem ingressis, ut in talibus obsequiis Deo studerent placere."

The *Fioretti* has several tales of the Brothers' care of the sick and lepers, such as cap. IV, cap. XXV, cap. XLII. A tale which is preserved in *Chronica XXIV generalium* shows us that the Brothers sometimes could be discontented with Francis: "qui fratres hinc inde transmittendo per hospitia leprosorum frequenter ab orationis studio distrahebat" (*Anal. Franc.*, III, p. 48). See also Eccleston's Chronicle (*Anal. Franc.*, I, p. 249): "dixit autem (fr. Agnellus), quod cum esset cum sancto Francisco in quodam hospitali commorans" and Bishop Theobald of Assisi's letter on the Portiuncula indulgence, *A. SS.*, Oct. II, p. 880, n. 6.

[1] *Tres Socii*, cap. XIII, n. 55. Celano, *V. pr.*, I, XVI.

perseverance of the Brothers aroused wonder, their pious way of life won approval. Wayfarers who passed by the shed at Rivo Torto heard the Brothers' voices in prayer by night. By day they were seen going to the hospital or working elsewhere, wherever they could get anything to do.[1] In spite of their poverty they always had something to spare for anyone who asked it, and if there was nothing else, they would give the hood off of their cloak or one of the sleeves. They showed no concern about money; a man once laid a considerable sum of money on the altar in the chapel in Portiuncula, but soon after found his mammon lying in a heap of dirt upon the highway.

Especially was it to be seen how they loved each other. Two of them once, while on a journey, were attacked by a wandering imbecile who had started to throw a stone at them. And they saw the Brothers shifting places constantly, because each wanted to be upon the side the stone came from, so as to protect his companion with his body. If it happened that one of the Brothers by a thoughtless or hasty word had hurt the feelings of one of the others, he allowed himself neither rest nor quiet until he had made peace with his Brother, and, at the behest of the offender, the offended one would have to put his foot on the mouth out of which an uncharitable word had issued. Never was impolite or even superfluous and worldly conversation heard among them, and if they passed by women on their way, they did not look upon them, but fastened their eyes on the dust with their hearts in heaven.[2]

That they did not seek after this world's vanity and nothingness is to be seen on an occasion when Otto of Brunswick went through the valley of Spoleto, in September, 1209, on his way to Rome to be crowned Emperor by Pope Innocent.

---

[1] "ut non starent otiosi, juvabant pauperes homines in agris eorum, et postea ipsi dabant eisdem de pane amore Dei" (*Spec. perf.*, cap. LV).

[2] *Tres Socii*, cap. XI. Anon. Perus., in *A. SS.*, Oct. II, pp. 587–588, nn. 224–225. Celano, *Vita prima*, I, cap. XV. Compare *Fioretti*, cap. III: "Come per mala cogitazione che santo Francesco ebbe contro a frate Bernardo, comandò al detto frate Bernardo, che tre volte gli andasse co' piedi in sulla gola e in sulla bocca." Still more severe was the punishment for uncharitable conversation to which Brother Barbarus condemned himself (2 Cel., III, 92).

The populace gathered from Assisi, Bettona, Spello, Isola Romana and all the other towns and villages of the mountain and plain, to see the gorgeous retinue. Only the Brothers from Rivo Torto were absent — with the exception of one who was sent by Francis to go and meet the Emperor Otto and say to him that the honors of this world are transitory and not to be regarded, — a saying whose truthfulness was soon to be shown in the very case of the Emperor himself.[1]

Meanwhile Francis had decided to go to Rome. In the solitude at Rivo Torto he had, as he tells in his Testament, "with few and simple words," written or had written the Rules of life, which he and the Brothers followed in their lives.[2] His present desire was to have this Rule, or *forma vitae*, as he used to call it, ratified by the highest authority of the Church. There was no need of this visit; it was the Fourth Lateran Council of 1215 which first made such ratification a requirement for the founding of a community in the Catholic Church. A custom which was not older than Valdes was now beginning, in virtue of which laymen used to seek permission from the Papal throne to participate in preaching, hitherto reserved for bishops and parish priests. Valdes had obtained such a permission, but with a strict command to be subject to the local churchmen. A similar permission had been given in 1201 to the Humiliates, and in 1207 to Durand

[1] Many modern biographers, on account of the sequence of events, as given in Thomas of Celano, have been led to believe that the occurrence with the Emperor Otto properly belongs *after* the journey of Francis and the Brothers to Rome and after the Pope's approval of the Rule of the Order, which they place accordingly in 1209. It was April 23, 1209, when Giles visited Francis, and consequently the two missionary trips (to the Marches and to Rieti, including Florence) come after this time. These journeys undoubtedly took several months, but Innocent III left Rome late in May, 1209, and went to Viterbo, whence he did not return until October for the crowning of Otto. The Brothers' visit to Rome must have occurred after this date, and belongs probably in the summer of 1210. See *Anal. Franc.*, III, p. 5, n. 8; Wadding: *Annales*, 1210; Sabatier: *Vie*, p. 100, n. 1; Hergenröther: "*Kirchengeschichte*," I, p. 797.

[2] "ego paucis verbis et simpliciter feci scribi; et dominus papa confirmavit mihi." *Opuscula*, p. 79. Compare Cel., *V. pr.*, I, XIII. *Chron. XXIV gen.* in *Anal. Franc.*, III, p. 6: "quandam regulam scripsit, ubi pene omnia mandata, quae Christus dedit apostolis, inseruit et omnes professores ejusdem, tam praelatos quam subditos, nominibus evangelicis nuncupavit."

of Huesca and his Catholic Valdenses.[1] Francis had reason to hope that Innocent would be accessible to his wishes also.

But Francis' devotion to the Apostles had drawn him to Rome with special power, to the grave of the Apostles and of their successors. The Apostles were Francis' model; all his thoughts went in the direction of the restoration of the apostolic life, as he saw it in the Gospels. It was "after the rule of life of the Apostles" that all property of the Brothers should be for the common use. "It was thus in the Apostolic Church," was an argument to which Francis always submitted himself.[2] The later legends tell of Peter and Paul showing themselves to Francis in the church of St. Peter as he was praying, and assuring him of the possession of "the perfect kingdom of the most holy poverty."[3]

One day in the summer of 1210, the little troop of penitents started from Rivo Torto, and took their way to Rome. Little is told us of their journey, except that Bernard of Quintavalle was sometimes their leader instead of Francis. Him they all obeyed, as they shortened the way with prayer, song and conversation. The Lord, says the legend, prepared resting places for them everywhere and never left them unprovided for.[4]

On their arrival in Rome, Bishop Guido of Assisi was the first to whom they presented themselves, who at this time, perhaps not without previous communication with Francis, was present in the Eternal City. The Bishop presented the Brothers to a friend of his among the Cardinals — John of St. Paul [5] — and the way to the Pope was made easy for them. Later stories tell us that Francis first tried to reach the Pope by his own efforts, but failed. What is historically certain

[1] Hilarin Felder: *"Gesch. der Studien im Franz. Orden"* (Freiburg, 1904), S. 40–41. Achille Luchaire: *Innocent III; les Albigeois* (Paris, 1905), pp. 104–113.
[2] *Tres Socii*, n. 43. Anon. Perus., p. 587, n. 223. — It was Francis who, in the Roman Breviary, instead of the usual invocation of "all the Apostles," had introduced a special invocation of the two Roman Apostles Peter and Paul. See Bernard of Bessa (*Anal. Franc.*, III, p. 672).
[3] *Fioretti*, cap. XIII. Wadding, I, p. 30. Compare Bonaventure, II, 7.
[4] *Tres Socii*, XII, 46.
[5] John of St. Paul, of the noble Roman family of Colonna, made cardinal by Celestin III and named as Sabine bishop by Innocent (Wadding, 1210, n. 7).

is only this much, that Cardinal John, after the Brothers had lived with him a few days, undertook to speak to the Pope about them. The Pope was Innocent III.[1]

An injustice is perpetrated if we, like Sabatier, reproach Cardinal John, because he in his capacity of representative of the Curia utilized the time Francis and the Brothers stayed with him, to investigate their intentions and prospects. The period was actually very critical for the Church, and the greatest foresight was a duty for its pilot.

It is with a very poor comprehension of the Middle Ages that anyone speaks of "the powerful Church of the Middle Ages," and especially is this idea faulty when the period is that of Innocent III. In fact the centuries of the Reformation and the Revolutionary days were scarcely more anti-Papal or more opposed to the Church than the epoch we speak of — about the year 1200. No one would in our days permit Pius X to be treated as Innocent III was treated more than once. He tells himself how, on Holy Thursday, April 8, 1203, on the way from St. Peter's to the Lateran, in spite of the Papal crown which he wore upon his head, he was insulted by the

---

[1] Not only Francis but also many others of the Brothers knew the Bishop of Assisi, Guido. This is said explicitly in *Leg. trium soc.*, n. 47: "ipse affectabat videre virum Dei et aliquos de fratribus suis." Sabatier has not been willing to accept this and similar testimony (Celano, *V. pr.*, I, XIII: "omnes fratres in omnibus honorabat et speciali venerabatur dilectione"). It certainly follows from Celano's biography that Guido did not know the cause of the Brothers' Roman journey (causam nesciens). But this does not exclude the possibility of a conference between him and Francis; certainly in any case the Bishop would not willingly have thought of the Brothers intending to leave Umbria ("timebat enim, ne patriam propriam vellent deserere . . . gaudebat plurimum tantos viros in suo episcopatu habere"). It appears to be a preconception, when Sabatier (*Vie*, p. 108) accuses Guido of only taking a lukewarm interest in Francis and his cause. Also from *Spec. perf.* (ed. Sab.), cap. X, it is clear that a good understanding existed between Guido and Francis.

The place in Bonaventure's legend (III, 9), in which it is told that Innocent first turned Francis away with disdain, and was converted by a dream and sent the next morning a messenger after him, when he was found in St. Anthony's Hospital near the Lateran, is due to Jerome of Ascoli, General of the Franciscan Order from 1274 to 1279, and later Pope under the name of Nicholas IV. In Wadding (1210, n. 8) a certain nephew of Innocent, Richard Hannibal de Molaria, Cardinal of S. Angelo in foro piscium, about 1274, is the authority for this story. This nephew should have had the story from Innocent himself. Compare *A. SS.*, Oct. II, p. 591, and *Chronica XXIV generalium* in *Analec. Franc.*, III, p. 365. The passage in question exists in many manuscripts. A similar but much expanded relation is found in Matthew of Paris.

Roman people with so offensive a word that he would not repeat it.

As early as 1188 the same Roman people had anticipated the French terrorists and abolished the Christian reckoning of time; they had established in its place a new era based on the restoration of the Roman senate in 1143. Time after time was Innocent chased out of Rome; the tower he and his brother had built for themselves as a secure refuge, and whose imposing remains still bear Innocent's family name (*Torre dei Conti*), was taken from him by the Romans and was declared communal property. From May to October, 1204, the Pope had to be a helpless witness of the devastation of Rome by his enemies of the Capocci party.

And in the small remains of power which the Hohenstaufens had left to the see of Peter, the power and authority of Innocent was also small. For to free themselves from the temporal domain of the Pope, men on all sides withdrew from his spiritual supremacy and broke away from the unity of the Church. In Orvieto such an independent faction chose an Albigensian for leader, and killed the *podestà*, Pietro Paranzi, sent to them by the Pope. Viterbo, in the face of the prohibition and threats of the Pope, had chosen open heretics as consuls. Interdict and ban were without effect on the rebellious populace; Narni, that against the Pope's ban had laid waste the little community of Otricoli, situated near it, lived untroubled for five years under excommunication. The republic of Orvieto, likewise in cold blood, overrode the Papal command when their army plundered and burnt the neighboring town of Acquapendente. In Sardinia the priests and even the Bishops were so inimical to the Pope that his legate, Blasio, in the year 1202, literally did not know whence he could procure food there. Eventually the Ghibelline Pisa took the island from the Pope. Even when Innocent won a victory over his opponents, the fruits of the victory were taken from him. Thus when Conrad of Irslingen had gone to Narni to make over the imperial castle in Assisi to the Pope, the inhabitants of Assisi destroyed the castle before the Pope could take it in possession. So far from punishing Assisi for this violence, Innocent did not dare to enter the city, when he passed near it, as he visited Perugia and Spoleto on his journey of homage through Umbria.[1]

Innocent III's era was thus in full rebellion against the Papal authority, and this rebellion was, just as in later centuries, at the one time religious and political. We seem to see Puritans, Independents, Illuminati, Rosicrucians, Freemasons shadowed forth in the more or less politically tinted sects with which the time was crowded. The church historians reckon whole ranks of sect-creators and heresiarchs in this century, — from the rigorous Peter Valdes and his "Poor Men from Lyons," to shameless pantheists like David of Dinant and Ortlieb of Strassburgh, Neo-Manichees like the Albigenses, Satanists like the *familiae amoris*, which celebrated the black mass even in Rome.[2]

The most dangerous of all these sects were the Albigenses. In the year 1200 they were to be found scattered all over Europe — from Rome to London, from the Black Sea to Spain, but especially along the lower Danube, in northern Italy and southern France, and in places along the Rhine. They bore different names in different countries: on the lower Danube Bulgari, Bugri, Publicans; in Lombardy Paratenes, Gazarenes; in southern France Cathari or Albigenses (after the city Albi in Languedoc). Everywhere they held the same doctrine, and this was a reiteration of the dualism of the Manichees. By way of the Bogomili and Paulacians of Bulgaria, they descended directly from the adherents of Mani.

The Albigensian theory of the universe rested on the old heathen doctrine of two gods — a good one who had created souls, a bad one who had created the material world. It was therefore essential, they taught, to hold aloof from all that is material — in theory they cast aside marriage, family life, all that could not be considered purely spiritual. The name they themselves adopted Cathari or "the pure," indicates this. To preserve this purity the most zealous among them starved themselves to death. In practice, marriage was

[1] See in this connection Achille Luchaire: *Innocent III; Rome et l'Italie* (Paris, 1905).
[2] Wadding, I (1731), pp. 3-4.

permitted for the great mass of the Cathari, and often the severe denial broke loose into unbridled sensuality — as with the German Luciferians.

The Cathari were therefore, with their entire philosophy as well as with their practice, born enemies of the Catholic Church. The war which the Church now took up, and which on the part of Rome was carried on as long as possible with spiritual weapons,[1] was therefore a fight for one of the most valued possessions of Christian culture — for theological *monism*. The unity of God — this was the truth for which the Church fought and which it saved by fighting. There is a bottomless abyss between the Manichees, for whom life is impure and unholy, and for whom nature is a work of a devil, a bad and detestable crime of the "Life-desire," and the Christian, who in matter sees a pure and holy work from the hands of an all-loving Creator, and only stained by the miserable crimes of little man. Rome had to decide on which side of this abyss Francis and his Brothers stood — if their strange asceticism was a product of the pride of the Cathari or of evangelic Christianity. That they came from Assisi could well awaken a suspicion; for among the communities where the Cathari had acquired political power, it was precisely this little city which in 1203 had chosen an Albigensian for podestà.

In Francis, it was to be feared, might be found a man of the same character as Peter Valdes, whose ideal had also been evangelical poverty. The well-known Lyonnese had in 1179 obtained permission from Alexander III to preach in public the conversion of sinners, and to live in apostolic poverty. Already in 1184 Lucius III had placed Valdes and his followers under the ban as rebels against the functions of the Church, and as renewers of Donatism. Only a few of the Valdensians were preserved as adherents to the unity of the Church, by the Spaniard, Durand of Huesca.

It took only a short time to convince Cardinal John that Francis and his friends were neither the one nor the other of these two sectaries.

[1] Consult in this matter Achille Luchaire: *Innocent III; La Croisade des Albigeois* (Paris, 1905), pp. 35-67.

That God is one — this was the foundation of Francis' piety, as it is the fundamental doctrine in the theology of the Church.[1]

There is only one God — the God of creation and of salvation, the God of the Cross and the God of holiness, the God of love and the God of nature — one God, as there is one world and one heaven — one God, glorious, thanked and praised by all, who moves and has the spirit of life, from worm to cherubim, through all the ages of eternity! Francis felt this, for he was no Manichee to deny life and to hate life, but a Christian who wanted to live, and loved life, — in its purity, in its golden goodness, in its deepest innermost sweetness, in its highest most divine plenitude. It was by these feelings that he was to be distinguished from the souls of pride, who haughtily called themselves "the pure," "the perfect," "the chosen," but who in reality had to vibrate between self-torture and degradation.[2]

Francis was no negative soul; neither was he a critical soul. The only criticism he understood was self-criticism. And this distinguished him completely from Valdes and his tendencies. As a modern historian has pertinently said: "Francis appeared as the herald of a holy life; Valdes of the divine command. Francis preached the love of Christ, and Valdes the prohibitions of the Lord. Francis overflowed with the happiness of God's children; Valdes punished the sins of the world. Francis collected those who loved amendment, and let the others quietly go their way. Valdes attacked the ungodliness of the ungodly and irritated the clergy."[3]

Such then was the distinctive peculiarity of Francis — this it was which separated him from all the contemporaneous reformers. Even those of them who were best disposed to the Church, such as a Robert of Arbrissel, fell before the temptation of turning their criticism against the priesthood and

---

[1] At the Lateran Council of 1215 this doctrine was most explicitly invoked in the case of the Cathari. See Denziger's *Enchiridion*, pp. 355 et seq.

[2] Such of the Cathari who had taken the so-called spiritual baptism (*consolamentum*) called themselves *perfecti* or *electi*. A good insight into Francis' monistic views is to be found in the last chapter of his *Regula prima*.

[3] Schmieder in "*Ev. Kirchenzeit,*" 1854, p. 288, quoted by Oppermann: *Kunst og Liv i det gamle Florens* (Copenhagen, 1895), p. 28.

their failings, instead of against the heart of the individual. With instinctive certainty Francis understood that without the reform of the individual all other reform is meaningless, and therefore he brought about that general reform of conduct which neither the bulls of excommunication of the Pope nor the thunders of the lay-preachers had been able to effect. Here it was shown, as so often elsewhere, that God was not working by stormy methods.

Cardinal John was not long in coming to a complete understanding of the deep-rooted idiosyncrasy of Francis. He felt that here he stood before a man unselfish in root and branch. He felt that there were no idle promises, no false pretences, when Francis, speaking of his plans, simply said: "God has called us to the help of his holy faith and of the Roman Church's priests and prelates." [1]

After the lapse of a few days the Cardinal found himself in the presence of Innocent and imparted the following information: "I have found a very perfect man who wishes to live after the precepts of the holy gospel, and in all things to adhere to the evangelical perfection. And I believe the Lord intends by him to renew the faith all over the world."

The Brothers from Assisi were then admitted to the Pope's presence. The Pope let Francis unfold his programme and then answered:

"My dear son, this life you and your Brothers lead seems too severe to me. I certainly do not doubt that you are all in a condition to live it, borne up by the first enthusiasm. But you should also think of those who come after you, and who may not have the same zeal."

To this Francis only answered thus: "Lord Pope, I depend upon my Lord, Jesus Christ. He has promised us eternal life and heavenly happiness, and will not deny us so trivial a

---

[1] *Speculum perfectionis*, cap. X, where also the motives are given: that Francis and his Brothers could do more to gain souls, when laymen and priests lived in unity, than when people were filled with anger against the priests. In the same place is to be noted this saying of Francis: "In the first days of my conversion God put his word into the mouth of the Bishop of Assisi, that he might advise me and fortify me in the service of Christ." (Sabatier's edition, p. 24.) This agrees perfectly with the *Legenda trium sociorum*, III, 10; see in this book, p. 85, n. 1.

thing as what we need here upon earth to maintain our life."

With the suspicion of a smile — one seems to see it through the words — Innocent answered:

"What you say, my son, is perfectly true. But the nature of man is frail and seldom holds to one purpose long. Go then and pray God to reveal to you how far what you want coincides with his will."

Francis and his Brothers left the presence of the Pope, who, in the next consistory, laid the affair before the Cardinals. As was to be expected, several of the old, practically minded ones had great doubts about an order whose principles seemed to exceed the powers of mankind.[1]

It was no purely contemplative order that Francis wished to found, to which utter poverty might be supposed to be annexed. Francis' ideal was indeed the apostolic life and especially the apostolic preaching. But how should this last-mentioned task be performed in a life of all kinds of work or one of begging from door to door? Even the Waldenses had had evangelical poverty on their programme; in reality they had laymen among them whose work took care of the needs of the preachers. The Humiliati, in spirit and life allied to the Waldenses, originally a brotherhood of Lombard cloth-makers, worked in common, kept what was most necessary for themselves and distributed the rest to the poor. The "Catholic Poor" founded by the converted German Catharus, Bernhard Primus, came the nearest to Francis' ideal; they lived by the work of their hands, received no money wages, but only food and clothes as compensation. This did very well as long as prayer and work were the Order's only effective obligations. But Francis came precisely to obtain the Papal permission to preach, and if this preaching could not be based on the work of lay-preachers, then necessarily they must be supported by a certain amount of study. To make this study possible there would be needed, no matter in how poor a shape, fixed abodes and a cloister life. And how was it possible to erect a cloister on the foundation of complete poverty?[2]

[1] Bonav., III, 9. Anon. Perus., in *A. SS.*, Oct. II, p. 590, n. 237.
[2] Compare Gustav Schnürer: "*Franz von Assisi*" (München, 1905), pp. 46-47.

There is scarcely need here to do more than call attention to the fact that the old monastic orders held their members to the obligation of poverty, but this was to be taken in a far different sense than that in which Francis used the word. It stood certainly in the Benedictine Rules that he who entered the Order should give first his goods to the poor,[1] and "the holy poverty" was glorified under this almost Franciscan title by Bernard of Clairvaux.[2] But however scornfully this great father talks of "silver and gold, the white and red varieties of earth that acquire their value from man's wickedness,"[3] yet the existence of the Cistercian convents as well as that of the Benedictine abbeys depended on large estates of land. The single monk owned nothing except what the abbot gave him, but his vow of poverty was not affected if the cloister was richly endowed. Even a certain degree of possession seemed necessary for the inmates of the cloister to be free to devote themselves to spiritual works, and not be troubled about their daily bread.

On this head Francis had an entirely different conception. What Peter and Paul had been able to accomplish — to announce the gospel to the world while they at the same time supported themselves by the work of their hands or by the gifts of the charitable — should still be possible. The Apostles had not sat quietly within the doors of a convent, and Francis did not want to be behind them in this respect.

In the College of Cardinals this wish of Francis aroused the liveliest opposition. All objections were met by John of Colonna's simple enunciation: "These men only want us to allow them to live after the gospel. If we now declare that this is impossible, then we declare that the gospel cannot be followed, and thus insult Christ, who is the origin of the gospel." These words had their effect and Francis was again invited to the Lateran.

In the night preceding this new meeting, the Pope is said to have had a curious dream. It seemed to him that he stood in the Lateran palace, in the place that is called *speculum*, because there is a wide prospect therefrom, and one looks out

---

[1] "Res si quas habet . . . eroget prius pauperibus" (*Reg. S. Bened.*, cap. 58).
[2] Ep. 103, n. 7. Ep. 141, n. 2. [3] *In Adv.*, Sermo IV, n. 1.

over the Lateran church dedicated to John the Baptist and John the Evangelist, "the head and mother of all churches." And then he saw with fear that the proud building shook, the tower swung, and the walls began to crack — soon must the old basilica of Constantine be a heap of ruins. Paralyzed with fright, with powerless hands, the Pope stood in his palace and looked on, wanted to cry out but could not — and what good would that have done? — wished to fold his hands in prayer but could not — and even that might have been useless.

Then a man came over the Lateran piazza — a small, common-looking man, dressed in peasant garb, barefoot and with a rope around his waist instead of a belt. And the poor little man, looking neither to right nor left, went right across to the falling church. Now he stood by one of the walls that leaned over him, as if ready to fall and crush him in the next minute. Wonderful to see, it seemed as if the little man suddenly became as tall as the wall he stood by. See! now he sets his shoulder in under the cornice of the wall, and with a mighty push straightens the whole falling church, so that it again stands up in perfect condition.

Involuntarily the Pope emitted a deep sigh of relief and loss of tension. As if the little man had only waited for this, he turned himself about with face directed towards the Lateran. And Innocent saw that he who so wonderfully had rescued the head and mother of all churches was no other than the little, poor Brother Francis from Assisi.

When Francis the day after stepped before the Pope, it was with a well-prepared tale.

"Lord Pope," said he, "I will tell you a story."

"Once there lived in a desolate place an extremely beautiful but very poor woman. She saw the king of the country, and she found favor in his eyes, and he asked her to marry him, hoping to have born to him beautiful children. But when they were married a long enough time, the woman had borne many sons. And she began to meditate within herself and said: 'What shall I a poor woman do with all the children I have? I have no inheritance from which they can live!' Then she said to the sons: 'Fear not, for you are the sons of a king! Go then to the court and he will give you all you want!' But as they came to the king, he wondered at their beauty and saw that they resembled him, and he said to them: 'Whose sons are you?' But they answered that they were sons of the poor woman in the desolate place. Then the king embraced them with great joy, and said to them: 'Fear not, for you are my sons. If I feed so many at my table, how much more should I feed you who are my lawful sons!' And he sent a messenger to the woman in the wilderness, that she should send him all her children to the court, so that he could support them!"[1]

After having ended this parable, Francis continued:

"Lord Pope, I am the poor woman in the wilderness. God has in his mercy looked upon me and I have borne him sons in Christ. And the King of kings has said to me that he will take care of all my offspring, for if he gives the stranger food, much more should he give it to the children of his house. God gives worldly goods to sinners, on account of the love they have for their children; how profusely will he not pour all his gifts upon those who follow his gospel and to whom therefore he owes that much?"

Thus Francis spoke, and Innocent understood that it was not the world's wisdom but the spirit and power of God. He broke out, turning to the Cardinals who sat there:

"Truly this is the pious and holy man by whom the Church of God shall be restored!"

And he arose, embraced Francis, blessed him and the Brothers and said to them: "Go with God, Brothers, and announce salvation for all, as the Lord reveals it to you! And when the Almighty has multiplied your numbers, then come back to me, and you will find me willing to give you further concessions and to charge you with a greater inheritance."[2]

All the Brothers knelt before the Pope and promised him obedience as their superior. Permission to preach was also given to Francis, and only through him to the others. As a conclusion to the audience the Brothers finally received the

---

[1] *Tres Socii*, XII, 50. Anon. Perus., p. 590, n. 238, has a somewhat different version of the occurrence. Compare Celano, *Vita secunda*, I, cap. XI.

[2] Celano, *V. pr.*, I, cap. XIII. Julian, *A. SS.*, Oct. II, pp. 590–591, n. 240. *Tres Socii*, XII, 49.

clerkly tonsure, which was given them by Cardinal John and which was the outer sign of the permission to preach the word.[1]

After a visit to the graves of the Apostles in St. Peter and St. Paul, Francis and the Brothers left Rome. Their way led them out over the Roman Campagna and past Soracte's white summits. They hastened quickly from the place, eager to be back in their accustomed surroundings once more to pursue the life and do the things for which they had so fortunately obtained the Church's permission from the mouth of the Vicar of Christ.

---

[1] Introduction to *Regula prima* (*Opusc.*, p. 24). *Tres Socii*, cap. XII, nn. 51-52. *Bonav.*, III, 10. Anon. Perus., p. 590, n. 240.

In the work referred to before on scientific studies among the Franciscans, Fr. Hilarin Felder remarks that the permission Francis obtained in 1210 only included the so-called *moral preaching*, but not *dogmatic preaching* (on faith, the sacraments, etc.), for which theological knowledge was required (ditto, p. 56).

CHAPTER III

RIVO TORTO

AFTER having wandered through the scorched Roman Campagna in the burning heat of a summer day, Francis and his companions approached the Sabine Mountains. Here they stopped for a while in the vicinity of the town of Ortis, in our day the junction point for the two great railroad lines which go to Rome each from its own side of the Apennines. They rested here for a space of two weeks in one of the mountain valleys through which the green-grey river Nera flows. The place was so beautiful, says Thomas of Celano, that the Brothers were near proving untrue to their newly sanctioned plan of life. By begging from door to door in Ortis they obtained for themselves the necessary daily bread — sometimes they got so much that they could lay aside some for the next day. Although this was not in accord with Francis' designs, the place was so lesolate and empty that there was no one to whom they could give for alms what was left over. An old Etruscan grave served them as storechamber. And so great a power had this isolated and solitary life in the midst of the mountains and of nature's loneliness upon the Brethren, that they seriously nourished the thought, if it were not better for the salvation of their souls to remain here for ever, and to forget the world and mankind in a severe ascetic life.[1]

Those who have lived among the Italian mountains will find it easy to understand this temptation. There is something in the nature of the Italian mountains that invites to the hermit life. For example, the limestone of which the Sabine Mountains are composed supplies natural caves and places of retreat for hermits. For the simple man in Italy, the two principal needs for his nourishment are *bread* and

[1] Celano, *V. pr.*, I, cap. XIV.

wine, and if the hermit has no wine the springs are bubbling and the brooks are flowing everywhere in the mountains. There is a real Italian feeling of enjoyment and contentment throughout the chapter in *Fioretti*, in which Francis and his Brother Masseo eat the bread they have begged together "on a fine big stone at the side of the clear spring," and thank God so devoutly for the happiness to be allowed to sit in the warm sunshine under the blue sky and appease their thirst and their hunger at Lady Poverty's table with simple healthy food. . . ."

This is why Italy's stories of her saints are so full of tales of hermits. St. Benedict of Nurcia himself began his career as a hermit in his grotto at Subiaco, where for three years he fasted and scourged himself, so that the herdsmen who discovered him regarded him first as a wild beast. And again, one hundred years after the time of St. Francis, Siena saw three of her most prominent and learned young men, Bernardo Tolomei and his two friends, withdraw to the cypress-grown heights of Mt. Oliveto and put on the white habit of the Benedictine hermit, separating them from the world.

This temptation to a life in lonely penance and prayer now drew near to Francis and his friends here in this isolated valley among the Sabine Hills, where no voice was heard except those of the birds and brooks. But the temptation was overcome. Francis, says his first biographer, never depended on his own insight, but asked in prayer for God's guidance in all things. And so he now chose not to live for himself alone, for it was made clear to him that he was sent out to save souls from the devil and win them for God. Soon the well-known places in the valley of Spoleto greeted Francis and his disciples, and they re-established their dwelling in the shed at Rivo Torto and in the woods around the Portiuncula chapel.

Soon after their home-coming they had the happiness to receive the priest of Assisi, Silvester, into their ranks. As before related, Francis' liberality, that day in St. George's churchyard, had made a deep impression on him, and he began to form another opinion about the significance of our life than what he had hitherto entertained. It came to pass that one night he saw in a dream a huge cross whose arms stretched over the whole world, and that came out of the mouth of

Brother Francis. This made him understand that the brotherhood Francis had begun to establish was to spread over the whole world of mankind and that its action was a divine one. After some period of deliberation he decided himself to ask to be received among the Brethren and thus became the first priest in the order.[1]

Francis, "emboldened by the power of the apostolic authority," prosecuted the missionary activity he had begun before the journey to Rome. His preaching in accord with the permission given to him was directed to the moral and social aspect of things — he preached conversion from evil ways, a life of goodness, peace with God and with one's neighbor. Presumably with the consent of Bishop Guido, the cathedral church in Assisi was given to him for his sermons; here he heralded the Christian ideal, without fear and without regard to other issues, because he never, as his biographers say, gave any advice to others which he had not first practised in his own person.[2]

For Francis the proverb did not hold, that the prophet is without honor in his own country. That his exhortations were not fruitless is witnessed by the large accessions his Order now received —"many of the people, noble and common, clerks and laymen, were seized by the spirit of God, cast aside all worldly distractions and followed the track Francis had trod."[3] Of these new disciples the majority were from Assisi and its vicinity.

But the preaching of Francis in San Rufino operated in a much wider circle. Thomas of Celano compares its effects to a star rising brightly over the horizon, and to the breaking of dawn after a gloomy night. He compares it to a seed's breaking forth from the ground with the coming of the flowers and spring. The whole aspect of the place was changed, he writes; like a river, rich in goodness and fruitfulness, Francis streamed through the place and transformed the gardens of the hearts of men so that they blossomed forth in virtue.

It is probable that Brother Thomas, in this carefully worked-

---

[1] *Tres Socii*, IX, 31. *Actus b. Francisci*, I, 38–43. Bonav., III, 5.
[2] Cel., *V. pr.*, I, XV. *Tres Socii*, XIII, 54.
[3] *Tres Socii*. ditto. Compare Celano.

out prose, alludes to an occurrence which really changed the whole condition of Assisi, and which can undoubtedly be ascribed to the sermons of St. Francis. I refer to the adjustment between the upper and lower classes, *majores* and *minores*, which was ratified in the great hall of the communal palace in 1210. We still possess the document which was drawn up on this occasion, and which begins thus:

"In the name of God. Amen.

"The grace of the Holy Ghost be with you.

"For the honor of Our Lord Jesus Christ, the blessed Virgin Mary, Emperor Otto and Duke Leopold."

After his introduction a whole series of stipulations follows, of which the most important is the agreement below:

"In all mutual agreements, no alliance shall be entered into, neither with pope or his nuncios or legates, nor with the emperor or king or their nuncios or legates, or with any state or fortification or with any magnate; but they shall be united in all things which are necessary for the welfare and progress of the city of Assisi."

In this, the *Magna Charta* of Assisi, almost all the citizens who hitherto had been bondsmen were released on payment of a very small ransom, which could be validly paid to the city authorities if their lords refused to accept it. Inhabitants of the environs of Assisi received the same rights as the citizens proper; the protection of strangers was provided for; the compensation of ambassadors for going on embassies was stipulated; finally, amnesty for the disturbances of 1202 was pronounced, and the proper authorities were strictly charged to carry out the work on the cathedral that had been under way since 1140.[1]

When we think of how the Italian republics, both in the thirteenth century and later, were rent by civil wars, then we can realize how eloquently such a document speaks for the peaceful growth and prosperity of Assisi. The biographers also picture Francis to us as the pacifier in other Italian states, such as Arezzo, Perugia, Siena.[2] Even the celebrated

---

[1] Cristofani, I, 123-130. Le Monnier, I, 165-167. Sabatier, 133-135.
[2] Arezzo: Bonav., VI, 9; Perugia: Celano, *Vita secunda*, II, 6; Siena: *Fioretti*, cap. XI.

Wolf of Gubbio is nothing without the tale, adorned in the legend, about the treaty of peace between a little Italian republic and one of those inhuman savage lords of a castle, who, like Knight Werner of Urslingen, could bear a shield on the breast with the inscription, "Enemy of God, of Pity and of Mercy."[1] An historical companion-piece to Francis and the Wolf of Gubbio is given by Anthony of Padua face to face with the tyrant Ezzelin.[2]

This aspect of Francis' activity is pictured in the legends as the expulsion of devils. In Giotto's pictures in the upper church in Assisi we see the demons flying in all sorts of horrible forms up the chimneys of Arezzo, while Francis' hand is lifted in blessing over the city. We, children of the twentieth century, have lost the power of representing the evil spirits in bodily form, as the artist and tellers of legends did in the Middle Ages. But can we say that their presence is less certain or their disagreeable propinquity in many fateful moments less real? Are there no times and places when the great power of darkness is felt, not only in but around one — where it is as if a real incorporeal voice whispered in the ear, when one is led off into the flames of hell hand in hand — when there is a low, penetrating voice that goes through one: "See that! Go there!" Ah, there are not only many places, but also many houses, where the need is real that one of God's friends should appear upon the threshold, and with mighty voice give the command: "In the name of the Almighty God and of his servant St. Francis I command you evil spirits to depart!"[3]

It was at this time that one day the Rules of the Order were being read aloud in the presence of Francis, and that the reader came to the part of the seventh chapter where is the expression: *et sint minores,* "and they shall be inferiors." The thought of a name for the Brotherhood had long occupied

---

[1] *Fioretti,* cap. XXI. Compare the legend of "Brother Wolf" on Mt. Alverna in Arthur's *Martyrlogium Franciscanum* for July 3 and in Wadding (1215, n. 16). See Translator's note, p. 410.

[2] Lempp: "A. v. P." in *Ztschr. f. Kgsch.* (Gotha), vol. XIII, p. 22, n. 3.

[3] ante portam civitatis coepit clamare valenter: "Ex parte omnipotentis Dei et jussu servi ejus Francisci, procul hinc discedite, daemones universi." Bonav., VI, 9.

Francis: the term "Penitents from Assisi," *viri poenitentes de Assisio*, was only an expedient to repress the curious. On hearing this placed in the Rules, the word *Minores* impressed him greatly — "Little people, Little Brothers, that name suits me and mine well!" *Ordo fratrum minorum*, "the Order of the Minor Brothers," it became.

Thomas of Celano, in his first biography of St. Francis, has given a sketch of the life of the Brothers in the shed at Rivo Torto, which, in the bright harmony of clear colors on a sort of ground of gold, remind one of Fra Angelico's altar-pieces. When they returned from their work at evening time (he writes) and were again together, or when they in the course of the day met on the road, love and joy shone out of the eyes, and they greeted each other with chaste embraces, holy kisses, cheerful words, modest smiles, friendly glances and equable minds. Because they had given up all self-love, they thought only of helping each other; with longing they hurried home, with joy they abided there; but separation was bitter, and leaving was sad. Dissension was unknown among them; there was no malice, no envy, no misunderstanding, no bitterness, but all was unity, peace, thankfulness and songs of praise. Seldom or never did they cease from praising God and praying to and thanking him for the good they had done, sighing and grieving for what they had done badly or had failed in. They felt that they were deserted by God when their hearts were not penetrated by the sweetness of the Spirit. So as not to fall asleep in their nightly prayers they wore belts, studded with iron points, whose pricking prevented them from sleeping. Filled with the Holy Ghost they not only prayed from the Breviary like the Catholic priests, but at intervals sang out with suppliant voice and spiritual melody, *Our Father who art in heaven*.[2]

The central point in all this brotherly intercourse was Francis. From him none of the Brothers kept anything hidden, but revealed the most secret thoughts and feelings of their hearts to him. They obeyed him, and with so loving

---
[1] Celano, *V. pr.*, I, XV. *Spec. perf.*, cap. XXVI.
[2] Celano, *V. pr..*, I, XV–XVIII.

an obedience that not only did each one fulfil his behest but also tried to read his wish in his slightest expression.

The power Francis exercised rested first and foremost on his personality. He was the Brothers' teacher, not only in word but also in action. When he warned them against enjoyment in eating, and even said that it was not possible to eat to satiety without danger of bearing the yoke of luxury, they understood his warning better when they saw him strew ashes on his own food or pour cold water on it to take away its savor. When he told them to fight heroically against all temptations, it was he who gave them an example by jumping in winter into the ice-cold river to put to flight a temptation of the flesh.

Every one who has had the happiness in his youth to have lived near a highly exalted personality will therefore understand that a young Brother named Ricerius had acquired the conviction that the good-will of Francis was an infallible sign of the satisfaction of God. But now it came to pass with him, the last to have come into the Order, that, while Francis showed himself friendly and loving to the others, he seemed to make an exception in his case only. When Brother Ricerius had once come by this warped imagining, naturally every occasion served only to implant it deeper within him. If he came out as Francis was going in, he would think Francis did so to avoid being with him. If Francis stood and talked with others, and they happened to look in the direction of Brother Ricerius, then he would think that they must be complaining at having taken him into the Order and were determining to ask him to take his leave again. Thus did this young Brother misjudge all and was almost desperate, certain that he was avoided and repelled by Francis and consequently by God.

The sight of Brother Ricerius' pained face and imploring, longing eyes seems, like a revelation, to have betrayed to Francis the poor youth's tribulations. One day, therefore, he had the young Brother summoned and said to him: "My dear son, let no evil thought disturb thee or tempt thee! Thou art my own dear child, and one of those I think the most of, and as deserving of my love as of my confidence. Come then and speak with me when thou wilt, and whenever anything weighs upon thee, thou art always thoroughly welcome!" Overcome, out of his senses with joy, with heart happily beating and eyes streaming with tears, the young Brother left the master and knew of nothing until he in a lonely place out in the woods fell down on his knees and thanked God for his happiness.[1]

Two other stories that are associated with Rivo Torto tell of the same refined, loving understanding of the special trouble of each individual Brother.

One night — thus it told in *Speculum perfectionis* — one of the Brothers woke from sleep with loud cries and shouted: "Oh, I am dying, I am dying!" All the others woke, and Francis said: "Let us get up, my Brothers, and light the lamp!" As soon as the light was lighted, he asked: "Who was that who cried out, 'I am dying'?" One of the Brothers answered: "It was I!" And Francis asked further, "What ails thee, my Brother, to make you die?" And he answered, "I am dying of hunger!"

Now this was in the early days of the Brotherhood, and they mortified and scourged their bodies beyond measure. Therefore Francis had the table at once spread and sat at the table with the starving Brother, lest he should be ashamed to eat alone, and he invited the rest of the Brothers to take seats at the table. And after they had eaten, Francis said to them:

"My dear sons, I truly say to you that every one must study his own nature. Some of you can sustain life with less food than others can, and therefore I desire that he who needs more nourishment shall not be obliged to equal others, but that every one shall give his body what it needs for being an efficient servant of the soul. For as we are obliged to be on our guard against superfluous food which injures body and soul alike, thus we must be on the watch against immoderate fasting, and this the more, because the Lord wants conversion and not victims."[2]

[1] Celano, *V. pr.*, I, XVIII. *Fioretti*, cap. XXVII. *Actus b. Francisci*, cap. XXXVII. — Brother Ricerius is author of a little work, which by many is placed as high as Thomas à Kempis' "Following of Christ": *Qualiter anima possit cito pervenire ad cognitionem veritatis.*
[2] *Spec. perf.*, cap. XXVII. Celano, *Vita secunda*, I, cap. XV.

A trait of the same kind is told of, when Francis rose early one morning and took a sick Brother, whom he thought it would benefit to eat grapes fasting, along with him into a vineyard, and there sat by his side and gave him grapes to eat in company with himself, lest the Brother should be ashamed of eating alone. It can be understood that, as the *Speculum* tells us, the Brother, as long as he lived, never forgot this attention of Francis', and that he never could tell the other Brothers this reminiscence of his youth without tears in his eyes.[1]

The residence at Rivo Torto came to an end in a manner as abrupt as drastic. One day, as the Brothers were in the shed, praying quietly each in his place, a peasant suddenly appeared with his ass, which without more ado he drove in, calling out in a loud voice: "Go in, long ears, here we can surely be comfortable." These words, which seemed to be more intended for the Brothers than for the ass, showed that it was his intention to at once change the house of prayer into an asses' stable. After a few minutes' contemplation of the man's untroubled demeanor, Francis broke forth:

"I know, Brothers, that God has not called us to keep a hotel for asses, but to pray and show men the way of salvation!"[2]

All then arose and left Rivo Torto for ever. From now on, Portiuncula was the central point of the Franciscan movement and soon put the first modest abode completely in the shade. And yet it was there that Francis and the mistress of his heart, the noble Lady Poverty, had spent their first and perhaps happiest days.

[1] *Spec. perf.*, cap. XXVIII. Celano, *Vita secunda*, III, 110. According to Wadding (1210, n. 50), this disciple was Silvester.
[2] *Tres Socii*, XIII, 55. Cel., *V. pr.*, I, XVI.

CHAPTER IV

PORTIUNCULA AND THE EARLY DISCIPLES [1]

THE small and ancient chapel of Portiuncula, as it exists to-day, is a long room, with a pointed arched ceiling and a semi-circular apse, a gable roof, a simple arched door in the façade, and another in one of the side-walls. According to a tradition that for the first time is given in Salvator Vitalis' *Paradisus Seraphicus* (Milan, 1645), the chapel was built by five hermits during the pontificate of Pope Liberius in the fourth century, who were returning home from the Holy Land with a relic of Mary's grave, which was given to them by St. Cyril. In any case there is found over the altar a picture of great age, which represents the assumption of the Blessed Virgin into Heaven; the many angels who float around Mary in the picture gave the popular name to the chapel of "Our Lady of the Angels." The designation *Portiuncula* — "little portion of earth" — dates from the Benedictines on Monte Subasio, to whom the chapel had belonged ever since 576. In 1075 the building was in such a ruinous condition that the monks abandoned it and withdrew to the mother-house upon the mountain. According to the legend, Pica had prayed in the deserted chapel, and here received the knowledge that she should have a son who would eventually rebuild the fallen house of God. After the putting of it in order, Francis and his Brothers usually kept themselves in the forest which surrounded the church, and it was a great joy to them when the abbey on Monte Subasio, which now belonged to the Camaldolites, gave the Brethren the privilege of using Portiuncula for ever. For Francis was unwilling to take possession of the chapel in fee simple, and strictly kept up the custom of sending every year a basket of fish to the monks as payment of rent.[1]

[1] Thode, as before referred to, 302–304. Wadding: *Annales*, 1210, nn. 27 and 30.

At the side of the chapel Francis and his Brothers built a hut of interwoven boughs, plastered over with mud and thatched with leaves. Sacks of straw served for beds, the naked earth was both table and chair, and the hedge served for convent walls.[1] This was the first Franciscan *luogo* — "place" — established, which according to Francis' expressed wish was to be a model for all the others. When the Franciscan Order began later to depart from his ideals, one of the signs of this departure was that the designation *luogo, locus,* was changed for the more stately *convento,* whence the less severe branch of the order took a name (Conventuals). It was a new brotherhood, the "Poor of Christ," the Jesuati, founded by St. John Colombini of Siena, who assumed the old Franciscan designation.[2]

Besides the original flock of disciples, there was now gathered here in Portiuncula a circle of new Brothers who could properly be called the new generation of Franciscans. By the side of Bernard, Giles, Angelo and Silvester, tradition and legend, from now on, placed a second series of names: Rufino, Masseo, Juniper, Leo. Yes, this younger set is near surpassing the others and casting the older ones a little into the shade. It seems as if many of the older ones had a certain inclination to isolate themselves, and set more of a price on solitude than on community life. Thus Silvester longed to keep himself in the caves of Carceri and there give himself up to prayer and meditation. Bernard was so wrapt up in God, when he was in the woods, that he did not even hear Brother Francis calling

[1] *Spec. perf.*, capp. V, VII, X.
[2] Three epochs can be distinguished in the history of the Franciscan convents. First the Brothers lived where they worked, especially in hospitals. Then they had their own *loci,* such as Portiuncula, Monte Ripido near Perugia, Alberino near Siena, La Foresta, Greccio and Poggio Bustone in the valley of Rieti, le Pugliole near Bologna. Coincident with these hermitages were established the more lonely places to which the Brothers sometimes withdrew themselves (*eremi, retiri*); this character was to be seen in Carceri near Assisi, Cerbajolo in Casentino, Celle near Cortona, Monteluco near Spoleto, Monte Casale near Borgo San Sepoloro, S. Urbano near Marni, Fonte Colombo in the valley of Rieti. Such was the condition of things, for instance, when Jacques de Vitry visited Italy. Finally, city convents were erected: 1235, in Bologna, 1236, in Sienna, and in Viterbo, Florence, Cortona, etc. (*Spec. perf.*, ed. Sabatier, p. 25, n. 1). For the Jesuati's *luoghi,* see Feo Belcari: *Vita d'alcuni Giesuati,* cap. I (ed. Dragonedelli, 1659, ed. Gigli, 1843).

to him. At other times "he wandered sometimes twenty, sometimes thirty days at a time alone, on the highest mountain summits, and saw the things which are on high."[1] Giles led a life of extensive travelling, was now in the Holy Land, now in Spain, now in Rome, now in Bari at the shrine of St. Nicholas.

Yet we will do wrong if we follow the legends and forget the works of early days on account of the newer members. This before all applied to Brother Giles, whom Francis called by the title, "the Knight of the Round Table," and in whom all of the original Franciscan spirit was vivified and stayed alive to the last. Until his death, which happened in the year 1262 on the festival of St. George, the anniversary of his reception into the Order, Giles continued to be God's good knight and a true St. George of the noble Lady Poverty. His life is especially a witness to the love of labor of the early Franciscans. His biography as it is written by his younger friend, Brother Leo, is full of such traits.

On his way to the Holy Land he came to Brindisi, and as there was no chance of embarking there at once, he had to stay several days in the city. Here he begged an old cart, filled it with water and dragged it through the city streets, calling out like the water-carriers: "*Chi vuole dell' aqua?* Who wants water?" As pay for water he took bread and such other things as were needed by him and his companions. On the return from the same pilgrimage he was put ashore at Ancona. Here too he found employment; he went out and cut osiers for baskets and rushes for covering bottles, he plaited them and sold them, not for money but for bread. He also carried bodies to the grave and earned thereby, not only a garment for himself, but also for the Brethren who accompanied him; such deeds he wished to pray for him while he slept.

Apparently it was during this stay in Ancona that a priest who saw him coming home to the town with a bundle of rushes uttered the word "hypocrite" as Giles passed him by. On hearing this, Giles was so cast down that he could not keep back the tears, and when the Brother who accompanied him

[1] *Fioretti*, capp. XVI, III, XXVIII.

asked him the reason of his distress, he answered, "Because I am a hypocrite, as a priest to-day said to me." "And does that make you believe that you are one?" asked the Brother. "Yes," answered Giles, "a priest cannot lie!" Then his companion had to teach him that there is a difference between priests as between men, and that, like a man, a priest can very likely do wrong, and thus comforted the unhappy Brother Giles.

During his visit in Rome Giles had arranged it so that he heard mass early in the morning, and then went out to a forest at some distance from the city. Here he gathered a bundle of wood which he carried back to Rome and sold for bread and other necessities. Once a lady wanted to give him more for the wood than he had asked, as she saw that it was a religious who was before her. But Giles now would not take more than half the former price. "I will not yield to avarice," he declared.

At the time of the wine harvest he helped pluck grapes, in the olive harvest he gathered olives. He often gleaned corn in the fields like other paupers, but gave most of it away, saying that he had no granary to keep it in. From San Sisto's fountain outside of Rome he brought water to the monks in the convent of SS. Quattro Coronati, and also helped the convent cook in mixing bread and grinding flour. Altogether he took part in all kinds of work by which he could support himself; he only had one invariable requirement, the time necessary to read his Breviary and for meditation.

In the midst of this life of ceaseless industry he was infused with the deep Franciscan goodness. Once he cut the hood off of his cloak, while on his way to San Jago di Compostella, and gave it to a poor person who had asked for alms; he went about for the next twenty days without any hood. As he went through Lombardy, a man beckoned to him. Giles thought that he wanted to give him something, and approached him, but with a grin the man stuck a pair of dice into his hand. "God forgive you, my son!" said Giles, and went his way. When carrying water to the monks in Santi Quattro Coronati, he was addressed by a wanderer on the Appian Way, who wanted a drink from his jar. Giles refused it, whereupon the man made an outcry in his wrath. Giles made no response, but as soon as he had reached the convent he got another jar, filled it, overtook the man and asked him to drink, saying, "Do not be angry with me, but I did not like to take the monks water that another had tasted of!"

Even when a guest with such noble people as the Bishop of Tusculum, Cardinal Nicholas, he went out and earned his bread, which he afterwards ate at the Cardinal's table. One day it rained in torrents and the Cardinal was rejoicing that Brother Giles for once would have to eat of his food. Meanwhile Giles went to the kitchen, found that it was dirty, and offered the cook to clean it for a price of two loaves. The offer was accepted, and the Cardinal was disappointed in his hopes. As it rained the next day also, Giles earned his two loaves by polishing all the knives in the house.

Under the title of "Brother Giles's Wisdom," there are collected a quantity of maxims and sayings, apparently mostly from his later years. Thus it is told that two cardinals once had paid him a visit and on leaving had politely recommended themselves to his prayers. "It is surely not necessary that I should pray for you, my lords," was his answer, "for it is evident that you have more faith and hope than I have!" "How is that?" asked the two princes of the church, astonished and perhaps a little anxiously, for Brother Giles was known for his wit. "Because you who have so much of power and honor and the glory of this world hope to be saved, and I who live so poorly and wretchedly fear in spite of all that I will be damned!"

Until his death Brother Giles lived true to the Franciscan ideals — poverty, chastity, cheerfulness. A sonnet which he composed in honor of chastity is preserved for us, as well as some fragments of other verse. In his little convent garden at Perugia he listened to the cooing doves, and spoke to them. And on beautiful summer mornings he would be seen wandering up and down among his flower-beds, singing the praises of God, and playing as if on a violin, with two sticks, one of which he scraped upon the other.[1]

[1] "pigliando il bastoncello cominciò a fare con esso a modo di viola, e di qua e di colà per l'orto discorrendo a modo di sonatore di citara cantava." Feo Belcari: *Vita di frate Egidio*, cap. XXV. (*Prose*, ed. Gigli, vol. 2, Roma, 1843.)

If the older Brothers lived thus much by themselves, we find the newer generation of Franciscans almost always in the company of Francis. Especially was Masseo of Marignano, near Assisi, the master's companion on many important journeys. While Francis was "a very insignificant man and of small size and therefore was taken for a poor being by those who did not know him," on the other hand Masseo was "large and fine-looking and had the gift of eloquence and could speak with people." When the two went together begging, Francis got "nothing but a few bits and remains of bread, and that dry," but Masseo "got good big pieces, and bread enough and whole loaves." Just the same the tall, fine-looking, eloquent Masseo offered his services up in Carceri, "to look after the door, to receive alms and to go into the kitchen" so that he alone would bear the whole burden of the house, while the other Brothers could give themselves undisturbedly to prayer and meditation. And once when he was walking with Francis and came to a cross-way where one could go to Florence, to Siena or to Arezzo, and Brother Masseo asked, "Father, which way shall we take?" Francis answered him, "The way God wishes." But Brother Masseo asked further, "How shall we know God's will?" And Francis answered: "That I will now show you. In the name of holy obedience I order you to start turning round and round in the road here, as the children do, and not to stop until I tell you to." Then Brother Masseo began to whirl round and round as children do, and he became so giddy that he often fell down; but as Francis said nothing to him, he got up again and continued. At last as he was turning round

---

He had learned this way of playing from his master, Francis. See *Spec. perf.*, cap. XCIII, and Cel., *V. sec.*, III, 67. Compare also *Anal. Franc.*, III, p. 101. The Sonnet to Chastity reads thus:

O santa castitate! Quanta e la tua bontate!
Veramente tu se' preziosa, e tale
E tanto soave il tuo ardore
Che chi non ti assaggia, non sa quanto vale.
Impero li stolti non conoscono il tuo valore.

See: *A. SS.*, Apr. III, pp. 220 et seq.; *Anal. Franc.*, III, pp. 74 et seq.: Celano, *Vita prima*, I, cap. XVII; Bernard of Bessa: *De laudibus* (in *Anal. Franc.*, III), p. 671; *Doc. Antiq. Franc.* (ed. Lemmens), I (Quaracchi, 1901), pp. 37 et seq.; *Vita di frate Egidio* and *Dottrina di frate Egidio* in appendix to *Fioretti*.

with great vigor, Francis said, "Stop and do not move!" And he stood still, and Francis asked him, "How is your face turned?" Brother Masseo answered, "Towards Siena!" Then said Francis, "It is God's will that we shall go to Siena to-day."

Francis exercised the tall impressive Brother Masseo with other such humiliations until he felt humble and small. And Masseo at last became so deep in humility that he regarded himself as a great sinner and very deserving of hell, although he daily waxed strong in all virtues. And this humility filled him with such an inward light that he was always full of joy. And often when he prayed he would give out a cry of joy, a monotone like the cooing of a dove, and with cheerful face and joyful heart he lived in the sight of God and yet regarded himself as the most insignificant of men. But it came to pass in his old age that young Brother Jacob of Fallerone asked him why he did not make a change in his way of rejoicing and make a new verse. Then he answered with great delight: "Because he who has all his happiness in only one thing should not sing but the one verse." [1]

Brother Rufino of Assisi among the younger disciples reminds us of Bernard of Quintavalle among the older ones. Like him he was of noble family—he belonged to the noble race, Scifi or Scefi. And like Bernard he had an inclination to be a hermit—an inclination which was so strong that finally he, on a single opportunity offering itself, was near leaving Francis, whose practical Christianity appealed to him less than a life in ascetic solitude, like that of the old hermits of the desert. He was often seen sunk in prayer and meditation, so that he could scarcely be roused out of it, and when he at last was awakened, there was no connection in what he said.[2]

On the other hand, Brother Juniper or *Ginepro* was entirely of Francis' spirit. Of him Francis said jokingly, "I wish we had a whole grove of such juniper trees!" It was he who one

[1] *Actus b. Francisci* (ed. Sabatier), cap. XI, cap. XII, cap. XIII, cap. XLI. *Chron. XXIV gen.* in *Anal. Franc.*, III, pp. 115-158. *Fioretti*, capp. XI, XII, XIII, XXXII.

[2] "Unde semel vocatus a sociis ut iret pro pane . . . respondit: *Frater a te imo mo molto volontire.*" *Actus*, cap. XXXIII. Compare *Fioretti*, capp. XXIX-XXXI; *Chron. XXIV gen.*, pp. 46 et seq. Rufino died, 1270, in Assisi.

day, when one of the Brothers who lay sick in Portiuncula convent expressed a desire for boiled pig's feet, sprang into the woods and cut off a foot from one of the swine which went there after mast, and served it to the sick Brother. After him came the peasant to whom the pig belonged, and complained to Francis, whose suspicion fell upon Brother Juniper. He was called, and answered freely about his action. "For," said he, "our Brother got so much good out of the foot of this pig that I would have no remorse if I had cut the feet off of a hundred swine!" With much difficulty Francis brought Brother Juniper to suspect the least wrong in such a wilful trespass upon a neighbor's goods. "Very well," said he at last, "I see that the man is angry with us, but now I will try to find him and pacify him." And he ran the best he could and found the peasant and told him the whole story — how the Brother who was sick wanted a cooked pig's foot, that pigs are made for man's use, for his nourishment and food, that everything belonged equally to all men, because no one can make so much as one little pig, but God alone can do it, and that therefore he had taken the one pig's foot because the sick man had wanted it so badly.

All this Brother Juniper told, very explicitly and with satisfaction, to the angry peasant, being now sure that all was understood and that he would be understood and that the amputation of the pig's foot would be forgiven. But it turned out otherwise, for the man began to abuse Brother Juniper, calling him an evil-doer, a loafer, a thief and robber, a simpleton and a fool. "Why, he cannot have understood me," thinks Brother Juniper, and begins anew his story, still more impressively than before. Then when he came to the end he fell on the neck of the peasant and cried out, "See, I did this for my poor sick Brother, that he might get well again, and you have helped me, so you must cease being troubled or angry, but let us together rejoice and thank the good God who gives us the fruits of the earth and the flocks of the field and the wild beasts of the woods, and who wants us all to be his children and to help one another like good brothers and sisters. Am I not right, my dear, good brother?" And thereupon Brother Juniper embraced the peasant and pressed him to his heart and kissed him, and the peasant thought over it, begged for forgiveness from God and from the Brothers with bitter tears for his hardness, and went away and caught a pig and slaughtered it, cooked it and brought it himself to the convent at Portiuncula as a gift to the Brethren.

The same Brother Juniper was once in a little convent, and the time came for the other Brothers to leave it to go each to his work. As they went off, the guardian Brother gave instructions to Brother Juniper and said to him, "Take good care of the house while we are away, and cook a little food before we return." "Depend upon me," answered Brother Juniper, and the others went on.

When he was alone he began to reflect over what he had been told, and said to himself as he went on chopping wood and gathering some twigs to make the fire with: "Is it not really unreasonable that a Brother should thus be in the kitchen every day and use up his time there without being able to pray a little bit? I shall certainly see to it, so that to-day there shall be prepared so much food, that even if the Brothers were many more they would have enough to eat for the next two weeks!" Having reached this determination Brother Juniper went to the neighboring city, and purchased there a lot of clay pots, together with meat, game, eggs and a quantity of vegetables. He lit a big wood fire, filled the pots with water and put all the food into them, chickens with the game, all unplucked, the vegetables without washing, and the rest in the same style.

The Brothers came home as Brother Juniper was in full blast with his cooking. A huge fire was roaring away, and Brother Juniper jumped from one pot to the other so that it was a joy to see him, and stirred them with a long stick, because the fire was so hot that he could not get near the pots. At last he rang the dinner bell, and red with his exertions and the heat of the fire, he carried in his dishes of food and set them down before the assembled Brethren, saying: "Eat now, and then we will go to our prayers! I have cooked so much food to-day that there is enough to last us for the next two weeks!" Meanwhile, none of the Brethren touched the food which Brother Juniper vainly with great eloquence offered them as a great feast. But as it dawned upon Brother Juniper what he had done he cast himself at their feet, kneeling and striking his breast, and blamed himself for having spoiled so much good food.

It was not always pure naïveté that was at the bottom of such actions. Sometimes Brother Juniper wished in this burlesque manner to give others of the Brethren a lesson which might be needed as they departed from the spirit of the Order. Possibly, the Brothers to whom he served the wild lobscouse had shown too great interest and had spent too much time in the cooking department. A reprimand of the best kind was given by Brother Juniper when, in the middle of the night, he served porridge with a big lump of butter in the middle to his superior, who had reproved him the preceding afternoon for his too great generosity in giving alms. "Father," said Brother Juniper as he stood before his door with the plate of porridge in one hand and a lighted candle in the other, "to-day when you reprimanded me for my fault I noticed that you were very hoarse from excitement. Now I have prepared this porridge for you and beg you to eat it; it is good for the throat and chest!" The superior, who understood the meaning of this untimely attention, harshly told Brother Juniper to go away with his foolish tricks. "Well," said he, "the porridge is cooked and has to be eaten, so you hold the light while I do the eating!" The other was enough of a Franciscan to answer this boldness by sitting down at the table with Brother Juniper and sharing the porridge with him.

Such actions resulted in making Brother Juniper famous, and people used to collect together when he was coming, to see him. It so happened that he was once sent to Rome, and several prominent persons — of the same type of the ladies rustling in silks and smelling of perfume, who in our days are seen lorgnetting the martyrs' graves in the catacombs — presented themselves at his door for the purpose of meeting him. Brother Juniper had been told about it and prepared at once to play a trick on their curiosity masquerading as piety. In a field by the roadside a couple of boys were playing seesaw, having placed a plank across a support, each sitting on his own end of the plank and going up and down alternately. So Brother Juniper took the place of one of the boys, and when the noble company came along, they were much surprised to find the man of God busily engaged in seesawing. None the less they greeted him with great deference and next waited for him to stop his play and come out to them. But Brother Juniper troubled himself little about their greeting and waiting; on the contrary, he gave the more energy to his seesawing. And after the strangers had waited thus a reasonable time, and Brother Juniper kept on seesawing, they went away irritated, as they mutually agreed that the so-called holy Brother was an entirely common peasant and lout, void of all culture. Then only did Brother Juniper leave his seesawing, and went on to Rome in peace and alone.

Like Brother Leo and Brother Angelo Tancredi of Rieti, Brother Juniper belonged to the small select circle who, after the master's death, associated themselves with St. Clara. Brother Juniper was present with the other two at the death-bed of St. Clara. "What is the news from God?" she asked cheerfully, as this loyal disciple of Francis showed himself at her bedside, and he sat down by her and spoke "flaming sparks of words."[1]

A chip of the same block as Brother Juniper was that Brother John, who bore the surname "the simple," whose calling to enter the order is told in the following recital:

"When the Brethren were living at Portiuncula and were now many in number, St. Francis went around to the towns and churches in the vicinity of Assisi, and preached to the people, that they should be converted, and he had a broom with him to clean the churches of dirt, for it made St. Francis very unhappy when he saw that a church was not as clean

---

[1] "Inter quos dum apparet frater Juniperus, egregius Domini jaculator" (undoubtedly *joculator*, compare *Spec. perf.*, cap. 100) ". . . nova hilaritate perfusa quaerit, si aliquid novi de Domino habet ad manum. Qui aperiens os suum, de fornace fervidi cordis flammantes verborum scintillas emittit." (*Vita S. Clarae, Acta SS.*, Aug. II, cap. VI, n. 51.) See also *Vita di frate Ginepro* in the appendix to *Fioretti* with the extract from *Chronica XXIV gen.* (*Analecta Franciscana*, III, pp. 54 et seq.). Brother Juniper died 1258; according to Wadding he entered the order in 1210. (Wadding, *Annales*, 1210, n. 36, 1258, n. 10.)

as he wished. And therefore he sometimes stopped in his preaching and gathered the priests around him in some retired place so that no one else should hear, and preached on the salvation of souls and especially on keeping the churches and altars clean and all that had to do with the celebration of the holy mysteries.

"And one day he came to a village in the environs of Assisi and started in all humility to sweep and clean it. But the rumor of who was there ran through the whole place, and a peasant who was ploughing his field also heard of it and came at once and found him busy sweeping the church. But the peasant, whose name was John, said to him, 'Brother, give me the broom and let me help you!' And he took the broom out of his hand and swept vigorously. Then they sat down together and he said to St. Francis: 'Brother, for a long time I have had a desire to serve God, and especially after I heard of thee and thy Brethren, but I never knew how I could meet thee. It has now pleased God to bring us together, so I will do all thou wishest.'

"When St. Francis perceived so great a zeal he rejoiced in the Lord, especially because at this time he had only a few Brothers, and it seemed to him that this simple and upright man could become a good Brother. Therefore he said to him: 'Brother, if you have it in your mind to live like us, you must free yourself of all the possessions you can dispose of, and you must give them to the poor after the counsels of the gospel, for thus have all my Brothers done each in his own way.'

"When he had heard this he turned back to the field where he had left the oxen standing in the plough, unyoked them, and brought one of them back to St. Francis. 'Brother,' said he to him, 'it is now many years that I have served my father and all in the house; I intend, therefore, as my portion by inheritance, to take this ox and give it to the poor, in the way that shall seem best to you.'

"But when his parents and his sisters, who were all younger than he, heard that he was going to leave them, they began to cry so strongly and so long that St. Francis was moved to pity, because they were many and could do nothing. Therefore he said to them: 'This your son wants to serve God, and that should not displease you in him, but you should rather rejoice over it. But so that you in the meanwhile shall not be without comfort, I will have him give you this ox, just as he would have given it to the other poor, as the gospel teaches us.' Then they were all comforted with the words St. Francis said, and still more that they had got the ox back. . . .

"But Brother John was clothed in the habit of the Order, and so great was his simplicity that he thought he was obliged to do all that St. Francis did. When therefore St. Francis was in a church or other place to pray, he watched him closely so as to follow all his ways and movements. And when St. Francis bent the knee or lifted his hands to heaven, or spit, or sighed, then he did exactly the same. But as St. Francis became aware of this, he scolded him very cheerfully about it. Then Brother John answered, 'Brother, I have promised to do all that you do, and therefore it is fit that I copy you in all things.'"[1]

Francis' special confidant and best friend among the younger ones, yes, among all the disciples at this time, was Brother Leo of Assisi, who filled the office of his amanuensis and secretary. Francis called him, perhaps with a wilful opposition to his name *Leone* (lion), *frate pecorella di Dio*, "Brother little lamb of God."

It was together with him that Francis — according to the *Fioretti* — was once in a place where they had no Breviary to pray out of. So as to spend the time in praising God, Francis proposed the following part-prayer: "I shall first say, 'O Brother Francis, you have done so much ill and committed so many sins here in the world, that you are worthy to go to hell. And to this you must answer: 'Yes, it is true that you deserve the deepest hell.'"

And blithe as a dove Brother Leo answered: "Willingly, Father. Let us begin in the name of God!"

Then Francis began to say, "O Brother Francis, thou hast

[1] *Spec. perf.*, capp. LVI–LVII. Celano, *Vita secunda*, III, 120. The village where Francis met the simple Brother John is called Nottiano, and is about three hours east of Assisi; the tale still lives in the mouths of the people as it is told here. Not far off, near a place called Le Coste, is seen a cave in which Francis is supposed to have dwelt. (*Le Specchio di perf.*, Assisi, 1899, p. 121.)

done so much evil and committed so many sins here in the world that thou art worthy to go to hell." And Brother Leo answered, "God will do so much good through thee that thou shalt come into paradise." Then Francis answered: "Do not say that, Brother Leo, but when I now say, 'Brother Francis, thou hast done so much wrong before God that thou art worthy to be damned!' then answer thus: 'Thou art certainly worthy to come among the damned!'"

And Brother Leo answered, "Willingly, Father!"

Then Francis began to sigh and groan and beat his breast, and said in a loud voice, "O Lord, God of heaven and earth, I have committed such wrong against thee and so many sins that I am worthy to be damned by thee." And Brother Leo answered, "O Brother Francis, God will do such things with thee that thou shalt be happy before all the Blest." But Francis wondered why Brother Leo was so set in not answering as he had been told to, and he scolded him for it, saying: "Why dost thou not answer as I told thee to? In the name of holy obedience I order thee to answer as I now will teach thee. Thus I say: 'O thou bad Francis, dost thou think that God will have pity on thee, that hast committed so many sins against the Father of mercy and God of comfort, that thou in no way art worthy to find mercy?' And thou Brother Leo, God's little lamb, answer: 'Thou art in no way worthy to find mercy!'" But as Francis said after this, "O thou bad Francis," etc., Brother Leo answered him, "The Father God, whose mercy is infinitely greater than thy transgressions, will show thee great mercy and will moreover manifest to thee much favor." Over this answer Francis was very angry and a little carried away, and he said to Brother Leo: "Why hast thou fallen so as to show thyself disobedient? Now thou hast so many times answered the opposite of what I told thee." But Brother Leo humbly and reverentially answered, "God knows, Father, that every time I have wished to answer thee as thou commandest me to; but God forced me to speak as it pleased him, and not as it pleased me." Francis wondered greatly over this, and said to Brother Leo, "I pray thee in charity to answer me this time as I have told thee." Brother

Leo replied, "In God's name I will certainly answer every time as thou wishest it." And with tears, Francis now said, "O thou wicked Brother Francis, dost thou believe that God can have mercy upon thee?" Brother Leo answered: "Thou shalt have great favors from God, and he shall raise thee up and glorify thee for all eternity, for he who lowers himself shall be exalted; and I cannot say anything else, for God is speaking through my mouth."

It was also in company with Brother Leo that Francis — always according to the *Fioretti* — went one winter day from Perugia to Portiuncula, and the great cold affected them severely. And Francis called to Brother Leo, who went ahead, and spoke thus to him, "Brother Leo, even if we Brothers over the whole earth give good examples of holiness and edification, mark it well and write it down, that in that is not the perfect happiness."

And Francis went a little further, and he called a second time and said: "O Brother Leo, even if we Brothers gave the blind their sight again, cured the lame, drove out devils, made the deaf to hear, the cripples to walk, the dumb to talk, and, what is still more, woke the dead after four days had passed, mark thou, that in that there is not perfect happiness."

And he went on a little and called out loudly: "O Brother Leo, even if we Brothers spoke all tongues and knew all wisdom and the whole of the Scriptures, and were able to reveal the future and the secrets of the heart, so mark thou, that in that there is not perfect happiness."

And Francis went on a piece more and then called with a high voice: "O Brother Leo, thou God's little lamb, even if we Brothers spoke with the tongues of angels and knew the courses of the stars and the powers of herbs, and all the treasures of the earth were revealed to us, and all the virtues and powers of birds and beasts and fishes and also the properties of mankind and of trees and stones and roots and water, mark thou this still, that in that there is not perfect happiness."

And Francis went on a little further, and then said with a loud voice: "O Brother Leo, even if we Brothers knew how to preach so that all the faithless would be converted to the faith of Christ, mark thou still, that in that there is not perfect happiness."

And thus he talked for more than half the way. But at last Brother Leo said with much wonder, "Father, I beg thee for God's sake to tell me where perfect happiness can be found." And Francis answered him:

"When we come to Portiuncula and are wet through with rain, and frozen with cold, and dirty with the mud of the road, and overcome with hunger, and we knock on the convent door, and the porter comes and is angry and says, 'Who are you?' and we say, 'We are two of thy Brothers,' and he says: 'You do not speak the truth, but are two highway robbers who go about and deceive people and steal alms from the poor; away with you!' When he speaks thus and will not open the door for us, but lets us stand out in the cold and snow and water and hunger, and the night falls, and when we endure such abusive words and such a wickedness and such treatment, and endure it without becoming angry and without quarrelling with him, and when we instead think in humility and love that the porter knows us as we really are, and that it is God who lets him talk against us — O Brother Leo, mark thou, that is perfect happiness!

"And if we keep on knocking, and he comes out and is angry and treats us like a pair of thieves and hunts us away with evil words and with ear-boxing, and says to us, 'Get out, ye shameless rascals, go to the lepers, here you will find neither food nor lodging!' and we bear this too with patience and cheerfulness and charity — O Brother Leo, mark thou, that therein is perfect happiness.

"And if we, driven by cold and hunger and by the night, knock again and beg him with bitter tears that he for God's sake will let us in, if only across the threshold, and he gets still more angry and says, 'You are certainly shameless vagabonds, but now you will get your deserts,' and he runs out with a knotted stick, and seizes us by the hoods and throws us to the ground and rolls us in the snow and nearly kills us with the stick; and if we endure all this so patiently, and think of the sufferings of Christ, the All-praised One, and of how much we ought to suffer for the sake of our love of him — O Brother Leo, mark thou, that in this is perfect happiness.

"Now hear the end of all this, Brother Leo! More than all grace and all the gifts of the Holy Ghost, which Christ vouchsafes to his friends, is the conquering of yourself and the willing endurance of suffering, injustice, contempt and harshness. For of the other gifts of God, we cannot take any credit to ourselves, for they are not ours but come from God; so that the Apostle says: 'What hast thou that thou hast not received? But after you have received it, why do you take credit for it, as if you had it of yourselves?' But of trials and sufferings and crosses we can take the credit to ourselves: therefore the Apostle also says, 'I will take credit for nothing except for the Cross of our Lord Jesus Christ.'"[1]

Ernest Renan has justly said that since the time of the Apostles there has never been a more powerful attempt to put the gospel into practice than in the movement started by Francis. It is no wonder then one night in a vision a pious man thought that he saw all men who were alive in the world, stand like blind people around Portiuncula and, with folded hands and faces lifted to heaven, call to God to give them back their sight, and as they stood thus the heavens opened, and a great light fell upon Portiuncula, and all who stood about it and who had been blind, opened their eyes and saw the light of salvation.[2]

[1] *Fioretti*, cap. IX and cap. VIII (which last seems to be a further development of the fifth of the *Admonitiones*, which Francis had written; *Opuscula*, Quaracchi, 1904, pp. 8-9). See further, *Chron. XXIV gen.* (*Anal. Franc.*, III, pp. 65 et seq.) Br. Leo died November 14 or 15, 1271 (Wadding, 1271, nn. 7 et seq.).

[2] *Tres Socii*, cap. XIII, n. 56. Celano, *Vita sec.*, I, 13.

CHAPTER V

ST. CLARA AND SAN DAMIANO

WHILE men sometimes must be satisfied to represent theory, practice, often outside of all theory, is the vocation of woman. No one ever realizes more fully a man's ideal than a woman, once she is possessed by it.

This must not be taken to intimate that Francis of Assisi did not put into practice the gospel which he preached — on the contrary! But if one wishes to see the Franciscan life in a form free from all enforced additions and unfavorable foreign influences, one must above all others turn to his great female disciple, St. Clara of Assisi. She was accustomed to call herself Brother Francis' Plant.[1] She is really the flower of Franciscanism, and he who visits the places where she has lived, inhales even after seven hundred years have gone the singularly pure and heart-gripping perfume of this flower.

Clara was born in Assisi in 1194, probably on July 11. Her father was Favorini dei Scifi, her mother Ortolana of the Fiumi family, belonging in Sterpeto. The family was noble on both sides, and the Scifi belonged to the most prominent family in Assisi.[2] Favorino bore the title of Count of Sasso-Rosso, the name of the cliff that rises over Assisi: his fortified palace is still shown to visitors, near the Porta Vecchia, not far from the church of St. Clara.[3] Ortolana gave him

[1] "Clara indigna ancilla Christi et plantula beatissimi patris Francisci." *Reg. S. Clarae*, cap. I (*Textus originales*, Quaracchi, 1897, p. 52).
[2] "Frater Rufinus Cipii . . . de nobilioribus civibus Assissii, consanguineus S. Clarae." (*Anal. Franc.*, III, 46.)
[3] This statement I have taken from Locateli's Biography of St. Clara; unfortunately I have only been able to use this work in a French translation (*St. Claire d'Assise*, Rome, 1899-1900), as the original Italian work is not obtainable (*Vita breve di S. Chiara*, Assisi, 1882). Other sources for the life of St. Clara are the following:
Her testament: published by the Bollandists in the second August volume

Photo: G. Carloforti

ST. CLARA OF ASSISI AND SCENES
FROM HER LIFE
(Ascribed to Cimabue. Fresco in Church of Santa Chiara, Assisi·

five children — a son, Boso, and four daughters, Penenda, Clara, Agnes and Beatrice.

It is told of Ortolana that she was a good and pious child, and among other things had undertaken such dangerous and prolonged pilgrimages as to the Holy Land, to Bari, and to Rome. Shortly before Clara was born, she is said to have received in prayer the promise of God that the child she was to bear would be a light for the whole world. As a sequence thereof the child was given in baptism the name Clara, the bright; in metaphorical rendering, the celebrated one.

Clara grew up in her home surrounded by the prosperity and order which are so favorable for the development of a sure and reasonable fear of God. Moral disorder leads almost invariably to poverty, while the fear of God is "useful for all things," and "has also promises for this life." It is not only in our days that the answer to the question, "How shall I get on in the world?" has been, "Fear God and keep his commandments." For up to a certain degree it is also true what the apologists evidently push too far, when they adduce, as a proof of the superiority of a religion, the statistics of its millionaires.

Little Clara at a very young age went far beyond the usual degree of piety. A favorite reading in her time was the stories of the lives of the old ascetics — *Vitae patrum*. Apparently Clara had made early acquaintance with these legends: in any case, we read of her that she as a little girl greatly longed to wear a garment of horsehair, and that she,

of the *Acta Sanctorum*, pp. 747 et seq., and by the Franciscans of Quaracchi in *Textus originales* (Quaracchi, 1897), pp. 273 et seq.

Alexander IV's Bull of Canonization *Clara claris* of September 26, 1255, *A. SS.* Aug. II, pp. 749 et seq.

Her Biography written by Messer Bartholomew, Bishop of Spoleto, in collaboration with Brother Leo and Brother Angelo of Rieti and revised for style by Thomas of Celano, to whom also the preface is due. It is printed by the Bollandists as above, pp. 754 et seq. See Cozza Luzi: *Il Codice magliabecchiano nella Storia di S. Chiara* in the *Bolletino della Società Umbra di Storia Patria*, I (Perugia, 1895), pp. 417–426.

Her four letters to Agnes of Bohemia, printed in *A. SS.*, March I, pp. 506–508, the first also (and from a better manuscript) in *Anal. Franc.*, III, p. 183, n. 7.

Several places in the biographies of St. Francis.

Letters to her from her sister Agnes, from Cardinal Hugolin. (Wadding, 1221; *Analecta Franc.*, III, pp. 175–177 and p. 183.)

just as the hermit Paul of Pherme in *Historia Lausiaca*, daily recited a great number of prayers which she kept count of with the help of little stones. While she thus did penance herself, she was, like all the pious of the Middle Ages, very zealous in giving to the poor.

Thus Clara grew up and became strong and beautiful. At the age of fifteen years she had her first suitor and one pleasing in the highest degree to her parents. When they spoke to their daughter about him, they met to their surprise a certain resistance. Clara would not hear of marrying, and when her mother pressed her for a reason, the daughter admitted that she had consecrated herself to God and wanted nothing of any man.

This was more piety than Favorino and Ortolana had counted on. The regular, everyday Christianity had — in the Middle Ages just as in our days — a great dislike for all that seemed to be "too much of religion." Over and over again we are witnesses in the history of those times of the bitter disputes which father and mother carried on with sons and daughters whose fear of God seemed to them to go beyond the proper bounds of a good citizenship.[1]

The sixteen year old Clara must now fight this battle, but she had the good fortune not to be without support in the contest. It was at this precise time that Francis, whose conversion had attracted such attention in Assisi, was re-

---

[1] Thus we read in Feo Belcari's *Vite d'alcuni Gesuati* the highly characteristic chapter XXIV. A young man in Arezzo, by name Donato, entered a convent of the Jesuati's Order, but was taken to his home by his family by force. Here his father locked him up in a room and for the sake of greater safety tied one leg to the wall. The son, however, remained true to his project, although father and brothers took away his Order's habit and gave him ordinary clothes; "You can change my clothes, not my heart," said he. Then the father sent a bad woman to him, who with word and *atti e scoprimenti vergognosi* tried to mislead him; he however struck her in the face, while he called her a sow and a devil. The father then arranged with a young girl of a good family and wanted to marry his son to her, but the son said "no" before the notary, and there was no marriage. Then the father sent five lusty fellows to Donato, who started to eat and drink, sing and play and invited him to join them. Then the young man began to weep, because he saw how determined his father was to destroy him, and he knelt down and begged God to take him away. And God sent a fever which in the course of a few days ended the young man's life; "with great joy and cheerfulness" he met his end. (Belcari: *Prose* ed. Gigli, II, Rome, 1843, pp. 106 et seq. See also cap. XXI in the same work.)

ST. CLARA AND SAN DAMIANO

turning from Rome with the Papal permission to preach, and now mounted the pulpit in San Rufino, a few steps from the Scifi palace. Here and in S. Giorgio's church Clara heard him speak, and from the first moment she saw him, was convinced that such a life as he led was to be hers, and that it was the will of God. The two Friars Minor, Rufino and Silvester, who were both of her family, paved the way for her, and followed by a female relative, to whom tradition has given the name Bona Guelfucci, she sought Francis and laid open her heart to him.[1]

Francis had already heard the rumors about Clara, and wished, as the legend says, "to rob the bad world of so noble a booty, and enrich his Lord therewith." He advised her, therefore, openly to despise the world, its vanity and perishability, not to yield to the wishes of her parents in the matter of her marriage, but to keep her body as a temple for God alone, and not to have any bridegroom but Christ.[2]

From now on Francis was Clara's spiritual guide, and under his direction she was seized by a stronger and stronger desire to take the final step, and let all things go that did not purely and entirely belong to the duty of man to his God. She could not see how it was any part of this obligation to give herself to a man because her parents wished it, and when she — it was in the Lent of 1212 — sat in St. George's church and heard Francis from the pulpit "speak so wonderfully of despising the world, of voluntary poverty, of pining after heaven, and of the nakedness of our crucified Lord Jesus Christ, and the insults and his most holy sufferings,"[3] her

[1] Clara's family tree is thus given by Locatelli:

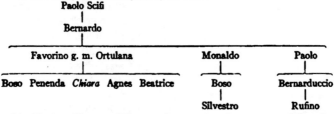

[2] *A. SS.*, Aug. II, p. 755 (*Vita*, cap. I, nn. 5–6) and p. 749, n. 51 (Alexander IV's Bull).

[3] *Fioretti*, cap. XXX.

heart burned in her the moment she left with the desire to take off her elegant clothes, and to live like Jesus and like Francis in contentment, labor, prayer, peace and joy.

At last her desire for the new life became so strong that she could not be any longer restrained, but must change the mode of existence she had hitherto followed. Francis set the night after Palm-Sunday as the time for her to "change the joys of this world for grief for the suffering of our Lord."

Clara utilized this feast-day (March 18, 1212) to say farewell to the world in the most solemn manner. Wearing her richest dress she went with her mother and sisters to church; no one among the women and girls of Assisi were in such festive attire as the beautiful, fair-haired Clara Scifi on that day.[1]

On Palm-Sunday the church commemorates the entry of Christ into Jerusalem. Olive branches, which represent palm branches, are consecrated that day by the priest and are distributed to the congregation, who go in procession through the church while the choir sings the beautiful old anthem: *Pueri Hebræorum, portantes ramos olivarum, obviaverunt Domino, clamantes et dicentes: Hosanna in excelsis!* "With olive boughs in their hands the children of the Jews went out to meet the Lord, crying out and saying: 'Glory be to God on high!'"

As the distribution of the consecrated olive branches was in progress, and all who were in the church came forward to the altar rail to receive a branch from Bishop Guido, who said mass, there was only one who kept back, and this one was Clara Scifi. Her emotions, on thinking of the great step she was about to take, may well have overcome the young girl. Here in the same church she had knelt so many mornings in the past years at the side of her mother and of her small sisters, and heard mass with them, and never thought that it could be different. And now to-day it was for the last time. On this very day she was to say farewell to them for ever, without their knowledge, and the following evening was to be the last she would spend in the home of her

[1] "in turba dominarum splendore festivo puella perradians." *Vita*, cap. I, n. 7.

childhood and youthful days. The thought of her mother's tenderness, of her young sisters' charms, affection and confidence overcame Clara; all the many happy and strong bonds, which years weave unnoticed around those who grow up in the same home, in this solemn hour cut into and wounded her heart, and she wept like the woman she was, wept the tears the bride weeps when she leaves father and mother. . . .

Bishop Guido saw her bowed head and sobbing form and understood her. It is probable that Francis had told him what was to take place. In any event, he took with fine sympathy the palm Clara had not taken, and brought it himself down to her in her place in the church.

Clara carried her flight into effect the next night. Out of a back door which was blocked by a pile of wood, which she had to remove herself, she got out upon the street and, led by Bona Guelfucci, took the road to Portiuncula. The Franciscans who have expected her went to meet her with torches, and soon she was kneeling before Our Lady's image in the little chapel, and gave to the world "for love of the most holy and loved Child Jesus, wrapped in poor rags in the manger," her letter of divorce which she had written long ago.[1] She gave her shining dress into the hands of the Brothers, and received in its place a rough woollen robe, such as the Brothers wore; she exchanged her jewelled belt for a common rope with knots upon it and, after her golden hair had fallen before the scissors which Francis plied, she let her high, stiff headdress lie upon the ground and covered her head instead with a tight black veil. Instead of her rich embroidered shoes which she had worn at the festival in the church, she put a pair of wooden sandals on her naked feet. She then took three vows of consecration, and promised, moreover, like the Brethren to obey Francis as her superior. After the change was over by which the high-born Lady Clara Scifi became Sister Clara, Francis took her the same night to the Benedictine Sisters' convent of St. Paul near the village of

---

[1] "amore sanctissimi et dilectissimi pueri pauperculis panniculis involuti, in paresepio reclinati . . . moneo . . . sorores meas, ut vestimentis semper vilibus induantur." *Reg. S. Clarae*, cap. II, § 18. "Mox ibi rejectis sordibus Babylonis, mundo libellum repudii tradidit." *Vita S. Clarae*, I, 8.

Isola Romanesca (now Bastia), where he had temporarily arranged for her reception.

It could not naturally be long unknown what had become of Clara. Favorino and his relatives had quickly discovered her refuge, and presented themselves at the convent to induce her to return. But the eighteen year old girl was immovable — neither prayers nor flattery nor promises availed, and when the father and uncles proposed to use force, she clung to the altar in the church, as she threw her veil aside and showed her cropped hair. For many days the family renewed their attempts to win back Clara, and Francis found it, at last, to be the wisest course to transfer her to another convent, Sant' Angelo in Panso, which also belonged to the Benedictine Sisters.[1]

Angry as Favorino had been, he now was more furious than ever, when his young daughter Agnes, sixteen days after Clara's flight, also left her home and went to Sant' Angelo to be there received into the Sisters' life. Of her he had had great hopes; she was engaged and the marriage already settled. And now she was taken also with the same madness! Wild with rage and indignation he asked his brother Monaldo to take twelve armed men and get Agnes back.

The nuns in the convent of Sant' Angelo drew back alarmed from the weapons that confronted them and deserted Agnes. The young girl, scarcely more than a child, made a vigorous resistance and the men had to adopt strenuous measures. Blows and kicks were hailed upon her, they pulled her by the hair, and thus drew her out of the convent. "Clara, Clara, come and help me!" the unhappy one cried in vain, as locks of her hair and bits of her clothes were left hanging on the bushes by the roadside.

Clara was in her cell and asked God to help her in this hour of need. And then it suddenly came to pass that twelve strong men were unable to bring Agnes' body one inch

---

[1] According to Cristofani (*Storia di S. Damiano*, cap. X) the Church Seminary in Assisi (*Seminarium Seraphicum*) occupies the same place as this convent. Locatelli thinks otherwise, that Sant' Angelo di Panzo was a mile outside of the city; then he identifies St. Paul's Convent with a portion of the Convent of S. Apollinaris now in Assisi. (*S. Claire d'Assise*, Rome 1899-1900, pp. 40 and 42.)

further. She became suddenly so heavy that she might have been of stone. The men pushed and pulled her, but in vain. "She has eaten lead the whole night," said one of them, grinning. "Yes, the nuns know what tastes good," answered another. But her uncle Monaldo became so furious over this unexpected obstacle, that he lifted his armored fist to crush with one blow the contumacious girl's head. But it came to pass that he too was petrified and stood powerless, with lifted but helpless arm. Meanwhile Clara came to the scene, and the half-dead Agnes was abandoned to her. The family made no further attempt to prevent the two young girls from following their vocation; later the third sister Beatrice joined them, and after Favorino's death, Ortolana also.[1]

The convent of Sant' Angelo could in the nature of things be only a temporary abode for Clara and Agnes. They were not Benedictines, did not wear the Benedictine habit, and did not follow the Rule of St. Benedict. Francis, in order to find a convent for them, sought his old benefactors, the Camaldolites of Monte Subasio, and who could paint his joy when these monks, who had already given him Portiuncula and who on April 22, 1212 had given to the city of Assisi the ancient temple of Minerva, changed into a Mary-church, as it is still seen on the city market-place, now showed themselves willing to give him San Damiano and the little convent belonging to the church. With "some few sisters"[2] Clara took possession of the building, within whose walls she for forty-one years — as her biographer says — "with the blows of the scourge of penance should break open the alabaster vase of her body, so that the whole Church was filled with her soul's perfume."[3]

For here it is that the life of prayer and labor, of poverty and joy, which I have called the flower of Franciscanism, unfolded itself. The example which Clara had given worked in a wide circle. There seems to have been among women in that time a desire, lying torpid, for a life above the plane of the senses, which is so well symbolized by the white walls of

---

[1] *Vita S. Clarae*, III, 24–26, and V, 45. *Anal. Franc.*, III, 175.
[2] *Test. S. Clarae* in *Textus originales*, p. 275.
[3] *Vita*, I, 9. Bull *Clara claris*, n. 50.

the cloister.[1] Maidens who were not yet bound to the world hastened to San Damiano to live there with her; those whose attachment to their families did not permit this, sought in secrecy to live as much of a convent life as possible. Noble ladies devoted their dowries to the building of cloisters, into which they themselves entered in sackcloth and ashes to do penance for their past lives. Marriage was no impediment, for man and wife went each to his own — the man to Francis and the woman to Clara.[2]

The conditions of entrance into San Damiano were the same as for the entrance into Portiuncula — to give all possessions to the poor. The convent could take nothing — that must always be "the fortified tower of the highest poverty," as Clara, with a warlike turn in the spirit of the time, expresses it.[3] The life of the Sisters was the same as that of the Brothers — work and begging. While some remained at home and worked, others went out and begged from door to door.[4]

Almost all the paragrahs of the *forma vivendi*, the rule of life which Francis now wrote for the Sisters, are devoted to these few points, whose principal contents were the obligation to evangelical poverty.[5] Apparently by the intermediation of Francis, Innocent III gave his approval to this Rule, even more formally than he had approved the Brothers' Rule. As Clara first in 1215, by Francis' express command, took the position as abbess in San Damiano,[6] it is not too bold an hypothesis to place the Pope's approval of the Sisters' Rule in this year. Hitherto Francis had been able to be the head of both Orders and their leader, but before Rome Clara had to stand as the Superior of the Sisters, just as Francis of the Brothers. Innocent III is said to have written with

---

[1] See for example Celano, *Vita secunda*, II, 7.
[2] *Vita*, II, 10–11. *Reg. S. Claras*, II, 3.
[3] *Vita*, II, 13.
[4] See the account in *Vita*, II, 12, of "famularum deforis revertentium" and of the reception Clara gave them (she took their feet and kissed them), quite analogous to Francis' treatment of the begging Brothers (see for example *Spec. perf.*, cap. XXV). It was not until later, when the Clares became an Order with full cloister, that they had male *eleemosynarii* (*Vita*, V, 37.)
[5] *Test. S. Claras*, 10–11 (*Textus originales*, p. 276).
[6] *Vita*, II, 12.

his own hand the first lines of the remarkable *privilegium paupertatis* — so different from the privileges for which courts are usually importuned — by which he accords to Clara and her Sisters the right to be and to remain poor.[1]

As Clara shared Francis' feeling about poverty as the foundation of Christian perfection, in conformity with the words "you cannot serve God and Mammon,"[2] so did she also share Francis' ideas about work. In spite of her dignity as abbess, it was she who most often served at table, poured water over the other Sisters' hands, and waited upon them. Rather than ask others to do for her, she would do things for herself. She personally took care of the sick and drew back from no work, however repugnant. When the other Sisters came home from outside the convent, it was Clara who would wash their feet. At night she would get up and put the covering on the Sisters who had uncovered themselves in sleep and were liable to become chilled. Francis often sent sick and weak people to San Damiano, where Clara took care of them and sometimes cured them. When it was she who was sick, she would not stop working; as soon as it was possible, she would sit up in bed with a cushion behind her back and embroider altar raiment. Thus she made — in Francis' own spirit — over fifty pairs of altar-cloths, of the kind called corporals, and sent them, laid into silk envelopes, to the churches upon the mountains and on the plain.[3]

As she surpassed the other Sisters by her good example in her work, so was it also in her religious life. When complines, the last prayer for the day in the Breviary, was over, Clara stayed long before the crucifix, the same whose voice Francis had heard, and before the little flame, which in all Catholic churches burns night and day in the perpetual lamp

---

[1] *Vita, II*, 14. Francis was in Rome in 1215.

[2] See her first letter to Agnes of Bohemia (*A. SS.*, March I, p. 506, and *Anal. Franc.*, III, p. 183, n. 7. The last text, after Nic. Glassberger's copy of 1491 of the *Chron. XXIV gen.*, is far the best).

[3] *Vita*, capp. IV-V. *Corporale* is the name of the linen cloth upon which the host lies during and after the consecration in the Mass.

After the stigmatization of Francis it was Clara who prepared a pair of specially arranged shoes, which made it possible for him to walk upon his perforated feet; she also saw to providing bandages for his wounds. Wadding, 1224, n. 3. *A. SS.*, Aug. II, p. 746.

before the sacrament of the altar. Here she gave herself up to the sympathetic contemplation of the sufferings of the Saviour, here she prayed the "Crucis Officium," the prayers in honor of the Cross of Christ, which Francis had arranged and taught her. But notwithstanding all this, she was up in the morning before all the others, herself waked the Sisters, lit the lamps, and rang the bell for early mass.

At the same time she did not spare her body, which by nature was full-blooded and strong. Her bed was in the first period in San Damiano a bundle of vine twigs, her pillow a log of wood. Later she lay upon leather with an uncomfortable pillow under her head, and finally, by Francis' express command, upon a sack of straw. He it was also who forbade her, in Lent and on St. Martin's fast, to eat only on three weekdays, and then only bread and water, a custom she had originally started. He had Bishop Guido order her, as a matter of duty, to eat daily at least one and a half ounces of bread. It was perhaps on account of the prohibition of this severe fasting that, in compensation, she for a while wore a garment of pig's skin, with the bristles inside, which garment she later exchanged for a penitential belt of hair-cloth.[1]

When she returned from church, after having prayed there for a long time, her face seemed to shine, and the words she spoke were full of joy. Once she was so seized by the significance of the holy water as a symbol of the blood of Christ, that she sprinkled the Sisters with it all day and pleadingly exhorted them never to forget the rivers of salvation that flowed from the wounds of Christ.[2] One Maundy Thursday evening she was absorbed in spirit and could not be waked for twenty-four hours. "Why are the lights still burning?" she asked, as she awoke, "is it not yet day?" One Christmas night she lay sick and could not follow the other Sisters to church, but heard in her bed the whole divine service in the convent church of S. Francesco, and saw the Child Jesus in the Christmas crib there.[3]

---

[1] *Vita*, capp. III-IV. Bull *Clara claris*, n. 54 (*A. SS.*, Aug. II, p. 750).
[2] Wadding, 1251, n. 14. *A. SS.*, Aug. II, p. 746, n. 36.
[3] *Vita*, cap. IV. There is half an hour's walk between S. Damiano and the church of S. Francesco.

It could be no secret to Francis in how high a degree he was an object of admiration to Clara and the other Sisters, and that a part of their religious feeling was intertwined with his personality. To turn the Sisters from this and direct their hearts to God alone, he imperceptibly, yet in adequate degree, withdrew into the background. His visits to San Damiano, which at first had been frequent, became little by little of rare occurrence. This action at last attracted the attention of his disciples and they assigned, as a reason for it, a lack of kindness to the Sisters. Francis explained to them his reason — that he did not wish to stand between them and Christ. For no consideration would he encourage the purely personal devotion to the priest or individual.[1]

Once he had agreed to come to San Damiano and preach. Clara was greatly devoted to sermons; when Pope Gregory IX at a subsequent time wished to prohibit the Franciscans from preaching in this convent, she impeded this prohibition by sending the Brothers away also, who, after the closure was in force at San Damiano about 1219, went from door to door and begged for the Sisters. "If we have to go without spiritual bread, we can even go without bodily bread also," she declared, and the Pope was obliged to take off his prohibition.[2]

Now Francis had permission to go to the Sisters and preach, and all were glad, not only at hearing God's word, but also at seeing their spiritual father and guide.[3] Francis entered the church and stood a while with uplifted eyes, absorbed in prayer. Then he turned to some of the Sisters, who were serving in the sacristy, and asked for some ashes. When the ashes were brought, Francis made a circle with them around himself, and what was left over he strewed upon his own head. Then only did he break the silence, not to preach, but only to recite the fiftieth Psalm of David, the great penitential Psalm *Miserere*. When he had said it to the end, he went quickly away

---

[1] "Non credatis, charissimi, quod eas perfecte non diligam. Si enim magnum esset eas in Christo fovere, nonne maius fuisset eas Christo junxisse?" Celano, *Vita sec.*, III, 132. Compare Cel., *V. pr.*, I, 8, and *V. sec.*, III, 133-134.
[2] *Vita*, V, 37.
[3] "Congregatis autem dominabus ex more, ut verbum Dei audirent, sed non minus ut patrem viderent." Cel., *V. sec.*, III, 134.

— he had taught the Sisters to see in him nothing but a poor sinner in sackcloth and ashes.

To the same order of thought may the tale be referred, which is preserved for us in the *Fioretti*,[1] of "how St. Clara eat with St. Francis and his Brothers in Santa Maria degli Angeli." It reads thus:

"When St. Francis was in Assisi, he several times visited St. Clara and gave her many salutary admonitions. And she had so strong a desire to eat with him, and asked him so many times about it, but he would not grant her the favor. But the Brothers, who had knowledge of this desire of St. Clara, said to St. Francis: 'Father, it seems to us, that this thy strictness is not after the divine precept of charity, that thou wilt not yield to St. Clara, who is so holy and pleasing to God, in so little a thing as it is to eat together with thee; especially when thou thinkest that she on account of thy preaching has left the kingdom and glory of the world. And even if she asked for a greater favor than this is, thou shouldst give it, for she is thy spiritual plant.' Then St. Francis replied, 'You think then that I should accede to her?' His Brothers answered, 'Yes, father, we think that thou owest her this favor and comfort!' Then St. Francis said: 'Since it seems so to you, it seems so to me. But for her greater comfort I will have this meal occur in Santa Maria degli Angeli here; as she has been long shut up in San Damiano, it will please and strengthen her to see Santa Maria, where her hair was cut off, and where she was betrothed to Jesus Christ, and there we will eat together in God's name.'

"And when the day for the meal came St. Clara left her convent with a companion and was taken by the Brothers to Santa Maria degli Angeli. And she made a devout reverence before the altar of the Virgin Mary, where her hair had been cut off, and where she had taken the veil, and then they took her around to see the convent, until the meal should be served. And meanwhile St. Francis had the table laid upon the naked earth, as was his custom. And when meal-time came, St. Francis and St. Clara sat down together, and one of the Brothers with the companion of St. Clara, and next all the

---

[1] Cap. XV. It is also found, later inserted, in Clara's *Vita* (V, 39-42).

other Brothers, and they humbly took their places at the table. And with the first dish St. Francis began to talk of God so lovingly, with such depth, so wonderfully, that the divine fullness of love descended upon him, and all were enraptured in God. And while they were thus transported with eyes and hands lifted towards heaven, the people in Assisi and Bettona and in the other neighboring towns saw that Santa Maria degli Angeli and the whole convent and woods, which then were at the side of the convent, seemed to be in a great blaze. And it looked as if there was a great conflagration, both in the church and convent and woods. And people from Assisi came running down there in haste to put out the fire, for they really believed that everything was on fire. But when they came to the convent and saw that there was no fire, they went in and found St. Francis and St. Clara and all the others transported unto God around the poorly furnished table. Then they understood that there had been a divine fire and no material one, when God had let Himself be seen there as a token to indicate and reveal the divine fire of love, with which the souls of the Brothers and Sisters were inflamed, and they went away with great comfort in their hearts and with great edification."

If Clara thus showed herself before Francis as the weak woman, who was one that longed for comfort and encouragement, she was in her relations to the Sisters the strong woman, the one who protected and defended the others. It was not for nothing that she was of old warrior blood.

This was seen on the two occasions when San Damiano was besieged by Frederick II's soldiers. During his war with the Pope this ruler had made an incursion into the Papal States, and had, with some degree of cunning, used his Mussulman archers, to whom the Papal excommunication was an object of indifference. From the elevated mountain fortification, Nocera, only a few miles from Assisi, these Saracens had darted out "like wasps" down over the valley of Spoleto and one fine day they attacked also the convent of San Damiano.[1] If the Mussulmen entered, the Sisters had not only death to fear, but also dishonor; they gathered trembling around Clara,

[1] "Saracenorum sagittariorum examina velut apum" (*Vita*, III, 21).

who — as so often — lay sick. Without losing courage she had herself carried to the locked door, so as to be the first who would be exposed to the danger. Next she had the silver and ivory ciborium brought from the church, in which the sacrament of the altar in the form of bread was preserved, and sank down in prayer to the Saviour. It then seemed to her that from the ciborium a voice issued, "like a child's," and this voice said, "I will always be your guardian." Strengthened and confident she rose from her prayers, and soon after the Saracens gave up the attack and went elsewhere.[1]

In another way Clara showed her indomitable spirit. When in 1220 the news reached Italy of the death of the first five Franciscan martyrs in Morocco, Clara was so inspired that she wanted also to go to the heathen to suffer martyrdom with her Sisters, and only an express prohibition of Francis prevented her from carrying out this plan.[2] Perhaps it was in the war she waged with the Pope himself that she might remain true to her vow of poverty that she showed herself most inflexible and most heroic. Over and over again her good friend Hugolin, who in 1227 became Pope with the name Gregory IX, sought with the best intentions to force upon her and her convent some property, on which they could live in peace and quiet like other nuns. She steadfastly refused, and he said that, if it was only for the sake of the promise she had made, he had power to release her from it. "Holy Father," was her answer, "free me from my sins, but not from following our Lord Christ!"[3] Two days before her death she obtained from Innocent IV the per-

---

[1] "Vox quasi pueruli ad ejus aures insonuit . . . Ego vos semper custodiam." *Vita*, III, 22. It is in reference to this event, which occurred in 1230, that Clara is often represented with a monstrance in her hand. The legend has since adorned the event. To-day, on the walls of S. Damiano, there is to be seen a half-obliterated fresco, that shows the frightened Saracens, who are thrown down from their storming ladders, as Clara meets them with the sacrament. Four years later (June 22, 1234) the troops of Frederick, this time under Vitale d'Aversa, were in a similar manner prevented not only from entering S. Damiano but also the city itself; the day is still celebrated in Assisi as a national festival.

[2] Wadding, 1251, n. 14. *A. SS.*, Aug. II, p. 746.

[3] *Vita*, II, 15. Innocent IV's Bull, *Clara claris* (*A. SS.*, Aug. II, p. 750, n. 55).

petual ratification of the right of her and her Sisters to be and to remain poor.[1]

Unlike Francis, and in spite of the austere life she led, Clara lived to an old age; she died in her sixtieth year, after forty-one years of convent life. In that time one great sorrow had reached her; this was Francis' death in 1226. As he lay at the last in the little poor sick-cell down back of Portiuncula, a message came from Clara that she wished to see him once more. But St. Francis sent word back and said to one of the Brothers: "Go and say to Sister Clara to give up all trouble. Now she cannot see me, but she must know this for certain, that before her death both she and the Sisters shall see me and take great comfort therefrom."

And then Francis died. But the day after his death the citizens of Assisi came and took his lifeless body and, along with the Brothers, carried it up to Assisi with hymns and songs of praise, with the blare of trumpets, and with olive-branches and lighted candles in their hands. And in the early October morning, as the violet mist still lay on the plain like a mighty sea, they ascended the sunlit height by San Damiano, the funeral escort stopped, and the bier with the lifeless body was taken into the church, so near to the grated window of the Sisters that they could see their dead spiritual father for the last time. "And after the grating through which the maid-servants of the Lord were wont to receive the sacred host and to hear the word of God was passed by, the Brothers lifted this holy body up from the bier and held it in their raised arms in front of the window, so long a time as My Lady Clara and the other Sisters wished it, for their comfort," the *Speculum perfectionis* tells us.[2] The little church now echoed the notes of sorrow and farewell, of grief and woe, for "who would not be moved to tears," says Thomas of Celano, "when even the angels of peace wept so bitterly?" . . .

Years passed, and Clara still lived. Francis was gone, but his near friends, Leo, Angelo, Brother Juniper, came fre-

---
[1] The Bull *Solet annuere* of August 9, 1253. Clara died August 11, 1253. In a later section the interesting but involved question of the development of the Rule of the Clares will be treated in connection with the history of the Rule of the Franciscans.

[2] Cap. 108. Compare Celano, *Vita pr.*, II, cap. X.

quently to San Damiano, and, together with them, Clara buried herself in memories of the time when the master still lived. Also Brother Giles, who otherwise always — as Bernard of Quintavalle tells us — "sat in his cell like a maiden in her room," gave Clara now and then a visit, and it was during one of these that the following real Franciscan trait occurred.

An English Franciscan, who was a Doctor of Theology, stood in the pulpit in San Damiano and gave a sermon which, with all his learning, seems to have been very different from the words that used to be heard from this place out of the mouth of Francis of Assisi. All felt it, and suddenly Brother Giles raised his voice and called out, "Be still, Master, and I will preach!" The English Doctor stopped speaking and Giles began, "in the heat of the Spirit of God" says the old legend. Then he resigned the pulpit to the foreign preacher again, and the latter continued. But Clara rejoiced over this, she said, more than if she had seen the dead brought to life again, "for this was what our most holy father, Francis, wanted, that a Doctor of Theology should have enough humility to be silent, when a Lay-Brother wished to speak in his stead."[1]

The time came at last when the call of death was heard also by St. Clara. For all of twenty-eight years she had been more or less a victim of sickness, and in the fall of 1252 she felt that her death was near. But as yet her life's work was incomplete — she had not obtained the final, unrestricted ratification of her privilege of poverty.

Exactly at this time Innocent IV returned from Lyons, whither he had fled before the army of Frederick II. The excommunicated Emperor died in 1250 in Fiorenzuola, and in September, 1252, the Pope took up his residence in Perugia. As soon as the Papal court came to rest in the Umbrian capital, the Sisters' well-wisher and protector, Cardinal Raynald, later Pope Alexander IV, visited San Damiano. Here he gave Clara the sacrament of the altar, and she begged him imploringly to obtain the ratification of the privilege from the Pope.

[1] *A. SS.*, April III, p. 239. *Vita di fr. Egidio* (Belcari), capp. XII and LVIII.

The Pope came with his court the next year to Assisi. He visited Clara on her sick-bed, and when she, as is the custom, wanted to kiss his foot, he set it on a stool so that she could do what she wished. She then prayed for the blessing of the Pope and for complete absolution of her sins. "Would to God, my daughter, that I had as little need of God's forgiveness as you!" said Innocent with a sigh. After his departure Clara said to the Sisters, who were collected around her: "Praise the Lord, my daughters! This morning I received Himself, and now I too have been considered worthy to see His Vicar on earth!"

After this the Sisters never left Clara's bedside. Agnes, who for thirty years had been separated from her sister as Abbess of Monticelli convent, near Florence, knelt weeping by her bed. Day after day the dying saint lay there; for over two weeks she had eaten nothing, but still felt strong. Her confessor exhorted her to be patient. "Since I learned to know the grace of my Lord Jesus Christ from God's servant Francis," she answered, "no pain and no penance has been too great for me, and no sickness too hard." She then sent messengers to her friends in Portiuncula, to Leo, Angelo and Juniper, telling them that they could read the story of our Lord's passion to her. They came, and Brother Leo knelt by the bed and kissed, weeping, the hard sack of straw, Brother Juniper opened his bundle of "News from God," Angelo comforted the weeping Sisters.

Then it was that Clara was heard to lift her voice in the tearful silence. "Go forth without fear," said she; "thou hast a good guide for the road! Go forth without fear, for He Who created thee has also sanctified thee, He has always protected thee, He has loved thee tenderly, as a mother loves her child. O Lord, I praise Thee, because Thou hast created me!"

Clara ceased her prayers and lay quiet a while, with open eyes. "Whom art thou talking to?" at last one of the Sisters asked her. "I am speaking," answered Clara solemnly, "with my blessed soul." "And do you not see," she added a moment after, "do you not see the King of Glory, Whom I now behold?"

With eyes blinded with tears all watched the dying one. But Clara saw them no longer. She constantly watched the chamber door — and behold, the door opened, and in white clothes, with golden bands around their shining hair, a flock of heavenly virgins entered, who had come to take Clara to the eternal Fatherland. One of them was taller and more beautiful than all the others, and her golden head shone, so that the dark cell was made more brilliant than the brightest day. And the beautiful, shining lady stepped out from the crowd of maidens to the bed of Clara, bent down over the dying one, embraced her and hid her as it were under a veil of light. In the arms of Mary, under the folds of the shining, luminous robe of the Queen of Heaven, Clara's soul went up to everlasting glory. But between the stiffening hands the dead saint held the Pope's bull, sent two days before — the final, solemn ratification of the right of Clara and of her Sisters to live after the Franciscan ideal.[1]

San Damiano's convent is still standing, almost as Clara and her Sisters left it. Here is the little, narrow choir where they prayed their Office; along the walls are seats, polished by wear, made of old rough woodwork, and in the middle of the creaking wooden floor the old desk with the great book of antiphones lying open upon it. Here is shown one of the bells Clara used when the Sisters were to be called to prayer, the tin cup out of which she drank after she had received the sacrament of the altar, the Breviary Brother Leo wrote for her, and out of which she prayed daily, and a copper reliquary given her by Innocent IV. Here too we see the refectory where Gregory IX was her guest, and where she by the command of the Pope blessed the rolls of bread, while on each roll as she blessed it a cross appeared. Here we see Clara's little, narrow, low bedroom; here we visit finally her so-called garden — a small strip of flagged ground between two high walls.

But from this bit of terrace there opens between the two walls, as if through the proscenium of a theatre, a beautiful view over the lovely Umbrian land — one sees Rivo Torto, Portiuncula, the white roads, the olive-grown fields, the little

[1] *Vita*, cap. VI. Bull *Clara claris*, n. 57.

town of Bettona over in the blue mountains. The garden proper consists of only a sort of wide terrace, filled with earth, in which flowers are growing. And as the old tradition goes, Clara would permit only three kinds of flowers here: lilies, which are the symbol of purity; violets, the symbol of humility, and roses, which signify the love of God to man.

BOOK THREE
GOD'S SINGER

> Quid enim sunt servi Dei nisi quidem joculatores ejus, qui corda hominum erigere debent et movere ad lætitiam spiritualem?
>
> *For what else are the servants of God than his singers, whose duty it is to lift up the hearts of men and move them to spiritual joy?*
>
> FRANCIS in *Speculum perfectionis*

CHAPTER I

THE SERMON TO THE BIRDS

IT seems almost as if Francis, after he had seen the quiet, introspective and happy life St. Clara and the first of her Sisterhood led in San Damiano, was again inspired with doubts as to his vocation. Again did the doubt arise within him if it were not better to withdraw altogether from the world and to live alone for his soul's welfare like the old anchorites. Many of his disciples had chosen this course — Silvester, Rufino, and to some extent Giles. And although Francis was well aware of the dangers of the hermit life — spiritual arbitrariness and ascetic pride (the characteristic description can be read in the *Fioretti*, Chap. 29) — yet it seemed to him incontrovertible that the wandering life as preacher was preferable to what he called the "accumulation of dust on the spiritual feet."[1]

To understand what Francis meant by this we must follow him on his great missionary journey, which he undertook in the years 1211-1212.

With Silvester he went to Tuscany, pacified the troubles in Perugia (see page 99), was joined in Cortona by Guido Vagnotelli and — if Wadding can be relied on — also by the celebrated and dreaded Elias Bombarone, established near the city a hermitage named Celle, and then wandered on to Arezzo and Florence. In the latter city a celebrated jurist joined himself to him, Johannes Parenti, a doctor of the University of Bologna and judge in Cività Castellana. Wadding, following Rudolphus, gives an anecdote about Parenti's entrance into the Order. When on a walking tour he heard a swineherd driving his grunting hogs into the pen with the words, "Hurry

[1] "spiritualium pulverisatio pedum." Bonav., XII, 2.

up into the sty, pigs, as lawyers hurry into hell!"[1] The old proverb, "Die Juristen sind böse Christen" (Lawyers are poor Christians), seems to have been current in the thirteenth century. In any case Parenti gave up his office and became a Franciscan,[2] at about the same time as another Bolognese lawyer, Nicolo de Pepoli, took up with interest the Franciscan mission in Bologna itself.[3] From Florence Francis went on to Pisa, where Angelus, the subsequent General of the Order, and Albert, later the leader of the Brothers' English mission, joined him. He then returned back to Assisi by S. Gimignano in the Val d' Elsa, by Chiusi and Cortona, and after a full year's absence he gave the Lenten sermons in the cathedral, as already alluded to (p. 125).

But this last part of Francis' journey was almost a triumphal march. As he would approach a city, the bells were rung, the people went out to meet him with palm-boughs in their hands, and conducted him in festival progress to the parish priest, with whom he always stayed. They brought bread for him to bless, to be afterwards preserved as a relic. And they repeated the cry which the Italians are so inclined to utter, "*Behold the Saint!*"[4]

Even the disciples found that this was too much. Sometimes they asked him — just as the chief priests and scribes had asked the Master — "Hearest thou what these say?" Francis used to answer that he regarded the homage paid him as analogous to the honor paid to pictures in churches, for the God-fearing man is only an image of God, and flesh and blood, like wood and stone, should not dare to ascribe to themselves the honor which belongs to God alone.[5]

---

[1] "Porci, ingredimini in antrum, sicut judices causarum intrant in infernum;" 1211, n. 21. Parenti was General of the Order from June 16, 1227 to 1232.

[2] Francis called him afterwards the "Florentine boxer" (*pugil florentinus*) a name with which he seemed to want to tease Parenti for his hardness of hand. (Cel., *V. sec.*, II, 138, ed. d'Alençon.)

[3] It is undoubtedly he who is spoken of in the *Actus*, cap. IV. Niccolo at last entered the Order in 1220. (See Brother Bonaventure's testimony of the year 1306, in Wadding, 1220, n. II.)

[4] Celano, *Vita prima*, I, VIII, 62. *Tres Socii*, XIV: "Et quando erat hora hospitandi, libentius erant cum sacerdotibus, quam cum laicis hujus saeculi." *Spec.* 45: "Iste est sanctus homo!"

[5] *Spec. perf.*, p. 81. Compare Barth, *Conform.*, f. 33b. Wadding, 1212, n. 7.

But eventually this was insufficient for him, and he sought therefore to abase himself, as well as he could. "Do not praise me too soon," he liked to say, "for soon I shall have sons and daughters!" Or he would break out: "Had God shown a street robber the love He has shown me, he would be much more thankful!" He heartily thanked the Bishop of Terni, when he once introduced one of Francis' sermons with a little introduction, in which he had developed the theme of how wonderful it was to see so insignificant and ungifted a man as Francis attain such great results.[1] To those who praised his severe way of life he said: "All that I do, a sinner can also do. A sinner can fast, can pray, can shed tears, can mortify the flesh. Only one thing a sinner cannot do — *be true to his Lord and his God.*"[2]

For such faithlessness to God Francis often upbraided himself, and never concealed it. Once he had been sick, and while sick had eaten some chicken. Scarcely was he well again when he put a string around his neck and had himself led stripped to the village pillory, and while thus led made the Brother who led him cry out, "Here you see the great glutton who ate chicken without your knowing about it!"[3] And as the people only broke out into greater praise of his humility, he ordered one of the Brothers to scold him vigorously so that for once he could hear the truth. Much against his will the Brother upbraided him as a rustic, a hireling and a useless servant, and with a contented smile Francis answered him: "God bless thee for the word! That is what the son of Pietro di Bernardone ought to hear!"[4]

On other occasions Francis sought to escape the homage of the people by withdrawing into solitude. Thus he passed the whole of Lent, 1211, on an uninhabited island in Lake Thrasimene,[5] and he seems to have passed a great part of the following winter in the high-lying hermitage Sarteano near Chiusi. The huts, made of branches, which he with a few Brothers built

---

[1] Cel., V. sec., III, 73. Spec. perf., cap. 43. Cel., V. sec., III, 80.
[2] Bonav., VI, 3.
[3] Cel., V. prima, I, 52. Spec. perf., 61. Bonav., VI, 2. Wadding, 1212, n. 53.
[4] Cel., V. pr., I, 53. Bonav., VI, 1. Spec. perf. places the residence in Assisi under Pietro dei Cattani's vicariate (1220-1221).
[5] Actus, cap. VI. Fior., cap. 7.

there, resembled mostly the dens of wild beasts, but Francis liked the place "partly for its wildness, partly for its loneliness, and finally because he could see from it Assisi in the distance."[1] In this loneliness he was visited by great temptations, sometimes to despair — an interior voice said to him, "There is salvation for all, except for a self-tormentor like you!" — sometimes to give up the state of celibacy and marry. Against this temptation he used an old practice of the anchorites — with the rope which he wore as a belt, he gave himself a dreadful beating on the bare back. But as "Brother Ass" — as Francis used to call his body — would give him no peace, he found another way. Outside of his cell the ground was covered with snow, and half naked as he was, Francis sprang out into the snow and began to build seven snow images. When the work was done he said to himself: "See, Francis — here is your wife, the big one over there — the four at her side are your two sons and two daughters, and the other two are your man-servant and maid. They are dying of cold — hurry up and put something on them! And if you cannot, then be glad that you have no one to serve except God alone."[2]

In one way or another the idea of withdrawing entirely from the world engaged Francis' thoughts. He often discussed it with the Brothers of the Order and weighed the pro and con. There was one thing that always prevented him from choosing the hermit life, and that was the example of our Lord. Jesus could have chosen to remain in his glory at his Father's right hand, but instead descended to earth to endure the vicissitudes of human life and to die the bitter death of shame on the Cross. And it was the Cross that had from the first been Francis' model, the Cross to which he applied with the rest of the Middle Ages God's word to Moses: *Fac secundum exemplar* — "Make it according to the pattern, that was shown thee in the mount."[3]

In his doubt Francis resolved to ask a decision from God

---
[1] Wadding, 1212, n. 1, after Mariano.
[2] Cel., *Vita sec.*, II, 82 (ed. d'Alençon). Bonav., V, 4. "A Brother, who had stayed up to pray, saw it all by the light of the moon," says the last-named. What a picture of Francis in the moonlight of the snow-white mountain loneliness, building snow images and talking to himself!
[3] Exodus, xxv. 40. Bonav., XII, 1-2.

THE SERMON TO THE BIRDS 149

and to follow it blindly, whatever it might be. On other occasions he had opened the Bible and taken the sense of the text that met his eyes. This time he decided to submit himself to the inspiration of two privileged souls. Brother Masseo was therefore sent away, first to St. Clara and then to Brother Silvester, who lived a hermit life in a cave on Monte Subasio, where now is situated the convent Carceri, in whose garden the first cells of the Franciscans are still shown. Francis determined to follow the judgment of Silvester and Clara.

"But Brother Silvester started at once to pray," we are told in *Actus beati Francisci*. "And in prayer he at once got the answer from God. And he went to Brother Masseo and said, 'This says the Lord, you shall tell Brother Francis that God has not called him for his own sake only, but also that he shall win many souls!' And then Brother Masseo went to St. Clara. . . . But she answered and said that she and another Sister had had the same answer exactly from God as Brother Silvester.

"But Brother Masseo went back to St. Francis. And St. Francis received him lovingly and prepared for them a meal, and when they had eaten Francis called him out into the woods. And St. Francis bared his head, crossed his arms over his chest, knelt down, asked and said, 'What does my Lord Jesus Christ tell me to do?' Brother Masseo answered that both Brother Silvester and Sister Clara and another had received the answer from Jesus Christ the glorious: 'that thou shalt go out and preach, for God has not called you for your own sake alone, but also to save others!' And then the hand of the Lord was lifted over St. Francis and he sprang up in the glow of the Holy Ghost, and inspired by power from on high, he said to Brother Masseo, 'Well, let us go!' And he took Brother Masseo with him and Brother Angelo, both of whom were holy men. . . . And they came between Cannara and Bevagna.[1]

"And St. Francis saw some trees by the roadside, and in these trees there was a multitude of birds of all kinds, such as never before were seen in this region. And a great quantity were on the ground under the trees. And when St. Francis

[1] Two small towns between Assisi and Montefalco.

saw all this multitude, the Spirit of God came over him, and he said to his disciples, 'Wait for me here, I am going to preach to our sisters the birds!' And he walked into the field up to the birds who sat upon the earth. And as soon as he began to preach all the birds who sat in the trees flew down to him, and none of them moved, although he went right among them, so that his cowl touched several of them. . . .

"But St. Francis said to the birds: 'My sister Birds! You owe God much gratitude, and ought always and everywhere to praise and exalt him, because you can fly so freely, wherever you want to, and for your double and threefold clothing and for your colored and adorning coats and for the food, which you do not have to work for, and for the beautiful voices the Creator has given you. You sow not, neither do you reap, but God feeds you and gives you rivers and springs to drink from, and hills and mountains, cliffs and rocks to hide yourselves in, and high trees for you to build your nests in, and though you can neither spin nor weave, he gives you and your young ones the necessary clothing. Love therefore the Creator much, since he has given you such great blessings. Watch therefore well, my sister birds, that you are not ungrateful, but busy yourselves always in praising God!'

"But after this, our holy father's word, all those little birds began to open their beaks to beat with their wings and stretch out their necks and bow their heads reverently to the earth, and with their song and their movements showed that the words St. Francis had said had pleased them greatly. But St. Francis rejoiced in his spirit as he saw this and wondered over so many birds and over their variety and differences and that they were so tame, and he praised the Creator for it and gently exhorted them to praise the Creator themselves.

"And when St. Francis had finished his sermon and his exhortation to praise God, he made the sign of the Cross over all the birds. And all the birds flew up at once and twittered wonderfully and strongly, and separated and flew away." [1]

[1] *Actus*, cap. XVII. *Fioretti*, cap. 16. Cel., *Vita prima*, I, 58. Bonav., XII, 3.

CHAPTER II

MISSIONARY JOURNEYS

IT was not now the intention of St. Francis to restrict himself to a new mission trip through Italy. He had greater plans, as he went out of Assisi this time, and in a sense it was his youthful dream of wars that returned to the man of thirty years. It was the time of the Crusades — not many years later John of Brienne, a brother of Francis' old-time hero, Walter, was to go to Damietta at the head of a great army of Christians. Francis too would go on a crusade, but with no other weapon than the gospel. What he had in mind was no less than to preach Christianity and conversion to the Saracens.[1]

First he wished to obtain the Pope's assent to his new proposal. It is said of St. Dominic that he "was always to be found on the road to Rome to obtain instructions."[2] The same applies to Francis. Two years after he had obtained Innocent III's verbal ratification of the Rules of the Order, we find him again in Rome to remind the Pope of the promises he had then given.[3] He could now well say that "God had multiplied his Brother's voice" and could therefore beg to have a greater mission given him.

We know little of Francis' third journey to Rome. On the way he visited Alviano, near Todi, where he, preaching in the market-place, is said to have ordered the swallows, swooping about and disturbing him with their cries, to be silent.[4] Perhaps he also went through Narni and Toscanella.[5]

In Rome Francis preached as usual in the streets and alleys. With these sermons he won two new Brothers — Zacharias,

---

[1] Cel., *V. pr.*, I, 55.   [2] Sabatier: *Vie de S. Fr.* (1894), p. 247.
[3] See p. 94.   [4] Cel., *V. pr.*, I, 59. Bonav., XII, 4.
[5] Cel., *V. pr.*, I, 65–66. Bonav., XII, 9.

who afterwards became a missionary in Spain, and William, the first Englishman who entered the Order.[1] Far more important for the whole future of the Order was the friendship Francis here contracted with a woman whom he later, on account of her manly character, called jokingly "Brother Jacoba"[2] — the wife of the Roman nobleman Gratiano Frangipani. Her name was Giacoma or Jacopa de Settisoli, and she was about twenty-five years old.[3]

The Frangipani family is one of the noblest in Rome; it is said to have sprung from the *gens Anicia*, which counts among its members in the course of years a Benedict of Nurcia, a Paulinus of Nola, and St. Gregory. In the year 717 Flavius Anicius Petrus, then the head of the family, by generous gifts of bread during a great scarcity of food in Rome won the name of "the Breaker of Bread." In the beginning of the thirteenth century the Frangipanis lived in Rome with extensive estates in the trans-Tiberian region and on the Esquiline, where they possessed, among the rest of their property, the castle-like remains of the *Septizonium* of Septimus Severus — a name which in a changed form still lives in the title of the Roman street *Via delle sette Sale* and from which Gratiano Frangipani's wife acquired her name *de Settesoli*.

Giacoma is said to have been of a mixture of Norman and Sicilian blood. She was probably born about 1190, for in 1210 she was married and had a son, Giovanni. Afterwards she had another son, Gratiano, in 1217, shortly after her husband's death. Already in the year 1212 she had made the acquaintance of Francis of Assisi — an acquaintance which on the next visit of the Umbrian evangelist to Rome was to develop into a true and inward friendship.

Francis had certainly little trouble in obtaining Innocent III's blessing on his work. He embarked on the sea, we do

---

[1] *Anal. Fr.*, III, p. 12. Wadding, 1212, n. 35, after Mariano.
[2] "Nam . . . fratrem Jacobam nominavit." Bernard a Bessa: *De laudibus, Anal. Franc.*, III, p. 687.
[3] I follow here Edouard d'Alençon: "*Frère Jacqueline.*" *Recherches historiques sur Jacqueline de Settisoli, l'amie de Saint François*, Paris, 1899. For the historical basis of her history, see also P. Sabatier: *De l'evolution des Légendes. A propos de la visite de Jacqueline de S. à s. François* in Suttina's "*Bull. critico,*" I, pp. 22 et seq.

nct know from which port. Storms drove the ship off her course, and she stranded on the coast of Slavonia. There was no way of embarking thence for the Orient — it was late in the year, and the weather was also unfavorable for the sea-crossing. Francis tried to get a ship for Ancona, but the seamen were unwilling to load a ship with him and his followers. They then formed the plan of hiding themselves among the ship's cargo without the crew knowing it; they emerged only after the ship was on the open sea, and as the voyage on account of unfavorable weather lasted longer than was expected, and the ship's rations became exhausted, the two hidden passengers obtained permission to share their rations with the crew.[1]

Hardly had Francis' feet touched Italian soil when he took up his old way of life and went preaching from city to city. In Ascoli his preaching had such effect that over thirty men, some priests, some laymen, sought to be received into the Brotherhood.[2] Everywhere he was surrounded as before by the jubilations and crowds of people; they strove at least to touch the skirt of his garment. Only the Cathari, also diffused through the Ancona region, kept away from him, for the kernel of his preaching — as of all his religious life — was the absolute, unconditional and in all unessential things blind obedience to the Roman Church, and the principal sequence thereof, a deep reverence for the priests of the same Church. It was with timely retrospect over this and similar missionary journeys that Francis in his Testament has written words about "the poor minor priests in the parishes about," whom he in spite of all will "fear, love and honor" as his masters and "not look upon their faults."[3]

This last was what the Cathari wanted; they expatiated long and loud over the sins of the priests, and thus took many out of that Church which the priests represented. Francis was of that rare nature that can discriminate between things

[1] Cel., V. pr., I, n. 55.
[2] Cel., V. pr., I, n. 62.
[3] "Et si haberem tantam sapientiam, quantam Salomon habuit, et invenirem pauperculos sacerdotes . . . in parochiis in quibus morantur . . . ipsos et omnes alios volo timere, amare et honorare sicut meos dominos; et nolo in ipsis considerare peccatum." (Opuscula, ed. Quar., p. 78.)

and persons, and he knew how to inspire the same spirit in his brethren. "But how can a priest lie?" Brother Giles asked in this spirit, incensed over so unreasonable a supposition.[1]

While in Ancona this time, Francis converted a celebrated man of that time, the troubador, Guglielmo Divini, called by the people, "the Verse-king."[2] Divini was on a visit to the village San Severino in the Mark of Ancona, where he had a relative, a nun. Francis was preaching in the convent at the time and the celebrated poet heard him there.

There was, according to all testimony, something very impressive in Francis' way of speaking. It was not so much a sermon, says Thomas of Spalato, as a *concio*, a lecture, that touched on practical and moral reform.[3] And Francis was an unbending moralist. He was not silent about wrongs that he saw, but gave everything its right name. In spite of his poor external appearance, he inspired thereby not only wonder but also fright; there was something of John the Baptist about him.[4] In his writings there is many a Woe to the sinner, whose wages are eternal fire![5] He was not afraid to threaten with God's judgment.[6] His words were compared to a sword that pierces through hearts.[7]

So Guglielmo Divini heard the celebrated preacher of repentance in the cloister in San Severino. The poet came from curiosity, and a crowd of the gay youth of the village with him. At first Francis did not impress them greatly. But the verse-king soon began to listen — it seemed to him as if the poor little man from Assisi talked to him alone, as if all the words he heard were directed to him, and one after another like well-aimed arrows, sent by a master-hand, thrust their points into his heart. . . .

What did Francis talk about? It was on his usual theme —

---

[1] Cel., *V. pr.*, I, 46. Compare *Anal. Franc.*, III, p. 79.
[2] "Vocabatur nomen ejus Rex versuum." Cel., *Vita sec.*, III, 49.
[3] Boehmer: "Analekten" (1904), p. 106.
[4] *Spec. perf.*, cap. 105. *Tres Socii*, cap. XIII.
[5] *Opuscula* (Quaracchi), pp. 51, 71, 95, 96–97, 114.
[6] Cel., *Vita sec.*, II, 6, and III, 121.
[7] "Verba acutissima, penetrantia corda," "separationis gladius." *Tres Socii*, cap. XIV. "gladium verbi Dei," "transverberat cor." Cel., *V. sec.*, III, 49.

to despise the world and to be converted so as to withstand the coming wrath. And when he was through, the simple and great thing at once happened, and Guglielmo Divini rose up, fell at the feet of Francis, and cried out, "Brother! take me away from men and give me to God!"

On the next day Francis clothed him in the grey clothes of the Order and girded his loins with the cord, and gave him the name *Pacificus*, because he had left the world's tumult for the peace of God.[1]

Thus, too, a century later, another much greater poet was to seek for peace among the children of St. Francis. One evening he, already grey and bowed down, stood before a lonely cloister in the Apennines and knocked at the door. And to the porter's question as to what he sought there, the great Florentine (Dante) gave only the one all-including answer, *Pace!* "Peace!"

Although Francis thus received every one with a troubled heart who came to him, and without further novitiate clothed him in the Order's garb — it was in 1220 that a year's trial or novitiate was established — he had a wonderful ability at discriminating among the many who began to wish to be received among the Brothers. A short period had elapsed after Pacificus' conversion when a young nobleman from Lucca sought Francis and with tears cast himself at his feet, and asked to be one of his sons. Francis addressed him with severity. "Your weeping is a lie!" he said, "your heart does not belong to God! Why do you lie to the Holy Ghost and to me?" Thus it appeared that the longing for the cloister was only a caprice of the young man, perhaps conceived in a moment of dissatisfaction with the conditions of home. When his parents came to beg him to come back, he readily complied.[2]

Especially was Francis on his guard with the book-learned, *viri literati*. "When such a book-man comes to me," he said

---
[1] Cel., *V. sec.*, III, 49. Compare III, 63. *Spec. perf.*, capp. 59–60. Bonav., IV, 50–51. Cel., *V. sec.*, III, 27, and III, 76. *Spec. perf.*, cap. 100. Brother Pacificus was sent to France at the head of the Franciscan mission in 1217. *Spec. perf.*, p. 122 (Sabatier's ed.). For Francis' way of preaching, see also Cel., *V. sec.*, III, 50. *Fioretti*, cap. 30.

[2] Cel., *Vita sec.*, II, 11, (d'Alençon's ed.).

openly, "I see at once if his intentions are sincere when his first prayer to me is this one: 'Behold, Brother, I have lived long in the world and never rightly knew my God. Give me a place far from the world's alarms, where I in the bitterness of heart can think over the years I have lost and squandered, to live a better life in the future.'"[1]

It was only for the disinherited of this world, the poor and oppressed, the unfortunate and lost, the lepers, thieves and robbers, that Francis' heart was open without reservation. It is true that the Benedictines' Rules contained at this time the words: "All strangers shall be received as if it were Christ," but Francis himself had found by trial in his youth that this command was not always lived up to, that it was observed in the case of guests who could claim a position in society, but that it was not observed in the case of those who needed it the most, the homeless, the tramps and the beggars. It is certain that with the experiences of his youth at St. Maria della Rocca in mind, Francis in his Rule at the very beginning wrote the beautiful words: "And whoever comes to the Brethren, Friend or Enemy, *Thief or Robber*, shall be kindly received."[2]

Even his most devoted disciples had trouble sometimes in following him in this matter. The *Speculum perfectionis* contains the following impressive tale, from the early days of the Order:

"In a hermitage over Borgo San Sepolcro" — *Monte Casale* is meant; Borgo San Sepolcro is a village about halfway between Mt. Alverna and Gubbio — "it happened that robbers who used to keep in the woods and fall upon wayfarers, came and asked for bread; but some of the Brothers said that it was not right to give them alms. . . .

"Meanwhile St. Francis came to this convent, and the Brothers asked him if it were right to give alms to robbers, and St. Francis answered them thus: 'If you do as I say,

[1] Cel., *Vita sec.*, III, 123 (Amoni). In *Verba Fratris Conradi* is a recital of how a learned man (*magnus doctor*) was first received into the Order after having worked for a month in the kitchen. (Sabatier: *Opuscules de critique*, I, pp. 381-383.)

[2] "Et quicumque ad eos venerit, amicus vel adversarius, fur vel latro, benigne recipiatur." *Reg. prima*, cap. VII. Compare p. 49 of this book.

then have I hope in God that I will save their souls. Go then and get good bread and good wine, take it out to them in the woods and say to them: 'Brother robbers! Come here! We are Brothers, and we come with good wine and good bread to you!' Then they will come at once and I will spread a cloth on the ground and set the table for them, and wait on them with humility and cheerfulness while they eat. But when they are through I will speak God's word to them, and finally I shall beg them to grant you a request in God's name, namely, that they shall promise you not to kill anyone and to do bodily harm to no one. If I ask everything of them at once they will answer, 'No,' but now for the sake of your humility and goodness they will promise you this.

"The next day, in requital of their good promises, you shall go out to them with bread and wine, eggs and fruit, and wait upon them while they eat. And when they have finished, you shall say to them: 'Why do you wander about all day and suffer hunger and endure so much, and in thought and deed perpetrate so many things, and imperil your souls? It is much better to serve the Lord; then he will give you what you need here upon earth, and at the same time you will save your souls!' Then the Lord will grant them that for the sake of your humility and patience they will be converted.

"But the Brothers did all, just as St. Francis had said, and the robbers, from thankfulness and with God's mercy, held point for point and jot for jot what the Brothers had enjoined them. Yes, for the sake of the humility and confidence of the Brothers, they helped them and carried wood into the hermitage, and eventually some of them entered the Order. But others confessed their sins, and did penance for their transgressions, and promised the Brothers solemnly, to live by the work of their hands, and never to do such things again."[1]

---

[1] *Spec. perf.*, cap. 66. In *Actus*, cap. XXIX (*Fioretti*, cap. 26), the same story is found more in detail. Here the guardian drives the robbers out of the convent door with scornful words. When Francis appeared "carrying a sack with bread and a bottle of wine," which he had begged, he scolded the guardian and told him as a penance to take the sack and bottle and search for the robbers "over mountain and valley," until he found them. "And then thou shalt kneel down before them and humbly beg them for forgiveness for thy rudeness and severity." (*Fioretti*.)

As this tale, one of the oldest remains we possess, lies before us, it gives us a full conception both of Francis' knowledge of men — he knew that it was useless to preach to a hungry man, he knew also that Rome was not built in a day — and of his unpharisaical love of men. Here is one of the moments in the history of Christendom, when the words of the gospel are understood exactly as they were said: "And if you love them that love you, what reward shall you have? Do not even the publicans this?" But do good without expecting anything from it! "And your reward shall be great, and you shall be the sons of the Highest, *for he is kind to the unthankful and to the evil.*"[1]

If Francis was thus indulgent to the last degree with great sinners, so on the other hand he put good people to a severe test. From those to whom much was given he expected much. The *Fioretti* have preserved for us many incidents which illustrate this characteristic in him, — such demeanor in the case of Rufino, who belonged to one of Assisi's best families, and whom he ordered to go naked from Portiuncula to the city, and to preach naked in the cathedral.[2] A similar command was that which he gave to Brother Agnolo near Borgo San Sepolcro, who belonged to that place and who like Rufino was of good family. He too was to go naked into the town and announce that Francis would come next day and preach there. But he was called back as he was approaching the city gate, and Francis promised him paradise for the readiness with which he had humiliated himself.[3]

Little is known with certainty of Francis of Assisi's journeys during the next few years. Wadding has with admirable sagacity tried to put into order all the fragmentary pieces which constitute the biographical material for these years, so as to form an artificial mosaic, but he failed in the attempt.

---

[1] Matth. v. 47. Luke vi. 35. This particular way of God made a deep impression upon Francis — see his own words in Bartholomew of Pisa: "Curialitas est una de proprietatibus Domini, que solem suum et pluviam suam et omnia super justos et injustos curialiter administrat" (*Actus*, Sabatier's ed., p. 205, n. 2).

[2] *Fioretti*, cap. 30.

[3] *Speculum vitae* (Antwerp, 1620), p. II, cap. 25. Compare Sab., *Opusc. de crit.*, I, p. 74, n. 2, and Wadding, 1213, n. 24.

MISSIONARY JOURNEYS

And when he, for example, assumes that Francis was sick in Assisi in the winter of 1212-1213, and sent out from his sick-bed his "Letters to all Christians," it confuses the occasion with much later events.

We can with some certainty believe that Francis pursued his journey through Italy. However this may be, we meet him in the beginning of 1213 on a similar mission — a journey in the province of Romagna. In this region, not far from the little republic of San Marino, there was in olden times a nobleman's castle called Montefeltro (now Sasso-Feltrio near the city of San Leo).

Francis and his companion — probably Leo — came to this city on a beautiful May morning just as the banners flying from the towers and the proud blare of the trumpets announced a great festival. Gaily dressed pages and men-at-arms hastened over the drawbridge, knights on powerful chargers, brightly caparisoned, thronged under the gateway, swinging carriages bore ladies, young and old, with laced bodices and high head-dresses up the steep road to the castle. Everything indicated that a festive tourney was to be held, to which all the nobility of the district was invited.

All the splendor here displayed did not irritate Brother Francis. Pious people are addicted to this failing, so that Francis was wont to warn his disciples against judging and despising those who went in costly clothes and lived in luxury.[1] "God is also *their* master," said he; "he can call them when he will and make them just and holy." Had not this happened to him?

Therefore he stood there a little while and looked at the banner that waved over the gate with the bearings of the barons of Montefeltro. He then turned with a smile to his companion.

"What do you think? Should we too go up to the festival? Perhaps we can win a good knight for God's cause!"

[1] "Admonebat etiam fratres, ut nullum hominem judicarent, neque despicerent illos, qui delicate vivunt ac superflue induuntur." *Tres Socii*, cap. XIV, n. 58. Compare *Regula sec.*, cap. II: "Quos moneo et exhortor, ne despiciant neque judicent homines, quos vident mollibus vestimentis et coloratis indutos, uti cibis et potibus delicatis, sed magis unusquisque judicet et despiciat semetipsum." (*Opusc.*, ed. Quar., p. 65.)

It was done as he said. The occasion of the festival was the knighting of a young soldier. All attended mass, during which the young man took the pledges of knighthood, and then Francis ascended some steps in the castle garden and began to speak. As his text he had chosen some words in the dialect of the people, a simple doggerel such as children use, the two following lines:

>Tanto è il bene ch' io aspetto
>Ch' ogni pena m'è dilletto
>
>*I hope that I so blessed will be
>That every suffering pleases me.*

One can easily imagine that Francis, grown up as he was in the atmosphere of the romances of King Arthur and the Knights of the Round Table, developed this text somewhat in the following manner:

"The knight," he began, "who wants to win a lovely dame, must be ready to undergo great and many sufferings. She may require of him that he shall go on a crusade against the sultan, perhaps that he shall bring her a horn of the unicorn or an egg of the bird called the roc. Perhaps that he shall set free a captive maiden, or ride a fully equipped charger over a bridge which is so small that one can hardly walk across it, while under it pours a wild torrent. And all these dangers and sufferings the true and noble knight is ready to undergo, only because his dear lady wishes it, and through all his tribulations he thinks only of her white hand that she will give him to kiss when he goes back with deeds well done, and immediately his despondency and gloom are over. . . .

"But now there is another and far nobler knighthood, to which all men are called, and not only those of noble birth. There is another battle, not to win the favor of an earthly beauty, but to do the will of the eternal and highest beauty, who is God. . . . For is not God far more beautiful than all the beautiful ladies — for they are all the work of His hands, made out of the dust of the earth? Is not He who made so much that is beautiful, is not He still more beautiful than all His creatures? Yes, He is that, and therefore He also deserves that you go out as knight-errants for Him, and fight valorously for His honor against the enemies who are the world, the flesh, and the Devil. And what will He not give us if we have been faithful to Him — like a knight to his ladylove — and do not permit ourselves to be cast down in His service by any obstacle or suffering? He gives us infinitely more than even the most beautiful dame can give. She has only herself, her hand, and her heart; but the hand shall wither, and the heart shall fail some time. But when God gives Himself as the prize for the victory, as the shining prize for the winner of the joust, then He gives us life, light and happiness in imperishable, immortal eternity."[1]

It was about in this way that Brother Francis spoke, and his words may well have moved many a young and noble heart. But one among them, and this was Duke Orlando dei Cattani of the castle of Chiusi in Casentino, approached Francis and spoke:

"Father, I want to talk to you about the salvation of my soul!"

But Francis, who gave God's Spirit time to work upon souls, had no haste, but answered:

"Go first and hold festivities with your friends, wherever you may be invited. After that we will talk in peace and quiet."

---

[1] When Sabatier so eloquently enlarges upon the contrast between him who serves God for love and him who does it for reward, and would regard the first as the true Franciscan, the other as the principle of the Church, he describes a contrast which does not exist. We see Francis on the contrary constantly preaching on the topics of reward and punishment. His words at the "Chapter of Mats" cannot be misunderstood (*Actus*, cap. 20: "Magna promisimus, majora vero promissa sunt nobis. . . . Brevis voluptas, perpetua poena. Modica passio, gloria infinita"). In the Letter to all Christians Francis descants in the same way with the expressions "merces," "praemium," "remuneratio": (*Op.*, p. 91), and he takes the same standpoint in the Rule of the Order of 1223, cap. IX, where he as the text of sermons especially recommends to the Brothers "Vitia et virtutes, *poenam et gloriam.*" "Non deterreat vos magnitudo certaminis et laboris immensitas, quoniam magnam habetis remunerationem," John of Parma has his *Domina Paupertas* say to her confidante (*Commercium*, ed. Alvisi, p. 40). The whole of this work, which is written from the extreme Franciscan standpoint, is charged with thoughts of "a reward in heaven," which appears to be so strongly repellent to Sabatier, but which he, if consistent, must object to in our Lord (Matthew vi. 1) and in St. Paul (Romans, viii. 18).

When the tourney was over the young duke again visited Francis, and they talked together; but at the end of the conversation the Duke Orlando said:

"I own a mountain in Tuscany, which is called La Verna, a very lonely mountain well adapted to meditation. If you would wish to build there, you and your Brothers, then for my soul's sake will I give it to you!"

"But St. Francis" — thus is it told us in the *Actus B. Francisci* — "greatly wished to find lonely places where it was good to pray. Therefore he thanked first of all God, who with his faithful took care of his lambs, and thereafter he thanked Lord Orlando, and said: 'Lord Duke, when you go back to your home I will send two of my Brothers to you, and you can show them this mountain, and if it seems suited to prayer and meditation, then I will be very grateful to you for your friendly offer.'"[1]

---

[1] *Actus*, cap. 9. Compare the *Consid. delle sacre stimmate* (in the Appendix to the *Fioretti*). — Casentino is the same as the upper Valley of the Arno. The ruins of Borgo Chiusi are still to be seen, not far from Mount Alverno. See Jörgensen's "Pilgrimsbogen," capp. XX–XXIV.

Francis did not wish to receive any written evidence of his right of ownership to the mountain. It was the sons of Count Orlando, who caused a formal letter of gift to be issued, of which Sbaralea in his *Bullarium Franciscanum* (IV, Rome, 1768, p. 156, note h) gives a copy after the original preserved in the archives of Borgo San Sepolcro. It is given here:

"In Dei Nomine. Amen. Anno Dni millesimo ducentesimo septuagesimo quarto Gregorio Papa sedente & Romano Imperio vacante die Lunae 9. Mensis Julii . . . Orlandus de Catanis quondam Domini Orlandi, Comes de Clusio, & Cungius & Bandinus & Guglielmus fratres et filii dicti Domini Orlandi, ejus verbo et auctoritate et qualiter ex certa scientia, et non per aliquem juris vel facti errorem, confitentes se lege Romana vivere et esse majores viginti quinque annis, confessi fuerunt, quomodo dictus Dom. Orlandus Clusii comes inter milites Imperatoris strenuissimus miles, et dictorum pater, oretenus dederit, donaverit atque concesserit libere et absque nulla exceptione Fratri Francisco, ejusque sociis fratribus, tam praesentibus quam futuris, de anno Domini MCCXIII, die octava Maji, *Alvernae* montem, ita ut praedictus Pater Franciscus, ejusque fratres ibi habitare possint, et per praedictum Montem *Alverniae* intelligimus . . . totam terram alboratam, saxosam et prativam absque ulla exceptione a supercilio praedicti montis usque ad radices a qualibet parte, quae praedictum montem circumdat cum suis annexis."

By their father's command the sons ratified the gift, that hitherto had been "in voce tantum et absque ulla scriptura." At the same time they made over to the convent at La Verna many relics of St. Francis, with the leather belt Francis had brought their father when he was taken into the Third Order of St. Francis ("habitum sumpsit").

For the present, Francis himself did not go to inspect the Duke Orlando's gift. For again did the crown of martyrdom beckon to him from afar. He had not succeeded in going to the Holy Land — now he thought of bringing the gospel to the Mussulmen on the further side of the Mediterranean Sea in Morocco. Sultan Mohammed ben Nasser, the *Miramolin* as the Christians by an anagram on the title — *Emir-el-Mumenin*, "the ruler of the faithful" — were wont to call him, had been beaten by the Spaniards at Tolosa, and was forced to retreat to Africa. Here Francis determined to visit him, and started on the journey, probably in the winter of 1213–1214.[1] He travelled across Spain, but he fell sick as he reached the end of his journey, and again had to return home with his object unattained. On reaching Portiuncula he took several new Brothers into the Order, among them Thomas of Celano.[2]

The year after this fruitless mission to the heathen, Francis seems to have been present at the Fourth Lateran Council.[3] He obtained in all probability on this occasion Innocent III's ratification of Clara's and her Sisters' privilege of poverty (see p. 131).

It was about the same time that the French prelate, Jacques de Vitry (see Appendix, p. 401), passed through Italy on his way to the Holy Land, and then made the acquaintance of the first Friars Minor. In a letter sent from Genoa in October, 1216 to his friends at home, the French Canon thus expresses himself:

"In the time that I spent at the Curia" (the Papal Court in Perugia) "I saw much that I was entirely dissatisfied with; all was so taken up with worldly and temporary affairs of

---

[1] "Post non multum tempus," i.e. after the return from Slavonia, says Celano (*V. pr.*, I, 20. Compare *Tract. de mir.*, V., 34). Sabatier would put the journey in 1214–1215. Compare *Etudes Franc.*, XV, p. 384, and XVI, pp. 60 et seq.

[2] *Vita pr.*, same place. The later biographers make Francis visit S. Jago da Compostella and establish a lot of cloisters in Spain, Southern France, and Piedmont (*Anal. Franc.*, III, p. 9). The Bollandists throw out all these traditions. It is certain that Luc de Tuy in his History of the World first for the year 1217 writes: "Eo tempore per totam Hispaniam ... Fratrum Minorum construunt monasteria." *A. SS.*, Oct. II, p. 603, n. 303.

[3] *Anal. Franc.*, III, 9.

politics and law, that it was hardly possible to get in a word of spiritual affairs.

"There was one thing, however, which comforted me in these surroundings: many men and women, among them many rich and worldly, have for Christ's sake forsaken everything and fled from the world. They are called Friars Minor, and stand in high repute both with Pope and Cardinals. But they take no heed of temporal things, but work day in and day out with zeal and diligence to draw souls away from the vanities of the world, so that they will not fall to the ground, and to take them along with themselves. And with the favor of God they have already reaped a rich harvest. . . .

"But they live after the example of the primitive man, of whom it is written: 'the multitude of the faithful were of one heart and one mind.' By day they labor and go into the cities and highways to capture souls, but at night they turn back to waste places and lonely regions, where they give themselves up to prayer. The women abide together in various retreats in the vicinity of the cities; they receive nothing, but live from the work of their hands. . . . But the men of this Order come together once a year with great provision to a predetermined place, to hold a feast together and to rejoice in the Lord, and with the support of good men they ordain and announce their laws, which the Pope ratifies. After this they disperse, and for the entire year are in Lombardy, and Tuscany, and Apulia, and Sicily. But a holy and God-fearing man, Nicholas, the Pope's secretary, recently forsook the Curia and went to them, but was called back because the Pope could not do without him."[1]

In the summer of 1216 the Papal Court was stationed in Perugia, and, as can be seen from the last lines of Jacques de Vitry's sketch, the movement started by Francis began to spread up to the highest hierarchy. The Bishop Nicholas here spoken of was Bishop of Tusculum, later Cardinal Nicholas Chiaramonti, of whom we know that he was very friendly to the Franciscans, and liked to have one of them with him.[2] Perhaps it was at the same time that another Cardinal paid his first visit to the Friars Minor; this was

[1] Boehmer: "Analekten," pp. 98-99. [2] *Anal. Franc.*, III, p. 83.

Cardinal Hugolin of Ostia, afterwards a friend and tireless protector of the Order. He came to Portiuncula — as we are told in the *Speculum perfectionis*, where the Brothers were holding a conference — with a large band of followers, both clerks and soldiers. But when he saw how poorly the Brothers lived, and that they slept upon straw, and ate from the bare earth, he was so overcome that he broke into tears and cried out, "How will it go with us who live so luxuriously day after day in superfluity and delights?"[1]

It is certain that the time was approaching for a nearer relation between Francis and the Papal Court to be established. The road from Perugia, where the Curia, as already said, was held for the greater part of the summer of 1216,[2] to Portiuncula is not long, and there seem to have been reciprocal visits.[3] It was in this summer that the majority of his biographers are unanimous in placing one of the most contested affairs in the life of Francis of Assisi — in the first days of the pontificate of Honorius III, God's poor little man from Assisi knelt before Christ's Vicar and begged for the celebrated *Portiuncula indulgence*.

[1] *Spec. perf.*, cap. 21.
[2] Potth., *Reg.*, I, nr. 5111 (May 20) — nr. 5327 (August 12).
[3] A single authority (Eccleston) considers that Francis was present at Innocent III's death-bed ("in cujus obitu fuit praesentialiter S. Franciscus"). *Anal. Franc.*, I, p. 253.

CHAPTER III

THE PORTIUNCULA INDULGENCE

IT is first of all necessary to observe that the Church of Rome, previous to the establishment of the Portiuncula indulgence, had only one plenary indulgence — the one granted to those who took up the Cross and joined the ranks of the Crusaders. Every one who did this, and fulfilled the requirements of confessing his sins and obtained absolution from a priest, obtained complete remission of the Church penances as well as of the punishment of Purgatory, so that his soul could appear before God directly after death.

This Indulgence of the Crusade — *Indulgentia de Terra Sancta* — was later extended, so as to apply to anyone who for one reason or another did not personally join the ranks of the Crusaders, but with money or with armed men sustained the Holy War. It was also the Franciscans — something which in this connection is of the greatest importance — who obtained from the Pope the right of distributing this indulgence, extended as above stated.[1]

Whenever the Church decreed an indulgence in other cases — as on the consecration of a church — it was done in a distinctively different form. The Lateran Council of 1215 had imposed further restrictions on this custom. On the consecration of a church — the Council decreed — an indulgence of only one year canonical penance should be granted, and on the recurring anniversaries of the consecration only one of forty days.[2] At the consecration of the church of St. Francis in Assisi there was granted as something quite extraordinary an indulgence of three years to all who had

---

[1] See, for example, several bulls of Clement IV of the year 1268 in Sbaralea, *Bull. franc.*, t. III, pp. 153 et seq., p. 164.
[2] Mansi, *Conc. coll.*, XXII, 1049 et seq.

come over the sea to take part in the festival, and of two years to those who had crossed the Alps, while the ordinary pilgrim had to be content with the usual indulgence of one year.[1]

What is it then, that Francis, in contrast to this, tried to get from the Pope, or better, did obtain from him? If we give credence to the authorities, he presented himself one fine day, accompanied by Brother Masseo of Marignano, before Honorius II and begged for the Portiuncula church the same indulgence granted to the Crusaders in the Holy Lands. "I desire," he is said to have announced to the Pope, "that every one who, with penitence for his sins, comes into this church and confesses his sins and is absolved by the priest, shall be free from all guilt and punishment for the sins of his life from the day of his baptism to the day when he entered the said church."[2] It was in vain that the Pope urged that the Roman Curia was not accustomed to grant such indulgences to any church; it was in vain that he offered to Francis one of the ordinary indulgences. Francis could not be moved, as he declared that the Lord himself had sent him in order to obtain this indulgence. Then the Pope suddenly, as if by the divine guidance, yielded the point, and now it remained to the Cardinals to restrict the new indulgence, as Honorius depicted the injury it might do to the Indulgence of the Crusade. It was to be valid for only one day in each year, from the vespers of the evening before through the full twenty-four hours following until sunset. Francis departed contented, and when the Pope asked him if he did not want a written authorization, he said it was superfluous, for "God will know how to bring his own work into the light."

With this relation for a foundation a group of legends has

---

[1] Wadding, 1230, n. 1. Potth., I, nr. 8556. P. A. Kirsch ("Theol. Quartalschrift," Tübingen, 1906: "*Der Portiuncula-Ablass,*" pp. 81 et seq. and pp. 231 et seq.) gives on page 225, note 1, a quantity of other indications of the status of this affair. — That Gregory's indulgence was regarded as a very great proof of favor by contemporaries is seen in Thomas of Celano's words (d'Alençon's ed., p. 445): "Clarificat (Gregorius) etiam locum ejus (i.e. Ecclesiam S. Francisci) indulgentiis et remissionibus plurimis, per quas fides et devotio populi quotidie magis accrescit."

[2] *Leg. tr. soc.*, ed. Da Civezza-Dominichelli, p. 157.

been built up, to which belongs the Rose-legend depicted by Overbeck on the façade of the Portiuncula chapel. These adornments of the recital first appear in works of the fourteenth century. What is given above can be referred to earlier sources.

At the first glance this narration seems very probable in itself. Every biographer of Francis tells us how he loved his dear Portiuncula, and we also know how zealous he was for the conversion of sinners. He once saw in a vision how men from all places near and far came in streams around the little Portiuncula,[1] and one of his disciples had a similar vision.[2]

Again, the dislike of documents is a characteristic of Francis. In 1210 he was satisfied with the verbal ratification of Innocent III, and at the Lateran Council he got nothing more. When Orlando dei Cattani gave him La Verna, this too was done "without any writing," as it is explicitly stated in the letter of gifts of the young Count Cattani in 1274. In his testament Francis forbids most definitely his Brothers to seek written privileges from the Curia, "whether for a church or for any other place."[3] It is perfectly clear that such an answer as Francis gave to Honorius, according to the old story, is quite in the spirit of St. Francis.[4]

It is quite another question if Francis really gave this answer; in other words, if such an interview ever took place.

First and foremost, we must here remark that none of the undoubtedly authentic authorities of the thirteenth century contain a single reference to the Portiuncula indulgence. Thomas of Celano knows the indulgence which Gregory IX granted to the church of St. Francis in Assisi, but neither he

---

[1] Cel., V. pr., I, cap. XI, n. 27.
[2] *Leg. tr. soc.*, XIII, 56.
[3] *Opusc.* (Quaracchi), p. 80.
[4] On the other hand, the boldness with which Francis here appears before Honorius accords only poorly with his humble words to the same Pope, when he later through Cardinal Hugolin obtained an audience with him. "Magnus timor," were the words used here, "et vericundia debet esse nobis, qui sumus magis pauperes et despecti ceteris religiosis, non solum ingredi ad vos, sed etiam stare ante ostium vestrum et praesumere pulsare tabernaculum virtutis christianorum." *Tres Socii*, c. XVI (Amoni's ed.), p. 92. Compare Cel., *V. tr.*, I, cap. XXVII, n. 75.

nor the old biographers of St. Francis have the least inkling of the existence of the Portiuncula indulgence. It is only much more recent authorities who assert that this indulgence could be gained every year since 1216, on days appointed by Honorius III, namely, from the evening of August 1 to the evening of the second. This remarkable silence of the official biographers may be regarded as the sequence of the non-existing Papal bull, or as a result of the opposition of Elias of Cortona and of his party to the "Portiuncula men" — the strict division of the Order. The biographers in question had to serve the party in power.

If this was the correct conclusion, on the other hand we should expect to find the Portiuncula indulgence in the place of honor in the legend originating in the ranks of the strict division — as in the *Speculum perfectionis*, or in the *Fioretti*. But it is in vain that one looks even here for a trace of the legend given above.

The tradition of the indulgence naturally can be referred, if not in the direct, then in the secondary line to Brother Leo and the other intimate friends of St. Francis. And in the first rank stands the testimony taken in the presence of numerous witnesses on October 31, 1277, and signed by a notary public in Arezzo, as given by two Franciscans, Brother Benedict of Arezzo, "who formerly was with St. Francis, when he still lived," and Brother Rayner of Arezzo, who declared himself a confidential friend of Brother Masseo from Marignano. In this document the two Franciscans testify that they had heard from Brother Masseo, who was "the truth itself," how he and Francis went together to Perugia and obtained from Pope Honorius the above described indulgence, "although the Pope said that the Apostolic throne was not wont to give such an indulgence."

The recital is very short, and the document is provided with a date which is quite complete and in all particulars correct.[1]

---

[1] "In anno Domini MCCLXXVII, nemine imperante, Papa in ecclesia romana vacante." Rudolph of Hapsburgh had been elected in 1273, but was not crowned in 1277. The Papal throne was vacant from May 20 to November 25, 1277, and the document is dated October 31. M. Paulus: *Die Bewilligung des Portiuncula-Ablasses* in "Der Katholik," 1899, p. 193.

The original is no longer in existence; Sabatier maintains that one of the copies now in Assisi dates from the end of the thirteenth century.

Various other recitals of the same period rest upon the testimony of Brother Masseo through the intermediary of Brother Benedict of Arezzo. Sabatier has inserted them in his edition of Francesco Bartholi's book on the Portiuncula indulgence of about 1435; but if they originate with Brother John of La Verna or with Brother Otto of Aquasparta, they contain nothing new. It is only a new appearance of the original source — Masseo-Benedict — which we find in various places. That an old man, Pietro Zalfani, in his youth claims to have been present at the consecration of the Portiuncula church, and that he says that he there saw Francis standing "with a paper in his hand," amounts to but little.

Another group of witnesses of about the same time depend upon Brother Leo instead of Brother Masseo. A nobleman of Perugia, Jacopo Coppoli, who on February 14, 1276 gave the Perugian Franciscans the hill on which their old convent Monte Ripido stands, testifies at about this same time, and in a similar form to that of Brother Benedict of Arezzo, that he had heard Brother Leo tell about the Portiuncula indulgence. In the narration of Coppoli the Pope offers to Francis an indulgence of seven years, without satisfying him. He then offered the indulgence *de terra sancta*, but the Cardinals caused him to limit it. After Francis had told this to Brother Leo, he told him to say nothing of the indulgence for the present, "for this indulgence shall remain hidden for a while, the Lord will in good time bring it out and reveal it."

Wadding places, and certainly correctly, this testimony in the year 1277.[1] This was two generations after the granting of the indulgence. It is clear that within the Order, or rather within its stricter party, to which Benedict of Arezzo belonged, the effort was made, first as strongly as possible to prove the existence of the Portiuncula indulgence, and secondly to explain why the indulgence was not announced sooner. For this reason Brother Benedict had his testimony affirmed by a notary, and Jacob Coppoli's testimony was given in the

[1] Note under 1277, n. 18.

presence of numerous witnesses before the provincial minister for Umbria, Brother Angelo (1270-1280).[1]

It was also about this time, or a little earlier, that Brother Francis of Fabriano obtained himself the Portiuncula indulgence, and he tells also that he received from Brother Leo the tale of how Francis obtained it from the Pope.[2] It is definitely certain that Francis of Fabriano wrote the work to which we refer, in his latter years, for he quotes a document which at the earliest may be of 1310. Brother Francis, who was born in 1251 and died in 1322, was sixty or seventy years old when he put down his reminiscences. There is no reason to doubt that Francis of Fabriano was in Portiuncula in the year referred to. We cannot set aside the explanation, that in his advanced age he may have had the indulgence as the object of his pilgrimage. From the beginning many Franciscans made the pilgrimage to the grave of their spiritual father and to Portiuncula, and in this connection it is of the greatest significance that Pope Nicholas IV — himself a Franciscan — speaks in a letter of May 14, 1284 of "the numerous crowd of Brothers" who streamed to Assisi, but never names the Portiuncula indulgence as the reason of their going. According to this Pope the church of San Francesco containing the saint's tomb, as well as the Portiuncula chapel, were the objects of pilgrimage, and not the indulgence, all being done "to honor the saint."

This accords with the fact that Angela of Foligno (1248-1309), soon after she entered the Third Order of St. Francis, made a pilgrimage to Assisi, but on this occasion never speaks of Portiuncula, but tells of two visits to the memorial church of San Francesco. And she is known to have been of the strict observance; the great chief of this party, Hubert of Casale, visited her shortly before her death and speaks of her in the prologue to his *Arbor vitae* with the greatest reverence. Naturally Angela's visit to Assisi may have fallen in a time of the year when the indulgence was not to be obtained; she may not have been there on the first or second day of August. Still it is strange that she never says a word about Portiuncula.

[1] *Coll.*, II, p. 52.
[2] Franz von Fabriano's Testimony in *A. SS.*, Oct. II, p. 89.

Everything indicates that the Portiuncula indulgence first began to be known only in the last quarter (in the last third if we accept Francis of Fabriano's words) of the thirteenth century. If it were allowable to apply modern conceptions to the ways of those days, we might be tempted to place the origin of the indulgence at the 50-year jubilee of the granting of the indulgence (1212-1262). (Francis of Fabriano's visit was made in 1268.) It is certain, that as soon as the indulgence became known it awakened opposition — hence the notarial declarations of Benedict of Arezzo, Rainer, Coppoli, Zalfani. Even the great leader of the strict Franciscan observance, Peter John Olivi (1248-1298), took up the question of the indulgence. In a small — unfortunately undated — pamphlet he strives to uphold its authenticity, first on dogmatic and then on historic grounds. Unfortunately the historic portion is lost.

It is not to be wondered at, that in this dispute several Catholic investigators doubted or even denied the origin of the indulgence to have been with St. Francis, so inadequately is it proved. Even the author of this book was once of the same opinion, and so expressed himself in the first edition of the same. According to my views at that time the Portiuncula indulgence was only a localized indulgence *de terra sancta* or Crusaders' indulgence. Thus when the Holy Land was lost (St. Jean d'Acre fell 1291, being the last stronghold of the Christians) the Indulgence of the Crusade, which the Pope had permitted the Franciscans to share, could only be obtained in Portiuncula. It was natural that the second of August should be chosen as the day for gaining the indulgence, as this was the anniversary of the consecration of the church. Such a choice was not un-Franciscan. On August 1 is celebrated the festival of "St. Peter's Chains." Francis of Assisi's reverence for the saint was well known. And in the mass of this day in the collect is this passage: "O God Who didst let the blessed Peter the Apostle depart free and uninjured from his bonds, we beg Thee to free us from the bonds of our sins."

In the little Portiuncula chapel, the new *terra sancta*, the Franciscans by virtue of the authorization already obtained shared on these days the same plenary indulgence which formerly belonged to the Crusaders, and led penitent pilgrims out of the valley of sin and punishment into the holy land of innocence.

In the four years which have passed since this chapter in my book was written, a most meritorious investigator of Franciscan history, Rev. Heribert Holzapfel in Munich, has developed new view-points for the consideration of this question.[1] Father Holzapfel agrees that in the lifetime of St. Francis the indulgence in question was little known and little used. "It must impress us," he writes, "that all later authorities . . . only mention the fact that the indulgence was secured by St. Francis, but never say that it was much frequented either in the lifetime of the saint nor during the first decade following his death. Some causes must then have been operative which, in the beginning at least, hindered the dissemination of the indulgence. In seeking these causes we are driven into the region of conjecture. I may be permitted to suggest the following solution for discussion.

"The Pope conceded the indulgence only after long persuasion. As we learn from later authorities, the Cardinals were decided enemies of the proposition, as were the Bishops of the vicinity" (i.e., in Assisi, Foligno, Perugia, Gubbio, etc.). "These Bishops," says Father Holzapfel, "did not wish such an extraordinary demonstration of favor for the insignificant Portiuncula chapel and expressed themselves to St. Francis on the subject in various ways, — and the more as they doubtless knew the feeling of the Curia." It would be in exact accord with the spirit of St. Francis that he would remain silent from his reverence for the priesthood. His was no combative nature, and here as in other instances yielded. "That he did it willingly we do not assert; it may have hurt him, like many another thing that he had to yield to and could not change. He will have spoken also of the disappointment with his trusted companions. . . . He will have comforted himself with the prospects of a better future and have exhorted them for the present to practise patient sub-

[1] "*Die Entstehung des Portiuncula-Ablasses,*" Archivum Franciscanum Historicum, I, Quaracchi, 1908, pp. 31–44.

mission. This does not exclude the possibility that the few Friars sharing his knowledge or similar people in the world may have used the indulgence as granted, only we must not think of a wide dissemination of it. The circle of those knowing of it would grow with time and consequently the frequentation of the indulgence, but also the opposition of its enemies. Then the Friars who were still living felt it their duty to leave authentic proof of what they knew so well. They need fear no longer the enmity of the Curia, which was very friendly to the Order, nor the enmity of the Bishops, at least not of the directly interested Bishops of Assisi, who for some time had been Franciscans.[1]

This hypothesis explains the silence of the biographers. If, moreover, the *Speculum perfectionis*, which was written in the year 1318, when the indulgence was perfectly known on all sides, never mentions it, why should the silence of the earlier biographers prove anything against the existence of the indulgence at the period when they wrote?

As in so many other questions of Franciscan investigation, we here have to refer to approved authorities of the olden times.

[1] A. a. O., pp. 43-44. Compare Lemmens in "Der Katholik," March and April, 1908: "*Die ältesten Zeugnisse für den Portiuncula-Ablass.*"

CHAPTER IV

CHAPTERS AND PROVINCES

THE community of Brothers, which Francis of Assisi had founded, was from the very first an order of *penitents* and *apostles*,[1] and Francis himself was the Superior of the Order. He it was who had written the Rules of the Order and had promised obedience to the Pope, he it was to whom the permission to preach was given, and through whom the others participated therein. It is certain that the first six Brothers had the same right as Francis to receive new members into the Order, but the new members were taken to Portiuncula, there to receive the robe of penitence from Francis himself.[2] This reception into the Brotherhood was regarded as equivalent in weight to the old-time *conversio* of the orders of monkhood — by it one left the world with its pomp and glory.[3] As a sign of this the supplicant gave his possessions to the poor.

Again, from the very first, Francis had liked to have his Brothers about him as much as possible. When the first disciples were sent out on their mission journeys, he had accordingly arranged a time (*statuto termino*) when they should all again meet at Portiuncula.[4] Later there were arranged once for all two such terms in the year, when all the Brothers

---

[1] "viri poenitentes de Assisio" (*Tres Socii*, cap. X). "Accedat frater Salomon de Ordine Apostolorum" (Eccleston in *Anal. Franc.*, I, p. 222).

[2] *Tres Socii*, XI, 41. Anon. Perus., *A. SS.*, Oct. II, p. 600, n. 291.

[3] "saeculo nequam cum pompis suis penitus derelicto intravit religionem." *Tres Socii*, XIII, 56. This is in entire disagreement with the theory of Karl Müller, Sabatier and Mandonnet making the origin of the Franciscan Order a brotherhood essentially from the Orders of the Church, of which they would call the so-called "Third Order" a relic. See W. Götz: "*Die ursprünglichen Ideale des hl. Frans*," "Hist. Vierteljahrschrift," VI (1903), pp. 19–50.

[4] *Tres Socii*, XI, 41.

should meet at Portiuncula — at Pentecost and on the feast of St. Michael (September 29).[1]

Of these two meetings — or, as they were called, using an expression from the older days of convent life, *Chapters* — Pentecost Chapter was the most important. "Then all the Brothers came together and discussed how best they should maintain the Rule." They held a feast in frugality and joy, after which Francis preached. His *Admonitiones* or Admonitions, which will be spoken of later, evidently originated at these Chapter-meetings. They explained perhaps a text from the Sermon on the Mount or sentences such as, "For he that will save his life, shall lose it," "I am not here to be served but to serve," he who "doth not renounce all that he possesseth cannot be my disciple." Most often and most willingly he spoke on his favorite theme—reverence for the sacrament of the altar, and the reverence for priests which flows from it. Sometimes he would have the Brothers kiss the head of the horse a priest rode on. "And always have peace in your hearts, you who come to bring others peace." If therefore any disciple felt disturbed by temptations, he went to the Master and took him into his confidence, and none went away uncomforted.

To the last Francis undertook the choosing of preachers whom he afterwards sent to the various mission-districts or *Provinces*, as the expression became later. In this choosing he was led only by considerations of the fitness of the one recommended, and sent out Lay-brothers as willingly as priests. With all his overflowing fatherly heart he finally blessed them all, and two and two they went off gladly into the world, "like strangers and like pilgrims," without other burden than the books they needed to say their Office out of.[2]

Francis' always strongly personal preaching at these meetings often approached the poetical. This passage from one of his admonitions unmistakably recalling the church

---

[1] *Tres Socii*, XIV, 57. We cannot be surprised that Jacques de Vitry only mentions one Chapter assembly; he only knew the Order from a visit of short duration. The Pentecost Chapter was, moreover, the principal one.

[2] *Tres Socii*, cap. XIV. Wadding states (1216, n. 1) that Francis held the first Chapter in imitation of the great Lateran Council (1215).

Maundy Thursday hymn, *Ubi charitas et amor, Deus ibi est*, may in this connection be cited here:
"Where charity is and wisdom is, is neither fear nor ignorance. Where patience is and humility is, is neither unquiet nor anger. Where poverty is and joy is, is neither cupidity nor covetousness. Where the fear of the Lord stands at the door, the evil enemy cannot enter. Where compassion is and prudence is, is neither waste nor hardness of heart."[1]

Like all model Christians Francis turned with special devotion to the Blessed Virgin and Mother of God, Mary. And troubadour as he was, he sang one of his most beautiful lauds in praise of all the virtues "with which the Blessed Virgin was adorned, and which should be the ornaments of all holy souls":[2]

"Hail, Queen Wisdom," he cries, "the Lord save thee with thy sister holy pure simplicity. Lady holy poverty, the Lord save thee with thy sister holy humility, the Lord save thee with thy sister holy obedience. All you most holy virtues, may the Lord from whom you proceed and come save you. . . . Holy wisdom confounds Satan and all his wickednesses. Pure holy simplicity confounds all the wisdom of this world and the wisdom of the flesh. Holy poverty confounds all cupidity and avarice and the cares of this world. Holy humility confounds pride and all men of this world and all things which are in the world. Holy charity confounds all diabolical and carnal temptations and all carnal fears. Holy obedience confounds all corporal and carnal wishes and keeps the body mortified to the obedience of the spirit and to the obedience of its brother and makes man subject to all men of this world, and not only to men, but even to all animals and beasts . . ."

From this praise of all virtues, which inevitably reminds one of Giotto's exaltation of "the holy obedience," "the holy chastity," and "the holy poverty" in the frescoes over the grave of St. Francis in Assisi, the poet takes his flight up to the throne of the purest Virgin:

---

[1] Admonitio XXVII.
[2] "De virtutibus quibus decorata fuit Sancta Virgo et debet esse sancta anima" (*Opuscula*, p. 21 + p. 123. Boehmer's "*Analekten*," p. 165 + p. 70).

"Hail Holy Lady, Most Holy Queen, Mary Mother of God, who art a Virgin for ever, chosen from heaven by the most holy Father, whom He consecrated with the most holy beloved Son and the Paraclete Spirit, in whom was and is all plenitude of grace and all good. Hail His palace. Hail His tabernacle. Hail His house. Hail His vesture. Hail His handmaid. Hail His mother and all you holy virtues, which by grace and illumination of the Holy Ghost may you pour into the hearts of the faithful, and may you make out of the faithless ones men faithful to God."

After having ended such a song of praise to Mary, taken as the Christian ideal, it may have been that Francis cried out:

"We Friars Minor, what are we other than God's singers and players, who seek to draw hearts upwards and to fill them with spiritual joy?"[1] To play good people into heaven, to sing before every one's door about the beauty and delight of serving the Lord — this Francis had tried personally in Assisi, and he assigned the same troubadour's ways to his Brothers. "Do you not know, dearest Brother," he asked Brother Giles, "that holy contrition and holy humility and holy charity and holy joy make the soul good and happy?"[2] There were many who in St. Francis of Assisi's time did not know this, and therefore God's singers, *joculatores Dei*, went out into the world to sing this into the hearts of men.

From the beginning the chapter-meetings were thus practically gatherings for mutual edification. The Order had no other organization — and what was there to organize? "They carry neither purse nor bag with them on their way, neither bread nor money in their belt not shoes on their feet. . . . They have no churches, no convents, no fields, nor vineyards nor animals nor houses nor property nor where they can harbor their heads. They use neither fur nor linen, but only woollen habits with hoods, neither cap nor cape nor over-garment nor any other raiment. If anyone asks them to a meal they

---

[1] "Quid enim sunt servi Dei, nisi quidam joculatores ejus, qui corda hominum erigere debent et movere ad lætitiam spiritualem?" "Et specialiter hoc dicebat de fratribus minoribus qui dati sunt populo Dei pro ejus salute." *Spec. perf.*, cap. 100.

[2] *Dicta b. Aegidii* (Quaracchi, 1905), p. 5. *Dottrina di Frate Egidio*, cap. L.

eat and drink what is set before them. If anything is given them for pity, nothing is kept for the next day. . . . And not only by their words, but by their holy life and perfect way of life they draw many of all classes to despise the world, to leave house and home and great possessions and put on the habit of the Friars Minor, which is a plain tunic and a rope around the waist."[1]

For men who lived thus, many laws and regulations were not necessary. Do the larks need more than a drink of water out of the spring and the food they can gather in the fields, to again fly up into the sky and sing the praise of God so exultingly that all must stop and look upwards? "Therefore Brother Francis loved also above all birds the bird which in everyday language is called the crested lark, and he said of it: 'Sister lark has a hood like us and is an humble bird, for it goes willingly along the wayside and finds a grain of corn for itself. . . . Its plumage is of the same color as the earth and is an example to us that we shall not have fine and colored clothes, but simple and plain. . . . But when they fly upwards they praise God so devoutly, like good Brothers of our Order, whose life is in the heavens, and whose pleasure is always in glorifying God.'"[2]

This happy unconfined bird-life could not be for ever. More and more joined the Brotherhood. And not only young men came to them, but women too, married and unmarried, even married men came. It was possible to help the young unmarried women; they were told to enter a convent, and one of the Brothers undertook temporarily to guide them and help them. But old married men came and said: "We have wives from whom we cannot separate! Teach us how to live!" And they too must be looked after — but in what way?[3]

---

[1] Jacques de Vitry: *Hist. orient.*, II, cap. 32 (Boehmer: "*Analekten*," pp. 103–104).

[2] *Spec. perf.*, cap. 113.

[3] *Anon. Perus.*: "Multae mulieres, virgines etiam non habentes viros, audientes praedicationem eorum, veniebant corde compuncto ad eos dicentes: Quid faciemus autem nos? Vobiscum esse non possumus. Dicite ergo nobis, quomodo salvare nostras animas valeamus. Ad hoc ordinaverunt per singulas civitates, quibus potuerant, monasteria reclusa ad poenitentiam faciendam.

The movement Francis had awakened bid fair to mount over his head. He did not like his Brothers to have the superintendence of nuns — "I am afraid the devil will give us Sisters around our necks in place of the wives we have given up for the sake of God," he may have said.[1] And in Cannara he himself had to restrain his hearers' zeal — all wished to follow him, men and women, married and unmarried, the whole population of the village. "Be not too hasty," he advised them, "I will think over what I can advise you for your salvation."[2]

The progress of the Order brought great difficulties with it. Francis on the one hand could only rejoice at the numbers of his army, but on the other hand he had no place to harbor them in. His net, like that of the Apostles, was ready to tear under the too rich draught of fishes.

The rules of the Order, he in his time "with few and simple words" had written, would answer for wandering evangelists and musicians, but would not suffice for nuns and still less for married people. A flock of larks Francis would willingly undertake to guide or to lead — the wild birds always gladly obeyed him! But men in the ranks of citizens, and maidens longing for the convent life, tame, useful beings and mystic doves, that cooed in the mountain clefts of Tabor or of Carmel — how should he, *simplex et idiota*, "the simple and foolish," give them rules of life or laws?

Involuntarily Francis looked for a helping hand. It was nearer to him than he thought — it was stretched out, white, well-kept and strong, adorned with the bishop's amethyst ring, stretched out to his help by the nephew of Innocent III, the Bishop of Ostia and Velletri, Cardinal Hugolin.

Constituerunt autem unum de fratribus, qui esset visitator et corrector eorum. Similiter et viri uxores habentes dicebant: uxores habemus, quae dimitti se non patiuntur. Docete ergo nos, quam viam tenere salubriter valeamus." *A. SS.*, Oct. II, p. 600, n. 291.

[1] Wadd., 1219, n. 45. Compare *Reg. sec.*, cap. XI: "Quod fratres non ingrediantur monasteria monacharum."

[2] *Actus*, cap. XVI, vv. 15-16.

CHAPTER V

CARDINAL HUGOLIN

HUGO or Hugolin, Count of Anagni, was when Francis first knew him a man of nearly seventy years, and of awe-inspiring and engaging appearance. He possessed all the highest polish of the day, had studied in Bologna and Paris, and was also characterized by an upright piety. His two principal interests were the freedom of the Church and the promotion of the cloister life. In 1188 he had, with danger of his life, defended the cause of the Church against the usurper Markwald (see page 22), and he stood in close and permanent relations with the Camaldolites, the monks of Cluny, the congregation of St. Flore (for whom he built two new convents), and also later with the Franciscans and the Dominicans. In his native land, Anagni, he founded a poor-house with church annexed thereto, and in October, 1216, gave it over to the Hospital Brothers from Altopascio in Tuscany.[1] In 1198 he was Papal Chaplain as well as Cardinal-deacon with the titular church of St. Eustachio. In May, 1206, he was nominated to the bishopric of Ostia and Velletri, the highest position in the Church next to Pope. It was not necessary to possess the power of a seer to see in him the coming Pope,[2] as it is said Francis did. Also as Gregory IX, Hugolin continued to be a true friend and benefactor of the religious orders — among other things he founded with his own means a Franciscan convent in Viterbo and a convent for the poor Clares in Rome (San Cosmiato). In Lombardy too and in Tuscany several convents owe their

---

[1] Joseph Felten: "*Pabst Gregor IX*" (Freib. i Bres., 1886), pp. 16-19. Götz in "Hist. Vierteljahrsschrift," VI (1903), p. 43. Achille Luchaire: *Innocent III et l'Italie* (Paris, 1905), *passim*.
[2] Cel., *Vita pr.*, I, V, n. 100.

existence to him.[1] To this man it fell — as his biographer puts it — "to find the Order of the Friars Minor in insecurity and formless and to give it form."[2]

As already told, the first acquaintance between Francis and Hugolin dates from the summer of 1216, when the Papal Court was established in Perugia. No closer relations were for the present established.[3]

Next year, on May 14, 1217, Francis held his usual Pentecost Chapter at Portiuncula.[4] He had made his appearance only with grave apprehensions. On his way thither he had opened his heart to a friend. "When I now come to the Chapter," said he, "the Brothers ask me to preach as usual, and accordingly I do so. But what if all the Brothers, when I am ready to begin, start to cry out against me: 'We do not want thee to rule over us any longer, for thou art not eloquent, as would become thee and as thou oughtest to be, and thou art too small and simple, and we are ashamed to have so simple and poor-looking a Superior over us, and therefore thou shalt no longer be called our supreme head!' And then they will cast me out with great scorn!"[5]

Anxious before the many accomplished book-learned people who now had come into the Brotherhood, Francis began to preach in his usual simple way. And a wonder happened — no one called out against him, on the contrary all the Brothers were greatly edified and filled with peace! Then Francis took courage and came out with his great plan: — that now, when the Brothers were so many, they ought to go out on missions, not only in Italy but also to countries on the other side of the mountains, to Germany, to Hungary, to France and Spain, yes, even to the Holy Land. This proposal was received with favor, and they started to divide, not only Italy but also the rest of the world into mission-

---

[1] Felten, p. 47.
[2] "minorum ordinem . . . sub limite incerto rogantem novae regulae traditione direxit et informavit informem." *Vita Gregor. IX* (Muratori), III, 75, quoted in Felten, p. 45, note 1.
[3] Cel., *V. pr.*, I, c. XXVII, n. 74.
[4] When Jordanus advances the date of this chapter to 1219 (*Anal. Franc.*, I, p. 2) it is due to one of those failures in memory for which he has already apologized.
[5] *Spec. perf.*, cap. 64.

districts, *Provinces.* The Holy Land was a province in itself, and over it a man was placed, for whom Francis had a great liking, Elias Bombarone.[1] For himself he chose to go to France, "because there, more than in all other Catholic countries, they have the devotion to our Lord's Body."[2] On leaving he held one of his usual sermons of admonition, in which he counselled the Brothers to go about in much silence and inward prayer, "just as if you were in a hermitage or a cell. For wherever we go or stay we have with us a cell. Brother Body is our cell, and the soul sits in it like a hermit and thinks of God and prays to Him."[3]

In the *Fioretti* this journey of Francis to France is described with many additions.[4] What is absolutely definite is that Francis in the latter half of May, 1217, came to Florence, and there sought Cardinal Hugolin.

Thomas of Celano is undoubtedly right when he says that the acquaintance between Francis and Hugolin was as yet not intimate.[5] They had each heard the other praised for goodness and piety and were thus prepared in advance to enter into closer friendship. Hugolin was sent by Honorius III as Papal Legate to Tuscany with the double task of establishing peace between the perpetually contending republics and to preach a crusade.[6] As soon as Francis on his arrival at Florence found out that the Cardinal was there, he sought him out — simply on the principle he followed of always

---

[1] Jordanus a Giano, *Anal. Franc.*, I, p. 4, n. 9. Compare *Anal. Franc.*, III, p. 10.

[2] *Spec. perf.*, cap. 65.

[3] "Frater enim corpus est cella nostra, et anima est eremita qui moratur intus in cella ad orandum Dominum et meditandum de ipso." *Spec. perf.*, Sab. ed., p. 121.

[4] Cap. XIII. *Anal. Franc.*, III, pp. 117 et seq. Francis went to Rome and visited the Apostles' graves, et al.

[5] "Nondum alter alteri erat praecipua familiaritate conjunctus, sed sola fama beatae vitae." Cel., *V. pr.*, I, XXVII, n. 74.

[6] Felten: "*Papst Gregor IX*" (Freib. i Br., 1886), pp. 31–35, p. 42. Compare *Archivio della R. Soc. Romana di Storia Patria*, vol. XII (Roma, 1889), p. 242, and Honorius III's Bull of January 23, 1217 (Potth., I, nr. 5430) and of March 6, 1217 (Potth., I, nr. 5487 and 5488), by which the Pope commends Hugolin's legation to the Church authorities in Lombardy and Tuscany as well as to the authorities of Pisa. In May, 1217, Hugolin stopped for a time in Genoa (*Mon. Germ. SS.*, XVIII, p. 138); thence he went to Florence.

seeking quarters with the clergy, rather than with lay-people.[1] The Cardinal received him with great cordiality, and a conversation began in which Francis lightened his burdened heart, as he had done in former days to Bishop Guido in Assisi. The end was that Francis cast himself at the feet of the reverend prelate and conjured him to take up his and his Brothers' affairs. This Hugolin promised with pleasure, and Francis from now on looked on him as his spiritual father, to whom he showed filial reverence and obedience.

The first effect of this new relation was that Francis abandoned his journey to France. "Brother Francis," said Hugolin, "I do not want you to go over the Alps. For there are many prelates in the Curia at Rome who do not feel well disposed towards you. But I and the other Cardinals, who feel well towards you, can help and protect you better if you do not go too far away."[2] In vain did Francis plead that he could not send his Brothers on missionary journeys to far and dangerous lands, while he stayed home and saved his own skin. The Cardinal was immovable, and Francis had, instead of going himself to France, to send there the "Verse-king," Brother Pacificus, along with many other Brothers.[3]

What now first of all attracted Hugolin and set his organizing spirit at work was the movement which the preaching of the Friars Minor started in the world of women.[4] Francis had taken care himself of Clara and her Sisters by procuring for them the Convent of San Damiano; he had promised to look after them, both in the spiritual and temporal

---

[1] Cel., *V. pr.*, I, XXVII, n. 75. Compare *Tres Socii*, XIV: "Et quando erat hora hospitandi, libentius erant cum sacerdotibus quam cum laicis hujus saeculi." (Amoni's ed., pp. 85-86.)

[2] Francis' earlier friend in the College of Cardinals, John of St. Paulo, Cardinal of S. Prisca and Sabine Bishop, died the year before. (Eubel: *Hierarchia cath. Medii aevi*, I, p. 36, and p. 3, n. 1, nr. 13.) Among the new friends of Francis of Assisi in the College of Cardinals, Leo Brancaleone takes a foremost place. In 1202 he was nominated Cardinal-presbyter with the titular church of S. Croce in Jerusalem. His signature is found on Papal bulls until May 23, 1224 (Eubel, p. 4). Compare *Spec. perf.*, cap. 67. Later (1219) the above mentioned Nicholas Chiaramonti was made cardinal (Eubel p. 37), and Francis had thereby obtained a new friend in the Curia.

[3] *Spec. perf.*, cap. 65.

[4] See pp. 179-180.

sense, as long as he lived.¹ But this promise could not be extended to include all of those who now came and asked for the Brothers to guide them to salvation!

The *Forma vivendi* or Rule of Life, which Francis had given Clara and her Sisters, simply told them to "live after the gospel," that is to say, in poverty, labor, and prayer. After having distributed their possessions to the poor, the Sisters in San Damiano could not again accept any property, either themselves or by an intermediary; the only exception was the convent itself with so much land around it as was required for its isolation. But this land was not to be cultivated, except as a garden for the needs of the Sisters.² This Privilege of Poverty was what Clara, apparently by Francis' intervention, in 1215 had had ratified by Innocent III.³

This was all the rule there was for Clara and her Sisters, and this Rule applied — this we must note well — *only to San Damiano*, for the simple reason that Francis had never thought of the possibility of more convents of the same kind.⁴ Now when there was talk of how to dispose of the many young women who gathered together in all the towns and wished to live a religious life, Hugolin was entirely free.⁵

In the course of the years 1217–1219 we find him therefore busy in establishing the Order which has since come to be called the Clares, but which in the documents of the time is called by the most varying names. Of the highest importance to the understanding of the evolution of the Order of the

---

¹ *Textus originales* (Quar., 1897), p. 92.
² The sisters were advised by Clara to observe their vow of poverty "in non recipiendo vel habendo possessionem vel proprietatem per se neque per interpositam personam . . . nisi quantum terrae pro honestate et remotione monasterii necessitas requirit; et illa terra non laboretur, nisi pro horto ad necessitatem ipsarum." *Reg. S. Clarae*, cap. VI. (*Textus orig.*, pp. 64–65.)
³ *Test. S. Clarae* (*Textus*, p. 277). Compare pp. 130–131.
⁴ "*Ipsis*" (Clara and her sisters) "beatus Franciscus formulam vitae tradidit," Hugolin himself says explicitly (*Bull. Franc.*, I, p. 243).
⁵ I lay great stress on this, like Lempp: "*Die Anfänge des Klarissenordens*," in Brieger's "Zeitschrift f. Kgsch.," XIII, pp. 181–245. Of "violent conduct" on Hugolin's part "against Francis' directions" (p. 243) there can be no reasonable discussion. S. Damiano and the Sisters there cloistered were one thing for Francis, the new convents which were now founded were something different; it was for S. Damiano alone that he had undertaken to care (Wadding, 1219, n. 44: "huius solius curam").

Clares, is a letter of August 27, 1218 from Honorius III to Hugolin. It is an answer to a letter from the Cardinal, in which he had informed the Pope that several maidens and other women wished to flee from the pomps and vanities of the world and to prepare for themselves abiding places where they could live without owning anything, with the exception of these houses and the chapel or church appertaining thereto. Several pieces of land had been offered to Hugolin for this object, and now he asked for full authority to accept these pieces of land in the name of the Church of Rome, so that the convents built thereon would be out of the jurisdiction of the local bishop and directly subject to Rome. Honorius granted this authority in his answer; no other churchly or temporal authority should have anything to say about these convents, and this position of exemption should continue as long as the Sisters affected by it should abide by their vow of poverty.[1]

Even before Hugolin had received this letter, Bishop John of Perugia, July 31, 1218, had given his permission for the erection of a convent for nuns of the above description, upon Monteluce by Perugia. In exchange for his renunciation of his jurisdiction over the convent he exacted only a tribute of a pound of wax to be given every 15th of August.[2] At about the same time Hugolin took steps for the establishment of three exactly similar convents — one in Siena, outside of Porta Camollia, one in Lucca (St. Maria in Gattajola), and finally one in Monticelli near Florence.[3]

At first the only requirement for the religious life in these convents was poverty. It was the Franciscan preaching and the Franciscan life which had drawn these women out of the world and into the convent.

When the problem was to establish a proper Rule for the

[1] Bull *Literae tuae* (Sbaralea, *Bull. Franc.*, I, p. 1): "quamplures virgines et aliae mulieres . . . deciderant fugere pompas et divitias hujus mundi et fabricari sibi aliqua domicilia in quibus vivant nihil possidentes sub coelo, exceptis domiciliis ipsis et construendis oratoriis in eisdem." (Potth., I, 5896.)

[2] Sbar., I, 635-636. The Sisters are there called *Ancillae Christi*. See Honorius III's Bull of September 24, 1222, to "Abbesses and nuns (*monialibus*) in the convent S. Maria of Monteluce," Sbar., I, pp. 13 et seq. (Potth., I, 6879c).

[3] Siena: Sbar., I, p. 11, Potth., I, 6879b; Lucca: Sbar., I, p. 10, Potth., I, 6879a; Florence: Sbar., I, p. 3, Potth., I, 6179.

Order for these new convents, the obvious thing for Hugolin to do was to consult the Lateran Council of 1215 and its *Interdiction of New Orders*. This great assemblage of the Church, taking into consideration the so frequently proposed new Orders and the resulting confusion, determined that for the future no new Rules of an Order should be approved by the Church, but that those who wished to found a new convent or establish a new Order should be instructed to accept one of the old and tested Rules.[1]

One of the first to whom this regulation applied was St. Dominic.[2] According to John of Saxony the Dominicans as well as the Friars Minor were definitely accepted by the Lateran Council, but neither of them obtained Papal sanction of their Rule. Dominic was even told to go home again and talk over with his Brothers as to which of the Rules, already in existence, they would decide to choose.[3] They chose the Premonstratensian Rule, and Honorius ratified this choice, when he explicitly defined the Dominicans as "a canonical Order after the Rule of St. Augustin."[4]

Exactly in the same way Hugolin had to proceed in the case of the nuns of St. Clare. As Dominic chose the Premonstratensian Rule for himself and his associates, Cardinal Hugolin now chose for the Franciscan Sisters the oldest and most respected of all the Rules of Orders of the West — the Rule of the Benedictines. What Francis expressly stood by

---

[1] "Ne nimia religionum diversitas gravem in ecclesia Dei confusionem inducat, firmiter prohibemus, ne quis de cetero novam religionem inveniat; sed quicumque voluerit ad religionem converti, unam de approbatis assumat. Similiter qui voluerit religiosam domum fundare de novo, regulam et institutionem accipiat de religionibus approbatis." (*A. SS.*, Oct. II. p. 604, n. 308. Labbe, XI, col. 165 and 168).

[2] Bierfreund's assertion in the first volume of his book on Florence, where he says that Dominic was the Pope's and Curia's great friend and obtained all the privileges he wanted, in distinction to Francis, is quite without ground. See *A. SS.*, Aug. 1, pp. 437 et seq.,

[3] "In quo concilio ordines fratrum prædicatorum et minorum, qui tunc recenter surrexerunt . . . recepti sunt, sed nondum confirmati; quia idem Innocentius ad eorum confirmationem durus fuit." *Vitae fratrum* 1., I, c. XIV (*A. SS.*, p. 604, n. 310).

[4] "ordo canonicus secundum beati Augustini regulam." Honorius III, Bull of December 22, 1216 (Potth., I, 5403). Echard therefore says also: "non tam ordinem novum erexit [Honorius] quam ordinem canonicum auxit in apostolicum" (*A. SS.*, Aug. 1, p. 458, n. 416).

SAINT FRANCIS OF ASSISI

as an inevitable basic principle, that the evangelical poverty must not be impaired, Hugolin adhered to accurately; not once could the Sisters acquire ownership of the ground on which the convents were built; they belonged to Hugolin in the name of the Church. In exactly the same spirit Francis had not wished to own Portiuncula, but continued to regard the land as belonging to the Benedictines, and to pay them a yearly rent for it.[1]

[1] *Spec. perf.*, cap. 55 (Sab. ed., p. 98). It is here clearly stated that Francis did not wish the Brothers to dwell in a place, which was not "subtus dominio aliquorum." Therefore Portiuncula is named even in 1244 in a document as belonging to the Abbey on Monte Subasio (Sab. ditto, p. 269). Not Hugolin, as Lempp would have it, but Francis himself introduced this difference between *dominium* and *usus*, ownership and use.

Lempp seems in his article to ascribe a singular meaning to the fact that Hugolin had a forest made over to the Sisters in Gattajola; he thinks that this must have involved a breach of their poverty brought about by Hugolin, because it was a source of revenue for them. In the same way the great Benedictine abbeys owned forests, pastures, lakes, etc. From the Bull in question it is clear that the requisite forest only is referred to, because the whole piece was covered with trees. The woods were cut down when the convent was built. ("Ostiensis episcopus a Rolandino Volpelli cive Lucanensi *silvam quamdam* quam habebat in loco, qui Gattajola dicitur . . . nostro nomine recepisset; et in *monasterio ibi constructo*," Honorius III writes. Sbaralea, I, p. 10.) Lempp admits that the Clares might own a convent with chapel. These could not float in the air, but the principle of poverty is preserved by having the title to the land stand in some one else's name (in this case the Roman throne). This was quite in Francis' spirit, and Lempp has gone wrong when he ("Zeitsch. f. Kgsh.," XXIII, pp. 626–629) declares categorically that this ordinance was something quite different from what Francis and Clara desired. (See also Lemmens in "Römische Quartalschrift," XVI, pp. 93–124.)

Lempp again goes wrong when he (ditto, p. 628), as proof that the convent of the Clares, erected with Hugolin's approval, really owned nothing in the old monastic and anti-Franciscan sense of the word, quotes Honorius' Bull of December 9, 1219 to the Clares in Monticelli. It reads: "Praeterea locum vestrum et ea quae in ipsius circuitu juste ac canonice possidetis, vobis . . . confirmamus. Ad praestationem" (read: a praestatione) "decimarum clausurae vestrae et de hortorum fructibus vos esse decernimus immunes." (Sbar., I, p. 4.) The Sisters in Lucca are similarly addressed in a bull ("locum vestrum cum omnibus pertinentiis suis et omnia, quae juste et canonice possidetis." Sbar., p. 11) as are those in Monteluce (p. 14).

Two things here are important, which Lempp entirely overlooks: (*a*) *locum* means in the older Franciscan terminology always a convent, and by "quae in ipsius circuitu" or "pertinentia" there is not meant the possession of surrounding lands, but of outhouses and the like belonging to the convent; (*b*) the Pope adopts in all three Bulls the expression "juste ac canonice." But *rightly and canonically* the Clares could own nothing except *domicilia* and *oratoria* (Bull of August 27, 1218). Finally, regarding the freedom from tithes for the fruits of

The outlines of the Rule of Life of the Clares was in accordance with that of St. Benedict. They were not bound literally to this Rule — as Innocent IV expressly declared at a later period[1] — they were only in general obliged to lead a life based on obedience, poverty and chastity. To this were added many rigid rules of cloister. The cloister could be entered by no stranger, and the active care of the sick, which, according to Jacques de Vitry, the Sisters were to have practised, must now in every case cease.[2] It is certainly Francis who wished the rigid cloistering for preventing the meeting of his Brothers and the nuns; Hugolin is said nevertheless to have wept from sympathy when he, with Francis, wrote down this requirement.[3] After Francis' death he modified several of the most rigid of the observances.[4]

After 1219 the Clares lived after the Rule of St. Benedict, but with the addition of the so-called "Observances of St. Damian."[5] In these last it is permissible to see with some degree of confidence the *forma vivendi* which Francis in his time had given Clara, and which now was put into the second position, but was by no means inoperative.[6] The core of these observances (*observantiae*) was presumably the privilegium of poverty, which Clara, after the custom of the

their garden, granted to the Sisters, and in which Lempp seems to see an indication of a definite ownership of the ground, the cultivation of the garden, with the uses of the convent always in view, was the only use of the ground Clara allowed. (*Textus originales*, p. 64.)

[1] Sbar., I, pp. 315 and 350.
[2] Boehmer, "*Analekten*," p. 98. *Actus b. Francisci*, cap. XLIII at end.
[3] "Hoc audivi ab antiquis patribus quod ipse" [Hugolin] "cum beato Francisco . . . ordinaverunt et scripserunt regulam sororum ordinis S. Damiani . . . propter cujus regulae arctitudinem partim devotione, partim compassione cardinalis ipse perfundebatur multis lacrymis in scribendo." (*Anal. Fr.*, III, p. 708.)
[4] Sbar., I, p. 101, p. 213, p. 215, p. 240.
[5] "Observantias nihilominus regulares, quas juxta ordinem dominarum sanctae Mariae de sancto Damiano de Assisio praeter generalem beati Benedicti regulam vobis voluntarie indixistis." Sbaralea, I, p. 4.
[6] For this must be thus understood, when Gregory IX, May 11, 1238, announced to the prioress of the Clares, Agnes of Bohemia, that Francis' *formula vitae*, after the Rule of St. Benedict was introduced, must be regarded as "postposita" (Sbar., I, p. 243). Francis, moreover, had not given out this rule of life publicly all at once, but after his habit in instalments ("*plura scripta* tradidit nobis," says Clara therefore. *Text. orig.*, p. 276).

time, tried to have confirmed on the accession of each new pope.

As long as Francis lived there was no complete new Rule given to the Sisters in San Damiano or to the community of Poor Clares in general. It was only after the death of Francis that Gregory IX tried to introduce modifications, first of all in the Regulation of Poverty. "On account of the unfavorable times" it might be well to own a little land, on which the convent could be firmly founded, instead of depending entirely on begging. These views of his he also brought to the attention of Clara, but was (see pp. 136, 137) definitely refused. On September 17, 1228 Clara obtained from Gregory — as she had from his predecessor — the privilege of poverty.[1] The Clares in Perugia had their privilege renewed June 16, 1229, and Clara's sister, Agnes, obtained the same for her convent of Monticelli, near Florence.[2]

Other convents were less constant, however. Many of them in this very year had the right of ownership granted by Gregory, and not only the right of usufruct, but of inheriting and owning.[3]

This defection filled Clara with anxiety and sorrow. As long as she lived, San Damiano would remain "the fortified tower of supreme poverty." But how was it to be when she was gone?

Thence came her ardor for replacing the Benedictine Rule and its proportion of the privilege of poverty with a completely new, real Franciscan Rule of the Order. There can be no doubt that she herself wrote it and that it was the one which Innocent IV ratified two days before her death.[4]

This Rule is, as far as possible, modelled on the Franciscan Rule. Like it, it is divided into twelve chapters, each of

---

[1] *Textus orig.*, p. 97. The original is still preserved in Assisi.

[2] Perugia: Sbar., I, p. 50. Monticelli: *Analecta Franc.*, III, p. 176 (letter from St. Agnes to her sister: "Inter haec sciatis, quod dominus papa satisfecit mihi . . . secundum intentionem vestram, et meam de causa, quam scitis, de facto videlicet proprii").

[3] In these cases it reads "vobis et per vos monasterio vestro concedimus et donamus." Sbar., I, 73. Bull of July 18, 1231. Compare Lemmens (as before), p. 107.

[4] See p. 136.

them not greatly differing from Hugolin's and Francis' Rule of 1219. But the point on which Clara's Rule is based is in the very first place the obligation of poverty. As she came to this section she ceased to be the impersonal lawgiver and began to speak from her heart.

"After the Heavenly Father," she writes, " had enlightened my heart with His grace, and had led me in the model of our most holy Father Francis on the way of penance, shortly after his own conversion, then I and my Sisters promised him willing obedience."

And as she turned her thoughts to these times, now so remote, when she first said good-bye to the world, one recollection after another pressed upon her. She remembered so many words that came from the mouth of the dear teacher and guide addressed to the honor of his Lady, the noble Lady Poverty, and wrote them down. And with strong hand she impressed the sentence, in which the ideal claim appears on record in all its rigor beyond all appeal:

"The Sisters shall own neither house nor convent nor anything, but as strangers and pilgrims shall wander through this world, serving the Lord in poverty and humility."

Under these words, as Clara was closing her eyes in death, Innocent set the inviolable seal of Rome.[1]

---

[1] *Reg. S. Clarae*, cap. VIII, compare cap. VI (*Textus*, p. 65 and pp. 62–63), in which Clara concedes "as much earth as is necessary for the isolation of the convent" and for a garden. Not all of the Clares accepted the Rule of August 9, 1253. Many continued to live after the version of Hugolin of 1247, confirmed by Innocent IV and in some particulars modified. (See the Bull in question in Sbaralea, I, p. 476, Potth., II, nr. 12635.)

CHAPTER VI

THE MISSIONARIES

WHILE Francis, together with Hugolin, was engaged with internal affairs of the Order, the missionaries of the Chapter of 1217 were gone each in his own direction. None of them had much success with it. Those who went to France were asked if they were Albigenses, and when they, not understanding the question, answered "Yes," they were treated accordingly; for Albigenses were heretics. The German mission went no better. It was a troop of sixty Brothers under the lead of John of Penna. They too were ignorant of the language of the country, but they had learned the word "Ja" (Yes). As they, by constantly using this as an answer to the questions addressed to them, obtained food and drink and lodging, they kept on using the magic word. But now it went wrong, for as they also answered "Ja" to the question if they were heretics, they were cast into prison, put in the stocks, and maltreated in other ways. In Hungary no better fortune awaited the Brothers; the peasants set their dogs on them and the pig-herds ran after them with their long sticks. "Why do they torment us so?" the Brothers asked each other in vain, and one of them thought that it might be that the Hungarians wanted their cloaks. Then they gave their tormentors their cloaks, but that did not help. Remembering the words of the gospel, they gave them next their robe. But even this did not satisfy the Hungarians. "Let us in God's name give them our breeches too," the patient Brothers said, and now they were permitted to go on naked. One of the Brothers had the fortune in this way — as we are told by John of Giano — to part with his breeches six times. At last they hit upon the plan of smearing their breeches with cow-dung, so that the peasants would not want them.[1]

All these Job's torments naturally filled Francis with care and disquiet. It was probably at this time that he is said to have had the following dream. He saw a little black hen and around it a whole flock of little chickens were running and chirping — so many were the chickens that the poor hen could not get them all under her wings. "The hen is I," he said to himself, as he awakened. "I am small and black, and it is evident that I cannot take care of my sons."[2] More than ever it was made clear to him that he must make over the care of his Order to the Church. This made it easy for Hugolin to persuade him to go to Rome and have an audience with the Pope. This probably occurred in the winter of 1217-1218; we know that in the interval between December 5, 1217 and April 7 of the next year Hugolin was in Rome.[3]

On this occasion the Cardinal seems to have had his doubts as to the impression which Francis would make upon the new Pope and his entire Curia. He had therefore persuaded him in preparation to study a speech, but when Francis started to say it he found that he had forgotten every word of it. This often happened to him; on such occasions he used to say to his audiences, at once, how it was, and he often would then speak much better than if he had given the discourse he had studied. If he found that he could say nothing, he would give the people his blessing and let them go.[4]

And so it happened as he stood before the Pope. Without being frightened, Francis knelt down at once and asked for his blessing. He then spoke and got into so ecstatic a mood that at last he began to move his feet in rhythmic movement, like David before the ark.[5] So far from finding this laughable,

---

[1] *Anal. Fr.*, I, p. 3 and p. 7. [2] *Tres Socii*, cap. XVI.

[3] Potth. I, nrs. 5629-5747. That this was Francis' *first* audience with Honorius III follows from the authorities — Hugolin was disturbed about Francis' ways and feared that he would cut a poor figure. (Cel., *V. pr.*, I, XXVII, n. 73: "episcopus Hostiensis timore suspensus est . . . ne beati viri contemneretur simplicitas.") For this he had no ground if Francis already a 1216 had stood before Honorius with authority as God's messenger and, so to say, had forced from him the Portiuncula indulgence.

[4] Cel., *V. pr.*, I, n. 73. Bonav., XII, 7.

[5] Cel., *V. pr.*, same place. *Tres Socii*, cap. XVI.

the Pope and Cardinals were deeply impressed by the remarkable man, and when Francis at last begged that Cardinal Hugolin might be made the special protector of the Order, the request was acceded to.

During his stay in Rome Francis made the acquaintance of St. Dominic; Hugolin brought them together. The Spanish founder of the great Order was seized with the greatest and most sincere admiration for the little barefooted Poor Man of God from Assisi. "Let us melt our Orders into one," he said to him, and as Francis would not accede, Dominic begged of him at least as a memorial the rope he wore around his waist. Soon after the two founders were to meet again at Portiuncula, and one year before Dominic's death they met once more in Rome. It was on this last occasion — in the winter of 1220-1221 — that Hugolin, with a reform of the clergy in mind, proposed to Francis and Dominic to have the higher ranks of the clergy filled with men of the two new Orders. Both Dominic and Francis refused to enter into such an arrangement. "My Brothers are *minores*, let them not become *majores*," was the rejoinder.[1] It was under the influence of Francis that Dominic, at the Pentecost Chapter, held in Bologna in 1220, introduced incapacity of ownership into his Order (only in 1218 he had sought Papal approbation of the possessions belonging to the Order), and on his deathbed he pronounced his curse on all who would impair his Brothers' evangelical poverty.[2]

In the year 1218 there was held the first Pentecost Chapter, at which Hugolin was present as the Order's protector. The Brothers met him in solemn procession and Hugolin dismounted from his steed, took off his fine clothes, and walked barefoot, and clad in the Franciscan habit, to Portiuncula. Here he sang mass in the little chapel, while Francis officiated as deacon and read the gospel. It may have been at the same Chapter that Hugolin afterwards helped the Brothers wash the feet of some paupers. Foot-washing here was more than

---

[1] *Spec. perf.*, c. 43. Cel., *V. sec.*, III, c. 86-87. Bernard a Bessa, *Anal. Franc.* III, p. 675.

[2] Jean Guiraud: *Saint Dominique* (Paris, 1901), pp. 164-168, p. 189. Dominicus died August 6, 1221.

a ceremony, and when the Cardinal did not succeed in getting the dirt off this particular beggar's feet, the beggar said angrily, without suspecting in the humble Brother waiting upon him the great Prince of the Church, "Go on your way, and let some one come that understands this!"

As already said, Dominic had seized the chance to again meet Francis; he found him in the Cardinal's suite. What he saw at the Chapter must have deeply impressed him. "For among so many men, none was heard to gossip or to speak unbecomingly, but wherever there was a group of Brothers assembled, they either prayed or said their Office or wept over their sins or over the sins of their benefactors. . . . And their beds were the naked earth, but some had also a little straw, and the pillow was either a stone or a piece of a tree. . . . And St. Francis said to his Brothers: 'In the name of holy obedience I bid you all who are here assembled, that none of you shall be concerned about what you shall eat, or what you shall drink, or what your bodies need, but think only of praying and praising God and leave to Him the whole care of your bodily welfare, for He will take care of you!' But St. Dominic, who was present all the time, wondered over the message Francis had given out and thought that he had borne himself very unreasonably, because, where so great a number of men were assembled, he asked that none should give attention to the things which are necessary for the body. . . . But the Lord Jesus Christ wanted to show that He loved His Poor with special love, and at once inspired the people in Perugia, in Foligno, in Spello, in Assisi and in the other towns in the vicinity to bring the holy assemblage both food and drink. And behold, at once men came from all these towns with asses, mules and horses loaded with bread, with fruit and with other good things to eat. . . . And besides they came with tablecloths, pots, dishes and cups and other such things, both large and small, which so large a crowd of men would require. And the more anyone was able to bring the Brothers, . . . the luckier he considered himself."[1]

[1] *Fior.*, c. 18 (*Actus*, c. XX). Compare *Tres Socii*, cap. XV, p. 88, Amoni's ed., Cel., *V. pr.*, II, V, n. 100, and Philip of Perugia's letter of 1305 to the General of the Order, Gonsalvo, in *Anal. Franc.*, III, p. 709.

In fact the generosity of the inhabitants of the vicinity at the time of these meetings was very great. Jordanus of Giano tells of a Chapter, at which he was present, where they had to remain two days over the time at the place to get all eaten up which was brought them.[1]

At the Pentecost Chapter of the next year (May 26, 1219) it was decided to again take up the mission work which two years before had failed so badly. Hugolin had employed the interval in preparing the way for the Brothers by sending out letters of introduction for them to the various regions whither they were going; he undertook to answer for them to the Bishops and declared them to be good Catholic men, who rejoiced in the approval of the Apostolic throne and who could be safely permitted to preach everywhere.[2] Then at the right moment — June 11, 1219 — came the document from the highest church authority, which it was Hugolin's fortune to have obtained: Pope Honorius' Letter of Commendation for the Brothers, addressed to all "Archbishops, Bishops, Abbots, Deacons, Archdeacons and other prelates" whom the Brothers might meet. The bearer of the Letter is declared in this Papal brief to be a good Catholic, who sows God's seed after the example of the Apostles and whose way of life is approved by the Holy See.[3] Armed with copies of this document and with Francis' permission to receive new Brothers into the Order, the missionary leaders went off each at the head of his little band.[4]

This time no missionaries were sent to Germany, so great was the Brothers' fear of the prisons and stocks of the Teutons. On the other hand Brother Giles and Brother Electus went to Tunis, Brother Benedict of Arezzo to Greece, Pacificus went back to France, and a small selected band undertook to carry out Francis' old plan and go to the miramolin of Morocco.

[1] *Anal. Franc.*, I, p. 6, n. 16.
[2] *Tres Socii*, cap. XVI, p. 94, Amoni's ed.
[3] Bull *Cum Dilecti*, Sbar., I, p. 2 (Potth., I, n. 608). A new bull, especially addressed to the French prelates, in whose dioceses the heretics were most prevalent, was published March 29, 1219. Sbar., I, p. 5. Potth., I, 6263.
[4] When it is said in the *Tres Socii*, p. 94, Amoni's ed., that the missionaries bore with them "litteras Cardinalis" "*regula bulla apostolica confirmata*," the Papal recommendation is meant.

The mission to Tunis had a sad end. Giles and his companion were put on board a ship by force, to be taken away. This was done by the Christians of the place, who were afraid that the presence of the missionaries would result in difficulties with the Mussulmen. And Brother Electus, who had just separated from the others, soon suffered martyrdom, which he accepted kneeling, with the Rule in his clasped hands, declaring his accountability for all the sins he might have committed during his life in the Order.[1]

Francis embraced with great affection the Brothers who were going to the miramolin. Their names were Vitale, Berardo, Peter, Adjuto, Accursorio and Otto. Before sending them Francis addressed them, and according to an old account his words were these:

"'My sons! God has ordered me to send you to the land of the Saracens to announce and make known there His faith and to combat the law of Mohammed. . . . Prepare yourselves, therefore, to fulfil the will of the Lord!' But they bowed their heads and said, 'Father, we are ready to obey thee in all things.' But Francis was rejoiced greatly over such complete obedience and said with love to them: 'Dearest sons, so that you can better fulfil God's command, see to it that there is peace and unity and indissoluble charity among you. Envy no one, for envy is the occasion of sin. Be patient in tribulations, be humble if all goes well with you. Copy Christ in poverty, obedience and chastity. For the Lord Jesus Christ was born poor, lived in poverty, taught poverty and died in poverty. And to show that He loved chastity, He wished to be born of a virgin, followed and counselled virginity and died surrounded by virgins. And He was obedient from His birth to His death, yes to His death on the Cross. Hope in God alone, He guides and helps us. Carry with you the Rule and the Breviary, and pray with completeness at the holy times. And all of you obey your great Brother Vitale. O my sons, well do I rejoice over your good will, but that I shall be separated from you, that grieves me in my heart. But the command of God must be obeyed

[1] Egidio (Giles): *A. SS.*, April III, p. 224. *Anal. Franc.*, III, p. 78. Electus: *Spec. perf.*, cap. 77. Cel., *Vita sec.*, III, 135. *Anal. Franc.*, III, p. 224.

rather than our will. And this I beg of you, that you may always have the sufferings of our Lord before your eyes, that will strengthen you and inspire you to suffer for Him!'

"Then these holy Brothers answered: 'Father, send us where thou wilt, for we are ready to do thy will. But you, father, help us with thy prayers to fulfil thy commands. For we are young and have never been out of Italy, and the people we go to we know not, but we know that they rage against the Christians, and we are ignorant and cannot speak Arabic. And when they see us in such poor raiment and with the rope, they will ridicule us as crazy men and will not listen to us; therefore we greatly need thy prayers. Ah, good father, shall we really be separated from thee: How shall we be able to do God's will without thee?'

"But St. Francis was greatly overcome, and with great power he said: 'Depend on God, my sons! He, who sends you, will also give you power and will help you, as that is His good pleasure!' Then all six fell on their knees and kissed his hand with many tears and asked for his blessing. And St. Francis wept also and lifted up his eyes to heaven and blessed them and said: 'The blessing of God the Father come upon you, as it came upon the Apostles; may He strengthen and lead you and comfort you in your troubles. And fear not, for the Lord is with you and will fight for you.'"[1]

This narration may in some particulars be more or less historic; one realizes at any rate an impressive conception of the relations between Francis and his Brothers. And then the six young missionaries went away — in accordance with the precept of the Bible, without staff or sack, without shoes on the feet, without silver and gold in their belts. Their way took them through Aragon — where Vitale fell sick and had to be left after them — through Castile and Portugal. Two years before this the Friars Minor had been in Portugal; King Alfonso's pious sister Sancia had received them in a friendly way, had given them a little chapel in Alenquer and had a house built for them. Soon after the queen, Urraca,

[1] "Qualiter beatus Franciscus eos misit Marochium" (*Anal. Franc.*, III, pp. 581-582. After a manuscript of the end of the fourteenth century. Compare pp. 15 et seq.).

gave them a convent in the vicinity of Coimbra. The five missionaries took their departure hence for Seville, which was then under Mohammedan control.

On arriving at Seville they began to preach outside the principal mosque of the city, and were at once seized and brought before the authorities. The miramolin, who resided in Morocco, was at this time Abu Jacob. After the defeat his father Mohammed el Nasir had suffered in 1212 at Tolosa, he was not inclined to displease the Christians, and by so much the less as he had at the head of his army a Christian leader, Dom Pedro, Infanta of Portugal, who because of discord with his brother, the reigning king, had accepted Mohammedan employment. Abu Jacob seems on the whole to have been a peaceful soul; his greatest enjoyment was to play shepherd and to drive personally his flock to the pasture. When the five Franciscans from Seville were sent to him, so that he could determine their fate, he seems to have had most pleasure in letting them go. In any case they were not cast by him into prison, but he let them live with their co-religionist, Dom Pedro.

The Brothers utilized this freedom now to preach in the markets and streets. They had learned a little Arabic, especially Berardo, who was leader of the band of missionaries. It happened that one day the miramolin, who was riding to his father's grave outside the city, passed by a place where Berardo stood and preached from a wagon. He ordered thereupon that the five Brothers should not be punished, but sent home to the Christian land.

The carrying out of this order was entrusted to Dom Pedro, who sent the five missionaries to Ceuta under guard, whence they were to sail home. Instead the Brothers turned about and went back to Morocco and began to preach again. Now the miramolin put them into prison, but set them free again, whereupon they were again taken to Ceuta, when they again, just as before, returned to Morocco. Dom Pedro took them with him on a warlike expedition into the interior of the country; both he and the other Christians living in the capital feared that the missionary activities of the Brothers would result in a persecution of the Christians. Accordingly after his return from this raid Dom Pedro had the Brothers carefully watched, but when they, one Friday, saw the chance to escape — this being the Mohammedan weekly holiday — and started to preach, where they knew that the miramolin would pass by, they could no longer be saved. After fearful torture — among other tortures they were rolled naked back and forth a whole night on a bed of broken glass — and after a hearing, where their answers remind us of the first martyrs before the Roman judges, they managed to arouse Abu Jacob's fury, so that he rose up and himself beheaded the five martyrs with his own hand. Dom Pedro saw to it that their lifeless bodies were taken to Coimbra, where Queen Urraca, at the head of the entire populace, went to meet the martyrs and laid them in the Church of Santa Cruz.[1]

The announcement of the deaths of these five martyrs was read at the Pentecost Chapter of 1221 — it was on January 16 of the preceding year that they suffered martyrdom — and Francis thereupon cried out, "Now I can truly say that I have five real Brothers."[2] When we think of his deep reverence for the crown of martyrdom, such an utterance from his mouth is quite credible.[3] According to another source he is said to have forbidden the reading of the account of the sufferings of the Brothers. "Let every one exult in his own martyrdom and not in that of others," he is said to have commanded, as he thought of the Brothers' pride in now having five martyrs in the Order.[4]

Be this as it may, it is beyond all doubt that Francis at this time himself went forth to win martyrdom. As early as 1218 he had sent Brother Elias away as a missionary to the Holy Land, and Elias had here, among others, received

---

[1] *Anal. Franc.*, III, pp. 583-593. A shorter version in Karl Müller: "*Die Anfänge des Minoritenordens*," pp. 207-210, and in *Anal. Franc.*, III, pp. 15-21.

[2] *Anal. Franc.*, III, 21.

[3] Compare his words in Celano, *Vita sec.*, II, 112 (d'Alençon's ed.): "Summam (obedientiam) . . . illam esse credebat, qua divina inspiratione inter infideles itur, sive ob proximorum lucrum, *sive ob martyrii desiderium*. Hanc vero petere multum Deo iudicabat acceptum."

[4] Jordanus, n. 8 (*Anal. Franc.*, I, p. 3). Jordanus himself was one of those who thus would be proud of what others had undergone — see his candid avowal same place, n. 18 (p. 7).

the first German into the Order — the learned, far-travelled clerk, Cæsarius of Speier.[1] In the summer of 1219 a strong attack was to be made on Egypt by the Crusaders by order of Honorius III. Francis decided in his own way to participate in this Holy War. After having placed Brother Matthew of Narni as his vicar in Portiuncula, where he was to remain and put the habit of the Order on the new Brothers, and appointed Brother Gregory of Naples as his vicar for the rest of Italy, Francis started for the Holy Land in company with his old friend Peter of Cattani.[2]

[1] *Anal. Franc.*, I, p. 4 (Jordanus, n. 9).
[2] "Matthaeum vero instituit ad S. Mariam de Portiuncula, ut ibi manens recipiendos ad ordinem reciperet, Gregorium autem, ut circumeundo Italiam fratres consolaretur." (Jordanus, n. 11. *Anal. Franc.*, I, p. 4.)

CHAPTER VII

THE FOREIGN MISSIONS AND THE CHAPTER OF MATS

THE Brothers who from love of Christ go to the heathen may act in two ways with them. The first way is, not to quarrel or dispute with words, but for the sake of God to be subject to all creatures and thus to let it be known that they are Christians. The other way is, that they, when they see that it pleases the Lord, shall announce the word of God and summon all to believe in God the Father, Son and Holy Ghost, and to let themselves be baptized and become Christians. And the Brothers must remember that they have given up themselves and their bodies to our Lord Jesus Christ, and that they, for love to Him, must not yield either to visible or invisible foes; for the Lord says, 'He that shall lose his life for my sake, shall save it!'"[1]

It is certain that it was with such feelings as these that Francis and his companion, Pietro dei Cattani, on St. John's Day, 1219, embarked on the Crusaders' fleet, sailed out of the harbor of Ancona and saw Italy disappearing behind them. The journey by sea to the Holy Land used then to last a month. At last in July, Francis went ashore at St. Jean d'Acre, where he was probably met by Brother Elias. Possibly Francis had brought some Brothers with him from Europe — the story about Brother Barbarus located in Cyprus points to this conclusion.[2] It may be that a number of the Brothers joined him in St. Jean d'Acre and followed him to the Crusaders' army, which lay before Damietta in Egypt.

[1] From *Legenda antiqua* (Sab., *Opusc. de critique*, I, pp. 102-105). Compare *Reg. sec.*, cap. XII.
[2] Cel., *Vit. sec.*, II, 115 (ed. d'Alençon).

The siege of this strong place had already lasted a long time (since May, 1218), and the end was not in sight. Nearly every day there was a new fight; just before Francis' arrival, namely, July 29, 1219, there had been a great battle, in which two thousand Saracens had bitten the dust. On July 31 the Crusaders accordingly ventured upon an attack by storm upon Damietta, but were beaten back with great loss by the Mussulmans under the two brave and able leaders, Melek el Kamel, sultan of Egypt, and his brother the sultan of Damascus, Melek el Moaddem, called Conrad by the Christians.

At first Francis found a large enough field of work in the army of the Crusaders. The Christian camp was very low in point of morals, and after the Crusaders' new, great defeat of August 29, where five thousand men were left upon the field, their minds were inclined to listen to Francis' preaching of conversion. Of the effect of this preaching Jacques de Vitry writes in his letter from Damietta to friends at home:

"Rainer, the Prior of St. Michael" (in St. Jean d'Acre) "has gone over into the Order of Friars Minor, which is spreading greatly over the whole world, because they so closely follow the life of the first Christians' congregations and on the whole of the Apostles. . . . Also my clerk Colinus the Englishman, and two other of my companions, namely Master Michael and Lord Matthews, to whom I had handed over the care of souls at the church of the Holy Cross" (also in St. Jean d'Acre), "and it is with the greatest difficulty that I can keep the cantor and Henryk and the others back."[1]

First of all Francis was attracted here to get an opportunity at last to put into practice his long-cherished dream — to come to stand face to face with the heathen and declare God's word to them. After the great defeat peace negotiations were commenced, and Francis may have taken advantage of this opportunity to visit Melek el Kamel with a single Brother

---

[1] Böhmer: "*Analekten,*" pp. 101-102. Wadding, 1219, n. 63. In my "Appendix," p. —, I have said that this letter was written in August, 1219. Sabatier (*Vie,* p. 122) places its date in November, 1219, immediately after the capture of Damietta (November 5); Böhmer ("*Anal.,*" p. 101) places it in March, 1220. The value of the letter as proof is equally great in either case. — Compare Cel., *Vita sec.*, II, 4. (Francis foretells the defeat of the Christians.)

— Bonaventure names Illuminato. On reaching the Saracen's outposts the two Friars Minor were not received particularly well, but Francis, by continually calling out, *Soldan! Soldan!* managed to induce them to bring them before the Ruler of the Faithful. He seems not to have taken their discourse unfavorably, but sent the daring evangelist away in peace with the words, "Pray for me, that God may reveal to me which faith is the most pleasing to Him!" According to Jacques de Vitry, Francis preached several days more in the Mussulman camp, but without great results.[1]

We do not know how long Francis stayed with the Crusaders' army. Damietta fell on November 5, 1220, and a sack of the town began, so wild and savage that it must have filled the mild evangelist with grief and horror. Is it not conceivable that he shook the dust from his feet and went off to visit the holy places, which were now so near and which must have exercised an irresistible force of attraction over him? How could he, Francis, have passed Christmas, 1220 better than in Bethlehem? Where the feast of the Annunciation of the Blessed Virgin the next year better than in Nazareth, and where could he have passed Good Friday and Easter better than in Jerusalem, in the Garden of Gethsemane and on Golgotha? His biographers are entirely silent about this time in his life, but when after his return home we find him keeping Christmas at the crib in Greccio, we can see in it a commemoration of a Christmas night in the real Bethlehem; and that which happened in La Verna, when the wounds of Christ were imprinted on his body, was that anything else than the completion of what he had already felt two years

---

[1] Jacques de Vitry in *Historia Occidentalis*, lib. II, c. 32 (Böhmer, pp. 104-105), and in the letter of 1219 (1220), (pp. 101-102). Jordanus, n. 10 (*Anal. Franc.*, I, 4). Compare Thomas of Celano, *Vita prima*, I, c. XX, Bonaventure, IX, 8, and *Actus*, cap. 27, in which we find it said: "Et dedit illis" (Soldanus) "quoddam signaculum quo viso a nemine laedebantur." The French orientalist Riant concludes from this and similar testimony that Francis must have received from the Sultan a letter of protection for himself and his Brothers, similar to the firmans which afterwards were issued for the Franciscans (first by Zaher Bibars I, 1260-1277). This should explain why the Pope preferred to use Friars Minor as ambassadors to the Mussulman ruler. In 1244 a Franciscan ambassador was sent by the sultan of Egypt to Pope Innocent IV. See Golubovitch in *Luce e Amore*, II (Florence, 1905), pp. 498-501.

earlier, kneeling on a Good Friday in the actual Place of Skulls (Golgotha)?

In this pilgrimage Francis was interrupted by a messenger from Italy, who brought bad news. It was a lay-brother by the name of Stephen, who without any order from his superior had gone on his way to the Holy Land to tell Francis what was going on at home during his absence in the Holy Land. What he had to tell was certainly very disquieting and showed Francis again how hard it was to guide so large a body, in which, as Jacques de Vitry rightly remarks, "not only the perfect, but also the young and imperfect, can find a reception without any preliminary trial or practice in the discipline of the convent."[1] At first his two vicars, Gregory of Naples and Matthew of Narni, together with the older Brothers in the Order (*fratres seniores*), at a Chapter, held probably on St. Michael's Day, 1219, had adopted a new explicit regulation of Fasts, of which there was no trace in the Rules of the Order.[2] Then Brother Philip, in his function as superior for the Clares, had been in Rome and sought to obtain that all who insulted these, his wards, should be excommunicated. Finally, Brother John of Capella gathered a whole crowd of lepers about him, gave them a Rule and thus wished to establish a new Order; he had even gone to the Pope to get his Rule ratified.[3]

Francis was sitting at the table, along with Peter of Cattani, when Brother Stephen came with his bad tidings — meat was already on the table, although it was one of the days on which by the new Rule meat should not be eaten. With a glance at the food, Francis asked:

"Lord Peter" (for Francis always called him "Lord" as a tribute to his learning), "Lord Peter, what are we to do now?"

"*Eh*," answered Brother Peter, with a real Italian inter-

---

[1] Böhmer, "*Analekten*," p. 101.

[2] This ordained fasting only on Wednesdays and Fridays, except for the fasts of the Church. The Brothers could by Francis' permission fast also on Mondays and Thursdays (Jordanus, n. 11).

[3] Lempp believes, curiously enough, that John of Capella's Order consisted exclusively of married people (*gens mariés*), and identifies it with the later Third Order! (*Frère Élie de Cortone*, Paris, 1901, pp. 42–43.)

jection, "*Eh*, Lord Francis, whatever you say, — for you have the power!"

"Then let us," answered Francis, "in accordance with the holy gospel, eat what is set before us!"[1]

Not only the prescriptions for fasting were repugnant to Francis, as against the gospel, and as impossible to keep in observance by an order of wandering preachers, but it disturbed him profoundly that no less than two of his disciples had dared to do what he was most opposed to — to plague the Roman throne about privileges.[2] He, who in his Rule had even obliged the Brothers to vacate their convent as soon as anyone wanted to take it from them,[3] must now yield to having the Clares protected by a Bull of Excommunication.[4] It was time for him to enter into affairs as quickly as possible, and Francis hurried back to Italy in company with Peter of Cattani, Elias of Cortona, Cæsarius of Speier and other Brothers.

They seem to have arrived the last of the summer, and at once went to Hugolin. By his influence the proposals of both Brother Philip as well as of Brother John of Capella were disapproved by the Holy See, and Francis called together thereupon a Chapter of the Order at Portiuncula for Pentecost, 1221.

---

[1] Luke x. 8. This entire description is found in all its details in Jordanus of Giano (*Anal. Franc.*, I, pp. 4–5).

[2] Even in his Testament he forbids this in the strongest terms (*Opusc.*, p. 80).

[3] *Reg. pr.*, cap. VII: "*nullum locum . . . alicui defendant.*"

[4] Also that a Franciscan was an inspector (*visitator*) for the Clares must have displeased Francis. He himself had in his time undertaken a supervision of the Sisters in San Damiano, but that was an exceptional case. For the new convents of the Clares he obtained from Hugolin that a Cistercian named Ambrosius should be made inspector. Ambrosius died during Francis' absence, and Philip had at the request of Hugolin taken up the office. He was strongly reprehended for it by Francis, and a certain Brother Stephen, who with permission of Philip had entered a Clares' convent, had to do severe penance. (Cel., *Vita secunda*, II, c. 156, ed. d'Alençon. Wadding, 1219, n. 48 and n. 45.)

After the death of Francis, Gregory IX at once made over the supervision of the Clares to the General of the Franciscans (Sbar., I, p. 36). Innocent IV accepted this ordinance in Hugolin's Rule when he ratified it in 1247. Even St. Clara's Rule of 1253 forms no exception ("visitator noster sit semper de ordine fratrum minorum"), while she appeals to the relation so necessary to the welfare of S. Damiano ("fratres . . . misericorditer a praedicto ordine fratrum semper habuimus," *Textus*, p. 74. Compare *Vita S. Clarae*, V, n. 37).

Even in 1227 the connection between the Cistercians and Clares was discernible (Potth., I, nr. 8027 and nr. 8048).

Francis now was certain of one thing — his Order must be reorganized from the ground up. It follows of itself that Hugolin stood by him in this; this is testified to explicitly by Bernard of Bessa.[1] Like a first stone for the new building, which was now to be erected — and indeed as a foundation stone — the Bull must be regarded by which Honorius III, on September 22, 1220, ordained that every one who wished to enter into the Order of Friars Minor must first go through a year's novitiate.[2] This closed the doors for all the more or less loose birds, whom Francis was wont to call by the name of "Brother Fly" — those vagabonds, so numerous in the Middle Ages, who ate well, slept well, but wanted neither to work nor to pray, and who, after spending some time with the Brothers, would depart again.[3] If once received into the Order, it was impossible for them to leave it, and strong measures were to be taken against all who put on Francis' habit and lived by their own hand, without joining the Order (*extra obedientiam*).[4] For the liberty allowed to a

---

[1] "In regulis seu vivendi formis ordinis istorum dictandis sanctae memoriae dominus papa Gregorius, in minori adhuc officio constitutus, beato Francisco intima familiaritate conjunctus, devote supplebat quod viro sancto judicandi scientia deerat." (*Anal. Franc.*, III, p. 686.) Compare Hugolin's own words when pope: "in condendo praedictam regulam . . . sibi" [i.e. Francisco] "astiterimus" (Bull *Quo elongati* of September 28, 1230, Sbar., I,'p. 68).

[2] Sbaralea, I, p. 6. Potth., nr. 6361. The Bull is addressed *prioribus seu custodibus fratrum minorum*. This is the first time the word "custodian" (in Franciscan language director of a convent) was used in an official document, and the Pope translated it accordingly by the universally understood term "prior."

[3] *frater musca*. Cel., *Vit. sec.*, III, 21. *Spec.*, c. 24. Bonav., VII, 3.

[4] It is curious to see Lempp (*Elie de Cortone*, p. 43, n. 5) assert that Honorius would hereby proscribe *les adhésions libres, celles précisément qui avaient été jusque-là possibles aux gens mariés*. Lempp is thinking of members of the so-called "Third Order," but these were anything but vagrants, married and home-living citizens as they were! No, the Pope referred to those vagabonds of whom it was spoken above and against whom Francis over and over again expresses himself, and in expressions which perfectly accord with the Papal bulls. Thus in the letter to the Chapter General: "Quicumque autem fratrum hoc observare noluerint, non teneo eos catholicos nec fratres meos . . . *Hoc etiam dico de omnibus aliis, qui vagando vadunt, postposita regulae disciplina*" (Böhmer, "*Analekten*," p. 61). And in the first Rule: "Et omnes fratres, quotiescumque declinaverint a mandatis Domini *et extra obedientiam evagaverint* sicut dicit propheta" (Ps. cxviii, 21) "sciant, se esse maledictos" (*Anal.*, p. 6). Honorius and Francis are here in accord, *n'en déplaise à M. le dr. Lempp*.

Brother Rufino or to a Brother Giles it would be impossible to grant to the crowds, who at a later period began to stream in to be received. Some words of Francis are still preserved for us which show how he at times looked upon this large and varied herd almost with dread, of which herd he was to be the shepherd.[1] During his stay in the Orient he had, moreover, acquired a serious affliction of the eyes, and one thing with another caused him at the Chapter on St. Michael's Day, 1220 *to resign his office as head of the Order.* As his vicar he named Peter of Cattani and, as this one soon after died (March 10, 1221), Elias Bombarone.[2] In this way he intended too to have freer hands for the work of organization which was before him. From now on Francis was no longer the head of the Order and its guide, but still was its lawgiver and, in the sight of Rome, always its real Superior.[3] Along with the accomplished scribe, Brother Cæsarius of Speier, in whom he, when in the Orient, seems to have acquired confidence, he went on with the task which first and foremost was to be attended to — to prepare a substitute for the few and brief rules written down in Rivo Torto, which Innocent III in his time had approved, to replace these by a new and complete Rule of the Order, to which Rome could give solemn and final approval.[4]

But before he started on this difficult task he was to have the joy of being together with more of the Brothers than ever before. During his absence the wildest rumors had gone through Italy — some said that he was a prisoner in the hands of the Mussulmans; others that he was drowned; others,

---

[1] *Spec. perf.* (Sab. ed.), p. 180: "Tam magni et multimodi exercitus ducem, tam ampli et dilatati gregis pastorem."

[2] Pietro dei Cattani's epitaph was found on the outside of the Portiuncula chapel and reads: ANNO. DNI. M.CC.XXI. VI. ID. MARTII CORPUS FR. P. CATANI QUI HIC REQUIESQIT MIGRAVIT AD DOMINUM ANIMAM CUIUS BENEDICAT DOMINUS. AMEN. A photographic reproduction in Schnürer: *"Frans. von Assisi"* (München, 1905), p. 99.

[3] See even in the prologue to the Rule confirmed by Rome in 1223: "Frater Franciscus" (not frater Helias) "promittit obedientiam et reverentiam domino papae Honorio. . . . Et alii fratres teneantur fratri Francisco . . . obedire" (*Opusc.*, Quar. ed., p. 63).

[4] Co-operation between Francis and Cæsarius is referred to by Jordanus, n. 15 (*Anal. Fr.*, I, p. 5).

again, that he had suffered martyrdom. When he now proved to be alive, the Brothers came in droves — priests and lay-brothers, the oldest in the Order and the newly received novices — all wished to see the newly returned master, to hear him, and to receive his blessing. This was the Chapter of the Mats, celebrated in Franciscan history, so-called because the Brethren who were there, to the number of three (five?) thousand, could not be accommodated in the houses, which the town of Assisi had prepared for them down at Portiuncula, but had to sleep in the open air or in huts of woven boughs or mats (*stuoie*).[1]

Hugolin was much occupied at this time with a new embassy to northern Italy, where he was to again preach a crusade; in the days of the Chapter he kept himself in Brescia and Verona. As his representative he had sent another cardinal, Rainer Cappoccio from Viterbo; with him were several other men of high spiritual dignity. A bishop among them sang the solemn Mass of Pentecost with its wonderful Sequence, *Veni, Sancte Spiritus*. Francis read the gospel, another Brother the epistle. Then Francis preached first before the Brethren on the text, "Blessed be the Lord, who strengthens my hands for the fight," and then to the people. "But St. Francis" — thus the *Fioretti* tell it — "preached with a high voice what the Holy Ghost inspired him with. And as text for his preaching he gave out these words: 'Little children, you have promised great things to God; still greater things are promised us by God if we keep to what we have promised Him and firmly expect He has promised us. The lust of the world is short, but the punishment which follows it is endless. The sufferings in this life are short, but the glories in the other life are endless!' And upon these words he preached with great devotion and encouraged all to obedience to Holy Mother Church, to mutual charity, to patience in adversity, to purity and angelic chastity, to peace and unity with God and man, to humility and mildness to all, to despising the world, to burning zeal for holy poverty, to attention and devotion in prayer and songs of

[1] The house at Portiuncula. *Spec. perf.*, cap. 7. Pentecost came this year on May 30; there was no difficulty in camping in the open air.

praise, and casting all care, both as concerns the body and the soul, upon the Good Shepherd, our Lord Jesus Christ the Blessed." [1]

It was a festival of meeting and of happiness, which Francis celebrated on this occasion with his Brothers and the people. It was at the expiration of this Chapter — and it lasted eight days — that the Brothers had to remain two days over the time at Portiuncula, to eat all the gifts of God with which they were loaded by the people.[2] It was coming to its end at last, when Francis pulled the skirt of the habit of Brother Elias, who had led the meeting and at whose feet he had sat, and told him he had something on his mind. Elias bent down to him and then said: "Brothers, *the Brother*" — this was the name given to Francis after his resignation — "the Brother asks me to speak for him; he is tired and cannot say anything more. There is a country called Germany, he says; there dwell many pious Christians, whom we often see coming here through the valley with long staves and large travelling bottles; singing the praise of God and His saints, in spite of the sun and their sweat, they go on to the graves of the Apostles. But as some of our Brothers were formerly badly treated in this land of Germany, none of the Brothers can be persuaded to go there: but if any will go there for love of God and zeal for the salvation of souls, then he will give him the same freedom of conduct as is given to those who go to the Holy Land — yes, even more. If, therefore, there is anyone present who wants to go there, let him stand up and go to one side." Then ninety Brothers stood up and declared themselves ready to go — as they thought — to certain death.

As leader of the German mission, Brother Cæsarius of Speier was very naturally selected. With him followed Brother John of Piano Carpino, who could preach in both Latin and Lombard; Brother Barnabas, who could preach in Lombard and German; Francis' future biographer, Thomas of Celano, and many other Brothers. Among the missionaries was also John of Giano, who himself, in his chronicle, has told with much humor how he, as a punishment for undue haste in making fine acquaintances — namely, with the

[1] *Fioretti*, cap. 18.   [2] Jordanus, n. 16.

outgoing martyrs *in spe* — was impelled to go with them.[1] In all there were twelve priests and thirteen lay-brothers that went, and we may believe that Francis blessed them "all that he could" with more fervor than usual, and not only them, but all who by their prayers would be won for the Order.[2]

The summer passed and the Brothers, who were to go to Germany, went their way. But it was not martyrdom they encountered. It is one of the most beautiful leaves of Franciscan history, the tale, as Jordanus has written it, of how he and the other Brothers went from Trent to Bozen, from Bozen to Brixen, from Brixen to Sterzing, and from Sterzing to Mittenwalde. It was evening as they reached this last-named town, and since morning they had eaten nothing, and they had travelled seven miles. To be able to sleep on such empty stomachs, they decided to fill them with water from a stream which was there. Next morning they resumed their travels, but by midday some of them began to fall sick; they found some wild apples, which they ate, and, as it was the time of the beet harvest, they begged some beets and ate them.

On the whole the Brothers were well received on their journey; they eventually settled for the time being in Strassburg, Speyer, Worms, Mayence, and Cologne, in Wurtzburg, Ratisbon and Salzburg. Following the old Francisan way, they took shelter where they found it — with the lepers, in a cellar or in an abandoned church. In Erfurt, Brother Jordanus was asked by the citizens, as he came there with some Brothers, if they should not build them a convent. "But as he had never seen a convent in the Order, he answered them: 'I do not know what a convent is, but if you want to do something, then build us a house near the water, so that we can wash our feet!' And so it was done."[3] And a characteristic story also is told of the Brothers in Salzburg, to

---

[1] Jordanus, n. 18.
[2] "Pater noster in capitulis fratrum solitus erat in fine semper capituli benedicere et absolvere omnes fratres presentes et venturos ad religionem . . . in fervore caritatis." *Spec. perf.*, cap. 87. Compare in Francis' Testament and letters the eloquent expressions in which his heart overflows: "My blessed Sons," "My beloved Sons," "I, Brother Francis, your servant, bless you all that I can" (*Analekten*, pp. 18, 40, 64; *Opuscula*, pp. 49, 107, 115).
[3] Jordanus, nr. 21–23, n. 43.

whom Cæsarius wrote that they could come to the Chapter in Speyer if they wanted to, or could let it go if they wanted to. As the Brothers did not want to have any desire of their own, they were troubled at this behest, and went to Speyer to find out what Cæsarius had meant in sending such a vague order.[1]

When all the Brothers at the Chapter of Mats had been distributed — some to the Italian provinces or to missions — one Brother stayed back, whom no one knew and whom no one seemed to trouble himself about. He had come to the Chapter with the Brothers from Messina, who too knew nothing of him, except that he was apparently a new member of the Order, that his name was Anthony, that he had a home in Portugal, and on the way home from Morocco had been blown out of his course way over to Sicily. At last the unknown Brother approached the Superior of the province of Romagna, Brother Gratian, and asked if he could follow him. "Are you a priest?" "Yes!" On hearing this answer, Gratian asked Elias for the unknown Brother, for at this early time priests were few among the Brothers. Anthony followed his new superior to Romagna, where he withdrew to the hermitage of Monte Paolo, in the vicinity of Forli. The lonely life of penance and prayer he led there he was later to leave and to become the great preacher to the people whom the Church has canonized under the name of St. Anthony of Padua.[2]

---

[1] Jordanus, n. 27.

[2] This disciple of Francis, in modern times perhaps the most famous, was born in Lisbon in the year 1195. At the age of fifteen he entered the Augustinian convent Santo Vicente de Fora in his native city and thence was soon transferred to the celebrated convent of Santa Cruz in the university city Coimbra. Here he studied, was ordained to the priesthood, and then in 1220 was attracted to the Franciscans, probably in consequence of what he had heard of the five martyrs of Morocco already spoken of. With the permission of his superiors in the Order he went over to the other Order and was received in S. Antonio d'Olivares in Coimbra. Hence he went to Morocco to become a martyr. As he failed in this — Abu Jacob seems to have become again indifferent — he wanted to return again to his own country, but instead came to Sicily and thence to the Pentecost Chapter of 1221. Of his relation to the Order we will speak later. All the sources for Anthony's biography are found up to 1904 collected in Léon de Kerval's excellent book: "Sancti Antonii de Padua Vitae duae quarum altera hucusque inedita," which contains much more than the title promises. The work constitutes Volume V of Sabatier's *Collection d'études*. See also Albert Lepitre: *St. Antoine de Padoue* (4th ed., Paris, 1905), and Lempp in "Zeitschr. f. Kgsch.," Vols. XI-XIII (1889-1892).

CHAPTER VIII

THE RULES AND ADMONITIONS

CÆSARIUS of Speier did not at once go to Germany with his Brothers. Francis had asked him to assist him in writing the Rules of the Order, and Cæsarius also wished before his departure to spend some time with Francis — it was so uncertain if they ever again would see each other. For one and the other of these reasons Cæsarius remained three months with Francis in the valley of Spoleto, as well as at Portiuncula and up in Carceri.[1]

The first Rule, which Francis wrote at Rivo Torto, was quite short and simple. "I had it written with few and simple words, and our Lord the Pope confirmed it for me," says Francis in his Testament. With this all the burden of testimony of the first biographers agrees.[2] A great part of this first Rule was made up of extracts from the Bible put together — first and foremost from Matthew x. 9-10, xix. 21, xvi. 24, and Luke ix. 3. Thence comes the name

---

[1] It is Jordanus of Giano who in clearly put words says this. The two following extracts can be compared: "Et videns beatus Franciscus fratrem Cæsarium sacris litteris eruditum, ipsi commisit, ut regulam, quam ipse simplicibus verbis conceperat, verbis Evangelii adornaret. Quod et fecit" (n. 15); and "His ergo" [fratribus] "frater Cæsarius assumptis, quia ipsemet, utpote homo devotus, beatum Franciscum et alios sanctos fratres invitus deseruit, de licentia beati Francisci socios sibi datos per domos in Lombardia divisit, ut in illis verbum suum expectarent. Ipse vero in Valle Spoletana moram fecit fere per tres menses" (n. 19). This alone is enough to prove the impossibility of what Karl Müller ("*Anfänge*," p. 13) and following him Sabatier, Lempp, and Schnürer have maintained, that Francis at the Pentecost Chapter of 1221 "laid before them the edition of the Rule, which he with the help of Cæsarius of Speier had worked out." (Schnürer: "*Franz von Assisi*," p. 99.) If this were so, Jordanus would certainly have told of it. But this mutual work began *after* the Chapter in question.

[2] For the Testament, see *Opusc.*, p. 79; Böhmer, p. 37. For testimony of biographers, Cel., *V. pr.*, I, c. XIII; Julian, in *A. SS.*, Oct. II, p. 588, n. 226; Bonav., III, 8.

Francis liked to use instead of the word "Rule"—*forma sancti Evangelii*, "the form of the Holy Gospel." In a few words, to observe the gospel was what he desired.

We have no longer this first Franciscan Rule, and of the ingenious attempts which have been made in the most recent times to recover it, none have succeeded. But these attempts were undertaken from a correct standpoint; namely, that we undoubtedly have in the so-called *Regula prima* (generally called after Karl Müller "the Rule of 1221") the original Rule of the Order, with additions and buried under a quantity of later additions, alterations and expansions.[1]

A suggestion of how the development went can be obtained from Jacques de Vitry's description of the Franciscan Chapter gatherings. Here he tells how the Brothers came together at these meetings, and "with the support of good men, wrote and promulgated good regulations."[2] But the good men who stood by the Brothers were undoubtedly cardinals; the closer relations between them and Francis were formed in the summer of 1216, when Jacques was still in the Papal Court. And moreover the accounts compare well with what we know from other sources, that "the Brothers came together at Pentecost at Portiuncula and consulted as to how they best should maintain the Rule."[3]

Francis naturally had a deciding voice in these discussions. "St. Francis," the authority just cited says, "admonished, censured and commanded as it seemed good to him in the Lord." If we have the Latin text at this place before us, the meaning is still clearer. It there is written *faciebat admonitiones, reprehensiones et praecepta* — "he made admonitions, reprehensions and precepts." But among the writings of Francis of Assisi we have one entire collection remaining, which bears the title of *Admonitiones*.[4] If we wish to find

---

[1] Karl Müller's first attempt at reconstruction in "*Die Anfänge*," pp. 185-188, and another in "Theolog. Litt. Zeitg.," 1805, pp. 182 et seq., are too elaborate. Böhmer, in "*Analekten*," pp. 88-89, has attempted to produce a briefer reconstitution of the primitive Rule.

[2] "consilio bonorum virorum suas faciunt et promulgant institutiones sanctas." Böhmer's "*Analekten*," p. 98.

[3] *Tres Socii*, cap. XIV, p. 80, Amoni's ed.

[4] In Böhmer, pp. 40-49.

the first additions to the original Rule, it is here we should look. The superscription tells as much: "In the name of the Father and of the Son and of the Holy Ghost. These are the holy words of advice of our honored father St. Francis to all the Brothers."

In these *Admonitiones* we find what Thomas of Celano, where he speaks of the Rule, calls "some few additional commands, which are entirely necessary for the purpose of a holy conversion."[1] They contain the following:

I. "On the Lord's body." The first thing Francis thought of enforcing upon his disciples and of placing deep within their hearts was to have great reverence and great love for the God revealed to the eye of faith in the Holy Eucharist.

II. "On the sinfulness of self-will." It is self-will that leads to falling into sin.

III. "On perfect obedience." He who does not renounce all things, even his own will, cannot be a disciple of Jesus.

IV. "That no one should strive after command." It is better to wash the feet of the Brothers, than to rule over them.

V. "That no one should be exalted, but should glory in the Cross of the Lord." The same order of thought that is developed later at length in the celebrated eighth chapter of the *Fioretti* (see pp. 117–121).

VI. "On following after the Lord." "We wish to be called the servants of the Lord, but we should be ashamed, because the saints have done great things, and we wish to be honored and esteemed, only because we tell of them and preach about them."

VII. "That wisdom must be followed by work." That wisdom only has value which leads to good works — a thought to which Francis constantly returns.

VIII. "To envy no one," especially to envy no one the good which God works in his soul.

IX. "On charity." He has really charity towards his

[1] Celano, *V. pr.*, I, c. XIII: "beatus Franciscus . . . scripsit . . . simpliciter et paucis verbis vitae formam et regulam, sancti evangelii praecipue sermonibus utens, ad cujus perfectionem solummodo inhiabat. Pauca tamen alia inseruit, quae omnino ad conversationis sanctae usum necessaria inveniebat."

enemies who, when he suffers injustice, thinks first of all of the harm the unjust one has done his own soul.

X. "To hold the body in subjection." There is an enemy we ought not to love, and that is the body. And if we vigorously and ceaselessly fight this enemy, then no other enemy, spiritual or material, can hurt us.

XI. "Do not participate in the effects of another's sin." By paying evil with evil, one takes the effects of a sin upon his own soul.

XII. "On signs of the Lord's spirit." The better a man really is, the worse he feels himself to be.

XIII. "On patience." One first sees how great his patience really is when he has cause to be impatient.

XIV. "On poverty of spirit." Poverty of spirit is not in much fasting and penance, but in turning the left cheek to him who has struck the right one.

XV. "On peace." Blessed are the peaceful!

XVI. "On purity of heart." He is pure of heart who despises the world, seeks heaven, and always has the Lord his God before his eyes.

XVII. "On being an humble servant of God" and not to demand more of one's neighbor than one is willing to grant to God.

XVIII. "On sympathy with our neighbor." Blessed he who bears with his frailties, as his neighbor has also to endure his.

XIX. "Of a good servant of God." Blessed he who does not look upon himself as better or greater when he is exalted and honored by men than when he is scorned and despised by them and is degraded by them, for a man is what he is in God's eyes, and no more.

XX. "On the good and bad Brother of the Order. Blessed the Brother whose whole joy is in doing the work of God and in speaking of God, and who thereby leads men to love God in peace and joy.

XXI. "On the empty and gossiping Brother of the Order." Woe to the Brother whose joy it is to make people laugh with empty and vain talk, and who in his actions does not correspond with the grace he has received from God.

XXII. "On correction." Blessed the Brother who is not eager to excuse himself, but who in humility is willing to be shamed and blamed, even if he has done nothing.

XXIII. "On humility." Blessed the Brother who is as humble to those who are under him as to his superior.

XXIV. "On real charity." Blessed the servant of God who loves his Brother as much when the Brother is sick and depends on him as when the Brother is well and can be of use and pleasure to him.

XXV. And blessed the servant of God who loves and fears his Brother as much when he is away from him as when he is near him, and says nothing behind his back which he could not in charity let him hear.

XXVI. "That God's servants ought to honor clerics." Blessed the servant of God who has faith in the clerics, who live after the law of the Holy Roman Church. And woe to those who despise them! Even if they are sinners, no one should condemn them, for they have power over the body and blood of Jesus Christ.

XXVII. "On virtues, that put vices to flight." This is the *laud* in honor of all virtues already given (p. 177).

XXVIII. "Not to boast of your virtue." God sees our secret thoughts, for him alone we shall do all things, and thus accumulate for ourselves treasures in heaven.

Haec sunt documenta pii patris one can say in the words of Thomas of Celano after having gone through these twenty-eight short chapters — "with these prescripts the pious father moulded his new sons."[1] Francis was certainly a remarkable "Master of Novices," as the technical expression of the convent has it, but these religious psychological aphorisms, often wonderfully fine, remind us but little of the Rule of an Order.

Of Francis' way of writing such a Rule we have, on the other hand, an idea through a little piece of regulation, which undoubtedly comes entirely from his own hand. "In the early days of the Order, when there were few Brothers and when there was no regular convent,"[2] the members of the

---
[1] Cel., *V. pr.*, I, cap. XV, n. 41. Bonav., IV, 3.
[2] *Fioretti*, cap. 4.

Order spent most of their time on missionary journeys and took shelter where they could find it. At intervals they wished to withdraw into solitude to pray in peace and strengthen the soul for new apostolic efficiency, as they, after the Master's example, "talked over with themselves what they preached to others."[1] In this way originated the first Franciscan "convents," but which were only ill-adapted to bear this honored name. At Portiuncula the "convent" was a collection of huts surrounded by a hedge; in Carceri it was a few caves; at Fonte Colombo and Mount Alverna it was the same, and time after time in the *Fioretti* we are brought round to these "little convents where the Brothers had only huts of leaves to sleep in."[2] Neither was the word *claustrum* used in speaking of the Franciscan abiding-places; Brother Jordanus, as we have seen, was greatly perplexed when in Erfurt it was proposed to build him a convent. Such a Franciscan habitation was called simply a "place" (*locus*), a hermitage (*eremo, erimitorium*), a retreat (*ritiro*). And for the Brothers, who for a period of time wanted to stay in such a hermitage, Francis now wrote the following Rule, or rather regulations, which is the more valuable because it undoubtedly comes in its entirety from his own hand, without the assistance of Cardinal Hugolin or of Brother Cæsarius. It is here given in full:[3]

De Religosa Habitatione in Eremo.
"<i>On Pious Living in a Hermitage.</i>"

"Those who wish to live piously in a hermitage must be three or at most four Brothers. Two of them shall be mothers and shall have the other two for sons or the one. But the mothers shall lead the life of Martha and the others the life of Mary.[4]

"The two who are mothers shall lead the life of Martha and the two sons shall lead the life of Mary and shall have

---

[1] Celano, *Vita prima*, I, XV, n. 36.
[2] *Fior.*, c. 17.
[3] Böhmer: "*Analekten*," pp. 67–68. The text in Quaracchi edition (*Opusc.*, pp. 83–84) is less explicit.
[4] Naturally a reference to the two sisters in Bethania.

an enclosure with a cell, where they can pray and sleep. And as soon as the sun has set, they shall pray the Compline and try to maintain silence, but at Matins they shall get up and say their Hours and 'seek first for God's kingdom and His justice.' And at the proper time they shall pray the Primes, and after the Trines they can break the silence and go to their mothers, and, if they wish, can beg an alms of them like other poor people for God's sake. And later they shall pray the Sext and Nones, and say Vespers at a suitable time.

"And they must permit no one to enter the enclosure where they are, and no one must eat there either. The Brothers who are mothers shall keep themselves away from all men, and, as their Superior has told them, guard their sons from all men, so that no one can speak to them. And the sons must not talk with anyone except their mothers and with their Superior, if he with God's blessing visits them. But the sons shall take over the mothers' task, when they find it mutually good, and busy themselves to carry out exactly all that has been said before."

This was a Rule such as Francis was able to write. How graceful is the picture of the Brothers, who live together up in the mountain wilderness of Fonte Colombo or on Monte Subasio, and of which the two, like Martha in the gospel, must look out for the temporal things, while the other two, like Mary, have permission to sit at the Lord's feet! And when it gets to be midday, then the two who had chosen the better part come and beg well and modestly for food — like polite children asking it of their good mother.[1]

Besides the short, original Rule of 1210 and the Rule for hermitages, we hear further talk of a special *Rule, valid for Portiuncula*. This is preserved in Chapter 55 of the *Speculum perfectionis* and recalls the Rule for hermits; thus we find it

---

[1] "dico tibi, fili mi, *sicut mater*," Francis writes to his favorite disciple Brother Leo, with whom he had staid so often in the hermitages (Böhmer, p. 68). And of Brother Elias we find in Thomas of Celano (*Vita pr.*, II, cap. IV, n. 98): "frater Helias . . . quem *loco matris* elegerat sibi (Francisco)." Compare Celano, *Vita sec.*, III, 99: "dixit Pacificus s. Francisco: Benedic nobis, mater carissima;" III, 113 (II, 136, d'Al.). The complaint is later made that many "eremiticum ritum" "convertunt in otium."

forbidden for strangers to enter the place. No worldly talk and no superfluous word must be heard in Portiuncula; the Brothers there shall be chosen from the best and most pious in the whole Order, and shall edify all by the exemplary recitation of their office. "And in this place nothing shall happen or be spoken that is useless, but the whole place shall be kept pure and holy in hymns and songs of praise." For the infringement of these regulations — as it is given later in the same book, Chapter 82 — the offender is obliged to say a *Pater noster* along with the prayer composed by Francis, *Laudes Dei*.

Francis' work as lawgiver was only occasional. At a Chapter it was told him that many of the Brothers tormented themselves with penitential shirts, iron rings and the like on the naked body. He forbade at once the use of such ascetic things by the Brothers.[1] Another time he had the following regulation put into writing: "Let the Brothers take care that they do not present the appearance of hypocrites, with dark and cast-down mien, but that they show themselves glad in the Lord, cheerful and worthy of love, and agreeable."[2] This place is found in the existing *Regula prima*, Chapter 7, and in the *Speculum* there is cited another regulation, which we may safely read in the text of those we still possess.[3] The last chapter in the *Regula prima* has as title *Admonitio fratrum*.

If in the Rivo Torto Rule is to be found the basis for the whole code of laws, so are these occasional regulations and the admonitions promulgated at Chapters to be regarded as the first framework. And others were built upon them, each as time or occasion required. In 1217 the great Franciscan missions began; to this period are certainly to be ascribed chapters such as the 14th and 16th in the *Regula prima*, "How the Brothers ought to go through the world" and "Of those who go to the Saracens and other heathen." This

---

[1] *Spec. perf.* (ed. Sab.), p. 56.
[2] "pro generali commonitione in quodam capitulo scribi fecit haec verba." Cel., *V. sec.*, III, 68.
[3] *Spec. perf.*, cap. 96, p. 189 = *Adm.* XX in Böhmer, XXI in Quaracchi edition.

sort of farewell admonition has been preserved for us in several examples by Francis' biographer — see for example in the *Speculum perfectionis*, Chapter 65, "Admonition to departing Brothers"; as well as several extracts from the Rules, beginning with the words *In nomine Domini*, "In the name of the Lord," the usual formula with which in those days every official paper began.[1]

That these admonitions, which later, when the Order developed, came to have a larger and larger scope, were written out, we can rest assured. They had all of them a very practical object, which was something Francis wished the Brothers to observe and be guided by. We see how explicit he is in his later letters that the Brothers should, by copying, have them in manifold, and each possess a copy in his Breviary along with him, "the better to follow them."[2]

If we want to understand what the co-operation of Francis and Cæsarius in the summer of 1221 in preparing the Rule of the Order was, we must recollect that they, excepting the original Rule of 1210 — had before them the collection of all the Admonitions and Regulations. Out of this material they were to put together a new Rule of the Order.[3] In reality they, for the time being, were content to link together old and new, often without sequence, and so did this collection, or better this selection, of valid Regulations result, which the older investigators call *Regula prima*, the newer ones "Rule of 1221," but which *in no sense has been accepted as the Rule of the Order.*

Without wishing to go into details, like Karl Müller or

---

[1] *Spec. perf.* (Sabatier), p. 120. *Reg. prima*, capp. IV, XXIV.

[2] "Hoc scriptum, *ut melius debeat observari, habeas tecum* usque ad Pentecosten." Francis' letter of 1223 to Elias (*Opuscula*, p. 110). Böhmer ("*Analekten*," p. XXXVI) has collected a quantity of references which show Francis' care in this regard.

[3] The dream Francis had at this time proves this. It seemed to him that all the Brothers stood around him and were hungry, and that he had nothing but a quantity of crumbs that escaped from his fingers. "Francis," a voice then said, "knead all these crumbs together into a host and give that to the Brothers." This dream he explained the next morning to the effect that the crumbs indicated *verba evangelica*, the host indicated the Rule which was to be formed out of them. (Bonav., *Leg. Major*, IV, 11. Cel., *Vita sec.*, II, c. 159, d'Al.)

Boehmer, it is quite impossible to form a general understanding of what part of this great collection of material comes from the original Rule, and of what are additions of a later period. Out of the Rivo Torto Rule, besides the introduction (Francis promises obedience to Pope Innocent) the following portions undoubtedly came: Chapter I (of the three vows of the Order: obedience, poverty, chastity), Chapter II (of the Brothers' reception and habit), Chapter III (of the Office and fasts), Chapter VII (of how the Brothers are to work and pray), Chapters VIII and IX (on not caring for money, on begging when it is necessary) Chapter XII (on avoiding women), Chapter XIV (on neither travelling nor sitting down with evil people), Chapter XIX (on reverence for priests). These chapters may have been differently arranged in the original Rule, but the meaning has been the same. The regulations for fasting seem to have been severer originally, than as preserved in the *Regula prima*.[1]

As later additions to the fundamental rules we must look upon the fourth chapter with the statutory beginning *In nomine Domini;* this treats besides of the ministers and of the duty of obedience of the Brothers to them, and must date from the Chapter-meeting, in which the first ministers were installed and the first division of provinces was arranged for. Some other chapters agree also with the Admonitions which are in existence; thus Chapter V and the fourth and eleventh Admonitions may be located, and Chapter XXII and the ninth and tenth Admonitions. A "Reminder" as referred to by Thomas of Celano is not to be found in the existing collection of Admonitions; on the contrary, it is in the *Regula prima*, where it is found in the eighteenth chapter.[2]

A third element in the *Regula prima* consists finally of what we may call religious poetry. To this belong first of all the Lauds or Songs of Praise already spoken of (p. 69), which

---

[1] *Reg. prima* prescribed only one weekly fast: Friday. (Böhmer, p. 4.) If Jordanus is to be believed (*Anal. Fr.*, I, 4, n. 11), there were in the original Rule two fast days in the week, namely Friday and Wednesday also. With special permission of Francis, the Brothers who wished to do so could also fast on Mondays and Thursdays.

[2] Cel., *Vita sec.*, III, 68. There is also an Admonition addressed to the sick in cap. X of *Regula prima*, in *Speculum perfectionis*, cap. 42.

Francis offered to his Brothers for singing in the towns as the Good God's Musicians, and where we find a rhythm that reminds us of the later Sun Song.[1] What Francis desired first of all was to inspire men for God. And after finally a last *Admonitio fratrum* — the old name is here kept in the title of the chapter — his and Cæsarius of Speier's work breaks forth in a great, swelling Song of Praise, that rises and rises irresistibly like a stronger and stronger flowing organ sound, and never stops until the highest summits are reached — there where all human speech must cease, all human thought must fail, and nothing remain except the angels' *Sanctus, Sanctus, Sanctus* and ceaseless *Alleluia* of the happy souls. It is thus the last Chapter sounds:

"Prayer, Song of Praise and Thanksgiving.

"Almighty, highest and Supreme God, holy and just Father, Lord and King of the Heavens and Earth, we thank thee for thy own sake, because thou by thy holy will and by thy only begotten Son with the Holy Ghost hast created all spiritual and material things and us in thy form and likeness, and thou didst place us in paradise. But we fell through our own fault. And we thank thee, because thou, as thou didst create us through thy Son, thus also through the true, holy charity, wherewith thou lovedst us, let him be born, true God and true Man, of the ever virginal, holiest Virgin Mary and through his cross and blood and death thou didst wish to free us poor prisoners. And we thank thee, because the same One, thy Son, shall return in the glory of his majesty and send the damnéd, who have not converted themselves and knew thee not, into everlasting fire, and will say to all who have known thee and prayed to thee and served thee in conversion: 'Come here, the blessed of my Father, and inherit the riches which have been prepared for you even from the beginning of the world!'

"And because all we poor sinners are not worthy to name

---

[1] "Beati qui moriuntur in penitentia quia erunt in regno coelorum.
"Ve illis, qui non moriuntur in penitentia, quia erunt filii diaboli . . . et ibunt in ignem eternum." (*Reg. pr.*, cap. XXI. Böhmer, p. 19.)
"Guai acquelli ke morrano ne le peccata mortali. Beati quelli ke trovarane le tue sanctissime voluntati, ka la morte secunda nol farra male." (*Canticum fratris solis;* Böhmer, p. 66.)

thee, so do we pray and implore that our Lord Jesus Christ thy beloved Son, in whom thou art well pleased, together with the Comforter, the Holy Ghost, will thank thee for all the great things Thou hast done to us through Him, Alleluia. And we humbly implore the most blessed Mother and Virgin Mary, the blessed Michael, Gabriel, Raphael and all the rest of the choir of holy spirits, Seraphim and Cherubim, Thrones, Dominations, Principalities, Powers and Mights, Angels and Archangels, the blessed John the Baptist, John the Evangelist, Peter, Paul and the Blessed Patriarchs and Prophets, the Holy Innocents, the Apostles, Evangelists, Disciples, Martyrs, Confessors, Virgins, the blessed Elias and Enoch and all the Saints, that have been or are to come, that they out of love to thee and as it pleases thee shall bear our thanks to thee, thou highest true, everlasting and living God, with thy Son, our dear Lord Jesus Christ, and the Comforter the Holy Ghost for ever and ever. Amen. Alleluia.

"And we Friars Minor, we useless servants, beg and pray thee all humbly, who in the Holy Catholic and Apostolic Church wish to serve the Lord God, all who are in orders, all priests, deacons, subdeacons, acolytes, exorcisers, lectors, ostiairs, and all the clerics, all monks and all nuns, all children, all women and maidens, all poor and needy, kings and princes, laborers, peasants, servants and masters, all virgins, all continent and all married, all lay-people, men and women, all infants, children, young and old, well and sick, all large and small and all kinds of people, races and languages, all nations and all men everywhere, who are now or are to be, we pray them all humbly that they will persevere in the true faith and conversion, for otherwise they cannot be saved. Let us all with all our heart, with all our soul, with all our mind, with all our strength and power, with all our reason and all our dispositions, all our striving, all our love, all our inner self, all our desire and will love the Lord our God, who has given us all of our body, all of our soul and all of our life, he who has created us and redeemed us, and out of pure mercy wishes to save us, he who has given and daily gives all good to us poor, corrupted, putrid, thankless and evil things.

"Let us therefore seek nothing else, wish for nothing else,

rejoice and be pleased with nothing else than our Creator and Redeemer and Saviour, the one, true God, who is the perfect good, all good, the whole good, the true and highest good, he who alone is good, pious and mild, happy and loving, he who alone is holy, just, true and righteous, who alone is good, innocent and pure, from whom and with whom and in whom are all pardon, all grace, all glory for all penitents, all just men, all the blest in Heaven. May nothing restrain us therefore, nothing separate us, nothing drive us from him. Let us all in all ways, at every time and place, daily and constantly, truthfully and humbly believe in God and keep him in our hearts, and let us love, honor, beseech, serve, obey and bless, praise and glorify, sing praises to and thank the highest and supreme eternal God, the Threefold and One, the Father, Son and the Holy Ghost, Creator of all, the Saviour of those who hope in him and love him, God without beginning and end, unchangeable, inconceivable, invisible, incomprehensible, inscrutable, blessed, glorified, extolled, highly exalted, mild, lovable, dreadful, and worthy to be loved and desired always and above all things forever and ever. Glory be to the Father, Son and the Holy Ghost, as it was in the beginning, is now and ever shall be. Amen."[1]

[1] Böhmer, pp. 23–26. *Opuscula*, pp. 57–61.

CHAPTER IX

SAINT FRANCIS AND LEARNING

TWO years passed before the final Rule of the Order was finished. In September, 1221, Cæsarius left and with his missionaries went to Germany, and first on November 29, 1223, Honorius III with his bull *Solet annuere* gave his ratification to the Rule. Between these two dates lies a whole series of events of which unfortunately there is left to us no satisfactory account, but during which there seems to have developed a great opposition between Francis on the one side and Brother Elias Bombarone and his adherents on the other side. Hugolin in this dispute had the difficult task of being intermediator and as far as possible of pacifying both parties.

For in order to understand the core of the dispute one must realize what a development the new Order had experienced in the last year.

On his resignation Francis had certainly preserved for himself a definite position of authority — at the Pentecost Chapter of 1221, for example, it was he who sent out the German missionaries, and there are other indications that he always sat there with an authority by no means small.[1] Francis meanwhile had never been addicted to exercising any real compulsion. "He wished rather to reach the goal with the good than with the bad," says Jordanus. If he could not carry through his wish, then in God's name he did not wish to rave and domineer "like the powers of this world." If he did not suc-

---

[1] "potestatem habetis vos," *his vicar*, Pietro dei Cattani, said to him in the Holy Land (Jordanus, p. 5). See ditto, pp. 7–8, the expressions "nullum ad ipsos ire *compellit* frater" (Franciscus), "eandem eis *obedientiam* dare vult," "de *licentia* beati Francisci."

ceed in making the Brothers do their duty, then he comforted himself by being personally doubly dutiful.[1]

Wills more energetic had full sway over a man of this disposition of mind. First and foremost was Elias of Bombarone, or as he was called later, Elias of Cortona, a will of this stamp, but behind him stood others who supported him and were on his side against Francis. One of them we know by name — it was Brother Petrus Stacia from Bologna. The others appear on the records only under the title "ministers," by which are meant more especially the Superiors of the Italian Provinces, or as the Franciscan expression has it, *ministri* of these provinces.[2]

I mentioned Bologna above, and in doing so I named the centre of the opposition which, within the Order itself, appeared against Francis. There was from old times a connection between the Franciscans and the celebrated University town. As early as 1212 Bernard of Quintavalle had preached there, and in 1213 this Friar Minor settled in a house which was called *Le Pugliole*, just outside the Porta Galliera. A number of the most important men within the ranks of the new Order had studied in Bologna, among them Francis' two first vicars,

---

[1] "Omnia per humilitatem maluit vincere quam per judicii potestatem." (*Anal. Fr.*, I, p. 5, n. 13.) "nolo carnifex fieri ... sicut potestates hujus saeculi." (*Spec. perf.*, cap. 71.) "nolebat contendere cum ipsis, sed ... volebat in se illud *implere*." (Ditto, cap. 2.)

[2] The whole area over which the Order was distributed was divided in 1223 into twelve provinces; each — following Francis' prohibition of the word *prior* — was subject to a "servant of the province" (*minister provincialis*, compare Matthew xx. 26). The single provinces were then divided into smaller districts (*custodiae*) under charge of a *custos* or watchman. The superior of a *locus* (convent) bore a similar title (*guardianus*). The minister of a province, for example of Mark Ancona, had under him custodes for the districts (*custodiae*) Fermo, Ascoli, Camerino, Ancona, Jesi, Fano, and Feletro. The custos for the custodia of Fermo, so often mentioned in the *Fioretti*, had under him guardians in Fallerone, Bruforte, Soffiano, Massa, Penna, Moliano; he was also guardian of the convent of Fermo. At the head of the whole Order was the General Minister, a name which was abbreviated to "General" (as the "Provincial Minister" became "Minister"), but he was still the "Servant of the whole Order." On this peculiarity of the Franciscan nomenclature the *Chronica XXIV generalium* says: "omnes professores ejusdem" (regulae) "tam praelatos quam subditos, nominibus evangelicis nuncupavit." Even the designation *fratres minores* (Friars Minor, lesser brothers) is traced to a place in the gospel (Matthew xxv. 40 and 45), where the Vulgate has the word *minoribus* (in English "lesser").

Pietro dei Cattani and Elias, and the most of the following Generals of the Order: Johannes Parenti, Aymon of Faversham, Crescentius of Jesi, John of Parma. It has been told already, that the University Professor, Nicholas of Pepoli, who from the beginning had been the advocate and benefactor of the Order, eventually entered it himself; Bologna's most celebrated lawyer, Accursius, called the great, at about the same time bequeathed to the Order his villa, La Richardina, outside the town, where the first convent was soon found to be too small. And finally Peter of Stacia opened a house of study for Franciscans, like the theological school opened in Bologna by the Dominicans.[1]

But this was displeasing to Francis. All his life he had been an *idiota*, as he used to call himself, an ignorant man. He had nothing against studies, and Sabatier is wrong when he ascribes to Francis a definite opposition to wisdom. In the form of an Admonition he once had the following written: "All theologians and those who serve us with God's word we should honor and revere, because they give us the spirit and life."[2] This study should have a practical object, however; it ought to serve the proclamation of the Divine Word. Accordingly only few books were required; in prayer, that which grips the heart is the best to learn. Francis himself liked to read the Holy Scriptures; his works show this. But as he grew older it seemed to him that he had read enough even of God's word, and that for the rest of his life he had enough to do in pondering over it — and in practising it.[3] For — and it was to this his thought always reverted — example is the best preaching. He recognized well in his Rule three classes of members — *praedicatores, oratores, laboratores* — and he placed the preachers above those who prayed and those who worked. But he says also, "all Brothers ought to preach by their actions."[4] And he goes on to warn against "the wisdom of

---

[1] Hilarin Felder: "*Geschichte der wissenschaftlichen Studien im Franciskanerorden*" (Freiburg im Br., 1904), pp. 123-131. The same words in his Testament (*Opusc.*, pp. 78-79).

[2] Cel., *Vita sec.*, II, c. 122 (d'Alençon). The same expression in his Testament (*Opusc.*, pp. 78-79).

[3] Cel., *Vita sec.*, II, c. 72.

[4] *Reg. prima*, cap. XVII (Böhmer, p. 16).

this world" and against those who are all word, and do nothing, against those who try to seem, not to be. "As for myself," he declares at last, "I know Jesus Christ and him crucified, that is enough for me."[1]

A tale is preserved for us in the *Speculum perfectionis*, which belongs to this time, and which gives the clearest possible illustration of Francis' attitude as regards useless and injurious book-learning.

A young novice had received permission from Brother Elias to have a copy of David's Psalms and to read them. When he came to know that it was not pleasing to Francis that his Brothers should be eager after learning and books, he wished, for his conscience's sake in reading his Psalter, to have also Francis' permission to own it. To his request for this Francis replied:

"The Emperor Charles, Roland, Holger and all the other heroes fought with the heathen with much sweat and labor and conquered them and were at last holy martyrs and fell in the strife for the faith of Christ. But in these days there are many who only by telling and preaching about what the saints have done, want to win reputation and glory."

The young novice was not satisfied with this answer, but still forced his request upon Francis. Francis looked up — he sat with the other Brothers by the fire warming himself — and answered:

"My Son! Once you have got the Psalter, then you will want a Breviary, when you have got a Breviary, you will want to sit in the high seat like a great prelate and say to thy Brothers, '*Bring me my Breviary.*'"

And displeased and filled with anxious thoughts of the future prospects of his Order, he reached down into the warm ashes, spread a handful upon the head of the Brother so fond of reading, rubbed the ashes around as if he were washing his head, and called out again and again, "*I* am thy Breviary! *I* am thy Breviary!"

"Brother," said Francis next as he sat down somewhat quieter, "even I have been tempted to collect books. But as

---

[1] "Non pluribus indigeo, fili. Scio Christum pauperem crucifixum." Celano, *Vita secunda*, II, c. 71.

I did not know God's will about these things, I took the Book of Gospels and prayed God to let me know his will. And I opened the book and at once found these words: 'To you it is given to know the mystery of the kingdom of God, but to the rest in parables.'"

Francis was silent for a moment and then added: "There are so many in our days who want to seek wisdom and learning, that happy is he who, out of love for the Lord our God, makes himself ignorant and unlearned." [1]

Undoubtedly Francis was right in thinking that the time in which he lived was more eager after learning than almost any other epoch. Not less than seventy new universities were established in the course of the half-century from 1200 to 1250 — of these eight in Italy alone (Reggio, Vicenza, Padua, Naples, Vercelli, Rome, Piacenza, Arezzo). The three great and earlier-established universities in Paris, Bologna and Oxford reached at the same time their full development, and the powerful uplift in knowledge began which characterized the later Middle Ages. In this movement the Dominicans took part from the beginning — it stood in their statutes inherited from the Augustinian choir-masters. Now the Friars Minor were to be drawn along in the same tendency of the day, and it was here that Francis for the first time seriously set himself in opposition, here he showed himself — as in the vision Brother Leo had — with claws and outstretched wings defending his Order.[2]

Francis' wrath first was excited by Peter Stacia and his house of study in Bologna. Certainly Peter had not established it by his own hand, but in co-operation with Hugolin, who in 1220 was in Bologna, and had himself recorded as owner of the requisite building.[3] Francis at once travelled thither, ordered the Brothers to leave the house in the name of obedience — even one of them who lay sick had to go out — and took his own abode among the Dominicans. Here the Broth-

---

[1] "Tot sunt qui libenter ascendunt ad scientiam quod beatus erit qui se fecerit sterilem amore Domini Dei." *Spec. perf.*, c. 4. The place quoted above is in Luke viii. 10. Compare Celano, *Vita secunda*, II, c. 147 (d'Al.).
[2] *Anal. Fr.*, III, 71.
[3] *Spec. perf.*, c. 6 (Sab. ed., p. 16).

ers sought him and promised penance and amendment with the exception of Peter Stacia, whom the otherwise so cheerful Francis is said to have cursed — a curse he never to the day of his death was willing to take back.[1]

It was not only evangelical simplicity which Francis found to have been impaired by Peter — it was also evangelical poverty, and therefore was Francis so inflexible. How was it possible to be a good Friar Minor, if one had to buy great, fine, learned, expensive books and have big, fine, costly houses to keep them in? Was it not written in the gospel — and therefore also in the Rule of the Order — "Take nothing with you on the way." "I understand these words thus," said Francis, "that the Brothers ought to have nothing except a habit with a rope and underclothing and shoes, as much as is necessary." "What shall I do?" a minister once asked him. "I have books that are worth more than fifty pounds of silver." "For the sake of your books I will not disobey the books of the gospel which I have promised to follow as my guide," answered Francis.[2] Therefore he did not neglect to insert in the ideal picture of a General of the Order, which he once produced, the minor but essential trait: "And he must not be a collector of books."[3]

But more will was needed to carry through this fight than Francis possessed. It was the others — those who were not content to honor wisdom at a distance, but wanted to have a part in it — who were the stronger. If Brother Leo is to be trusted, Elias and his party even made a direct attempt to have the Rule written by Francis invalidated, and to accept in its stead the Dominicans' Rule, for example, in which study occupied a much more prominent place. At a Chapter of the Order, perhaps in 1222 or 1223, they secured Hugolin for their plan. Francis heard the carefully framed remarks of the Cardinal. Without answering, he seized his hand, drew him out among the assembled Brothers and cried out in a loud voice:

[1] Angelo Clareno, quoted by Hilarin Felder, p. 125, n. 1. *Actus B. Francisci*, cap. 61.
[2] Cel., *Vita sec.*, II, 32 (d'Alençon). The passage of Scripture referred to is Luke ix. 3. Fifty pounds in modern money is about 450 dollars. (Hilarin Felder, p. 80, note 2.)
[3] "Non sit aggregator librorum." *Spec. perf.*, p. 156.

"My Brothers, my Brothers, the Lord called me to travel the paths of humility and simplicity and with me all those who want to follow and copy me. Do not then speak to me either of the Rule of St. Benedict or of St. Augustin or of St. Bernard or of any other. For the Lord said to me, that he wished me to be a fool and a simpleton, the like of which was never seen before, and that he wished to bring us on another road than that of wisdom. But God wants to put you all to shame with your wisdom and knowledge, and I expect that he will send his master of discipline and punish you, so that whether you will or not you must with shame turn back to your place."[1]

Was Francis justified in his fear of knowledge? It is true that the Apostle says, "Knowledge puffeth up; but Charity edifieth," but it is also true, what has been said in our day, that this word must often cover over something far different from holiness.[2] Purely and simply to seek the truth and nothing but the truth is also a cultivation of God, and the disinterested seeking of truth exercises a strengthening and purifying influence on the entire moral being of man. To be open to all truth is in reality a sign of a will open to all good. It is with justice that the Apostle speaks in another place of the "holiness of truth" — he knew that holiness in the will is a fruit of truth in thought, and that only *the full disposition for truth is the full disposition for holiness.*

What most displeased Francis was, perhaps in his innermost heart, the pride of intelligence, egoism, the perversion of wisdom to a means of flattering the vanity of the *ego*. He did not desire that man should adorn himself with wisdom so as to be looked at and esteemed of men. It was much better,

---

[1] *Spec. perf.*, c. 68. "Et dixit mihi Dominus quod volebat me esse unum novellum pactum." The correct reading is undoubtedly Pazzum (Ital. Pazzo); this is found also in a MS. of the fourteenth century edited by Lemmens, the *Verba S. Francisci*: "dixit mihi Dominus, quod volebat, quod ego essem unus novellus pazzus in hoc mundo" (*Doc. Ant. Franc.*, I, Quaracchi, 1901, p. 104). Bartholomew of Pisa (ed. 1513, fol. 32b) in a like sense has Fatuellum. Francis was clearly enough thinking of that *nuova passia* Jacopone da Todi was to sing of — that madness of the Cross, which Elias and his followers never knew or understood.

[2] *L'adage* "Scientia inflat," *cher à quelques saints et à beaucoup de paresseux.* (The Bollandist van Ortrov in *Analecta Bollandiana*. Quoted from memory.)

he felt, to fall on the knees and pray to God for your fellow men, alone and unknown in a grotto or a hermitage high up among the mountains, than in a cathedral with a soul full of vanity over what a fine fellow one is.

"These are my *Knights of the Round Table*," Francis was in the habit of saying with one of the wonted expressions from the days of his youthful knighthood-mania, "who live far away in desert places in prayer and meditation and weep over their own and the sins of others and live in simplicity and humbly. For when their souls will go before the Lord, then will the Lord show them the fruit and recompense for their work, namely many souls, whom they by their examples, prayers and tears have saved. 'My dear sons,' he will say, 'others preached with their learned words, but I saved souls by your merits; take the payment for your work and the fruit of your merits, which is the eternal kingdom of heaven.' But those who have not troubled themselves about anything else than to know and to show the way to others and have done nothing for themselves, they must stand naked and empty and to their shame before the judgment seat of Christ." To this illustration, which Francis was accustomed to give the Brethren at the General Chapters, he was accustomed to add an extract from the first book of Samuel (ii. 5): "the barren hath borne many: and she that had many children is weakened."[1]

Prayer and life in its entirety, not words or theory, was for Francis the essential in spite of everything — the essential on which he and his Brothers especially had to depend. Others might take the way that pleased them, he neither condemned nor criticized them, as little as he condemned or criticized those who went in gay and costly clothes. He believed that he knew only what it was that he and his were called to make straight on the earth, and if he finally — as some think — gave Anthony of Padua (whose Portuguese University acquirements had been discovered and were to be utilized) permission to teach theology to the Brothers in Bologna, then it certainly happened in the form preserved by tradition:

"To my dearest Brother Antonius greeting in Christ from Brother Francis. It pleases me that thou readest theology

[1] *Spec. perf.*, cap. 72.

for the Brothers, provided they do not for the sake of this study give up their prayers and slacken the spirit of devotion, as it stands in the Rule. Farewell."[1]

Francis here alludes to the final Rule in which this precept is found in the fifth chapter. This chapter may have then stood in the Rule, but the Rule as a whole may not have been as yet accepted and recognized. It was first on November 29, 1222 that it was so accepted, and Anthony left Bologna in 1224 to go to Montpellier. If his lectures may have extended over any considerable space of time, they must have begun earlier, and it would seem probable that this permission was given in the summer of 1222, when Francis is known to have been in Bologna. Anthony at the time was stopping in Forli, in the province of Romagna, to which also the learned University city belonged.

That Francis, moreover, in spite of all internal changes in his order, continued to be greeted by the people with the same inspiration as before, and that his simple sermons even in the learned Bologna had made the deepest impression, is made known to us by an eyewitness' tale. In Thomas of Spalato's *Historia Pontificum Salonitanorum et Spalatensium*, which was written before 1268, the author gives the following:

"The same year"—i.e., 1222—"on the holiday of the Assumption" (August 15) "as I was a student in Bologna, I saw St. Francis preach in the market-place in front of the court-house, where nearly all the town were gathered. But the beginning of his sermon was, 'Angels, Men, Devils.' He now spoke so well and skilfully on these three kinds of reasonable spirits, that many learned men who were present were not a little astonished to hear an unlearned man (*idiotae*) speak thus. But the whole theme of his discourse was to assuage enmities and to create peace. His habit was dirty, his appearance insignificant, his face not handsome. But

---

[1] Böhmer, "*Analekten*," p. 71. Compare Thomas of Celano, *Vita sec.*, II, c. 122 (d'Al.). "Et beato Antonio cum semel scriberet, sic poni fecit in principio litterae: Fratri Antonio episcopo meo." This address, so characteristic of Francis' politeness, is not to be found in the existing text; but there is no reason to doubt the authenticity of the letter. It is found for the first time in the *Chron. XXIV gen.* of the last half of the fourteenth century. (*Anal. Franc.*, III, 132.)

God gave his word such power, that many noble families, between whom there was much old-time enmity and spilled blood, allowed themselves to be induced to make peace. And all felt such great devotion and reverence for him, that men and women in crowds precipitated themselves upon him, and tried to tear off bits of his habit or even to touch the hem of his garment."[1]

It is impossible to read without emotion this old account by one who himself had seen and heard St. Francis. It seems as if Francis first wanted to impose upon his learned audience a little in choosing so academic a theme as the different kinds of intelligent beings, Angels, Men, Devils. But soon it was the old Francis again, the preacher disappeared, the people's speaker remained. And then did his words seize, attack and inspire for God just as in the old days in Assisi or Arezzo, or when he established peace between the Wolf of Gubbio and the citizens of the town. Old hatreds were written in the Book of Lethe, death and assassinations were stricken from the tablets, hands were clasped in forgiveness for recent bloodshed. Near as he was to his death Francis was the same as on the first day, when he stood upon the steps in the market-place of Assisi to exhort to peace. He is still *the Herald of the Great King*, and his message is exactly the same as fifteen years before — it is the greeting Jesus Himself had taught him: *Dominus det tibi pacem*, the Lord give thee peace.

---

[1] Böhmer, p. 106. Thomas was archdeacon in Spalato (Dalmatia) in 1230 and died May 8, 1268. Hitherto the date of this sermon of Francis has been given as 1220, following Wadding, but Böhmer (*"Analekten,"* p. 61) has definitely proved that it first was given in 1222. According to the *Actus b. Francisci*, cap. 36, during this stay in Bologna Francis converted two students of the Mark of Ancona, Peregrine of Fallerone and Ricetius from Muccia, who afterwards became Friars Minor. "And although Brother P. was very learned and very advanced in canon law, he would never want to be considered a clerk, but a simple lay-brother." This was quite in the spirit of Francis. See also *Fioretti*, cap. 27.

CHAPTER X

THE LEARNED FRANCISCANS AND THE THIRD ORDER

THE development Francis had opposed went its inflexible and unchangeable way. More and more did the Friars Minor become a learned Order of students like the Dominicans.

After the Pentecost Chapter of 1219 Brother Pacificus and his companions went back to France, provided with the Papal Letters of Introduction of June 11 of the same year. This time their intention was to stay in Paris, whither they seem not to have gone in 1217, on their first mission journey. The French clerics seem not to have been satisfied with the letters brought by the Brothers, and inquired about them in Rome. The result of this inquiry was a new Papal commendation, addressed directly to the French prelates and dated May 29, 1220.[1] This authorized the Brothers to settle in a house in St. Denis outside of Paris; they had there not even a chapel, but attended divine service in the adjacent parish church. Already in 1234 they had obtained their own large convent in St. Germain des Prés, and here a seminary was erected to accommodate 214 students. The number of applicants soon became so great, that often for long periods many had to remain enrolled upon the waiting lists, until the departure of students who had taken their examination gave room for others.

Franciscans of the old type saw only with doubt and reluctance this new departure. Especially was Brother Giles tireless in opposing it. Time after time he used his sharp wit against the learned Brothers who seemed to him false children

[1] *Pro dilectis filiis.* Sbar., I, p. 5. Potth., I, nr. 6263. Hilarin Felder: "*Gesch. der wissensch. Studien,*" p. 159.

of St. Francis. "There is a great difference," said he, "between a sheep which bleats and one which grazes. For braying does no one any good, but grazing does itself good. It is so with a Friar Minor who preaches, and one who prays and works. A thousand and again a thousand times better is it to teach oneself than to teach the whole world."

Another time he broke out thus: "Who is the richer — he who has only a little garden and cultivates it, or he to whom the whole world was given and who does nothing with it? So much wisdom does not help to salvation, but he who really wishes to know much must work much and bow his head low."

A Brother came to Giles and wished to have his blessing for preaching in the market-place in Perugia. "Yes," answered Giles, "provided thou wilt limit thy preaching to saying, 'A great cry and little wool is what I give!'" [1]

Once Giles went into the garden in front of the hermitage of Monte Rípido near Perugia, where he lived for thirty years after the death of Francis. He heard some laborers in a vineyard getting scolded by their master, because they talked instead of working. *Faite, faite, e non parlate,* "Work, work, and don't talk," the master of the vineyard said to them. This was just the word for Giles. He left his cell and sought the other Brothers: "Hear this now, what the man says, 'Work, work, and don't talk!'"

Another time Giles heard a turtle-dove cooing in the garden. "O sister dove," said he, "I will learn from you how to serve the Lord! For thou sayest always *Qua, Qua,* not *La, La,* — here, here on earth, and not there, there in heaven, are we to serve God. O sister dove, how beautifully thou cooest! O children of men, why do you not learn from our sister dove?"

In such moments, it seemed to Brother Giles as if the old times were back again, when he and Francis, as God's musicians, wandered through Italy. Inspired by the thought, he sang his songs in honor of his queen, Poverty, and her sister the noble lady Chastity, while he kept moving up and down among

---

[1] "docuit eum frater Aegidius quod sic diceret in sermone: *Bo, bo, molto dico e poco fo.*" (*Anal. Franc.,* III, p. 86.)

his flower-beds and played as if on a violin with two sticks, one of which he scraped across the other.[1]

But soon Brother Giles awakened from his memories and dreams and saw that the good old times were irrevocably gone, that Francis was dead, and he himself an old man whose ideas did not interest anyone. It was as if the sun was extinguished for him, and the flowers in his little garden smelt sweetly no longer, and the turtle-doves ceased their cooing. Then Brother Giles sighed deeply and long: "Our ship leaks and must sink; let him flee who can! Paris, Paris, thou ruinest St. Francis' Order!"

This sigh found its echo from now on among the best of the sons of St. Francis. "Paris, thou hast ruined Assisi" was the song of Jacopone da Todi.[2] And when Giles in his old age was placed before the General of the Order, St. Bonaventure, the first question he asked this learned man was the following: "Father, can we ignorant and unlearned men be saved?" "Certainly," answered St. Bonaventure kindly. "Can one who is not book-learned love God as much as one who is?" asked the old Franciscan again. "An old woman is in a condition to love God more than a master in theology" was Bonaventure's answer. Then Giles stood up, went to the wall of his garden and called out to the wide world, "Hear this, all of you, an old woman who never has learned anything and cannot read can love God more than Brother Bonaventure!"[3]

This true disciple of Francis of Assisi died soon after;

---

[1] *Anal. Franc.*, III, p. 86, p. 101. The song praising Poverty reads: "O mi fratello, o bel fratello, o amor fratello, fami un castello, che no abbia pietra e ferro. O bel fratello, fami una cittade, che no abbia pietra e ligname." For the sonnet in praise of Chastity, see p. 109, n. 1.

[2] "Mal vedemmo Parigi, che n' ha destrutto Assisi, con la lor lettoria l'hanno messo in mala via." (Jacopone da Todi: *Poesie spirituali*, ed. Tresatti. Venice, 1617, I, I, satira 10. Quoted by Felder, ditto, p. 234.)

[3] *Anal. Franc.*, III, p. 86, p. 101. Bonaventure, who in his writings often alludes to Brother Giles and puts him on the same plane with St. Augustin or Richard of St. Victor, has not forgotten this incident. In his *Collationes in hexaemeron* it is thus told: "Sic ecce, quod una vetula, quae habet modicum hortum, quia solam caritatem habet, meliorem fructum habet quam unus magnus magister, qui habet maximum hortum et scit mysteria et naturas rerum." (Bonav., *Opera*, t. V, Quaracchi 1891, p. 418, n. 26.) These *collationes* date from the years 1267-1273 (l.c. *Prolegomena*, p. XXXVI).

Giles joined his master and those friends who had gone before him on April 22, 1262 — the eve of the feast of St. George, the same evening on which he, over fifty years before, had sat by the fire in his father's house in Assisi and had heard him tell about Francis and had made up his mind to seek him. Through a long life he had kept his heart faithful to the first and only love of his younger days.[1]

The development of the Order in the direction of study had taken a greater impulse after the Franciscans went to England, September 10, 1224. This mission went out from France and was led by Agnello of Pisa, who had been *Custos* in Paris. The Brothers settled first in Canterbury, but as early as November 1, 1224 had established themselves in Oxford. Here they received a large accession of students and candidates from the celebrated University, and study was nowhere more eagerly pursued than among the English Brothers. Eccleston tells how they, on their bare feet, went long distances in frost and cold or in unfathomable mud to go to the lectures. At the same time they adhered most strictly to the Franciscan vows of poverty; they also had the Franciscan joy with them in their house; as soon as they saw each other they must laugh, and even in the church this ecstatic joy would seize them, so that for sheer happiness they could not say their choral prayers.[2] The Franciscanism of the English Brothers was thus in some ways very genuine, and Elias of Cortona, when General, had no more fixed opponents of his violations of the Rule than the learned Friar Minor, Adam of Marsh.[3] None the less it was an Englishman, Aymon of Faversham, who as General of the Order from 1240 to 1244 ordained that none except the book-learned should be officers in the Order.[4]

Brother Giles' and Brother Juniper's type was on the point of dying out. And how could it be otherwise? At the Pentecost Chapter of 1221 there were present three thousand of the Brethren. But could Francis expect that all

---

[1] Fr. Gisbert Menge: "*Der selige Agidius von Assisi*," Paderborn, 1906, pp. 114–116.
[2] *Anal. Franc.*, I, pp. 217–218, pp. 226–228.
[3] *Anal. Franc.*, III, pp. 229–230.
[4] "Hic generalis frater Haymo laicos ad officia ordinis inhabilitavit, quae usque tunc, ut clerici, exercebant." *Anal. Franc.*, III, p. 251.

these, like the first twelve disciples, were to be "Knights of the Round Table"? Jordanus of Giano tells very honorably of himself that he, instead of being an adventurous warrior of God's army, energetically set himself in opposition when it was proposed to send him as a missionary to Germany.[1] Brothers like this were no longer heaven-soaring larks; Francis saw justly in them chickens, who sought shelter under protecting wings.

The same tendency became manifest in the Third Order at last, the Order founded by Francis for married men and women.

If we believe Thomas of Celano, it came to pass that St. Francis, after having preached to the birds at Bevagna, came to a town called Alviano, between Orte and Orvieto, near Todi. Here he and Brother Masseo stopped in the market-place and were going to preach. But it was now evening, and the many swallows, who still build their nests in the old grey walls and ruinous towers of Alviano, circled to and fro with ceaseless twittering and glad little cries in and out of their nests under the eaves. Francis and Masseo, as was their custom, sang their Laud, *Timete et honorate*,[2] and the people collected and stood expectantly in silence, while the singing lasted. But those who did not keep silence were the swallows. Lower and lower they swept across the market-place in ever thicker flocks, and their twittering and cries increased until at last no sound could be heard. Then Francis looked up with his patient countenance and said very cheerfully: "My sister swallows, it seems to me now that the time has come when I should have a chance to speak; now you have said enough! Hear therefore God's word and keep still and quiet while I preach!" And at once all the swallows were silent and made no sound, as long as Francis preached.

"But on account of this miracle and on account of the glowing words Francis spoke, all the inhabitants of the town wanted to follow Francis and be his disciples. But Francis restrained them and said, 'Be not too hasty, I will ordain for you what you shall do to be saved.' And from that time on," the *Actus b. Francisci* goes on to say, "he thought of

[1] *Anal. Franc.*, I, p. 7.   [2] *Reg. prima*, cap. XXI.

establishing a third order *qui dicitur continentium*, which is called the abstainers."[1]

More than once such things happened to Francis. As an instance there was a parish priest who, after he had heard Francis, wished to live the same life as he did, without, however, abandoning his field of work. Francis conceded to him to remain in his church and only ordered him each year, when he had collected his tithes, to give the poor what might be left of the tithes of the preceding year.[2] It was a Franciscan renunciation of possessions modified to suit the circumstances of the case.

On one of his wanderings Francis met in the town of Poggibonsi in the valley of Elsa (between Florence and Siena) a merchant named Luchesio, whom, it seemed to him, he had known in early youth. Like the Sienese, John Colombini, who figured later, Luchesio had hitherto been a hard and penurious man, with one exception in his sparing ways. He was generous with the poor, gave lodging to pilgrims, received and helped widows and orphans. Francis seems to have had no influence in his conversion, but only to have given him and his wife, Bona Donna, a rule of life and a penitential garment. After this Luchesio devoted all his time to works of charity, took care of the sick in the hospitals and went out with an ass loaded with medicines into the fever-laden Maremma, to bring succor to the many fever patients there. If he was home, he worked in a little garden he had retained after parting with his other possessions, and whose fruits he sold. If this way of life did not bring him enough, he would go out and beg. Bona Donna seems for a while to have resisted vigorously these proceedings of her husband, but like John Colombini's wife, she is said to have become converted by a miracle. After this they lived in unity together and died at an interval of a few hours, April 28, 1260.[3]

---

[1] Cel., *V. pr.*, I, XX, 59. In *Actus b. Francisci* (Sab. ed., p. 57) the scene of this incident is laid in Cannara between Foligno and Bevagna. Bonaventure (XII, 4) gives Alviano. The same name might suggest Laviano in the valley of Chiana, but Wadding declares positively for Alviano near Todi (see 1212, n. 32). *Fioretti* (cap. 16) calls the town Savurniano.

[2] Bernard a Bessa (*Anal. Franc.*, III, pp. 686–687).

[3] *A. SS.*, April III, pp. 610–616. Count Orlando dei Cattani of Chiusi received a garment of penance from Francis also (see above p. 162, note 1).

Around Luchesio as a centre a circle of people of similar inclination collected in Poggibonsi, and in the same way, in other Italian cities, there were formed what Gregory IX was to designate as *Poenitentium collegia*, "communities of penitents."[1] It is to be believed that, as in the case above, Francis gave these penitents a Rule of Life; this was ever his custom with all who asked him for spiritual guidance. None of these Rules are in existence, and it is only by the help of later sources that we can acquire an idea of their actual scope and contents.[2]

It was characteristic of the Penitential Brothers — the expression Tertiary, i.e., Member of the Third Order of St. Francis, only appeared later — that they sought in their life in the world to imitate the ways of Francis and his Brothers. They were to be *in* the world, but not *of* the world. As soon as they entered the Brotherhood they pledged themselves to give back all unjustly acquired goods — which in many cases meant to give up everything — to pay the tithes for which they might stand in arrears, to make their wills in time to prevent strife among their heirs, not to take an oath, except in special, extraordinary cases, and not to accept public office. They wore a poor and distinctive habit and divided their time between prayer and deeds of charity. They generally lived with their families, but sometimes, like the Friars Minor, withdrew into solitude.

These Penitential Brothers very soon came in conflict with the public authorities, on account of their principles. Impressive in this aspect is an incident that occurred in the

[1] Gregory IX to Agnes of Bohemia, May 9, 1238 (Sbar., I, p. 241).
[2] I follow here Karl Müller's fundamental studies in "*Die Anfänge des Minoritenordens*," pp. 130 et seq., as well as Le Monnier: *Histoire de S. François*, II, pp. 1-40. The *regula et vita fratrum vel sororum poenitentium* found by Sabatier in the Franciscan convent in Capistrano in the Abruzzi and published in *Opuscules*, I, pp. 16-20, comprise probably the Rule written by Francis and Hugolin in co-operation for the Penitential Brothers and in any case date from 1228, except for a few later additions. The papal bulls in favor of the Brothers, quoted by Karl Müller as above, pp. 132 et seq., are about the best proofs. See also Mandonnet in Sabatier's *Opuscules*, I, pp. 143-245, Sabatier in *Coll.*, II, pp. 157-163, Götz: "*Die Regel des Tertiarierordens*," and Karl Müller: "*Zur Geschichte des Bussbrüderordens*," both in "Zeitschr. f. Kgsch.," Vol. XXIII (1902), pp. 97-107 and 496-524.

city of Faenza (near Rimini). Here the citizens had joined the local Brotherhood in great numbers, and when the mayor wished them to take the usual oath of obedience, by which they would oblige themselves to take up arms when the authorities ordered it, they refused to swear, under the claim that to swear such an oath involving the taking up of arms was against their Rule. By every means of compulsion the mayor tried to force the Brotherhood to take this oath, and apparently they turned in their need to Francis' friend, Cardinal Hugolin. This is the only supposition by which we can explain the fact that Honorius III, in a document of December 16, 1221, ordered the Bishop of Rimini to take the Penitential Brothers in Faenza into his protection.[1]

This dispute between the Penitential Brothers and the authorities soon spread over the whole of Italy. As a sort of punishment the cities subjected the Penitential Brothers to special taxes, or forbade them to give their property to the poor. In a circular letter to the Archbishops of all Italy, Honorius orders the clergy to take the side of the Brothers against the public authorities and to see that they are not injured in any way, and scarcely had Gregory IX become Pope when he time after time threatened the enemies of the Penitential Brothers with "the anger of God and of the holy Apostles, Peter and Paul."[2] More fortunately situated than the Quakers and Adventists of a later time, the Penitential Brothers could bring about at least a partial disarming in the quarrelsome Italian republics and in some degree pave the way for future days of greater peace. And thus it fell to Francis' lot, or to that of the movement instituted by him, to tame the wolves of the Middle Ages.

As soon as the dissension in Faenza broke out, it very naturally occurred to Hugolin to unite the scattered Brotherhoods into a united and therefore more powerful body. In the late summer of 1221 he still resided in Bologna and in its environs

---

[1] *Significatum est nobis* (Sbaralea, I, p. 8. Potth., I, 6736).
[2] In his letter of March 28, 1230 (*Detestanda humani generis*, Sb., I, p. 39, Potth., I, 8159) Gregory IX quotes his predecessor's bull. For Gregory's other utterances in favor of the Penitential Brothers see Sbar., I, pp. 30 and 65.

and therefore had much to do with the citizens of Faenza in various ways.[1] Francis and Hugolin apparently at this time wrote in common the first Rule for the Penitential Brotherhood or, as they were already called by Bernard of Bessa, the Third Order.[2] "The Third Order," the secretary of St. Bonaventure writes, "is equally for clerics and layfolk, maidens, widows and married people. The intention of the Brothers and Sisters of Penance is to live honorably in their residences and to busy themselves with pious actions and to flee from the vanities of the world. And among them thou seest noble knights and others of the great ones of the world in humble costume acting so beautifully with the poor and rich that thou canst well see that they truly are God-fearing."[3]

As has been said, the original Rule of the Third Order, which Francis and Hugolin wrote, has not been preserved for us. But it certainly was the foundation of the Rule of 1228,

[1] Böhmer has collected the proofs of this ("*Analekten*," p. XXXV).
[2] The Friars Minor are the first, the Clares are the second.
[3] *Anal. Franc.*, III, 686. Compare *Tres Socii*, cap. XIV end, as well as Mariano of Florence's work, hitherto only existing in manuscript, on the Third Order (MS. Palatin 147 in the National Library in Florence, studied by Sabatier in *Coll.*, II, pp. 157–163). It says in it of St. Francis: "Havendo adunque fornito la oratione et sentendosi pieno di divino spirito et con el consiglio et adiuto di messere Ugolino cardinale Ostiense che fu poi papa Gregorio nono compose et scripse una breue vita in quatordici rubriche distinta, la quale comincia: *Viri et mulieres hujus fraternitatis* etc. et intitulola: *memoriale propositi fratrum et sororum de poenitentia in domibus propriis existentium.* Sancto Francesco in comporre questa regola essendo col sopradetto cardinale quello che lo spirito li dictava al cardinale porgeva, et el cardinale con sua propria mano alcune cose soperendo scriveva. La quale regola con breve parole scripta in se grande substantia contiene et e comune a chierici et layci, homini et donne, soluti et coniugati, vergine et vedove et in conclusione contiene suoi professori honestamente vivino nelle lore case in penitentia e che dieno opera alle opere della pieta fugendo le mondiale pompe. . . . Et cosi scripta la regola comincio in decta citta di Firenze a ricevere al decto ordine li huomini et donne et questo achade lanno del Signore 1221 ad di venti di maggio."
We see how well Mariano's description of the Order agrees with that of Bessa. When the Florentine chronicler wishes to claim that the Third Order originated in Florence, perhaps it is his local patriotism which makes him do it. But it is also conceivable that the original Latin text employed by Mariano contained — as Böhmer maintains — the word "Faventia" (Faenza), and that he read it "Florentia." The Rule of 1228, found by Sabatier, which almost certainly originated in Faenza, has the exact title given by Mariano: *Memorale propositi fratrum et sororum de poenitentia in domibus propriis existentium.* Moreover, the date of publication is here found as 1221, and Chapter I begins *Viri qui huius fraternitatis fuerint.*

the merit of bringing which to light is Sabatier's, and which was valid in the Ravenna district, perhaps in Faenza. This Rule had the following contents:

The first to the fifth chapter gives directions about clothing, fasts, prayers; the sixth chapter, paragraph 1, is devoted to the Brothers' confessions and communions, which are fixed at three times in the year (July, Easter, Pentecost). Paragraph 2 inculcates conscientious payment of tithes; paragraph 3 contains the prohibition against bearing weapons; paragraph 4 forbids oaths (oaths of allegiance and oaths in court are excepted); paragraph 5 is directed against cursing and swearing. Chapter VII treats of Meetings of the Order (once a month; mass is read, there is preaching and a collection). Chapter VIII on the sick; they are to be visited once a week, to be helped corporally as well as to be admonished spiritually. Chapter IX on praying for the deceased members and attending the burials. Chapter X, paragraph 1, on making one's will within three months of the day of reception; paragraph 2, to observe peace among themselves; paragraph 3, how to meet the attacks of the public authorities (the Heads of the Brotherhood shall have recourse to the Bishop). Paragraph 5 of this chapter treats of the requirements for being a Brother or a Sister — that one shall make peace with his neighbor, return ill-gotten goods, and pay arrears of tithes. Chapter XI, paragraph 1, no heretic can be received; paragraph 2, married women must not be received without their husbands' consent. Chapters XII and XIII treat of the maintenance of discipline in the Order; especially are to be noted Chapter XIII, paragraphs 8 and 9, in which it is ordered that the member who has given open scandal and injured the good name of the Order shall acknowledge his offence before the assembled Brethren and accept his punishment. If the offence is very great, the offender can be expelled from the Order. In paragraphs 13 to 15 it is forbidden to take a complaint against a Brother or a Sister to the courts; all disputes must be settled within the Order. Paragraph 12 gives finally an addition to the command to return ill-gotten goods; if it is not known any more who has been wronged or who his heirs are, then by a public crier, or by posting on the church pillars, all and every one who has been injured by the newly entering Brother shall be invited to make known his claim.[1]

[1] The Rule of 1228 in Sabatier, *Opusc.*, I, pp. 16-30; Böhmer, "*Analekten*," pp. 73-82.

The Rule for Tertiaries in Florence (Faenza?) given by Mariano in the manuscript referred to differs, as far as a provisional judgment can go, not a little from the Rule contained in the Capistrano manuscript. See the list of chapter-headings in Mariano's version of the Rule given by Sabatier (*Coll.*, II, p. 159) and the comparison based thereon with the Capistrano Rule by Walter Götz in "Zeitschr. f. Kgsch.," XXIII (1902), pp. 100-101. As the Third Order, as already stated, was formed by the union of originally independent brotherhoods, there is nothing to preclude the belief that local interpretations existed along with the general Rule.

For the wider development of the Third Order see Karl Müller's (not unassailable) presentation in "*Anfänge des M. O.*," pp. 145 et seq.

The Third Order of the present day was reorganized by Leo XIII in 1883 by the Constitution *Misericors Dei filius*. See Rev. Eugène d'Oisy's *Directoire des Tertiaires de St. François*, Paris, 1905.

CHAPTER XI

ELIAS OF CORTONA AND THE FINAL RULE

THE co-operation of Francis and Hugolin on the Rule of the Friars Minor seems to have gone on in the same way as their co-operation in the Third Order's Rule. "St. Francis," says Mariano of Florence, "said to the Cardinal what the inspiration of the spirit told him, and the Cardinal wrote it down with his own hand and then added some things."[1]

A tale preserved for us in the *Legenda antiqua* gives a description of Hugolin's influence and of the correction he introduced. Francis, for instance, wanted to put into the Rule that if the ministers did not see to it that the Brothers followed the Rule literally and verbally, then the Brothers should be at liberty to follow the Rule, even against the desires of the ministers. Such a permission Francis had, among others, once given to Cæsarius of Speier; he alone or with others of the same mind had Francis' permission to separate themselves from such of the Brothers who might appear unfaithful to the Rule, and to be at liberty "to follow it literally and without interpretation."[2]

Undoubtedly Francis by this determination wanted to open a way of escape for the Brothers who in the questions of knowledge and poverty did not want to go with the stream. Hugolin was opposed to such a permission as being the sure road to the splitting up and dissolving of the Order. But

---

[1] *Coll.* (Sabatier), II, p. 161. Compare Hugolin's own words in the bull *Quo elongati* of September 28, 1230: "in condendo praedictam regulam . . . (Francisco) astiterimus" (Sbar., I, p. 68), and Bernard a Bessa in *Anal. Franc.*, III, p. 686.

[2] "ad litteram sine glossa" (compare Francis' strong prohibition in his Testament against interpreting the Rule and saying "it shall be thus understood," *Opuscula*, p. 82). Sab., *Opusc.*, I, pp. 96-97.

Francis strongly advocated that the necessary permission should be embraced in the Rule, whereupon Hugolin said, "I will arrange it so that the intent of the Order shall not be changed, but only the expression." Francis agreed to this, but what eventually appeared in the Rule is only a very weak replica of his thought.

In Francis' drawing up it was permitted, and even commanded absolutely in the name of obedience, that the Brothers should disobey their superiors as far as it was necessary for obeying the Rule *litteraliter*, for the Rule was above the minister and the oath of obedience was one of obedience to the Rule, not to the ministers.[1] In Hugolin's version the very Brothers in whom Francis saw his real sons, and to whom he had, in the person of Cæsarius of Speier, given his benediction, became a sort of Scrupulists, whom the ministers were exhorted to speak to with consideration and to exert persuasion upon. Those who in the eyes of Francis were the warriors of the good cause, in Hugolin's Rule become patients.[2]

In addition to Hugolin, Brother Elias had also a great influence, as the Vicar of the Order, on the final form of the Rule. We have a proof of this in a letter which Francis wrote to him in the winter of 1222–1223.

Elias had openly gone to Francis with a complaint against some Brothers and with pious wishes for their amendment. Francis answered quite out of his usual trend of thought:

"I will tell thee my ideas as well as I can: namely, that thou regardest it as a blessing only, both when the Brothers

---

[1] The same order of thought is to be seen in Thomas of Celano's expression "obedientiis cunctis Franciscum omnino propono." *V. sec.*, II, 84 (d'AL).

[2] We can compare the two texts:

"ad suos ministros debeant et possint recurrere [fratres], ministri vero teneantur eisdem fratribus per obedientiam postulata benigne et liberaliter concedere; quod si facere nollent, ipsi fratres habeant licentiam et obedientiam eam" [*sc.* regulam] "litteraliter observandi, quia omnes tam ministri quam subditi debent regulae esse subjecti" (Sab., *Opusc.*, I, p. 94).

"Et ubicumque sunt fratres qui scirent et cognoscerent se non posse regulam spiritualiter observare, ad suos ministros debeant et possint recurrere. Ministri vero caritative et benigne eos recipiant et tantam familiaritatem habeant circa ipsos ut dicere possint eis et facere sicut domini servis suis. Nam ita debet esse quod ministri sint servi omnium fratrum" (*Reg. sec.*, cap. X).

and other men oppose thee. . . . Thou must wish that it should be just so and not otherwise. . . . I know with certainty that in this there is true obedience. And love those who are opposed to thee, and wish nothing else for them than what the Lord will give thee. And herein show thou thy charity, that thou shalt *not* wish them to be better Christians. And that shall be more for thee than to withdraw to a hermitage." [1]

In the same deep spirit of charity that accepts *everything* from God's hand and will not even extricate itself from disagreeable surroundings or wish the betterment of one's fellow-men from the desire of effecting their improvement personally, Francis treats of another question, which undoubtedly often came upon the stage with him and Elias. It is the question of what shall be done with the Brothers who are fallen into sin. Elias, who was so anxious to improve his neighbor, was naturally in favor of strong measures — "It takes strong lye for a scurvy head" is one of the merciless popular proverbs. Francis, on the other hand, writes:

"As sure as thou lovest the Lord and me, His servant and thy servant, see thou to it that no Brother in the whole world, let him have sinned as he may, in any way, is permitted to go from thee without forgiveness, if he asks for it. And if he does not ask for forgiveness, then ask him if he does not want forgiveness. And if he comes a thousand times even before thy eyes with sin, then love him altogether more than thou lovest me, that thou mayest draw him to the Lord, and be always merciful to such. . . .

"But of all the chapters there are in the Rules and that treat of deadly sins, we will, with the help of the Lord at the Pentecost Chapter, together with the Brethren, make a chapter to this effect: 'If any Brother, prompted by the evil enemy, falls into deadly sin, then he is obliged to reveal it to his guardian. And all Brothers who know that he has sinned must not put him to shame or attack him, but must show

---

[1] "et non velis quod sint meliores christiani. Et istud sit tibi plus quam eremitorium" (Böhmer, p. 28). This is the reading of the three best manuscripts. A single MS. (S. Isidoro $\frac{1}{1}$) in Lemmens' *Opuscula* has (p. 108) the opposite: "in hoc dilige eos, ut velis, quod sint meliores christiani."

him great mercy and keep their Brother's sin very secret, for the healthy need no physician, only those who suffer illness. Likewise they are obliged to send him with a companion to the guardian (custos). And the guardian shall mercifully help him, as he himself would want to be helped if he were in a similar case. And if a Brother falls into a venial sin, then he shall make it known to one of the Brothers, who is a priest, and if there is no priest, he shall make it known to his Brother, until he can find a priest, who can give him true absolution; but no other penance shall be given him than this: 'Go forth and sin no more!'

"But that thou canst better comply with this letter, so keep it with thee until Easter. Then thou wilt be with thy Brothers. And then with the Lord's help we will see that a treatment is provided for everything lacking in the Rule."

Few parts of Francis' writings give a better insight into the unbounded mildness and patience of his disposition. He was not one to extinguish the feeble flame or to break the bending branch. If we examine the regulation adopted at the Pentecost Chapter of 1223, alluded to by Francis, it almost frightens us to see how little remains of what he desired. It runs thus short and dry:

"If any Brother, incited by the evil enemy, falls into mortal sin, and if this is one of the sins which only the minister of the province can absolve, he is obliged to go to his provincial minister immediately. And if the minister is a priest, he shall prescribe a penance for him and absolve him, but if he is not a priest, then he shall let another priest in the Order give him a penance, as it seems to him most serviceable in the Lord. And the ministers ought to be on their guard that they are not angry or irritated over the sins of others, for anger and irritation are hindrances to Christian charity."[1]

This leads up to a correct canonical mode of procedure, with some admonitions which belong elsewhere,[2] but which were given a place here to appease Francis in some measure. And what has become of all of the deep evangelical charity of Francis' letter—the charity which, face to face with the obdurate

[1] *Reg. secunda*, cap. VII.   [2] *Admonitio* XI.

or perhaps defiant sinner, is seized by innermost pity for his poor unfortunate soul and goes to him, falls on his neck, and whispers in his ear, "Brother, dear, dear Brother, *wilt* thou not pray for forgiveness?" What is there left of the prescriptions in Francis' draught that no Brother shall cast a stone at the sinner, that all shall keep silent about his fault and help him, as they themselves will some time need to be helped, and that if it is only a venial sin (*peccatum veniale*), then shall nothing be said to him other than the word of Jesus to the sinful woman, "Go and sin no more!"

It often happened to Francis that what he had written was erased or changed beyond all recognition. Thus the great reverence he had for the sacrament of the altar caused him to ordain that if the Brothers ever found a piece of paper on which the words of consecration of the mass, or even the word "God" or "Lord," was written lying in an inappropriate place, they should reverentially take up the paper and preserve it with reverence. This unceasing fine character of reverence, that could not bear to see holy words in wrong places, the leaders of the Brotherhood did not openly entrust to the Brothers — the reason given to Francis was that it would be difficult for them to observe such a command! To him it was almost a real sorrow of the soul that the word of the gospel, which had once had so great an effect upon him and his first friends — the words which had spoken to him in the Mass of St. Matthias at Portiuncula, and which he had afterwards found in the Scripture with Bernard of Quintavalle — that the words "Take nothing for your journey; neither staff, nor scrip, nor bread, nor money" were not to be allowed to stand in the Rule he was finally to give the Brethren. This was mercilessly omitted, and in spite of all Francis' humility this was very hard for him to endure. The line drawn through these words of the gospel went like a sting through Francis' heart; yes, he felt as if all that he had lived for, and for whose carrying into practice he had devoted his life, was now pronounced a cobweb of the brain and an exaggerated theory, and by those who should stand closest to him and should be the ones to carry out his work. From this time to the end Francis was, as his truest friend Leo has put it, a man deathly sick and marked for death, *erat prope mortem et graviter infirmabatur*.[1]

As in a great picture the later legends have preserved the memories of the entire strife between Francis and his opponents.

Francis—thus we are told in the *Speculum perfectionis* and by Conrad of Offida — had betaken himself to the hermitage of Fonte Colombo in Rieti, there to give the last touches to the Rule of the Order with fasting and prayer, and he had chosen Brother Leo and Brother Bonizio as his companions.

"And Francis was in a cave in the mountain side a stone's throw from the others, and what the Lord revealed to him in prayer, that he told them. And Brother Bonizio dictated and Brother Leo wrote. . . .

"It happened that there was a great commotion among all the Brothers in Italy, because Francis was writing a new Rule, and the one minister excited the next. And all who were in Italy went to Brother Elias, who was then Vicar, and said to him: 'We have heard that Brother Francis is writing a new Rule, and we are afraid that it is too hard to be followed. For he is very strict with himself and could easily command things we cannot observe. Say this to him, therefore, before it is ratified by the Pope!'

"Then Elias answered that he would not go alone to Francis, and they went together. And they came near to the place, and Brother Elias called out, 'The Lord be praised!' Then Francis came out and saw them and asked Brother Elias, 'What do these Brothers want? Have I not said that no one was to come here?' Brother Elias answered, 'It is all the ministers in Italy, who have heard that thou writest

---

[1] *Spec. perf.*, cap. 11. See also cap. 3: "licet ministri scirent quod secundum regulam fratres tenerentur sanctum evangelium observare nihilominus fecerunt removeri de regula illud capitulum *Nihil tuleritis in via*." Cap. 65: "Voluit etiam poni in regula quod ubicumque fratres invenirent nomina Domini. . . . Et licet non scriberentur hæc in regula, quia ministris non videbatur bonum, ut fratres hæc haberent in mandatum." Cap. 2: "fecit [Fr.] in regula plura scribi, quae cum assidua oratione et meditatione a Domino postulabat pro utilitate religionis, affirmans ea penitus esse secundum Dei voluntatem, sed postquam ea ostendebat fratribus videbantur eis gravia et importabilia. . . . Et nolebat contendere cum eis." Compare Cel., *Vita secunda*, III, 122: "Hoc sane verbum voluit in regula ponere, sed bullatio facta præclusit."

a new Rule, and now they say that thou shalt write it so that they can obey it, for if thou dost not do this, they will not bind themselves by it, and so thou canst write it for thyself and not for them!'

"Then St. Francis lifted up his voice and cried out, 'O Lord, answer thou for me!' And then all heard the voice of Christ in the air, which said: 'Francis, there is nothing in the Rule of thine but it is all mine, whatever it is, and I wish that the Rule shall be literally obeyed, literally, without interpretation, without interpretation, without interpretation! And whosoever will not obey it may leave the Order!' Then St. Francis turned to the Brothers and said to them, 'Have you heard that? Have you heard that? Or shall it be said once more to you?' But the ministers went away terrified."[1]

This relation, which is also found in Ubertino of Casale, is evidently not intended to refer to the Rule ratified by the Pope in 1223. I reached this conclusion at the time (1903) I wrote about Fonte Colombo in my "Pilgrimsbogen" ("The Pilgrim's Book"), and I argued hotly with Paul Sabatier in its introduction. The Rule, to which the above relation refers, and which Christ in apparition approved, is quite clearly an earlier Rule: that, namely, of which Bonaventure speaks in his biography, saying that Brother Elias received it from Francis and *soon after said that he had lost it*.[2] It was after this that, at a new residence at Monte Colombo, the Rule

[1] *Spec. perf.*, cap. 1. *Verba fr. Conradi*, I (Sab., *Opusc.*, I, pp. 370-374). A description of Fonte Colombo, "the Franciscan Sinai," is given in Jörgensen's "Pilgrimsbogen" (Copenhagen, 1903), chapters VIII to X.

[2] "Volens igitur confirmandam regulam . . . ad compendiosiorem formam . . . redigere, in montem quendam cum duobus sociis . . . conscendit, ubi pane tantum contentus et aqua, ieiunans conscribi eam fecit, secundum quod oranti sibi divinus Spiritus suggerebat. Quam cum de monte descendens, servandam suo vicario commississet, et ille paucis elapsis diebus, assereret per incuriam perditam." *Leg. major*, IV, 11. The whole description tallies with *Spec. perf.* and originated with Brother Illuminato or possibly with Brother Leo himself. The *Spec. perf.* also says (cap. 1) that "secunda regula, quam fecit B. Franciscus, perdita fuit." That Brother Elias was not particular in the means he adopted is seen from his most evident invention ("frater Helias dixerat, se fuisse receptum ad ordinem sub alia regula domini Innocentii non bullata; et ideo, quia . . . non voverat paupertatem (!) poterat recipere pecuniam, ut dicebat." *Anal. Franc.*, III, p. 231. On the preceding page is Elias' assertion that, in accordance with Francis' wish "quam secreto didici," he built the basilica over his grave!).

was produced which Honorius III approved on November 29, 1223, and which Francis wrote because he "feared to irritate the Brothers and did not wish to contend with them, but with better knowledge he acceded to them and excused himself before God. And as for the word of the Lord which it was given him to announce, that it might not remain without fruit, so would he live after it himself, and therein he found at last rest and comforted himself therewith."[1]

The above is not to be understood as if the Rule approved by Rome was quite lacking in the Franciscan imprint. On the contrary, if we knew no other and had no suspicions of the changes it has undergone, it would never occur to us that it was not the Rule written by Francis' own hand. In it we find the essential maxims characteristic of St. Francis — first and foremost, in the very prologue, the obligation to "live after the gospel, in obedience, poverty and chastity." And here and there in the twelve chapters, of which the Rule, in accordance with Francis' reverence for the Twelve Apostles, consists, are found a whole series of real Franciscan principles. Thus we may cite the absolute prohibition to accept money (cap. IV) and to own nothing (cap. VI), the command to work (cap. V), without shame to ask for alms (cap. V), to wear simple clothes, which it is allowed to patch with sackcloth and other rags (cap. II) without the Brothers in the pride of poverty daring to condemn those who dress in fine clothing and live in luxury and happiness (same chapter). As the Brothers wander through the world they should be mild, peaceful, modest, humble, friendly to all. They shall not contend among themselves and shall judge no one. When they enter a house their greeting shall be *Pax huic domui*, "Peace be to this house," and what is put before them, in accordance with the gospel, they have permission to eat (cap. III). The Brothers must not preach if the Bishop of the place is opposed to it (cap. VI). They must not enter a nuns' convent (cap. XI). Those who are priests shall say their office after the custom of the Roman Church, but

---

[1] *Spec. perf.*, cap. 2. Especially is the expression to be noted: "condescendebat invitus voluntati eorum." Francis was brought to this in opposition to his character and principles.

lay-brothers shall say the *Pater noster* (cap. III). Those who cannot read shall preferably not try to learn to do so, but they shall recollect that what they before all came here for is to refrain from all pride, all vanity, all envy, all slander and complaining, all covetousness and all the troubles of the world, to have the spirit of the Lord and do God's work, always to pray to Him out of a pure heart and preserve humility and patience in persecutions and sickness, and to love them who hate us and torment us and sue us, for the Lord says: "Love your enemies and pray for them who persecute you and slander you. Blessed are you who suffer persecution for justice's sake, for yours is the kingdom of heaven. And he who endureth to the end shall be saved." (Cap. X.)

Thus in spite of all, even to-day in the Rule of the Friars Minor there burns a flame of the holy fire Francis came to the world to kindle, and down through time the best and noblest among the Franciscans have devoted their lives to keeping this flame pure. *Sine glossa, sine glossa,* these words of Christ to Brother Elias at Fonte Colombo were their war-cry — "without interpretation, without change" they wished to live after the law which for them was "the book of life, the hope of salvation, the seed of the gospel, the way of the Cross, the state of perfection, the key of paradise, a first taste and an aspiration after the eternal life."[1] Down through the centuries one form after the other is to be seen, in whom Francis seems to have again come to life — John of Parma, Hubert of Casale, Peter John Olivi, Angelo Clareno, Gentile of Spoleto, Paolo Trinci, St. Bernardine of Siena, Matteo da Basci, Stefano Molina. Again and again crowds of barefoot Brothers gather around these men who in their coarse brown robes, with rope around their waists, go to the old hermitages where Francis and his first Brothers prayed, and where they can chant the old, half-forgotten chapters of the Rule as if it were a new and unheard song, telling them to "wander through the world as pilgrims and as strangers without other possessions here upon earth than the inalienable treasure of the most exalted poverty" (cap. VI).

[1] *Spec. perf.*, cap. 76. Written by an Umbrian Spiritual (i.e., a Franciscan of the strict observance. See Appendix, p. 390)..

There is a tone of Portiuncula and Rivo Torto that over and over again exerts its great power, and like the Swiss sentinel who on Strassburgh's rampart heard the *Kuhreigen* of his childhood's days sung across the Rhine, the Friars Minor cast all things away which might hinder them in swimming over the rapid stream to their fatherland and home.

CHAPTER XII

THE LAST VISIT TO ROME AND THE CRIB AT GRECCIO

FRANCIS was last in Rome in the year 1223, to obtain the Papal ratification of his Rule, and Hugolin was helpful to him in this. "When we still occupied a lower office we were with St. Francis when writing the Rule, and obtained the confirmation of it by the Holy See," he says himself in 1230 after he was Pope.[1]

During this visit Francis undoubtedly again visited "Brother Jacoba," Jacopa de Settesoli, who in 1217 had become a widow. She was one of the two women with whose features, according to his own statement, he was acquainted (the other was St. Clara).[2] In her house he felt that he was welcome — it was his own Bethania, and Jacopa was Mary and Martha combined. She prepared for him the aliments he liked — among others the almond cream which he in his last sickness thought he would like to taste.[3] In return he gave her a legacy, which was exactly in his way of thought. He could never bear to see a lamb led to the slaughter-house; it reminded him of Jesus, as he was taken to Golgotha, and he

---

[1] "quum ex longa familiaritate, quam idem confessor Nobiscum habuit, plenius noverimus intentionem ipsius; et in condendo praedictam regulam obtinendo confirmationem ipsius per Sedem Apostolicam sibi astiterimus, dum adhuc essemus in minori officio constituti." (Gregor IX's Bull *Quo elongati* of September 28, 1230 in Appendix to Sabatier's *Spec. perf.*, pp. 315–316.)

[2] Cel., *Vit. sec.*, III, c. 55 (Amoni).

[3] "Illam autem comestionem vocant Romani mortariolum quae fit de amygdalis et zucario et de aliis rebus." *Spec.* (ed. Sab.) p. 221.

Sabatier identifies this favourite food of Francis with the well-known stone-hard Roman mostaccioli (see Jörgensen's "Pilgrimsbogen," p. 61). On the other side f. Edouard d'Alençon: *Frère Jacqueline*, p. 19, n. 2; in *mortariolum* (in Old French *mortairol*) he sees rather "cette crème d'amandes bien connue aujourd'hui sous le nom de frangipane," a name in which he finds an allusion to Jacopa's name (her married name was Frangipani).

always tried, when he could, to obtain its freedom. Thus he succeeded in the Mark of Ancona in getting a merchant to buy the lamb, with which he next presented himself before the Bishop of Osimo. It was only after long explanations that Francis succeeded in making this prelate understand why he came in such a procession, and the lamb was then given to the Nuns of San Severino. Out of its wool a habit was made, which was sent to Francis at the next Pentecost Chapter.[1] On another occasion Francis gave his cloak as ransom for two small lambs which a peasant was carrying. "For when Francis heard the lambs bleating his heart was moved, and he went and caressed them and comforted them like a mother who comforts her crying child. And he said to the peasant, 'Why do you torment so my brothers the lambs?' But the peasant answered, 'I am going to market with them to sell them.' 'And then what will they do with them?' 'Those who buy them will slaughter and eat them!' 'That will not soon happen,' said Francis, and bought them straightway from the man."[2] At Portiuncula he long had a tame lamb which followed him everywhere, even into church, where its bleatings were mingled with the songs of the Brethren.[3]

Also in the same way in Rome, Francis had procured a lamb for himself, which upon his departure he gave to Jacopa. In her house it lived long, and it is told that it followed her to mass in the morning and that, in its eagerness to go to church, it would wake its mistress with little friendly buttings of its head when she was late in getting up.[4] Out of its wool Jacopa spun and wove the habit which, in the autumn of 1226, she took with her to Portiuncula, and in which Francis died.[5]

It was not only the kind hospitality of Jacopa de Settesoli that Francis shared, he was also guest among the Cardinals.

[1] Cel., *Vita prima*, I, XXVIII, n. 78.
[2] *ibidem*, n. 79.
[3] "ovis autem . . . audiens fratres in choro cantare, et ipsa ecclesiam ingrediens . . . vocem balatus emittens ante altare Virginis, Matris Agni, ac si eam salutare gestiret" (Bonav., VIII, 7).
[4] Bonaventure, *ibidem*.
[5] E. d'Alençon: *Frère Jacqueline*, p. 24.

He followed in this respect his Brothers' example. Already at an early period of the development of the Order several Cardinals had wished to have a Friar Minor with them, "not for the sake of any use or service, but for the devotion they nourished for the holiness of the Brothers."[1] Thus Brother Giles lived for a time with Cardinal Nicholas Chiaramonti,[2] Brother Angelo Tancredi with Cardinal Leone Brancaleone.[3] It could be termed a pious custom at the Papal Court to have a Friar Minor in the house; Thomas of Celano censures sharply the idleness and life of luxury of these "Court-Brothers."[4]

In Francis was lacking the material for such a Court-Brother (*frater palatinus*). In Hugolin's house he never forgot to go out and beg his food and *to bring* the bread thus acquired to the Cardinal's table.[5] And scarcely had he with the domesticated Brother Angelo installed himself with Cardinal Leo, where there was given them a lonely tower which the Cardinal said was as good as a hermitage, when the tormentors of the demon came on the first night and fell upon Francis.

"But the next morning Francis said to Brother Angelo: 'Why have the demons beaten me, and why has the Lord given them power over me? The demons are our Lord's chastisers, for as the civil authorities send their *guastaldi*[6] to punish those who have done wrong, thus does the Lord chastise and punish by his *guastaldi*, who are the devils, those whom he loves. For the Lord really loves those for whom he leaves nothing unpunished in this life.

"'And I am now firmly of opinion, that with God's grace I have offended in nothing, without having done the utmost therefor to have my injustice absolved and make it good again. But it may be that this punishment is sent to me

---

[1] "unusquique eorum" [*i.e.*, cardinalium] "desiderabat habere in curia de ipsis fratribus non pro aliquo servitio recipiendo ab ipsis, sed propter sanctitatem fratrum et devotionem qua fervebant ad eos" (*Tres Socii*, cap. XV, ed. Amoni, p. 88).
[2] See page 109.
[3] *A. SS.*, Oct. II, p. 605, n. 322.
[4] *Vita sec.*, II, 84 and 85 (d'Alençon).
[5] *Spec. perf.*, cap. 23. Cel., *Vita sec.*, II, 43 (d'Al.).
[6] A Lombard word, corrector or provost.

because I have accepted the Cardinal's friendly invitation. For even if I can accept it, then my Brothers will hear of it, who wander in foreign lands and suffer hunger and many troubles, and my other Brothers who live in hermitages and in poor little huts will hear of it, too, and then they will complain about me perhaps and say, "We have to suffer while he is in comfort!" For I am given to the Brothers for a good example, and it is of more edification to them if I am with them in their poor little houses, and they will bear their lot more patiently when they see that I have no better lot than theirs.'"[1]

On that very day Francis bade farewell to the Cardinal and his tower, and although it was a bitter cold December day, when the rain pours almost constantly down from the Roman sky, he was not to be held back. Porta Salara was soon behind him and Francis went to the north, on the miry road, in blasts of wind and teeming rain. Notwithstanding the grey sky and the rainy weather his heart was filled with sunlight all at once, and he involuntarily went ahead faster so as soon to see his dear valley of Rieti and again to be among the faithful Brothers in Fonte Colombo.

And now another comfort awaited him above, among the wild Sabine Hills.

Since his trip to the Holy Land and his visit to Bethlehem, Francis had a special devotion to the Christmas time. One year the festival fell on a Friday, and Brother Morico propounded to the Brothers the opinion, that for that reason meat might not be eaten on Christmas day. "If it is Christmas it is not Friday," replied Francis. "If the walls could eat flesh, I would give them it to-day, but as they cannot, I will at least rub them over with it!" He often said of this day: "If I knew the Emperor, I would ask him that all would be ordered on this day to throw out corn to the birds, especially to our sisters the larks, and that every one who has

---

[1] *Spec. perf.*, cap. 67. Compare for Francis' relation to the demons *Spec. perf.*, c. 59 (he was disturbed by them at night in the church of S. Pietro di Bovara, near Trevi); Bartholi, cap. 8 (*Coll.*, II, p. 18; in the church *Quatuor Capellae*, outside of Todi, Francis was tempted to give up his life of penance); *Actus*, c. 31 (Francis saw that it was the devil who showed himself to Rufino in the form of Christ).

a beast in the stable should give them a specially good feed for love of the Child Jesus born in a manger. And this day the rich should feast all the poor."[1]

In the year 1223 Francis himself celebrated Christmas in a way the world had never seen the match of. In Greccio he had a friend and well-wisher, Messer John Vellita, who had given him and his Brothers a wood-grown cliff up above Greccio, for them to live there. Francis now had this man called to Colombo and said to him: "I want to celebrate the holy Christmas night along with thee, and now listen, how I have thought it out for myself. In the woods by the cloister thou wilt find a cave, and there thou mayest arrange a manger filled with hay. There must also be an ox and an ass, just as in Bethlehem. I want for once to celebrate seriously the coming of the Son of God upon earth and see with my own eyes how poor and miserable he wished to be for our sakes."

John Vellita looked after all of Francis' wishes, and at midnight of Christmas eve the Brothers came together to celebrate the festival of Christmas. All carried lighted torches, and around the manger the Brothers stood with their candles, so that it was light as the day under the dark vaulting of the rocks. Mass was said over the manger as the altar, so that the Divine Child under the forms of bread and wine should himself come to the place, as bodily and discernibly he had been in the stable of Bethlehem. For a moment it seemed to John Vellita that he saw a real child lying in the manger, but as if dead or sleeping. Then Brother Francis stepped forward and took it lovingly in his arms, and the child smiled at Francis, and with his little hands stroked his bearded chin and his coarse grey habit. And yet this vision did not astonish Messer Giovanni (John). For Jesus had been dead or else asleep in many hearts, but Brother Francis had by his voice and his example again restored the Divine Child to life and awakened it from its trance.

As the Gospel was now sung, Francis stepped forward in his deacon's vestments. "Deeply sighing, overcome by the fullness of his devotion, filled with a wonderful joy, the

[1] Cel., *Vita sec.*, II, 151 (d'Al.). *Spec. perf.*, cap. 114.

holy one of God stood by the manger," says Thomas of Celano.[1] "And his voice, his strong voice, and glad voice, clear voice and ringing voice invited all to seek the highest good."

Brother Francis preached on the Child Jesus. "With words that dripped with sweetness, he spoke of the poor King who is born in the night, and who is the Lord Jesus in the city of David. And every time he would name the name of Jesus, the fire of his love overcame him, and he called him instead the Child from Bethlehem. And the word Bethlehem he said with a sound as if of a lamb that bleats, and when he had named the name of Jesus, he let his tongue glide over his lips as if to taste the sweetness this name had left there as it passed over them. The holy watch-night only ended late, and every one went with joy to his home.

"But later the place where the manger stood was dedicated to the Lord for a temple, and over the manger an altar was erected to the honor of our blessed Father Francis, so that where the dumb animals formerly ate hay out of the manger, there men now receive the spotless lamb, our Lord Jesus Christ, for the salvation of their soul and body, he who in unspeakable love gave his blood for the life of the world, and who with the Father and the Holy Ghost in eternal divine glory lives and rules for ever and ever. Amen."

[1] *Vita prima*, I, c. XXX. Compare *Tractatus de miraculis*, c. III, n. 19.

BOOK FOUR
FRANCIS THE HERMIT

> Corpus est cella nostra, et anima est eremita qui moratur intus in cella ad orandum Dominum et meditandum de ipso.
>
> *The body is our cell, and the soul is a hermit who stays within in the cell for praying to the Lord and for meditating on him.*
>
> FRANCIS in *Speculum perfectionis*.

CHAPTER I

THE WRITER

FROM this period to the day of his death Francis had two things to live for — to live himself in accordance with the gospel to the last degree of perfection and thus by his example to show the Brethren the right way, and next by new writings to supply what was wanting in the Rule approved by the Pope, and what he was not permitted to say in it. Those days in which Francis, at first alone and then with a following of the Brothers, went about like an evangelist and one of God's singers, were past and gone; in the years which were left to him, he was to work with his pen and in private life.

A considerable part of these his last years Francis spent in the valley of Rieti. This valley, traversed by the river Velino, stretches from Terni down towards Aquila, is bordered on the one side by the Sabine Hills, on the other by the mighty, cloud-covered and snow-clad Abruzzi, and had been the scene of one of Francis' earliest mission journeys. Every one of the little towns which now as then hang on the mountain side or cover the mountain tops recalled to him the time before any of his illusions had vanished, and when he had still entertained the possibility of throwing a bridge across from heaven to earth *to take* all mankind with himself into paradise. He had now fully learned of what stuff men are made, and that some, as in the gospel, are taken up with their oxen, others with their crops, when the invitations go out for the great supper. But Francis knew also, what again is to be found in the gospel — that the master in the heavenly kingdom was enraged and said to his servants: "Go out quickly into the streets and lanes of the city, and bring in hither the poor, and the feeble, and the blind . . . that my house may be filled!" With greater faith than ever Francis took up the precepts of the Sermon on the Mount: "Blessed are the poor, Blessed are the peacemakers, Blessed are the pure of heart!"

After this, when he spoke to his Brothers it was not as one having authority over them. He still can be disturbed by ministers and prelates who send his Brothers where he does not want them to go, and in the emotions of the moment he can break out: "Who are you that have dared to take my Brothers away from me?"[1] But he depends on God and on His *guastaldi;* if the Friars Minor fall away from their ideal, men will despise them, yes, persecute them and thus drive them back into the right paths.[2] He himself is no longer obliged to do more than pray for the Brethren and by his example hold up the ideal before their eyes, so that no excuse can be offered for remissness. Can God well ask more of a sick man?[3]

And this is the place to speak of Francis' sickness or sicknesses, as especially they afflicted him in the last years of his life. His health had, as we know, never been very good. We see him in his youth attacked by one fever after another. Since then his many and long fasts had undermined his constitution. Demons could drive him to the border of despair by saying to him, "There is salvation for every sinner, except for him who has ruined himself by excessive penances!"[4] He seldom ate food that was prepared, and dusted it in such case by throwing ashes on it, saying, that "Sister ashes was chaste." He slept but little, and then by choice sitting, or with a stone or log of wood for a pillow.[5] In Carceri and later at La Verna his bed was the bare rock. After he had led this life for twenty years his body was all broken down; he had hæmorrhages from the stomach and the Brothers often believed his end was near.[6]

To this must be added the misfortune, that Francis during his stay in the Orient had contracted the Egyptian eye-sickness, so that at times he was nearly blind. It was no

[1] *Spec. perf.*, cap. 41. Cel., *V. sec.*, III, 18 (Amoni).
[2] *Spec.*, c. 71.   [3] *Spec.*, c. 81.   [4] Cel., *Vita sec.*, II, c. 82 (d'AL).
[5] Cel., *V. pr.*, I, c. XIX. Bonav., V, 1.   [6] Cel., *V. pr.*, II, VII, n. 105.

wonder then, that in a letter, written in that year, he signs himself as *homo caducus*, "a decrepit man."[1] It was almost a matter of necessity for him to be restricted to an apostolate by letters in which his zeal for leading men to heaven found expression up to the last. In this last epoch of his life Francis sent out five letters or circular epistles — a letter to all Christians, a letter to a Pentecost Chapter at which he could not be present (1224), a letter to all clerics, a letter to all guardians (custodes) and a letter to all Superiors. To these must be added his testament, the testament to the Clares, and finally his religious poetry — above all his Song to the Sun. To the same time we may certainly assign a little autograph writing or letter to Brother Leo.

But now we must not expect to find in the letters of Francis of Assisi new and surprising thoughts. It was precisely the old thoughts he wished to inculcate. The letters, moreover, are addressed to various circles, so that Francis had no reason to avoid repetition. A careless reader will find the five letters, therefore, poor in ideas and tiring with their constant repetition of two or three topics, but — Boehmer remarks — "if one thinks of the personality that stood behind the words, the simple and unlearned man from Assisi in all his naïveté and abounding love, then do the dead words become loving flesh, and the poverty of spirit reveals itself as richness. For the little which Francis possessed was not learned or prepared, it filled and possessed him completely, and therefore his words, notwithstanding all outer lack of elegance, acted on men with the power of a revelation."[2]

If we read through these letters of Francis, we find in reality nothing else in them than what we already are familiar with in his *Admonitiones* and in his *Regula prima*, and in his letter to Elias. There are the same precepts to serve and love God, to live a life of conversion, to fast — also in metaphorical sense to fast from sin and crime[3] — to love and help our enemies, not to seek worldly wisdom or exalted positions, to pray much, to confess and approach the altar, to try to

---

[1] *Ep. ad. cap. generale* (Böhmer, "*Analekten*," p. 57).
[2] "*Analekten*," 52–53.
[3] "Debemus etiam jejunare et abstinere a vitiis et peccatis" (*Anal.*, p. 52).

do good where we have been doing evil. The last precept gave Francis a chance in one of his documents, in a letter we might call a contemplative epistle, to introduce a description of how a sinner dies (*De infirmo qui male poenitet*).[1]

"The body sickens, death approaches," Francis writes. "The relatives and friends come and say, 'Prepare thy house!' And his wife and children, his nearest ones and his friends, act as if they wept. And the sick one looks around and sees them weep and is moved by a false emotion and thinks to himself, 'Yes, I will give over myself with soul and body and all that I have into your faithful hands!' Truly the man is damned, who gives his soul, his body and all he has, into such hands and depends upon them! Therefore the Lord says through the prophet, 'Cursed is he who depends upon a man!' And at once the priest is brought. And the priest says to him, 'Dost thou wish to do penance for all thy transgressions?' The sick man answers, 'Yes.' And the priest asks, 'Wilt thou give reparation to all whom thou hast defrauded and betrayed, as far as thou canst?' He answers 'No.' And the priest says, 'Why not?' He answers, 'Because I have given all to my family and to my friends.' And thereby he misses his goal, and dies without having done reparation for his injustice. But what all must know is this, that where and however a man dies in grievous sin without having made good his injustice, when he could have done it, but would not, such a soul the devil at once takes, and how great his sorrow and pain becomes no one knows, except he who experiences it. And all motion and all power, all knowledge and wisdom he thought he had, all that is taken away from him. And he leaves after him his property for his family and his friends, and they take and divide it up among themselves and say thereafter, 'May his soul be cursed, that he has not earned more for us and left us more!' And thus he loses all in this world, and in the other is tormented in everlasting hell."

There is in this picture a bitterness in the comprehension of mankind, that is elsewhere not to be found in Francis. It is no comfortable picture, he sketches, of these selfish

[1] *Ep. ad omnes fideles*, § 12 (*Anal.*, pp. 55–56).

"nearest ones," who stand around the bed of the dying man, and willingly let him go to hell, as long as they can get him to make a will in their favor. And when they have by their hypocritical emotions induced the man they pretend to love to end his unjust life with a last irreparable crime, they curse him, as soon as he has closed his eyes on this life and has opened them in everlasting torments, because he has not scraped together more for their benefit. All through his life they have seen in him only a work-slave whose wages they were to get, indifferent whether they were justly or unjustly earned. That he risked his eternal salvation to accumulate money enough, that never for a moment occurs to them — why should they think of that now in his last moments? We feel as if we were reading one of Leo Tolstoy's most gripping novels — for example, the short story which is called, "Before the Judgment Seat of Death," and which treats of how Ivan Ilitsch under his long last illness lay and discovered that he never had been loved, that his wife had never seen in him anything as far as she was concerned but a source of money for her and nothing else, and perceivèd that his children were trained to the same, to regard him as the old man who was good to "touch," and who now unfortunately was "going off." But more unfortunate than Ivan Ilitsch, the dying man of Francis of Assisi's little tale does not get his eyes opened before it is too late — and too late for ever.

In the letter to the Brethren assembled at the Chapter of Pentecost, 1224, in the letter to the clerics and to the guardians (Superiors of convents), Francis especially seeks to emphasize the precepts which had been omitted from the Rule. He exhorts the Brethren to great reverence for the sacrament of the altar; if a number of priests are together only one mass is to be said, which the others can be content at being present at; he says to pick up every piece of paper on which holy words may be and to preserve such with reverence; the Office is to be said with more regard to inner devotion than to melody of voice,[1] the sacred vessels and the altar-cloths

[1] "non attendentes melodiam vocis, sed consonantiam mentis." ("*Analekten*," p. 61.)

should be kept shiningly clean, and the most holy sacrament should be preserved with reverence. And when it is offered on the altar in the mass, all shall kneel down, praise and glorify God, and the church bells are to be rung so that all near can participate in this giving of praise.

"And I, Brother Francis, your little servant, pray and beseech you in charity, which is God himself, and with the desire to kiss your feet, that you with humility and charity accept these and other of the words of our Lord Jesus Christ and practise them and keep them perfectly. And they who cannot read, let them often have them read for them and have them with them and live after them to the end with holy actions, for these words are spirit and life. And whoso does not do this shall be called to account at the last day before the judgment seat of Christ. And all those who accept the word with joy and embrace it and live after it, an example to others, and persevere to the end, may they be blessed by God the Father, Son and Holy Ghost. Amen."[1]

It seems to have been at this time that Francis conceived the idea of sending Brothers out to all the provinces with beautiful, bright ciboria (*pyxides*), and everywhere where they found the Lord's Body improperly preserved, they should give the priest of the place one of the new altar-vessels. Other Brothers he would send out with good, ornamented host-irons to make beautiful and pure altar-bread with.[2] It is certain, that none of these plans was widely carried out; yet in the convent of Greccio a host-iron is to be found, which it is said was presented by Francis.[3]

The letter to all authorities, namely, "all podestàs, consuls, judges and rectors," originated in Francis' anxiety to work also upon the community. Religion was for him no private affair — it was also an affair of the public at large. He therefore exhorts all those who are in authority not to forget

---

[1] *Ep. ad omnes fideles* in fine. (Böhmer, pp. 56–57.)
[2] *Spec. perf.*, cap. 65. Cel., *Vita sec.*, II, c. 152 (d'Al.).
[3] On page 29 is given a sketch of the design which is engraved on this iron. As I have often been told, the inscription is I H C (= I H S, the three first letters of the Greek Jesus) except that the H is so separated by the engraving of the ornament, that it seems to be I I I C, which I (and with me the Fathers in Greccio) would actually read as a number.

in the presence of their manifold tasks the one thing needful. When death comes what is there left? As Verlaine was to sing seven hundred years later — *et puis, quand la mort viendra, que reste-t-il?* Therefore Francis exhorted all the mighty lords to approach the altar just like common men, and as power is for the present given to them, let them make a good use of it by means of a herald, or in some other way have a signal given, and when people hear that signal they shall all praise and glorify God.[1]

The letter to Brother Leo seems to have been written at the time when the indignation and grief over the many alterations and erasures in the Rule were still fresh both with him and the master. It is not written in nearly so carefully labored a style as the great circular letters, in which possibly also Cæsarius of Speier, who on June 11, 1223 was back from Germany, was a collaborator.[2] The whole letter reads:

"Brother Leo, thy Brother Francis sends thee greeting and peace!

"I speak thus to you, my son, and as a mother, because all the words which we spoke upon the road I arrange in this word and advice, and in case thou hast to come to me for advice afterwards, for thus I do advise thee: In whatever way it seems better to thee to please the Lord God and follow in His steps and poverty, do so with the blessing of the Lord God and with my obedience. And, if it is necessary to thee on account of thy soul or of other consolation of thine, and thou desirest, Leo, to come to me, come."[3]

[1] "*Analekten*," p. 71. We can here see the germ of the later Franciscan Angelus prayers. The General Chapter in Pisa (1263) ordered an *Ave Maria* said when the evening bell rang (*Anal. Fr.*, III, p. 329). In 1295 a Provincial Chapter for Padua, Venice, Verona, and Friaul ordered three *Aves* to be said at the same time of the day. (See C. A. Kneller: "*Zur Geschichte des Gebetsläutens*" in the "Ztschr. f. kath. Theol.," 1904, pp. 394 et seq.) — The letter to all Superiors is found for the first time in Gonzaga (*De orig. seraph. relig.*, pp. 806 et seq.) from a Spanish translation.

[2] Jordanus, nn. 30–31 (*Anal. Fr.*, I, p. 11).

[3] "F. Leo F. Francisco tuo" [Italianism for: Franciscus tuus] "salutem et pacem. Ita dico tibi, fili mi, et sicut mater, quia omnia verba, quae diximus in via, breviter in hoc verbo dispono et consilio, et si te post oportet propter consilium venire ad me, quia ita consilio tibi: In quocumque modo melius videtur tibi placere Domino Deo et sequi vestigia et paupertatem suam, faciatis

Francis gives evidently here a permission to Brother Leo of the same sort as the one he had given Cæsarius. The plural number employed in the letter (*faciatis*) might indicate — as Sabatier thinks — that the permission was not only accorded to Leo but also to others of like mind. Strictly speaking, Francis could not do this, for the law-making power was no longer his, or not his alone. And it appears that he was not always clear in his mind about this; thus Eccleston relates that Francis, after the Rule was established, sent out an order in virtue of which the Brethren, when they ate outside of the convents, should not take more than three mouthfuls so as not to irritate lay people by showing too great an appetite.[1] For more than one Brother Francis continued to be the real Head of the Order, and directly after his death the contention, that lasted for centuries, broke out between those who wished in accordance with the permission granted by the saint to follow the Rule literally,[2] and those who wished to accept the leniencies granted by Rome.

cum benedictione Domini Dei et mea obedientia. Et, si tibi est necessarium propter animam tuam aut aliam consolationem tuam, et vis, Leo, venire ad me, veni." ("*Analekten,*" pp. 68–69.)

In the rendering, two sentences, separated in the text but belonging in connection to each other, are put together. — The letter to Leo is preserved in the original and is to be found since 1902 in the Dominican convent in Spoleto. The photograph is in Falocci-Pulignani: *Tre autografi di S. Francesco*, S. Maria degli Angeli, 1895, and in *Misc. Franc.*, VI, pp. 33–39.

[1] "Haec fuit autem prima constitutio, quam sanctus Franciscus fecit post regulam bullatam." *Anal. Fr.*, I, p. 227.

[2] Thus Angelo Clareno, who "exivit extra obedientiam ordinis, ut regulam beati Francisci servaret" (*Bernardini Aquilani Chron.*, ed. Lemmens, Romae, 1902, p. 5).

CHAPTER II

THE SPIRITUAL LIFE

FRANCIS did not wish to preach by word only, but by actions above all. "And all are to preach by their example," he had already told the Brothers in his Rule, and was the first to follow this order. He was the same in his life as in his speech, says Thomas of Celano.[1]

The last years of his life in Rieti show time and again fresh proofs of this species of honesty. In the days of Advent of 1223 or 1224 he was once spending some time in a hermit cave at Poggio Bustone.[2] As his poor digestion did not permit him to eat anything that was prepared with oil, he had to have special food that was prepared with lard (*lardo*). Francis personally accused himself of this infraction of the rules of Advent when he preached on Christmas Day to the people. "You are come hither," he at once said, "because you think that I am so pious and God-fearing. Therefore you must know that I in this fast have eaten food that was prepared with lard."

It was a trait of the same kind when he, in the winter of 1220–1221, during one of his frequent attacks of sickness, recuperated by eating a little meat-soup and boiled meat. He had hardly recovered when, after he had preached in the cathedral, he had himself dragged half-naked by his vicar, Peter of Cattani, with a rope around his neck, down through the town to the pillory on the market-place. Before the thronging populace Francis confessed publicly his indulgence.[3]

---

[1] "idem lingua et vita." Cel., *V. sec.*, II, 93 (d'Al.). *Reg. prima*, cap. XVII: "Omnes tamen fratres operibus praedicent."
[2] 10 miles north of Rieti. See Jörgensen's "Pilgrimsbog," cap. XIII.
[3] *Spec.*, cc. 61–62. Cel., *V. sec.*, II, 93–94 (d'Al.). Bonav., VI, 2.

Another time he was induced by the Brothers, also for the sake of his infirmity, to have a piece of skin sewed on the inside of his habit to warm his stomach. "But sew also a piece on the outside," said Francis, "so all can see that I am wearing furs!"

"I do not want to be different in secret," he was wont to say, "from what I am in public!" If he had been invited into any place and had eaten anything special, he told of it immediately to the Brothers when he returned. If, as he went through the streets of Assisi, he gave an alms and felt a certain selfish pleasure at having done something good, he confessed it at once to the Brother who accompanied him.[1] In the image which he drew of the ideal General of the Order, he accordingly required that this one should not eat good food in retirement, but must always let the Brothers see what came to his table.[2]

Above all was he devoted to poverty. It is blessed to give alms, he declared, but it is blessed also to receive them. Bread that was begged was "Angels' bread." The Brother who came home from begging should therefore come with song. Francis had constantly in his mouth the Psalms and texts of the gospels which praise poverty. When a Brother once in a hermitage had said to him, "I come from *thy* cell," Francis would not stay in it any longer. A house of hewed planks was too much for him, a hut of cane and mud was enough for him, but he liked best to live in caves like the foxes of the gospel (Matthew viii. 20). The stone house the citizens of Assisi had built down by Portiuncula he started to tear down, and had already got a part of the roof torn off when the podestà sent down a protest to the effect that Francis thus was destroying the property of the community. To provide to-day for the needs of to-morrow was something that might do for the well-to-do; therefore he commanded the Brothers not to put green vegetables in water in the evening to keep for the next day, just as they were not to collect more in alms than they could eat on the same day. To make his habit really poor in appearance he liked to have common

---

[1] *Spec.*, cc. 62–63. Cel., *V. sec.*, II, pp. 93–94 (d'AL).
[2] Cel., *V. sec.*, II, p. 308, L. 23–26 (d'AL).

rags sewed upon it here and there. If he wanted a new one he would wait until he could beg one.[1] The Brother who objected to going after alms was in danger of being called "Brother Drone," because he wanted to eat the honey in the combs, but did not want to fly out and gather it.[2]

With all this striving after poverty, Francis could never find that he and the Brothers were poor enough. "We ought to be ashamed of ourselves," said he when he encountered a real ragged beggar; "we want to be called poor and to be celebrated all over the world for our poverty, and here we see one who is much poorer than we, but does not boast of it!" Such a beggar was sacred in the eyes of Francis, and he would not allow any Brother to speak ill of such or to insult their poverty. Francis the voluntary pauper willingly gave all he had to this the real pauper — his hood, a piece of his habit, even his breeches. "They properly belong to them," he declared, "and I would have to look upon myself as a thief if I kept their possessions from them!" "Let us give back to our brother Poor-man what we have borrowed from him" was one of his regular expressions on such an occasion. When anything was given to him, he always held himself ready to give it up to some one more in need of it. The Brothers thus often had their work cut out for them in keeping the clothes on their master's back, especially because he would not wear new clothes, but always insisted on having those which had already been worn. Sometimes one Brother would give half of his habit to Francis, and another the other half. Now and then the Brothers tried to get back his clothes from those to whom he had given them, but Francis discovered this and thereupon warned the beggar possessing them not to give them up without ample return in the shape of money. At Celle the Brothers had to buy back Francis' hood from an old woman.[3]

---

[1] *Spec. perf.*, cc. 5, 14, 16, 7, 8, 9, 19. Cel., *Vita sec.*, II, cc. 26, 27, 29, 39, 40 (d'Al.). *Tractatus de miraculis*, V, n. 35. Bonav., *Legenda major*, VII, 2, 8.
[2] Cel., *Vita secunda*, II, c. 45 (d'Al.).
[3] *Spec. perf.*, cc. 29–31, 33–35, 37. Cel., *V. sec.*, II, cc. 51–55, 57, 148 (d'Al.). Bonav., VIII, 5.

He often had a special object in his alms; thus when he in Colle near Perugia met a man he had formerly known and who now was reduced to poverty. In their conversation the poor man complained especially at having been unjustly treated by his master, towards whom he accordingly bore a bitter feeling. "I will give thee willingly my hood, if thou wilt forgive thy master his injustice," said Francis. And the other's heart was moved; he forgot his hatred and was filled with the sweetness of God's spirit.[1]

In Rieti Francis once discovered a poor woman who, like himself, had poor eyes; he helped her, not only with clothes, but also with a dozen loaves of bread.[2] Another poor woman, who had two sons among the Brothers, came to Portiuncula and complained of her need. Francis gave her the New Testament which was used in the divine service, so that she could sell it. "I believe," said he, "that the Lord will be better pleased that we thus help *our mother* than if we keep the book and let her go away without help." By the title "our mother" he designated every woman who had given the Order a son.[3]

It was in Portiuncula that the altar was menaced with the loss of its ornaments. To get food for the many Brothers who now were joining the Order, Peter of Cattani proposed that the novices should no longer, as hitherto, give their property to the poor, but that a part should be made over to the Order. "By no means," answered Francis; "that is forbidden in our Rule!" "What shall I do then?" asked the uncertain vicar. "Take the ornaments of the altar and sell them! It is better to have a bare altar and keep to the gospel than to have an ornamented one and depart therefrom!"[4]

Thus did Francis try to keep his path clear and to follow the gospel in reality and not only in appearance. Nothing, therefore, could displease him more than when he thought the Brothers used the alms laboriously begged in the name

---

[1] *Spec.*, c. 32. Cel., *V. sec.*, II, 56 (d'Al.). Colle is a little village on the road from Assisi to Perugia just before the Ponte S. Giovanni is reached.
[2] *Spec.*, c. 33. Cel., I, c. II, 69.
[3] *Spec.*, c. 38. Cel., II, 58.
[4] Cel., *V. sec.*, II, 37 (d'Al.). Bonav., VII, 4. *Regul. secunda*, cap. II.

of God in a way unbecoming to poor people. The celebrated Bishop Ketteler of Mayence once caught a family by surprise who used to receive much assistance from him, and who were eating roast goose and red wine. All the Bishop said was that he was glad to see that his gifts had given them a pleasant evening; Francis on such occasions was much severer.

It happened that on another Easter Day, in the convent at Greccio, the Brothers, in honor of the feast-day and of one of the ministers who had come as a guest, had covered the table with a cloth and had set out glasses instead of the tin cups. A little before midday Francis came along and saw the whole preparation; he quietly crept out, put on an old hat which a beggar had left after him, and with staff in hand knocked at the door just as the Brothers were taking their seats. His appealing voice was heard at the door: *Per l'amor di messer domenedio, faciate elimosina a quisto povero ed infirmo peregrino!* "For the love of God, give alms to this poor and infirm pilgrim!"

On the Brothers' friendly invitation Francis entered. He sat down on the floor by the fireplace, had a dish of soup brought to him and a piece of bread, and began to eat. None of the Brothers said anything, and none could get down a mouthful — it was hard enough to sit there with that finely spread table while Francis, like a male Cinderella, with his dish on his lap, crouched down in the corner. Soon Francis laid down his spoon and said to himself: "Now I am sitting as a Friar Minor ought to sit! But when I came in here and saw the fine spread upon the table, I did not think I was with poor members of the Order that had to go every day and beg their bread from door to door!" The Brothers could stand it now no longer; some of them began to weep, others rose and went to Francis as he sat there.[1]

On another occasion there was a similar scene. It was Christmas time; Francis sat at the table with his Brothers. One of them spoke of how poor the Child Jesus had been, and of how sad it must have been for Mary to have her child put in the stable, without a bed except the manger, with only hay

[1] *Spec. perf.*, c. 20. Compare Cel., *V. sec.*, II, 31 (d'Al.) and Bonav., VII, 9.

and straw for pillow and mattress, with no warmth in the cold winter night other than the breathing of ox and ass upon the tender child. Francis sat in silence and listened until he suddenly burst out into lamentation, took his bread and sat down upon the cold floor of earth so as to eat there, where it was no better than it had been with Jesus and Mary.[1]

So unaccustomed did Francis become to any kind of comfort that at last he felt it an annoyance rather than a satisfaction. Thus the Brothers in Greccio, after he had been burnt with a hot iron on the temples as a treatment for his eye sickness, induced him to use a pillow to rest his head on at night. The morning after Francis appeared and said: "Brothers, I have not been able to sleep for your pillow! Everything swam around me, and the legs tremble under me — I believe there is a devil in the pillow!" He then ordered a Brother to take the pillow outside and throw it carefully behind him without looking after it.[2]

This was not the first time Francis believed himself to be attacked by the powers of darkness. Of an evening, when he lingered in lonesome prayer in an empty church or in a cave, it would often seem to him as if some one was behind him, as if hurried, soft steps were stealing and moving around him, as if a horrid head looked over his shoulder and wanted to read with him out of his prayer book.[3] Then he would hear voices in the storms whistling through the mountain forests, the demons would laugh at him, while the owl screeched outside his cell; but worst of all was the almost inaudible whispering which, in the deathlike stillness of the hours of the night, would sound in Francis' ears, as if whispered by hateful and spiteful lips, "It is all in vain, Francis! Thou canst implore and pray all thou wishest — yet dost thou belong to *me!*" Then would Francis fight for his eternal life, and the Brothers who came in the morning to look after him found him pale and exhausted, wearied by the fight with the devouring powers

---

[1] Cel., *V. sec.*, II, 151 (d'Al.).
[2] *Spec. perf.*, cap. 98. Cel., *V. sec.*, II, 34 (d'Al.).
[3] "In sero, cum dicebam completorium, sensi diabolum venire ad cellam (*Spec.*, ed. Sab., p. 193). *Spec.*, c. 99. Cel., *V. sec.*, II, 81 (d'Al.). *Spec.*, cc. 59–60. Bonav., X, 3.

of darkness. "I feel I am the greatest sinner that ever has existed," he once said, after such a night, to Brother Pacificus. But the King of Verse (Pacificus) also saw in a dream the kingdom of heaven opened and the throne, whence Lucifer had been cast down, standing ready for Francis on account of his deep humility.[1]

[1] *Spec.*, ed. Sab., p. 110. Bonav., VI, 6.

CHAPTER III

THE TRUE DISCIPLE

FRANCIS, with all these experiences in the spiritual life, was a good teacher and guide for his disciples. He taught them not to fear temptations. "No one," said he, "ought to consider himself a true servant of God who is not tried by many temptations and trials. Temptations overcome are a sort of betrothal ring God gives the soul." On other occasions he turned back to his favorite conception of the demons as God's *guastaldi* (note 6, p. 259). "Brother Bernard of Quintavalle," he declared, "is visited by the most deceitful spirits of hell, who are trying to get him to fall like a star from heaven. Now he is oppressed and bowed down under their attack, but when death draws near the storm will cease and there will be a great peace." And so it happened. In the last days of his life Brother Bernard's soul was quite separated from earthly things, and he "snatched his food in the air like swallows," said Brother Giles. "And twenty or thirty days at a time he wandered by himself on the highest mountain tops and contemplated the things that are above." But in his dying hour he said to the assembled Brothers, "Not for one thousand worlds as beautiful as this would I have served any other master than my Lord Jesus Christ," and beaming with very great gladness he went into the eternal fatherland of all the saints.[1]

Another of the early disciples, Brother Rufino, was attacked by great temptations. It was with him as with the master — "the old enemy whispered to his heart that he was not of the number of those who are destined to eternal life, and that all he did was therefore in vain." Yes, it even seemed to him

---

[1] Cel., *V. sec.*, II, 19 and 83 (d'Al.). *Fioretti*, capp. 6 and 28.

that the Saviour appeared to him and said: "O Brother Rufino, why trouble Me with prayer and penance, since thou art not destined to eternal life? And believe thou Me, for I well know whom I have chosen and predestined! And this so-called Francis, son of Peter Bernardone, is also among the condemned, and all who follow him will suffer for ever in hell. Therefore seek no advice from him any more, and listen to him in nothing!" Then was Brother Rufino all dark of soul, and he lost all faith in and love for his hitherto trusted master, and sat dark and alone in his cell and would pray no longer nor go to the Brothers' divine service. What good was it all — he looked for nothing else than the everlasting fire and the devil and his angels!

It was in vain that Brother Masseo, at Francis' behest, took the message to Rufino to come. The unhappy man's answer sounded angry and short: "What have I to do with Brother Francis?" Then Francis went personally to get Brother Rufino out of his dark cloud. "And already at a distance Francis began to cry out, 'O Brother Rufino, thou miserable man, whom hast thou believed?' And he showed to him clearly that it was the devil and not Christ who had shown himself to him. But if the devil should again say to thee, 'Thou art lost!' then answer him quietly, 'Open thy mouth and I will blow into it!' And it will be a sign that it is the devil that when thou hast answered thus, he will fly away at once: And thou canst know by this that it has been the devil, because he has hardened thy heart against all good, which is precisely *his* doing, whilst Christ the Blessed One never hardens a living man's heart, but makes it tender, as he says by the mouth of the prophet: 'I will take thy heart of stone from thee and give thee a living heart instead!'"

Then Brother Rufino saw how he had been deceived, and the heart softened in his breast, and he began to weep bitterly and cast himself down before Francis and once more gave himself into his master's care. Weeping but happy, strengthened and comforted, he arose, and when the devil again showed himself to him in the likeness of Christ, he answered him courageously, as Francis had taught him. "Then the devil was so furious, that he at once went away with so great a blast and movement of the stones on Monte Subasio (for this happened up in Carceri) that they flew a long ways, as one can see to-day. And while they were rolling down the ravines, they struck sparks, and Francis and the Brothers came out in alarm to see what was going on. But Christ blessed Brother Rufino and restored to him such a spiritual joy and sweetness and exaltation of soul that day after day he was out of himself and entranced in God. And from that same hour he was so fixed in grace and so sure of his everlasting salvation that he became another man, and if he could have obtained permission for it, he would have given himself up to prayer and meditation on the things which are above. Wherefore Francis used to say that Brother Rufino was sanctified by Christ during his actual life, and that, if only he himself would not hear it, he, Francis, would not hesitate to call him St. Rufino, although he was yet living on the earth."[1]

In this environment of his faithful Brothers, living and conversing with them constantly, Francis forgot in the world-remote peace of Rieti all that was upon the other side of the mountains — the Brothers in Bologna, the Brothers in Paris, the Brothers at the Curia and the Brothers at the University, the Brothers who were in all other places than just where Francis wanted them to be, and did all things differently than Francis wanted them to. As a counterpoise to it all Francis issued a letter *On the Ideal Friar Minor*, a letter which was not carved out of the air, but in which he employs traits of character of all his most faithful disciples. "The perfect Friar Minor," said Francis, "must be as true to poverty as Bernard of Quintavalle, simple and pure as Leo, chaste as Angelo, intelligent and eloquent by nature as Masseo; he must have a mind fixed on high, like Giles; his prayer must be like that of Rufino, who always prays, and whether he wakes or sleeps, his mind is with God; he must be patient as Brother Juniper, strong in soul and body as John de Laudi-

---

[1] *Fior.*, c. 29. *Actus*, cc. 31 and 35. *Anal. Franc.*, III, pp. 48–52. The word Francis taught Rufino to say to the devil is worse than what is given above (*Apri la bocca metteti caco* = "Aperi os tuum et faciam intus faeces"). Compare a tale of how Francis cured a Brother of conscientious scruples, in Celano's *Vita secunda*, II, c. 87 (d'Alençon). Compare II, c. 6.

bus, loving as Roger of Todi, and like Brother Lucidus he must not settle in any place, for when Brother Lucidus had been more than a month in one place, and found that he was beginning to like it, then he would at once leave it, saying, 'Our home is in heaven.' "[1]

Francis rejoiced in being able also to count in this flock of the most faithful others than those who were nearest to him. Thus he once heard with great joy a priest returning from Spain speak of the Spanish Franciscans. "Thy Brothers," said the traveller, "live there in a little hermitage and have so arranged things that one half of them spend the week taking care of the house, while the other half give their time to prayer. The next week the two divisions change about. It so happened one day that the dinner bell rang, and that one of the Brothers did not come. As this was a day on which the food was unusually good, the others went in search of him. They found him prostrate, with face against the ground, with arms extended like a cross, apparently lifeless, completely carried away in an ecstasy. The Brothers went silently away, and after some time the favored one came in. But as if nothing unusual had happened to him, he knelt down humbly and begged forgiveness because he came too late!"

Such an occurrence was exactly in harmony with Francis' wishes. "I thank thee, O Lord," he cried out, "because thou hast given me such Brothers!" And as he turned towards the quarter of the heavens where Spain lay, he blessed with a great sign of the Cross his faithful and distant Brothers.[2]

Such a pair of true Franciscans were also those two Brothers who had gone to the pains of traversing the long road to the other side of Greccio to see Francis. Now it had become so, in the last years of Francis' life, that when he had withdrawn from the other Brothers to pray in solitude, no one dared to approach him and disturb him, and the Brothers took care of any business that might present itself.[3] When the two pilgrims came, Francis had just gone, and it was uncertain when

---

[1] *Spec. perf.*, c. 85.
[2] Cel., *V. sec.*, II, c. 135 (d'Al.).
[3] Cel., *V. pr.*, c. VI. *Actus*, IX, 28–31. *Verba fr. Conradi*, I, 11 (in *Opuscules de critique*, I, p. 373).

he would come back. The strangers, who had no time to stay, were much cast down by this and said to each other: "This is on account of our sins! We are not worthy to be blessed by our father Francis!" As they were so unhappy over the affair, the other Brothers accompanied them on the road down from the convent, comforting them as well as they could. Suddenly a cry from above was heard — the road went zigzag down from the lofty caves where the Brothers lived, and as they turned around they saw Francis standing up in the entrance of his cell.[1] The two strange Brothers fell upon their knees, and with faces turned to the master received the blessings he gave them, with a large, slow sign of the Cross.[2]

In the various descriptions of his life are still preserved many a trait of Francis' fine feelings and tenderness for the Brothers and of his deep knowledge of the soul. He understood others so well because he understood himself, and the Brothers often felt that he was reading their hearts. This was the case with one of his countrymen, Brother Leonard from Assisi. Weary of long walking, Francis had complied with the advice of a sympathizer and had mounted an ass and ridden a part of the way. Brother Leonard walked by his side and presumably was also tired; in any event he thought to himself, "Why should Peter Bernardone's son ride, whilst I, who am of much better ancestry, have to walk?" How surprised he was when Francis stopped his steed, dismounted, and said as he did so, "It is not becoming, Brother, that thou, who art of much better family than I, should walk, while I ride!" Red in the face, Leonard resisted his uncharitable thoughts and helped Francis to mount again.[3]

Against such and all other trials and temptations Francis over and over again advised his Brothers to use three remedies — the first was prayer, the second was obedience, such that

[1] He lived "in cella ultima post cellam majorem," says *Spec. perf.* (cap. 98).
[2] Cel., *V. sec.*, II, c. 16 (d'Al.).
[3] Cel., *V., sec.*, II, c. 5. Compare same, cap. 2 (Francis sees through a Brother who under guise of holiness, to preserve complete silence, will not even write), and *Actus*, cap. 11 (Francis reads in Masseo's heart that he is angry that they left Siena without paying the Bishop a farewell visit). Compare Bonav., *Legenda major*, XI, 8, 10, 13.

one willingly did another's will, the third was the evangelical joy in the Lord, which drives away all evil and dark thoughts. In these three precepts Francis set the best example to his Brothers. Ever since he resigned the leadership of the Order he always had a Brother with him, whom he obeyed as his guardian. It mattered nothing to Francis who it was; he was as willing to obey the youngest novice in the Order as Brother Bernard or Brother Peter of Cattani. He was always pleased with his surroundings, and if anyone happened to do anything displeasing to him at any time, he would go apart and pray, until the natural irritation over the incident had subsided, and never spoke of it to anyone. "Teach us to be perfectly obedient!" the Brothers asked him once. Then Francis answered: "Take a corpse and bring it where thou wilt! It makes no resistance, does not change its attitude, does not wish to move. If thou placest it on a throne, it looks down and not up; if thou dressest it in purple, it appears only paler than before. It is so with the really obedient; he never asks whither he is sent, he never is concerned as to how he came here, does not seek to be taken away. If he acquires honors, they only increase his humility, and the more he is praised, the more unworthy does he consider himself." [1] Francis wished to be like a corpse, subject, without resistance, to all, and his true Brother should follow him in this as in all other things. *Per lo merito della santa ubbedienza*, "by the merit of holy obedience," Francis once made Brother Bernard stamp upon his mouth in punishment for some evil thoughts he had nourished about him.[2]

In one utterance of Francis this conception of his of obedience attains an almost Buddhistic character. "Holy obedience," it says, "annihilates all will of the body and flesh and causes a body to be dead to itself and ready to obey the soul and to obey its neighbor, and makes a man subject to all men here in the world, and not only to all men, but also to all tame and wild beasts, so that they can *do with him what they will, as power for this is given them by the Lord*."[3] This undeniably

[1] *Spec.*, cc. 46-48. Cel., *V. sec.*, II, cc. 111-112 (d'Al.).
[2] *Fioretti*, cap. 3.
[3] *Opuscula*, p. 21. Böhmer, "*Analekten*," p. 65.

reminds us of Sakyamuni's disciples, who let themselves be torn to pieces by tigers rather than resist the evil. And that this was not a momentary idea of Francis which found expression in these words is seen in the tales of how he did not want to put out the fire that was burning his clothes, and of how he upbraided himself for having taken a skin away from "Brother Fire" which it wished to "eat!"[1]

The first great means of bringing about peace for Francis was obedience, taken as the complete abandonment of all personal will, the perfect subjection to every command and every power. "If anyone strikes thee on one cheek, then offer him the other, and if anyone takes thy cloak from thee, then do not keep thy habit from him. . . . And if anyone takes thy property from thee, ask it not again from him. . . . Therefore if anyone comes to me and does not hate his own body, he cannot be my disciple. For he who will save his life shall lose it, but he who loses his life for my sake, he shall save it."[2]

The other means of obtaining peace was prayer, constant and persevering prayer, prayers "without intermission." Francis himself, as Thomas of Celano says, was not one who now and then prayed, but "his whole being was changed to prayer" (*non tam orans quam oratio factus*). It was as if there was only a thin wall between him and eternity and he often, as it were, heard the sound of the eternal song of praise on the other side of the wall. In such moments he suddenly became silent, broke off the conversation, if he was with the Brothers, and covered his face with his hood or at the least with his hands. The disciples then would hear him sigh deeply and murmur something or other, they would see him also nod his head, as if he answered some one, and they would steal away. They knew that the master did not want to be noticed when he prayed; it is told that the Bishop of Assisi once lost his voice as punishment for surprising Francis at his prayers. Francis tried to conceal his piety as much as possible, got up in the morning as quietly as possible before the others, so as to escape remark, and went out in the woods to be free from dis-

---

[1] *Spec. perf.*, cap. 116–117.
[2] Luke vi. 29–30; xiv. 26; ix. 24.

turbance. Sometimes one of the Brothers stole out after him, and the curious one would sometimes see a great light, and in this light Christ, Mary and many angels would show themselves and would talk with Brother Francis. When he at last came back from his prayers, there was never anything to notice about him, and he also used to say to his disciples: "When God's servant receives comfort from God in prayer, he should, before he ends his praying, lift up his eyes to heaven and with folded hands say to God, 'Lord, thou hast sent thy comfort and sweetness from heaven to me an unworthy sinner; I give them back to thee again, that Thou mayest keep them for me!' And when he then returns to the Brothers, he must show himself the same poor sinner he is wont to be!"[1]

Besides prayers in solitude Francis also used zealously prayers in common with others. In the *Fioretti* we see him praying together with Brother Leo. In his letter to the Brothers assembled at the Pentecost Chapter he gives them rules for saying the prayers in their Breviaries.[2] In spite of his physical weakness he never was willing to lean against a wall or partition when he chanted the Psalms in company with the others. If he was travelling and it was time to pray, he stopped the requisite time; if on horseback, he dismounted. When, in December, 1223, he was on the journey home from Rome, he stood thus in a pouring rain and let himself get wet through, as he prayed from his Breviary to the end of the prescribed portion. "Does not the soul need a quiet time for eating as well as the body?" he asked his companion, who remonstrated with him.[3] Once he had carved a little cup in his leisure moments, and when it was just finished it was time for saying the Tierce (the fourth of the canonical times of the day; it is said at nine o'clock in the morning). During the prayer his eyes wandered contentedly to the completed work; yes, so taken up with it was he that he hardly paid any attention to the Psalms he was saying. Suddenly he realized his distraction, and in his zeal he seized the beaker

[1] Cel., *V. sec.*, II, c. 61, cc. 65–66 (d'Al.). *Fior.*, c. 17. *Actus*, c. IX, 32–51.
[2] *Opusc.*, p. 106. "*Analekten*," p. 61.
[3] Cel., *V. sec.*, II, 62 (d'Al.). *Spec.*, c. 94.

that had taken his thoughts from God and threw it into the fire.[1]

Prayer was thus something which he took seriously. Christians are often profuse in promises to pray for each other — promises which are seldom kept. Francis was not like this. The abbot of the convent of St. Justin in Perugia had once recommended himself to Francis to be remembered in his prayers, when taking leave of him. Francis regarded this as more than a phrase; he had gone only a few steps when he said to his companion, "Let us pray for the abbot, as we promised him."[2]

Above all, Francis loved to hear mass every day. When he was stopping in a town, this was easy to do; out in the hermitage it was otherwise. It is a long road from Carceri down to Assisi or from Celle in to Cortona. For Francis it was certainly the best Christmas present he ever received when Honorius III, in December, 1224, permitted the Friars Minor to have their mass read out in their hermitage at an altar they could transport from place to place with them.[3] After this Francis had Brother Leo or Brother Benedict of Prato, who were both priests, say mass for him. When neither of these was there, he would have at least the gospel of the day read aloud; this one of the Brothers was glad to do just before midday.[4]

[1] Cel., *V. sec.*, II, 63 (d'Al.). Bonav., X, 6.
[2] Cel., *V. sec.*, II, 67 (d'Al.): "Mos enim iste semper [ei] fuit, ut orationem postulatus non post tergum projiceret, sed cito hujusmodi promissum impleret." Bonav., X, 5.
[3] Such a portable altar consists of the altar-stone only, that can be placed on a suitable support, where it is to be used. Honorius III's permission was given December 3, 1224 (Sbar., I, p. 20. Potth., I, nr. 7325).
[4] *Spec. perf.* (ed. Sab.), p. 175, concerning Benedict of Prato. Compare in note 2, same page, the quotation from Brother Leo's words written in *the Breviary which had belonged to Francis* and which is still preserved in the church of Santa Chiara in Assisi:

"Beatus Franciscus acquisivit hoc breviarium sociis suis fratri Angelo et fratri Leoni eoque tempore sanitatis suae voluit dicere semper officium sicut in regula continetur, et tempore infirmitatis suae quum non poterat dicere volebat audire et hoc continuavit dum vixit. Fecit etiam scribi hoc evangelistare ut eo die quo non posset audire missam occasione infirmitatis vel alio aliquo manifesto impedimento faciebat sibi legi evangelium quod eo die dicebatur in ecclesia, in missa, et hoc continuavit usque ad obitum suum. Dicebat enim: 'Quum non audio missam, adoro corpus Christi oculis mentis in oratione quemadmo-

The third means for obtaining peace, which Francis pointed out to his disciples, was constant cheerfulness.

"Let those who belong to the devil hang their heads — we ought to be glad and rejoice in the Lord," said he. Melancholy was "the sin of Babylon," because it led back to the abandoned Babylon of the world. "When the soul is troubled, lonely and darkened, then it turns easily to the outer comfort and to the empty enjoyments of the world." Therefore Francis repeated over and over again the words of the Apostle: "Rejoice always!" He never wanted to see dark faces or sour visages — his Brothers should not be mournful hypocrites, but glad children of light. To those who asked how this was possible, he answered, "Spiritual joy arises from purity of the heart and perseverance in prayer!" Only sin and torpidity are able to extinguish or darken the light in the heart. "When the soul is cold," said Francis, "and gradually becomes untrue to grace, then it must be flesh and blood that are seeking their own!"[1]

To keep free not only from every sin but from every blemish, from every trespass though ever so little, these were the conditions for living in the divine joy. The least grain of dust in the eye is enough to stop one from seeing the light. Francis taught his disciples to be on their guard against such grains of dust, and he especially warned them against confidential intercourse with women. When talking with persons of the opposite sex, he liked to look down on the earth or up into the sky, and when the conversation was too prolonged, he broke it off abruptly. At Bevagna he and a Brother were once entertained by a pair of pious women, a mother and her daughter, and Francis in recompense had spoken some edifying words to them. "Why dost thou not look at the pious

---

dum adoro quum video illud in missa.' Audito vel lecto evangelio, beatus Franciscus ex maxima reverentia Domini osculabatur semper evangelium." Compare *Spec. perf.*, cap. 117: "volebat (Franciscus) semper audire evangelium quod in missa legebatur illa die priusquam comederet, quando non posset audire missam."

St. Clara owned a Breviary written by Leo, which is still preserved in S. Damiano. See Aug. Cholat: *Le Bréviaire de Ste. Claire* (*Opusc. de critique*, II, pp. 31-96, Paris, 1904).

[1] Cel., *V. sec.*, II, cc. 39, 88, 91 (d'Al.). *Spec.*, cc. 95-96.

young girl who hangs upon every word from thy lips?" the Brother asked Francis, as they left the place. "Why should one not be afraid to look upon the bride of Christ?" answered Francis. Every pious woman in Francis' eyes was the betrothed of Christ, to whom he as the poor servant of Christ did not dare to lift his eyes.[1]

In recompense for this complete renunciation, Francis accepted also perfect joy. There were times and hours when there was a perfect song within his soul, and he would begin at last to hum the melody he heard within himself, hum it in French as in the old days when he went out with Brother Giles to announce the gospel. Clearer and clearer would the melody sound to him, and stronger and stronger did it rise in him — next he would snatch up a couple of pieces of wood or two boughs, place one to his chin as if it were a violin, and draw the other one across it as the bow is used in playing the violin. Louder and louder would he sing, more and more eagerly did he carry out his imitation playing whose melody none but himself could hear, while he rhythmically rocked his body back and forth with the tune. Finally his feelings would overcome him, and letting the violin and bow fall he would burst into scalding tears, and sink into his own soul as into a great wave.[2]

---

[1] Cel., *V. sec.*, II, cc. 78, 80. Compare c. 81 (parable of the Two Pages, of whom one was bold enough to look upon the king's bride and for that was cast out of the castle).

[2] *Spec. perf.*, c. 93. Cel., *V. sec.*, II, c. 90 (d'Al.).

CHAPTER IV

LA VERNA AND THE STIGMATA

DURING the summer of 1224 Francis' health seems to have improved, and in August he left Rieti. The goal of this journey was the mountain La Verna in Casentino, which had been given to him by Orlando dei Cattani in 1213; he wished along with the most faithful Brothers — Leo, Angelo, Masseo, Silvestro, Illuminato — to celebrate the Assumption of the Blessed Virgin (August 15) and then to prepare himself by a forty days' fast for the feast of St. Michael (September 29). In common with the rest of the people of the Middle Ages, Francis nourished a special devotion to this Archangel, *signifer sanctus Michaelis*, the standard-bearer of the Heavenly Host, and the one who with his trumpet was to wake the dead in their graves on the Last Day — "Sjaele-Mikal" (Soul-Michael), as he is called for that reason in the old Norsk *Draumkvaede*.[1]

Immediately after having received the Alverna hill as a gift, Francis had sent a couple of Brothers there to take possession of it. With the help of the Duke Orlando's people the Brothers had established themselves upon a plateau high up on the cliff, and had built some huts of clay and interwoven branches, as Francis liked it; next the Duke Orlando built a little church which received the same name as the

---

[1] Cel., *V. sec.*, 149 (d'Al.). Compare Brother Leo in Francis' Blessing (Appendix, pp. 347-348). "Beatus Franciscus duobus annis ante mortem suam fecit quadrigesimam in loco Alverne ad honorem beate Virginis Marie matris Dei et beati Michaelis archangeli a festo assumpsionis sancte Marie virginis usque ad festum sancti Michaelis septembris." Besides this fast in honor of St. Michael, and the lenten fast, and the fast prescribed in the Rule of the Order from All Saints' Day to Christmas, Francis appears to have fasted forty days in honor of Sts. Peter and Paul, ending with their feast-day, June 29, and finally in honor of Mary from June 29 to August 15 (Bonav., IX, 3. Compare Cel., *V. sec.*, II, 150 (d'Al.), on Francis' devotion to the Blessed Virgin).

Portiuncula chapel, namely, *Santa Maria degli Angeli*, "Our Lady of the Angels."[1]

During the trip to La Verna, Francis' strength again failed him, and the Brothers went into a farmyard to borrow an ass for their master. When the peasant heard who it was that wanted to use the beast, he came out himself. "Art thou the Brother Francis there is so much said about?" he asked. Receiving an affirmative answer, he added, "Then take care that thou art as good in reality as they say, for there are many who have confidence in thee!" Stirred to his innermost depths, Francis cast himself down and kissed the peasant's feet in thanks for his reminder.[2] May it not have been the same peasant who himself undertook to guide Francis and the Brothers to La Verna? Whoever it was he was seized by an overwhelming thirst in the burning summer heat, and during the long hard ascent from the river Corsalone to the convent. When he complained of his thirst to Francis, the latter kneeled down with him in prayer, and a moment after he was able to lead the peasant to a spring.[3]

"But as now Francis and his Brethren climbed the mountain, and rested a little at the foot of an oak" — the *Fioretti* tell us — "there was at once a flock of the birds of heaven in the place, and greeted them with cheerful song and fluttering of their wings. And some rested on Francis' head, and others on his shoulders, and again others on his knees and hands. But when Francis saw this wonder, he said: 'I believe, dearest Brothers, that it is the pleasure of our Lord Jesus Christ that we establish a residence on this lonely mountain, where our sisters the birds rejoice so much over our coming.'

"But when the Count Orlando heard that Brother Francis and his Friars were going to build on Mount Alverna, he was highly pleased over it, and the next day he went there with many from his castle, and they came and brought bread and wine and other things with them, to Francis and his Friars. And as he approached the place he found them praying, and he went up and greeted them. Then Francis arose and received Lord Orlando and his followers with great love and

---

[1] See page 105. [2] Cel., *V. sec.*, II, 103 (d'Al.).
[3] Cel., *V. sec.*, II, 17 (d'Al.).

joy, and they sat down to speak together. And after they had spoken together, and Brother Francis had thanked Count Orlando for the mountain he had given him, and had preached a little, the evening fell. And Lord Orlando took Francis and his Brethren aside and said to them: 'My dearest Brothers, it is not my intention that you shall suffer from want on this wild mountain, and therefore I say to you once for all, that if you are in need of anything you shall only send a messenger to me after it, and if you do not do so I will be very angry about it.' And after he had said this he withdrew with his followers to his castle.

"Francis then made the Friars sit down and determine how they were to live, and he especially impressed upon them the keeping of holy poverty in their hearts, and said to them: 'Do not pay so much attention to Lord Orlando's friendly offering as to break the troth you have promised our Lady, the holy Poverty!' And after many beautiful and pious words about this thing, he concluded, saying: 'This is the way of life I lay upon you and myself. For as I see that my death approaches, I wish to be alone with God and lament my sins. And Brother Leo can bring me a little bread and a little water, as seems fit to him, but if anyone comes, answer for me, and let no one come to me!' And when he had said these words, he gave them his blessing and went to his hut, which was under a great beech tree, and the Friars remained in their huts."[1]

There are still shown by La Verna the places where St. Francis stopped — the great overhanging stone, *Sasso* or *Masso spico*, under which he used to pray, the dark damp cave where he had his hard bed on a projecting shelf, Brother Leo's grotto high up on the mountain side, where Francis many a morning in the early hours attended his friend's mass and prayed to the body and blood of our Lord in the white Host and golden chalice, lifted on high in Brother Leo's hand as the only comfort for poor pilgrims in this vale of tears.

For again Francis seems to have become disquieted, troubled, and bowed down with thoughts of the future. How was

[1] *Fioretti*, 1ª e 2ª considerazione delle sacre sante stimmate. *Actus*, cap. IX.

it all going to end? They had taken his Brothers, his sons, from him, and whither were they taking them now? They were going there where Francis did not wish them to go, and he had to look on without power. . . .

In vain did Francis issue his Ideal Image of what a perfect Friar Minor, a perfect Provincial Minister, a perfect General of the Order, should be — he knew well that the facts were widely different. Brother Elias and others of his mind were not, as Francis would have it, satisfied with "a book and an ink-horn and one pen and a signet,"— they collected books and studied church law, and it was only waste of time to exhort them to act towards their Brothers in the spirit not in the letter of the law. Again and again might Francis sigh to God: "Lord, I commit to thee the family thou hast given me — I cannot lead them any longer myself!"[1] But again and again the beautiful dream would return, that all was as in the old days, when nothing stood between him and his dear children, and they were united in harmony again and were to be separated no more.[2]

One day Francis awaked out of this his constant dream, and realized anew the truth, and had recourse to a method he had used before, to lift the edge of the veil that hides the future. He ordered Brother Leo to take the Book of Gospels and in honor of the Holy Trinity to open it in three places. Leo did as his master desired, and all three times it opened at the Passion of Christ. Then Francis understood that there was nothing for him but to suffer to the end, and that his days of good fortune were gone for ever. And he resigned himself to God's will.

In the night which followed, Francis could not sleep. In vain did he turn on his hard bed — in vain did he listen for the call of the Friars of La Verna, announcing the hour for saying matins. "All will be as it should be in heaven,"

---

[1] "Domine, recommendo tibi familiam, quam dedisti mihi!" *Spec. perf.*, c. 81. "Sufficiant autem sibi pro se habitus et libellus, pro aliis vero pennarolus cum calamo et pugillari et sigillum. Non sit aggregator librorum." Cap. 80. Compare cc. 71 and 85, and also Cel., *V. sec.*, II, cc. 139-140 (d'Al.).

[2] "si secundum voluntatem meam fratres vellent ambulare . . . nollem quod alium ministrum haberent nisi me usque ad diem mortis meae." *Spec.*, p. 138. Cel., *l.c.*, c. 141.

Francis said to comfort himself; "there, at least, there is eternal peace and happiness!" And with these thoughts he fell asleep.

Then it seemed to him that an angel stood by his bed with violin and bow in hand. "Francis," said the shining denizen of heaven, "I will play for thee as we play before the throne of God in heaven." And the angel placed the violin to his chin and drew the bow across the strings a single time only. Then Brother Francis was filled with so great a joy, and his soul was filled with such living sweetness, that it was as if he had a body no longer, and knew of no secret sorrow. "And if the angel had drawn the bow down across the strings again," thus Francis told his Brothers the next morning — "then would my soul have left my body from uncontrollable happiness." [1]

After the Feast of the Assumption, Francis withdrew from the Brothers into still greater solitude. The place he had selected for himself was on the far side of a deep ravine, and to cross over to it, a felled tree-trunk had to be used as a bridge over the abyss. Here Francis installed himself in a hut, and had made the arrangements with Brother Leo that he should visit him twice in the twenty-four hours, once by day to bring bread and water, once by night at matins. As Leo stepped upon the bridge he was to say aloud the words with which the recitation of the Breviary begins — the verse of the psalm, "O Lord, thou wilt open my lips" (*Domine, labia mea aperies*). If Francis from the other side gave the proper response: "And my mouth shall declare Thy praise" (*Et os meum annuntiabit laudem tuam*), then Leo was to go across the bridge and say the matins with Francis. But if he got no answer he was to go quietly home again. "But Francis said this because he was sometimes in such a state of rapture that he could not speak for a whole day, he was so occupied with God," says the *Fioretti*.

For a while Brother Leo carried out his master's commands

---

[1] *Fioretti*, 2ᵃ e 3ᵃ consid. — Of a falcon whose scream used to wake Francis in the morning, see Cel., *V. sec.*, II, c. 127. When Francis was sick or tired, it there tells us, the falcon noticed it and waked him at a later hour. Compare Celano, *Tract. de miraculis*, IV, 25, and Bonav., VIII, 10.

for "the pain of my Lord Jesus Christ!" And so great, so real was his unhappiness, that even the other began to weep.

To honor the Cross was the object of the prayer Francis had prescribed for his Brothers. "We pray to thee, O Lord, and praise thee, because with thy Holy Cross thou hast redeemed the world!" And he would never permit the Brothers to step upon two straws or two twigs that were lying across each other.

And the others thought of him under the symbolism of the Cross. Silvester dreamt that a cross of gold went out of the mouth of Brother Francis and over the world, and Brother Pacificus saw him in a dream in the form of a cross pierced by two swords. Leo once saw a great gilded cross going in front of Francis.[1]

In the Mass of the Feast of the Exaltation of the Holy Cross it is as if places in the Liturgy were given for all the words of the Church and gospel referring to the Cross. "This sign of the Cross," it says, "shall stand in heaven when the Lord comes to judgment." Or, in the words of Paul: "We should be glorified in the Cross of our Lord Jesus Christ, in whom is our salvation, life, and resurrection." Or the following: "Christ, our Saviour, who saved Peter on the sea, save us, have mercy on us by the power of thy Cross." "Thou strong Cross, thou noble Cross, nobler than all the trees, no woods produce thy equal, a tree with such leaves and flowers," is in a hymn for that day. And again about the Cross, to the Cross: "Thou art fairer than the cedars of Lebanon, thou art the tree of life in the middle of the garden of paradise." "Behold the Cross of the Lord! Let all its enemies fly! The Lion of Judah's stem hath conquered, Alleluia!"

Penetrated by all these strong words, Francis lay in prayer outside his cell on the morning of the fourteenth of September. It was not yet day, but while awaiting the sunrise he prayed, with face turned to the east, with hands upraised and extended arms:

"O Lord Jesus Christ, two favors I beg of thee before I

[1] *Actus*, cap. 38. Compare *Verba fr. Conradi* (*Opusc. de critique*, I, pp. 380-381.)

Photo: Anderson

ST. FRANCIS OF ASSISI
From the fresco attributed to Cimabue at Assisi

die. The first is, that I may, as far as it is possible, feel in my soul and in my body the suffering which thou, O gentle Jesus, sustained in thy bitter passion. And the second favor is, that I, as far as it is possible, may receive into my heart that excessive charity by which thou, the Son of God, wast inflamed, and which actuated thee willingly to suffer so much for us sinners."

"And as he long prayed thus," says the old story, "he felt a certainty that God would vouchsafe him these two things, and that it would be given him to receive both parts, so far as it was possible for a creature. And after he had received this promise, he began with great devotion to meditate on the sufferings of Christ and on the boundless charity of Christ, and the glow of piety grew so strong in him, that with charity and pity *he was all transformed to Jesus.*

"And as he lay in this prayer and burned with this flame, behold, it came to pass that he in the same morning hour saw a seraph coming down from heaven with six luminous wings. And the seraph slowly approached Francis, so that he could discern and clearly see that it bore an image of a crucified man, and its wings were so placed that two were raised over the head, two were extended for flight, and with two it covered its body.

"But when Francis saw this vision he was much frightened, and at the same time he was filled with joy and sorrow and wonder. For he had great joy in the gentle Jesus who showed Himself to him so intimately and looked so lovingly upon him, but it gave him inexpressible sorrow to see the Lord fastened to the Cross. And, moreover, he wondered over so unusual and astonishing a vision, for he knew that mortal suffering is not compatible with a seraph's immortal spirit. But as he wondered thus, it was revealed to him by the one before him that this vision by a special provision of God was granted him that he should understand that it was not by bodily martyrdom, but through an inner flame, that he should be transformed entirely into the likeness of Christ the Crucified.

"But now after the wonderful vision had finally disappeared, an excessive glow was left in Francis' heart, and a living love of God, and in his body the vision left a wonderful image and imprint of Christ's sufferings. For at once in his hands and feet marks like nails began to appear, so that they seemed perforated in the middle, and the heads of the nails were within the palms of the hands and on the top of the feet, and the points of the nails were on the backs of the hands and under the feet, and they were bent over, so that there was space between the flesh and points of the nails for a finger, as if in a ring, and the nails had a round, black head. And so in his left side the image of a lance-thrust appeared, without cicatrice, but red and bleeding, out of which blood often issued from Brother Francis' breast and saturated his habit and clothes.

"But Francis said nothing of this to the Brothers, but hid his hands, and he could not put the soles of his feet to the earth any more. And the Brothers found that his habit and clothes were bloody when they went to the wash, and then they understood that he bore the image and likeness of our Lord Jesus Christ the Crucified in his side and likewise on his hands and feet."[1]

[1] *Fioretti*, 3ᵃ considerazione. I use this late authority as I think that it is essentially based on what Leo, Masseo, Angelo, and the other Brothers have imparted either in writing or orally. We know from Eccleston that Brother Leo willingly told the younger Brothers in the Order about the stigmatization — see *Anal. Franc.*, I, p. 245. It is impossible to doubt that he had also among his *rotuli* several relating to the event at La Verna; some of these have appeared as part of the *Actus beati Francisci* (c. IX, c. XXXIX). Moreover, we possess directly from Leo's hand the most authentic testimony of Francis' stigmatization — his remarks on the blessing Francis wrote and gave him at La Verna (see Appendix, p. 347). The description of the stigmatization in Thomas of Celano's *Vita prima*, II, c. III, and in the *Mirac. trat.*, c. II, n. 4, presents, in spite of the much shorter form, an unmistakable resemblance to the relation in the Fioretti, and this is not surprising when we recollect that Celano always worked in company of Leo and the other confidential friends of Francis. (Appendix, pp. 352, 368–369.) Compare Bonaventure, XIII, 3, where essentially the same relation is found.

Since the appearance of Sabatier's defence of the stigmatization of Francis (*Vie de S. Fr.*, pp. 401–412) the general view among historians has been turned in the direction of accepting it. Of Karl Hampe's attempt to separate the stigmatization from the vision of the seraph on Mount Alverna and to transfer it to a time no more exactly stated shortly before Francis' death, something will be found said in the Appendix. Hampe's article ("*Die Wundmale des hl. Frans v. Assisi*") appeared in the "Historisches Zeitschrift," 1906, pp. 385–402.

CHAPTER V

THE FAREWELL TO THE BRETHREN

FRANCIS could not long keep the wonder a secret that had come to him. For one thing he was in the midst of a circle of inspired and devoted friends whose central object he inevitably was, and who were constantly occupied with him. On the other hand, the miracle caused him such great pain and made his existence so difficult, that he had to have recourse to the assistance of others. Probably Leo was the first one he initiated into the secret. That Francis might be able to move his hands and feet, bandages had to be wound around the projecting parts of the nails. Leo shifted these bandages daily, except — as it is said — from Thursday afternoon to Saturday morning, because Francis wished to suffer with Christ. Bróther Rufino, too, who washed for the master, found out all about the mystery, when he found the left side of the clothes saturated with the blood from the wound in the side. It was later that he, by a trick, managed to touch and see this wound.[1]

Of the state of Francis' soul, after he had received the wounds, it is hard to form a conception. From now on he is so high above ordinary mankind, that the best we can do — like Brother Leo, who often thought he saw the master floating among the tree-tops — is to cast ourselves down, kiss

---

[1] *Actus*, cc. 39 and 34. Cel., *V. sec.*, II, cc. 98-100. Thomas of Celano says here explicitly of Rufino: "Hic solus vidit in vita, caeterorum nullus usque post mortem" (d'Alençon's ed., p. 274). It cannot, therefore, be regarded as a deceit of Brother Elias of Cortona, that Brother Thomas gave credence to, when we find in the *Vita prima* (II, c. III, n. 95): "felix Helias, qui dum viveret sanctus, utcumque illud videre meruit; sed non minus felix Rufinus" etc. Brother Pacificus by a trick managed to let a friar from Brescia see the stigmata in the hands. (Cel., *V. sec.*, II, cap. 99, d'Al.)

the dust once trod by the blessed one's feet, and ejaculate with the faithful disciple: "God be merciful to my sins and let me by the intercession of this holy man find pity with thee!"[1]

The first effect of the stigmatization seems to have been a great joy, a complete liberation from all care and dejection. This feeling of inner happiness refound was what gave itself voice in the Song of Praise Francis wrote immediately after he had received the wounds, "in thanks for the grace that had befallen him."[2] In its entirety the Laud reads thus:

"Thou art holy, Lord God. Thou art the God of Gods, who alone doest wonderful things. Thou art strong, thou art great, thou art most high, thou art omnipotent, thou art Holy Father, the King of heaven and earth. Thou art three in one, one Lord God of Gods. Thou art goodness, all goodness, the greatest goodness, living and true Lord God. Thou art charity, thou art wisdom, thou art humility, thou art patience, thou art beauty, thou art security, thou art quietude, thou art joy, thou art our hope, thou art justice . . . and temperance. . . . Thou art all our riches to satiety. . . . Thou art gentleness. . . . Thou art the protector, thou art the guardian and defender. . . . Thou art our refuge and strength. Thou art our faith, hope and charity. Thou art our great sweetness. Thou art infinite goodness, great and admirable Lord God Almighty, pious and merciful and Saviour."[3]

At this very time when Francis felt himself raised to the highest summits of Christian joy, and like Moses on Nebo, already saw the promised land afar off, his best friend was the

---

[1] "'Deus, propitius esto mihi peccatori et, per merita hujus sanctissimi viri, fac me tuam sanctissimam misericordiam invenire.' Quum tantum elevatum aspiceret quod ipsum tangere non valebat, se sub sancto Francisco prosternens, orationem [talem] faciebat [fr. Leo]." *Actus*, c. 39, 6-7.

[2] "propter visionem et allocutionem seraphym et impressionem stigmatum Christi in corpore suo fecit has laudes . . . et manu sua scripsit, gratias agens Domino de beneficio sibi collato." Brother Leo's testimony concerning Francis' blessing given to him. See Appendix, pp. 347-348.

[3] For the Latin text see Appendix, p. 349, n. 1. I also refer to Faloci-Pulignani's monograph: *Tre Autografi di S. Francesco* (S. Maria degli Angeli, 1895).

object of a great temptation, — not of bodily, but of spiritual kind, we are told by the authorities without any further enlightenment. Was Brother Leo perhaps tempted by a feeling of envy of the master? Did he feel jealous and disquieted in seeing his friend penetrate into regions where he could not follow him? In any case he seems to have sought for a proof that he was not forgotten, an assurance that the old relations, in spite of the wonder that had happened to Francis, were still as strong as ever. Leo thought of the times when Francis wrote to him in such a friendly manner, and every one who knows what effect a dear and well-known handwriting on a letter can have, will understand Brother Leo's longing to have something from Francis' hand. He was to be seen every day, but what good was that, when it seemed as if the old-time friendship between them was no longer in existence?

With his usual delicate perception Francis seems to have known what was troubling his friend's spirit. One day therefore he called for Leo, and bade him bring parchment, pen and ink. While Leo in expectation stood by his side, Francis wrote down first the Song of Praise given above, then turned the sheet over and inscribed upon the back in large letters the Patriarchal Benediction from the Old Testament:

"The Lord bless thee, and keep thee. The Lord show his face to thee, and have mercy on thee. The Lord turn his countenance to thee, and give thee peace!"

For a moment Francis paused — then he finally added, "The Lord bless — Brother Leo — thee!" And instead of his name he put beneath the whole the Old Testament symbol of the Cross, T (Thau), erected on Golgotha over a human skull as emblem of death conquered by Christ.

With glance and smile both charged with goodness, Francis handed the inscribed parchment to Brother Leo. "Take this," he said, "and keep it with thee to the day of thy death!" Then all of Brother Leo's evil thoughts left him, and with tears in his eyes he seized the pledge of inviolable friendship which the master gave him. Even until he became an old man — Leo died in 1271 — he carried next to his heart this parchment from La Verna, and after his death it went as an inheritance to the Franciscan Church in Assisi, where it is to the present day preserved in the sacristy.[1]

On the thirtieth of September, Francis with Brother Leo left Mount Alverna. Duke Orlando had sent an ass on which the stigmatized one who could not use his feet was to make the journey. Francis heard mass early in the morning with his Brothers in the little chapel, and gave them a last admonition. Then he took leave of each one in turn — of Masseo, Angelo, Silvestro, Illuminato. "Live in peace, dearest sons, and farewell! My body is to be separated from you, but my heart remains with you! I go forth with Brother Little Lamb of God to Portiuncula, and I come back here no more! Farewell, sacred mountain: farewell, Mount Alverna: farewell, thou Angel mountain! Farewell, dearest Brother Falcon, who used to wake me with thy screams, thanks for thy care of me! Farewell, thou great stone, beneath which I used to pray; thee I shall see no more! Farewell, Santa Maria's Church — to thee, mother of the Eternal Word, I commend these my sons!" Whilst the Brothers who remained behind broke into lamentations, Francis went forth for the last time from the mountain, where so great a thing had befallen him.[2]

Francis rode to Borgo San Sepolcro; after he had taken leave of Duke Orlando in the neighboring town of Chiusi he

[1] Cel., *V. sec.*, II, c. XX. Bonav., XI, 9. — The words of the blessing are taken from Numbers vi. 24-26. On the letter *Thau* see Ezechiel ix. 4. On Francis of Assisi's use of the same see Bonav., IV, 9, and Cel. *Tract. de miraculis*, c. II, n. 3.

[2] I quote here the *Addio di S. Francesco alla Verna*, said to have been written by Brother Masseo. All internal evidence points to the authenticity of the document, but the copy of it, found in the so-called *Capella dell' Ascensione*, and which is the only existing manuscript, dates only from the sixteenth century. It is a parchment 27 x 13 cm. (10.8 x 5.2 in.) and begins: *Pax XPI. Giesu Mã speranza mia. fra Masseo peccatore indigno servo di Giesu XPO Compagno di fra Francesco da Assisi huomo a Dio gratissimo*, and ends: *Io fra Masseo ho scritto tutto. Dio ci benedica.* Sabatier, who did not know of this document, heard it spoken of as an original autograph (*Spec. perf.*, pp. 303-304); he gives a copy not differing more than the above and following the oldest printed copy (of 1710), ditto, pp. 305-308; the concluding words are worthy of notice: "Io fr. Masseo ho scritto *con lagrime*," which indicates that the words were written under the influence of Francis' recent departure. *L'Addio di S. Francesco* is also found printed in Amoni's Italian translation of Celano's *Vita secunda*, Rome, 1880, pp. 314-315, without statement of the source.

crossed the River Rasina, followed by Brother Leo, and took the road over Mount Arcoppe, Mount Foresto and Mount Casella. He stopped on the top of Mount Casella, whence the last view of La Verna is to be had, and he dismounted and knelt down. And with his glance directed to the distant La Verna, that far away lifted its ridge up under the heavy autumn clouds, he made the sign of the Cross over it and broke out into a last farewell, a last thanksgiving and a last blessing.

"Farewell, thou mountain of God, thou holy mountain, *Mons coagulatus, mons pinguis, mons in quo bene placitum est Deo habitare!* Farewell, Mount Alverna — God the Father, God the Son, God the Holy Ghost, bless thee! Live in peace, but I shall never see thee more!"[1]

Francis then mounted his placid steed and rode down to Monte Casella. He was absorbed in his thoughts for the rest of the journey, so that he passed through Borgo San Sepolcro without knowing it; the town was already behind them when he awoke from his revery and asked if they were yet near Borgo.[2]

The journey became a triumphal procession. The populace met Francis everywhere with olive boughs and the cry *Ecco il Santo!* "Here comes the Saint!" He had to give his hand to be kissed, and miracles were wrought by him; yes, a woman who lay in agony and whose life was in danger was cured by laying the bridle of the ass upon her, the same he had held in his hands.[3] From Città di Castello, where Francis stopped a whole month, and where he among other things by a simple command cured a woman who was raving with hysterics, he went at last to Portiuncula. It was now November, 1224, and the snow in the Apennines was already deep. And now it happened that Francis, Brother Leo and the peasant who had lent them the ass, one evening could find no human habitation, but had to spend the night in the mountains. The snow gathered in drifts and they had only

---

[1] Amoni's work named above, p. 315. In La Verna these words are to be found in a manuscript dated September 30 (also anniversary of the departure), 1818.

[2] Cel., *Vita sec.*, II, c. 64 (d'Al.).

[3] *Fioretti*, 4ᵃ considerazione. Cel., *Vita prima*, I, c. XXII, n. 63. Compare the quite similar miracle in the succeeding paragraph (64).

a projecting rock to take shelter under. For the two Brothers this was not so bad, but the peasant cursed and scolded — this was the reward for his foolish kindness; he might have remained at home and now be lying in his comfortable bed, etc., etc. Francis managed at last to quiet and calm the angry man, and when morning came the peasant announced himself quite satisfied, that he never had slept better than out here among the rocks and drifts of snow.[1]

Scarcely was Francis back at Portiuncula when he went out at once on a missionary trip. It seems as if all of the zeal of his youth was returned; he talked anew of wanting to do great things.[2] For a while it seemed to him that it was not too late to begin all over again. "I will go to the lepers again and serve them and be despised of all men," said he.[3] Riding on his ass, he often visited in one day four or five towns and preached in them;[4] and where he found lepers he waited on them. The story in the *Fioretti* certainly belongs to this period, which tells of the impatient leper patient whom the Brothers who took care of him could in no way please, but he abused them with word and blow, and reviled and abused God and all the saints, so that none could bear to listen to him.

"But St. Francis himself approached this abandoned leper and greeted him and said, 'God give thee peace, dear brother!' But the leper answered, 'What peace can I have when God has taken everything from me and has made me all decayed and malodorous? And even then I would not complain of my disease, but the Brothers thou hast given me to wait upon and look after me do not do it as they ought!'

"Then Francis said, 'Son, since thou art not contented with the others, shall I take care of thee?' 'I would like that,' answered the sick man; 'but what couldst thou do for me more than the others?' 'I will do all thou wishest,'

---

[1] Cel., *V. pr.*, I, c. 26. *Fior.*, 4ᵃ consid.
[2] Cel., *V. pr.*, II, c. 6: "Proponebat, Christo duce, ingentia se facturum."
[3] ditto, "Volebat ad serviendum leprosis redire denuo, et haberi contemptui, sicut aliquando habebatur."
[4] Cel., *V. prima*, II, c. 4: "Replebat omnem terram evangelio Christi, ita ut una die quatuor aut quinque castella vel etiam civitates saepius circuiret." "Cum per se ambulare non posset, asello vectus circuiret terras."

answered St. Francis. Then the leper said, 'Then I want thee to wash me all over, for the odor is such that I cannot stand it.'

"St. Francis thereupon had warm water with many aromatic herbs in it prepared; he undressed the sick man and began to wash him with his hands, and another Brother helped. And by a miracle from God it came to pass that where St. Francis touched him with his blessed hands the leprosy disappeared and the flesh became entirely well. And as the flesh began to be cured, the soul was also cured; for when the leper saw that he was well he was overcome by great sorrow and emotion over his sins and began to weep bitterly. And when he was entirely healed in soul and body, he began in humility to accuse himself and said, weeping, in a loud voice, 'Woe to me, I have made myself worthy of hell by the injustice I have done the Brothers, and by my impatience and blasphemy!'

"But St. Francis thanked God for so great a miracle and went away to distant regions, for from humility he wished to flee from all honor and sought in all things only God's honor and glory and never his own."[1]

[1] *Fior.*, c. 25. On the relation between Francis and the lepers see also *Speculum perfectionis*, cc. 44 and 58, with the numerous parallel citations in Sabatier's edition.

CHAPTER VI

FRANCIS, THE LOVER OF NATURE

THE light which is soon to go out flares up for a last time, and such a last flaring was Francis' new zeal. The spirit indeed was willing, but as he sat upon his ass he seemed more a dead man than a living one, and for Brother Elias, who for a time was with Francis in Foligno, it was clear that the master had only a couple of years to live.[1] The eye sickness he had brought from Egypt, and which he had never attended to, now got the mastery, and not only Elias, but also others of the Brothers, begged him to try medical aid.

This did not accord with Francis' ideas. In one of his *Admonitiones* he himself had advised his sick Brothers not to strive too eagerly for a cure, but to thank God for everything and not wish to have things better than God wanted them, for God chastises those He loves.[2] Instead of consulting a physician, he sought solitude again, and this time it was to San Damiano that he withdrew himself. In the vicinity of the Sisters' convent St. Clara had placed a wattle hut, in which Francis could live.[3]

It was in the summer of 1225, and the blinding Italian sun had evidently been bad for Francis' eyes. For a time he was quite blind and was incidentally plagued by a swarm of field-mice, who probably had their home in the straw walls of the hut, and who eventually ran over his face, so that he had no peace by day or night. Apparently never before had Francis been more depressed and unfortunate. And yet it was precisely in this wretched sickness, in the midst of the

---

[1] Cel., *Vita pr.*, II, c. 8.
[2] *Spec. perf.*, c. 42. *Reg. prima*, c. 10.
[3] *Spec. perf.*, c. 100. *Fior.*, c. 19.

darkness of blindness and of the plague of mice, that he composed his wonderful masterpiece, *Canticum fratris solis,* the Canticle of our Brother Sun.

To understand the Sun Song we must understand Francis' relations to nature. Nothing would be more unjust than to call him a pantheist. He never confounded himself or God with nature, and the pantheist's alternations of wild orgies and pessimistic melancholy was quite foreign to him. Francis never, like Shelley, wished to be one with the universe; neither did he, with *Werther* or Tourguénieff, shudder as feeling himself abandoned to the blind inevitableness of things and to nature's "everlastingly ruminating monsters." Francis' standpoint as to the conception of nature is entirely and only the first article of faith — he believed in a *Father* who was also a *creator*.

And out of this common relationship with the one and same Father he saw in all living beings, yes in all that is created, only brothers and sisters. In the kingdom of the heavenly Father there are many mansions, but only one family. This thought is not Greek and is not German, but it is true Hebraic and therefore truly Christian. The song of praise which Ananias, Azarias and Misael sang in the fiery furnace of the Babylonian tyrant, and which has gone down to the Church, as it were an inheritance from the synagogue, contains the following:

"All ye works of the Lord, bless the Lord: praise and exalt him above all for ever.

O ye angels of the Lord, bless the Lord: . . .
O ye heavens, bless the Lord: . . .
O all ye waters that are above the heavens, bless the Lord:
O all ye powers of the Lord, bless the Lord: . . .
O ye sun and moon, bless the Lord: . . .
O ye stars of heaven, bless the Lord: . . .
O every shower and dew, bless ye the Lord: . . .
O all ye spirits of God, bless the Lord: . . .
O ye fire and heat, bless the Lord: . . .
O ye cold and heat, bless the Lord: . . .
O ye ice and snow, bless the Lord: . . .
O ye nights and days, bless the Lord: . . .

O ye light and darkness, bless the Lord: . . .
O ye lightnings and clouds, bless the Lord: . . .
O let the earth bless the Lord; let it praise and exalt him above all for ever.
O ye mountains and hills, bless the Lord: . . .
O all ye things that spring up in the earth, bless the Lord: . . .
O ye fountains, bless the Lord: . . .
O ye seas and rivers, bless the Lord: . . .
O ye whales, and all that move in the waters, bless the Lord: . . .
O all ye fowls of the air, bless the Lord: . . .
O all ye beasts and cattle, bless the Lord: . . .
O ye sons of men, bless the Lord: . . .
O let Israel bless the Lord: let them praise and exalt him above all for ever.
O ye priests of the Lord, bless the Lord: . . .
O ye servants of the Lord, bless the Lord: . . .
O ye spirits and souls of the just, bless the Lord: . . .
O ye holy and humble of heart, bless the Lord: . . .
Blessed art thou in the firmament of heaven, and worthy of praise and exalted above for ever."[1]

There is no tone missing in this symphony of all creatures, where all sing together in the great song of praise from cherubim to atom. Morning after morning, year after year, Francis, alone or with the Brothers, had sung out of their Breviaries daily this hymn of all creatures to the Creator. The poetry of it had won him early; in 1213 he raised a little chapel between S. Gemini and Porcaria, and had sentences such as these painted on the antependium of the altar: "All who fear the Lord, praise Him! Praise the Lord, heaven and earth! Praise Him, all rivers! All creatures, praise the Lord! All birds of heaven, praise the Lord!"[2] Francis' preaching to the birds at Bevagna is based on the same ideas: the birds are obliged to praise and bless their good Creator, who has cared so well for them; for all beings it is

[1] Daniel iii. 57-67, 70-87 and 56.
[2] Wadding, 1213, n. 17. The church in the custodianship of Todi was called *L'Eremita*, according to Rudolph of Tossignano there cited.

undoubted happiness to exist, and it is their simple, filial duty to thank their Father for life.

Francis' feelings about nature gave him a predilection for all, that justified such an optimism. He turned with special joy to all the lightsome, beautiful and bright in his surroundings — to the light and fire, the pure running water, flowers and birds. This feeling about nature was half symbolic — Francis loved the water because it symbolized the sacred penitence by which the soul is purified, and because baptism is effected by water. Therefore he had such great reverence for water that, when he washed his hands, he turned so that the drops which fell could not be trod under foot. Over stones and rocky ground he went with special carefulness, while he thought of him who is called the chief corner-stone. The Brother who cut wood in the forest he ordered to leave a part of the tree standing, so that there might be some hope of its putting forth branches again — in honor of the Cross of Christ. He had the gardener arrange a bed where flowers would grow — to remind the Brothers of Him who is the Lily of Sharon.

But he possessed an entirely direct love of nature. Fire and light seemed to him so beautiful that he never could endure having a candle extinguished or a lamp put out. There was to be a place in the convent garden, not only for the kitchen vegetables, but also for the sweet-smelling herbs and for "our brothers the Flowers," so that every one who observed their beauty would be induced to praise God. He tenderly bent over the young of "our brothers the Robins" in Greccio, and in Siena built nests for turtle-doves. If he saw an earthworm lying on the road and twisting about helplessly, he would take it up and carry it to the side, so that it would not be crushed. In winter he put honey into the beehives for the bees to feed on.

Every being was for Francis a direct word from God.[1] Like all pious souls he realized in the highest degree the worth of all things and had reverence for them as for something precious and holy. He understood God's presence

[1] "Omnis enim creatura dicit et clamat: Deus me fecit propter te, homo." *Spec. perf.*, c. 118.

among his creatures; when he felt the immovable firmness and strength of the cliffs and rocks, he directly felt that God is strong and is to be trusted. The sight of a flower in the silence of the early morning or of the mouth of a little bird confidently opened revealed to him the pure beauty of God and his purity and the endless tenderness of the Creator.[1]

This feeling infused Francis with a constant joy in God, an uninterrupted tendency to thankfulness. In these thanks all beings were to participate and were to appear to have pleasure therein. "Our Creator be praised, Brother Pheasant," thus Francis addressed the rare bird, which a wellwisher had sent him, and the pheasant stayed with Francis and did not want to be with anyone else. "Sing the praise of God, Sister Cicada," he exclaimed under the olive trees at Portiuncula, and Sister Cicada sang until Francis bade it be silent. The wild animals often kept him company; for example, a hare on an island in Lake Thrasimene, a wild rabbit at Greccio. Near Siena he was surrounded by a flock of sheep; the gentle animals gathered around him and bleated, as if they wanted to tell him something. Sailing on Lake Rieti he was presented with a living fish; he put it into the water, and for a long time it followed the boat. A bird which was captured in the same place and given to him would not leave him until he explicitly commanded it to.[2]

But above all things Francis was thankful for the sun — the sun and fire.

"In the morning," he was wont to say, "when the sun rises, all men ought to praise God, who created it for our use, for all things are made visible by it. But in the evening, when it is night, all men ought to praise God for Brother Fire, which gives our eyes light at night. For we are all like the blind, but God gives our eyes light by means of these two brothers."[3]

[1] *Spec. perf.*, cc. 116, 118. Cel., *Vita sec.*, II, cc. 18, 124 (d'Al.). *Actus*, c. 24. *Fioretti*, c. 22. *Spec. perf.*, p. 232: "nos qui cum eo fuimus, in tantum videbamus ipsum interius et exterius lætari quasi in omnibus creaturis, quod ipsas tangendo vel videndo non in terra, sed in coelo ejus spiritus videbatur."
[2] Cel., *Vita sec.*, II, cc. 126, 129–130. *Tract. de mirac.*, IV, 23–31 (d'Al.). Bonav., VIII, 7–10.
[3] *Spec. perf.*, c. 119.

The Sun Song had its origin in this idea. In his hut in San Damiano Francis lay like a blind man and could endure neither sunshine nor the light of a fire. And one night his sufferings were so great that he called out to God, "Lord, help me, so that I can bear my sickness with patience!"

Then in spirit it was answered him: "Behold me, Brother; would you not be very glad if some one for these sufferings of thine gave thee so great a treasure that the whole world in comparison therewith is worth nothing?" And Francis answered, "Yes." But the voice went on, "Then be glad, Francis, and sing in your sickness and weakness, for the kingdom of heaven belongeth to thee!"

But Francis arose early the next morning and said to the Brothers who sat about him: "If the Emperor had given me the whole Roman kingdom, should I not be greatly rejoiced? But now the Lord, even while I am living here below, has promised me the kingdom of heaven, and therefore it is proper that I should rejoice in my trials and thank God the Father and Son and Holy Ghost. And therefore I will in his honor and for your comfort and the edification of our neighbors compose a new song of praise about the creatures of the Lord whom we daily make use of, and without whom we could scarcely live, and whom we nevertheless so often misuse and thereby offend the Creator. And we are constantly ungrateful and do not think of the grace and beneficence which every day is shown us, and we do not thank the Lord, our Creator and the Giver of all good things, as we ought to do."

And Francis sat down and thought. A moment after he broke out in the first words of the Sun Song, *Altissimo, onnipotente, bon Signore*, "Highest, almighty, good Lord!"

But when the song was composed in full, his heart was full of comfort and joy. And he wished straightway that Brother Pacificus should take some other Brothers with him and go out into the world. And wherever they found themselves they were to stop and sing the new song of praise, and then as servants of God they should ask for compensation from their hearers, and the compensation should be that they who listened should be converted and become good Christians.[1] But the Sun Song itself is this:[2]

Altissimo, onnipotente bon signore,
Tue so le laude, la gloria, el honore et onne benedictione.
Ad te solo, Altissimo, se konfano,
et nullu homo ene dignu te mentouare.
Laudato sie, Misignore, cum tucte le tue creature,
spetialmente messor lo frate sole,
lo quale iorno et allumini noi per loi.
Et ellu e bellu e radiante cum grande splendore
de te, Altissimo, porta significatione.
Laudato si, Misignore, per sora luna e le stelle
in celu lai formate clarite et pretiose et belle.
Laudato si, Misignore, per frate vento
et per aere et nubilo et sereno et onne tempo,
per lo quale a le tue creature dai sustentamento.
Laudato si, Misignore, per sor aqua,
la quale e molto utile et humile et pretiosa et casta.
Laudato si, Misignore, per frate focu,
per loquale enallumini la nocte,
ed ello e bello et iocundo et robustoso et forte.
Laudato si, Misignore, per sora nostra matre terra,
la quale ne sustenta et governa
et produce diversi fructi con coloriti flori et herba.
Laudate et benedicete Misignore et rengratiate
et serviateli cum grande humilitate.

Most high omnipotent good Lord,
Thine are the praises, the glory, the honor, and all benediction.
To thee alone, Most High, do they belong,
And no man is worthy to mention thee.
Praised be thou, my Lord, with all thy creatures,
Especially the honored Brother Sun,
Who makes the day and illumines us through thee.
And he is beautiful and radiant with great splendor
Bears the signification of thee, Most High One.
Praised be thou, my Lord, for Sister Moon and the stars,
Thou hast formed them in heaven clear and precious and
  beautiful.
Praised be thou, my Lord, for Brother Wind,
And for the air and cloudy and clear and every weather,
By which thou givest sustenance to thy creatures.
Praised be thou, my Lord, for Sister Water,
Which is very useful and humble and precious and chaste.
Praised be thou, my Lord, for Brother Fire,

---

[1] *Spec. perf.*, capp. 100, 119. *Actus*, c. 21. Cel., *Vita sec.*, II, c. 161 (d'Al.)
[2] *Spec. perf.*, cap. 120. I repeat here only the original Sun Song (from Böhmer, p. 65, L. 23–31; p. 66. L. 1–13 and 24–25). The two later additions will be given further on.

*By whom thou lightest the night,
And he is beautiful and jocund and robust and strong.
Praised be thou, my Lord, for our sister Mother Earth,
Who sustains and governs us,
And produces various fruits with colored flowers and herbage.
Praise and bless my Lord and give him thanks
And serve him with great humility.*

CHAPTER VII

FRANCIS' LAST TESTAMENT, ILLNESS AND DEATH

IN the end of April, 1225, an uprising in Rome had forced Honorius III to leave the city, and after a short stay in Tivoli he transferred his residence to Rieti, where he remained until the beginning of 1226.[1] More urgently than ever Brother Elias begged Francis to go to the Papal Court, in which request he was supported by Cardinal Hugolin, to have his eyes treated by the skilful physicians who were there.[2] At last, in the summer of 1225, Francis left San Damiano and said farewell to Clara and the Sisters. It may have been on this occasion that he left them his last will in the following form:

"I, Brother Francis, wish to follow after the life and poverty of our highest Lord, Jesus Christ, and of His most holy Mother, and I will hold out in this to the last. And I pray you, my ladies, and counsel you, that you always remain in this holiest way and in poverty. And be very careful that you do not in any way give up this way of life on anyone's advice or teaching."[3]

This time Francis must have travelled on foot; while he was at San Damiano Clara had prepared a pair of shoes for him such that he, notwithstanding the stigmata, could manage to walk. From Terni he followed the old road through the valley, a way well known and dear to him. Between Poggio Bustone and Rieti he stopped with the priest of the little church of San Fabiano (now the convent of La Foresta), and as soon as the news of his arrival had been told in the

---

[1] Potth., I, n. 7401–n. 7526.
[2] Cel., *Vita pr.*, II, cc. IV–V. *Actus*, c. 21. *Fior.*, c. 19. Compare A. Bournet: *S. François d'Assise, étude sociale et médicale* (Paris, s.a.), pp. 118–123.
[3] *Textus originales*, p. 63: "paulo ante obitum suum iterum scripsit nobis ultimam voluntatem suam, dicens: Ego frater Franciscus," etc.

town, people came out in great crowds to see him. Now unfortunately the road to the house where Francis was stopping ran through the priest's little vineyard, and the crowds from the town slaked their thirst by eating the poor priest's ripe grapes, with the usual disregard to be expected on such occasions. The priest saw this pillaging only with sorrow and finally complained to Francis. "The vineyard always gave me thirteen kegs of wine," he said sadly, "and that was all I used in the whole year." Francis comforted him and promised him that this season too he would have his wine, and in fact it is told that the vines this year bore more profusely than before, so that the priest in the end got twenty kegs out of them.[1]

After this Francis stayed a short time in Rieti, in the house of Thedaldo the Saracen, according to what Wadding says.[2] It was here that Francis one evening called Brother Pacificus and told him to borrow a cithern and sing the Sun Song to its accompaniment. Pacificus was, however, afraid of arousing a disturbance in the house with his song and playing and said so. "Then we will let the thought go," said Francis; "one must give up much to avoid irritating one's weak brother!"

The following night Francis lay awake and could not sleep for pain. Outside he heard the last belated wanderers going home; finally all was still, only the church bell from time to time sounded through the night. Then Francis heard outside his window the soft vibrations of a cithern's strings, and some one began to play outside. The playing lasted a long, long time — now quite near, now a little distant, as if the player was going back and forth under the window. Enraptured, carried away, overcome by the music, which continued to stream out upon the still, hot autumn night, Francis lay there and listened, and when morning came he said to Brother Pacificus: "The Lord did not forget me this time either, but comforted me, as He always does. Instead of thee, he sent me an angel, who has played for me all night."[3]

[1] *Spec. perf.*, c. 104. *Actus*, c. 21. *Fioretti*, c. 19.
[2] 1225, n. 2 (Mariano is the authority).
[3] Cel., *Vita sec.*, II, c. 89 (d'Al.). Bonav., V, 11.

It was only when winter came that Francis left Rieti, going to the hermitage of S. Eleutherio, where, in spite of his illness and of the severe cold which prevailed, he would not consent to have his habit lined with fur.[1] Probably about Christmas time he went to Fonte Colombo.

Meanwhile the Papal physicians had tried every conceivable remedy upon him — bindings, salves and plasters — and nothing did any good. They had also tried to reform his whole way of living, and in this they succeeded to some extent. "Has not thy body all through thy life been a good and willing servant and ally?" they asked Francis, and he could not avoid giving "Brother Ass" a good character. "Then how hast thou treated it in return?" was the further question, and Francis had to acknowledge that his treatment had not been the best. Smitten with sorrow, he entered into himself and exclaimed, "Rejoice, Brother Body, and forgive me; now I am ready to humor you in your wishes!"[2] As in so many cases of repentance, this also came too late.

The physicians decided to adopt heroic measures and undertook the application of red-hot irons to both temples. According to the views of the time such treatment should be very efficacious; it was used among other cases for hydrophobia.[3] When the physician and his assistant approached Francis with the brazier, in which the glowing irons lay, Francis made the sign of the Cross over them and said: "Brother Fire, thou who art nobler and more useful than most other creatures! I have always been good to thee and always will be so for love of him who has created thee! Now show thyself gentle and courteous to me and do not burn me more than I can stand!"

The physician started the burning, and all the Brothers fled when they heard the flesh hiss under the iron. Francis only said, when it was over, "If that is not enough burning, then burn it again, for I have not felt the least pain!"[4]

This physician seems to have formed a real friendship with

---

[1] *Spec. perf.*, c. 16.
[2] Cel., *Vita sec.*, II, c. 160 (d'Al.).
[3] Bournet, *l.c.*, p. 122.
[4] *Spec. perf.*, c. 115. Cel., *V. sec.*, II, c. 125 (d'Al.).

Francis. He often and willingly talked with the Brothers about their wonderful master. "It is singular," he once said; "I can remember well the sermons of others, but never the sermons of Francis. And even if I do remember something of them, it nevertheless is no longer *it!*"[1]

Once, when the consultation was lasting a long time, Francis wished to keep the physician to dinner. The Brothers said meanwhile that they did not have enough for themselves, and certainly not enough to offer a stranger. "Go and set out what we have," ordered Francis, "and do not let me have to say it twice!" And hardly had they sat down at the table when there was a knock at the door and a woman stood outside with a basket filled with the best food — fine bread, fish, pies, honey and grapes.[2]

It was probably on the suggestion of the same physician that Francis later in the winter changed the bleak Fonte Colombo for Siena, already in the Middle Ages renowned for its mild air. It was on the way thither that Francis and the Brothers, on the plain between San Quirico and Campilia, met three women, who all looked exactly alike, and who as the little group went by bowed the heads in greeting and in one voice said, "Hail to thee, Lady Poverty!" This meeting and this remarkable greeting for a long time occupied Francis' and the Brothers' minds.[3]

The treatment in Siena did no more good than that in Rieti, but the stay seems to have benefited Francis. He lived in the hermitage of Alberino (now Ravacciano, a little north of Siena), and it was here that he one day, among others, received a visit from a Dominican who, perhaps not without reference to Francis' own condition, asked for an interpretation of the words of Ezechiel, If thou dost not announce to the ungodly his impiety, "I will require his blood at thy hand."[4] "For I know many who live in mortal sin," declared the troubled Dominican, "and I say not this to them. Shall all these souls be required of me?" Francis answered, in

---
[1] Cel., *V. sec.*, II, c. 73 (d'Al.).
[2] *ibid.*, c. 15.
[3] Cel., *V. sec.*, II, c. 60 (d'Al.). Bonav., VII, 6.
[4] Ezech. iii. 18.

his usual way of thought, that a life of goodness was the best sermon for the wicked, and that God's message to the prophet was most completely corresponded to by such an example.[1]

The question of the Dominican had made more impression upon Francis than he wished to acknowledge. One night he awakened the Brothers and said to them: "I have begged God to say to me, *when* I am his servant and *when not*, for I neither wish nor desire anything else than truly to serve him. And the Lord has shown me grace and answered me: 'Thou art really and truly my servant, when thou thinkest, speakest and doest all, as it is becoming!' Therefore you have permission to despise me, if I do not do that."[2]

In accordance with this was the incident, when in Siena he inculcated anew the Brothers' obligation of poverty. A certain "Sir Bonaventure" had presented a piece of ground for a new convent; Francis gave the following rules for its erection:

The Brothers must for the present accept no more land than what is strictly necessary. Next they must not build without the permission of the local Bishop — "for the Lord has called us to the help of the priests of the Roman Church" and not to work in opposition to them. Francis had himself given the best example of this, when in Imola he let himself be turned away by the Bishop, whom he asked for permission to preach in the city, but who answered him, "Brother! It is enough when *I* preach!"

After they had got the permission of the clerical authorities, the Brothers were to dig a deep ditch around their ground and to plant a good hedge behind the ditch, but they were to build no wall. In front of the hedge the cells were to be built of mud and wattles, and there was to be no large church, but only a poor little chapel.[3]

The improvement which was apparent in Francis' health was of no duration. One night he had bad hæmorrhages, and the Brothers thought he was going to die. Weeping

---

[1] *Spec. perf.*, c. 53. Cel., *V. sec.*, II, c. 69 (d'Al.). As early as 1225 the Dominicans had a convent and church, S. Domenico, in Siena.

[2] *Spec. perf.*, c. 74. Cel., *V. sec.*, II, c. 118.

[3] *Spec. perf.*, c. 10. The convent of S. Francesco, erected in Siena in 1236, does not correspond with this description. — For the Bishop of Imola, see Cel., *V. sec.*, II, c. 108 (d'Al.).

they knelt around his bed and begged for his last blessing. As soon as Francis came back to his senses he ordered his mass-priest, Brother Benedict of Prato, to bring parchment, pen and ink. "Write," he then said, "that I bless all my Brethren who are in the Order, or who are going to enter it, from now until the end of the world. And as a sign that they have received this my blessing, and for memory of me, I leave them this testament, that they ought always to love each other, as I have loved them and still love them; that they should always love and honor our Lady Poverty; that they should always be true and obedient to the clerks and prelates of our holy Mother Church." After having dictated these words, Francis blessed them all, "as he had been wont to do at the Chapter Meetings" many of the Brothers thought, and as they again burst forth in sobs, he wearily closed his eyes.[1]

The end was not yet — six months were to pass before Francis in earnest could bid "Sister Death" welcome. For the present he had enough to do with "Sister Sickness."[2] By Brother Elias' arrangement he was transported to Celle near Cortona; here a dropsy was added to his troubles so that his underbody, legs and feet swelled up. The stomach could retain no more food; then came severe pains in spleen and liver.[3] Francis had only the one wish, to see Assisi again before he died, and in this Elias complied with his desire. For fear that the inhabitants of Perugia should by an actual attack get possession of the sick man (and thereby of the true saint all saw in Francis), Elias transported home by a circuitous route the body of his master, that already in full life was a relic to be striven for. By Gubbio and Nocera they approached the place, not far from Bagni di Nocera, where now the convent of *l'Eremita* stands; here they were joined by a body of armed men sent from Assisi to meet them and to guard them for the rest of the way. At midday of the same day they entered the territory of Assisi and stopped in the village of Satriano (now a lonesome village below Sasso Rosso, very

---

[1] *Spec. perf.*, c. 87. Compare Celano, *Vita prima*, II, c. VII, n. 105.
[2] Cel., *Vita sec.*, II, c. 161 (d'Al.). Bonav., XIV, 2.
[3] Cel., *V. prima, l.c. Spec.*, p. 183 (ed. Sab.).

near to Babbiano). Francis was here received as a guest in a private house; the soldiers meanwhile wished to go into the village and buy food for themselves. No one would sell them anything, and sullen and hungry they returned. "Yes, this is what you get, when you depend upon your useless money (*muscae*, lit., flies). But try now and go from door to door and beg for a little in God's name, and you will see that you will get what you need!" This proved to be true.[1]

Towards evening the procession entered Assisi. The invalid was brought to the Bishop's residence, and a watch was set around the house to prevent all attempts of the Perugians upon the saint of Assisi.

If the churchly and civil authorities of Assisi were thus united when it came to the question of securing Francis' person, there were other topics where there was no such unity of sentiment. The first knowledge Francis acquired of the home relations was, that the podestà and Bishop were in open strife, and that the Bishop had placed the ban upon the podestà, and the podestà in return had forbidden all citizens to have anything to do with the Bishop. "It is a great shame for us, God's servants," said Francis to his Brothers, "that no one makes peace here!" And to do what he could he composed two new verses for his Sun Song, and then sent a messenger to the podestà to come to the Bishop's residence, and one to the Bishop to meet him. The summoned ones came and gathered together on the Piazza del Vescovado — the same place where, nineteen years before, Francis had given back his clothes to his father. And when all were there, two Friars Minor stepped out and sang the first Sun Song, as Francis had originally written it, and then the new verses:

> Laudato si, Misignore, per quelli ke perdonano per lo tuo amore
> et sostengo infirmitate et tribulatione,
> beati quelli kel sosterrano in pace,
> ka da te, Altissimo, sirano incoronati.

> "Praised be thou, O Lord, for those who give pardon for thy love
> and endure infirmity and tribulation,
> blessed those, who endure in peace,
> who will be, Most High, crowned by thee!"

[1] *Spec. perf.*, c. 22. Cel., V. sec., II, c. 47 (d'Al.).

Whilst the two Brothers sang, all stood with folded hands, as if the Gospel was being read in church. But when the song was ended, and the last *Laudato si Misignore* had ceased to be heard, the podestà made a step forward, cast himself down before Bishop Guido and said: "Out of love to our Lord Jesus Christ and to his servant Francis I forgive you from my heart and am ready to do your will, as it may seem good to you!"

But the Bishop leaned over and drew up his enemy, embraced him and kissed him and said: "On account of my office I should be humble and peaceful. But I am by nature inclined to anger, and thou must therefore be indulgent with me."

But the Brothers went in and told Francis of the victory he had won over the evil spirits of dissension with his song.[1]

By this time the invalid could not but realize that he had but little time left. One day he asked the physician who attended him, a native of Arezzo named Bongiovanni, for the exact truth.[2] "With God's help things can go much better," was the evasive answer. "Tell me the truth, *Bembegnato!*" said Francis, who used to call the physician by this name, because the use of his real name "Good John" seemed to him in conflict with the words of the gospel, that "One is good, God" (Matthew, xix. 17). On similar grounds Francis would call no one master, so as not to be in conflict with the citation in Matthew, xxiii. 10.

When the physician realized that it was the truth that had to be told to Francis, he answered without reservation: "I consider that thou still canst live till the last of September or the beginning of October!" Francis was silent for a moment — then he stretched his hands upward and cried out, "Then be welcome, Sister Death!" And as if by these words he had opened up again the fount of poetry in his soul, he added to his Sun Song these last verses:

> Laudato si, Misignore, per sora nostra morte corporale,
> da la quale nullu homo vivente po skappare.
> Guai acquelli ke morrano ne le peccata mortali.
> Beati quelli ke trovarane le tue sanctissime voluntati,
> ka la morte secunda nol farra male.

[1] *Spec. perf.*, cap. 101.
[2] Concerning this physician see Bournet, *l.c.*, p. 125, n. 2.

*"Praised be thou, O Lord, for our Sister Bodily Death,
from whom no living man can escape.
Woe to those who die in mortal sin.
Blessed those who have discovered thy most holy will,
for to them the second death can do no harm!"*[1]

From this moment Francis wanted Brother Angelo and Brother Leo to be always with him, in order to sing to him about Sister Death, when he would desire it. And now it was in vain that Brother Elias came and warned him not to give scandal by the constant singing — "there is a watch set below, and they do not think that thou art a holy man, when they hear singing and playing always in thy cell!" Francis had now for a long enough period submitted and yielded; now when he was about to die, he wanted at least to have leave to die in his own way. "By the grace of the Holy Ghost," said he, "I am so completely united with my Lord and God, that I may well be allowed to be glad and rejoice in him!"[2]

But it was not only a time for singing — it was also time for Francis to put his house in order. In the last weeks his thoughts flew constantly to two places — to the faithful Brothers in La Verna and in Rieti, at Portiuncula and Carceri, and to Clara and her Sisters in San Damiano.

The road from the episcopal residence in Assisi down to San Damiano is not long, yet Francis had trod it for the last time. It was in vain that Clara sent messengers to him and told him to come, so that she could bid him farewell — it was no longer possible. He had to be satisfied to send her his last blessing in writing. "Say to Sister Clara," he said to the Brethren who were to go with the letter, "that I absolve her for every transgression of the commands of the Son of God or of mine, which she may have been guilty of, and that she now must put aside all care and tribulation, for now she cannot get to see me, but before she dies, both she and her Sisters shall see me and have great comfort therefrom."[3] Probably Francis had himself arranged that his body — as it did

---

[1] *Spec. perf.*, capp. 122-123. Compare Cel., *Vita sec.*, II, c. 163 (d'Al.).
[2] *Spec. perf.*, cap. 121. *Actus*, c. 18.
[3] *Spec. perf.*, c. 108, c. 90.

happen — was to be taken up to San Damiano after his death.

All that remained was to leave a word of farewell to the Brethren. And this the Testament did — that remarkable document in which Francis from his death-bed looks back over his life, with melancholy and joy dwelling on the first hours of his conversion's dawn, while he also thought with sadness of what the coming years were to bring his faithful disciples. Once again he collects here in short, impressive sentences all the admonitions from the General Chapters and from letters.

"The Lord thus gave to me, Brother Francis, to begin to do penance, because when I was in sin it appeared too bitter to me to see lepers; and the Lord himself led me among them, and gave me pity for them. And leaving them, that which seemed to me bitter was changed for me into sweetness of soul and body. And afterwards I remained a little and left the world. And the Lord gave me such faith in churches that I would simply pray and say: 'We adore thee, Lord Jesus Christ, here and in all thy churches, that are in the whole world, and we bless thee, because by thy holy Cross thou hast redeemed the world.'

"Afterwards the Lord gave me and gives me still such faith in priests who live by the form of the holy Roman Church on account of their holy orders, that, if they should do persecution upon me, I would wish to have recourse to them. And if I would have as much wisdom as Solomon had, and would find the very poor priests of this world, I would not wish to preach without their desire in the parishes in which they live. And I wish to fear, love and honor these same and all others as my lords; and I wish to see in them no sin, because I see the Son of God in them, and they are my lords. And I do it for this, because I see nothing bodily in this world of the very highest Son of God except his most holy body and blood which they receive and they alone administer to others. And these most holy mysteries I wish above all things to honor, to venerate and to be placed in precious places. The most holy names and his written words, wherever I may have found them in improper places, I wish to gather, and I ask that they be collected and be placed in a becoming place. And all theologians and those who minister the most holy divine words we ought to honor and venerate as those who minister to us spirit and life.

"And after the Lord gave me some Brothers, no one showed me what I ought to do; but the Most High himself revealed to me that I should live according to the form of the holy gospel. And I had it written in a few words and simply; and the Lord Pope confirmed it for me. And those who came to receive this life gave all they had to the poor, and were content with one tunic, patched inside and out, if they wished it, with a girdle and breeches. And we were unwilling to have more.

"We clerics said the Office like other clerics, the laymen said the Pater noster; and we remained willingly enough in the churches. And we were simple and subject to all. And I worked with my hands and wish to work; and all the other Brothers I strongly wish that they may work at labor which is of honest nature. And when the price of our labor is not given to us, we return to the table of the Lord in seeking alms from door to door.

"The Lord revealed to me a salutation, that we should say: 'The Lord give thee peace.' Let the Brothers beware, that they do not accept on any account churches, poor habitations and all other things which are built for them, unless they are such as suits holy Poverty, which we have promised in the Rule, always living here as strangers and pilgrims.

"I make it a firm precept of obedience for all the Brothers, that wherever they are they do not dare to seek for any letter from the Roman Curia by themselves or by a substituted person, neither for a church nor for another place, nor under the guise of preaching, nor for the persecution of their bodies, but, wherever they may not have been received, let them fly into another land to do penance with the blessing of God. And I wish firmly to obey the General Minister of this Brotherhood and the other guardian, whom it may please him to give me. And thus I wish to be a captive in his hands, that I may not go a step or act outside of obedience and his wish, because he is my lord. And although I may be simple and weak, nevertheless I wish to have a cleric who will perform the Office for me as it is contained in the Rule.

"And let all the other Brothers be obliged thus to obey their guardians and to do the Office according to the Rule. And those who may have been found, who did not do the Office according to the Rule, and wish to vary in other ways, or are not Catholics, let all Brothers, wherever they are, be obliged by obedience, that, whenever they will have found any of these, they should declare to the nearer guardian of that place, where they may have found him.[1] And the guardian is firmly obliged by obedience to guard him strictly like a man in bonds by day and by night, so that he cannot be taken out of his hands until he shall in his own person place him in the hands of his own minister. And the minister is firmly obliged by obedience to send him by such Brothers who will guard him day and night like a man in bonds, until they present him to the lord of Ostia, who is the lord, protector, and corrector of the whole Brotherhood.

"And let not the Brothers say: 'This is another Rule;' for this is a remembrance, an admonition and an exhortation, and my Testament, which I, Brother little Francis, make for you my blessed Brothers for this, that we may observe in a more catholic way the Rule which God has put before us. And the General Minister and all other ministers and custodes, let them be held by obedience not to add or diminish anything in these words. And let them always have this writing along with them together with the Rule. And at all Chapters they hold, when they read the Rule, let them read these words. And I make it a firm precept of obedience for all my clerical and lay Brothers, that they do not apply glosses to the Rule nor to these words by saying, 'They ought to be understood thus'; but as the Lord gave it to me to tell and write the Rule and these words purely and simply, so are you to understand simply and purely and observe unto the end with holy operation.

---

[1] "proximiori custodi illius loci, ubi ipsum invenerint, debeant representare." The affair is so important, that the Brothers shall not keep within the limits of the custodian, but seek the nearest custodian, whether the convent is in his jurisdiction or not.

"And whoever will have observed these things may be filled with the blessing of the most high Father in Heaven, and on earth be filled with the blessing of his beloved Son with the most Holy Ghost the Paraclete and with all virtues of the heavens and all the saints. And I, Brother Francis, your little one and servant, as far as I can, confirm to you within and without this most holy blessing. Amen.[1]"

Francis had now taken care of the future as well as he could. In the Middle Ages even a Papal bull was not always certain of obedience, and Francis perhaps had not any great confidence in the obedience which the Brethren would give to his last will. But his conscience was quiet — he could do no more.

With a touching charity he continued to love his Brethren to the last. Like all sick people, Francis lying prostrate now had one desire and now another. Once he could hardly eat anything; "but if I had a little fish," said he, "I believe I could get it down." Another time he had the desire in the middle of the night for some leaves of parsley; he thought that would do him good. It was only unwillingly that the Brother in charge went to do what seemed to him useless work, plucking parsley in pitch darkness.[2] More than once Francis must have seen a cloud of impatience on the Brother's countenance, and eventually as he lay there he formed scruples in the matter. "Perhaps I lie here," he thought, "and am the cause of my Brother sinning by anger. It might be, that if they did not have me to look after they could pray much more and live in a more regular way." Accordingly one day he called the Brethren to his bed and bade them not to be weary of all the inconvenience he occasioned them; it was not he alone in his person whom all this trouble concerned, but in and with him it related to all the Order. "And when you are weary of me, keep always before your eyes that the Lord will reward you for all that you do for me."[3]

To occasion the Brothers less trouble Francis finally decided

---

[1] *Opuscula* (Quaracchi), pp. 77–82. "*Analekten*" (Böhmer), pp. 36–40. *Speculum perfectionis* (Sabatier), pp. 309–313.

[2] The fish, *Spec. perf.*, c. 111. The parsley, Cel., *V. sec.*, II, c. 22 (d'Al.).

[3] *Spec. perf.*, c. 89.

to have himself carried down to Portiuncula. Bishop Guido was away — gone on a pilgrimage to Monte Gargona, perhaps as a penance for his strife with the podestà.[1] And the citizens in Assisi did not oppose the move, but merely let the guard accompany the party to Portiuncula.[2]

Accompanied by a great crowd of men the Brothers carried the sick man out of the city. From the episcopal residence the party went through *la Portaccia*, a principal gate now walled up, between Porta Mojano and Porta S. Pietro. By a road which here follows the city wall, S. Salvatore delle Pareti is reached, the leper hospital about half-way between Assisi and Portiuncula (now *Casa Gualdi*). As this place so memorable in the story of Francis' conversion was approached, the invalid asked to have the litter set down. "And so turn me with my face to Assisi," he said.

There was a moment of deep silence, whilst the sick man with the assistance of his Brethren was raised up. Above on the mountain side lay the city wall of Assisi and its gates and row after row of houses, surrounding the towers of San Rufino and Santa Maria della Minerva. Over the city, just as to-day, the bare cliff of Sasso Rosso hung with the German tower on top. Further away Monte Subasio was blue in the distance, where Carceri lay, and at whose feet San Damiano hid itself. And between Francis and the city was the great plain where, when young, he had taken his lonely rides and dreamt of doing great things. From this land and this city he had set forth, to this land and this city he was going back to die.

With his half-blind eyes Francis stared for a long time at the town, over the mountains, over the plain. Then he slowly lifted his hands and made the sign of the Cross over Assisi. "Blessed be thou of the Lord," he cried, "for he has chosen thee to be a home and an abode for all those who in truth will glorify him and give honor to his name!"[3] Then he dropped back upon the litter, and the Brothers carried him on to Portiuncula.

[1] Cel., *Vita sec.*, II, c. 166 (d'Al.). The Bishop was on his way home when Francis died.
[2] This follows from Celano's *Tractatus de miraculis*, IV, n. 32: "Custodes civitatis, qui sollicitis vigiliis custodiebant locum."
[3] *Actus*, c. 18. *Spec. perf.*, c. 124.

The invalid was taken into a hut which was a few paces behind Portiuncula chapel. Here it was that he had the comfort of receiving a visit from "Brother Jacoba," Jacopa de Settesoli. Just as she arrived Francis was going to dictate a letter to her asking her to come. The rumor of the master's incurable sickness had reached Rome, and Lady Jacopa brought with her the cowl she had woven for him, and which was to be his shroud, together with wax candles and incense for the solemnities of the interment. No woman was allowed to enter Portiuncula, but an exception was made for "Brother Jacoba." With tears she fell upon the bed of the beloved master — "like Magdalen at the feet of Jesus," the Brothers whispered to each other. The visit enlivened Francis, and to please him still more Jacopa prepared his Roman dainty, of which he in his sickness had often spoken and wanted to have. Not only did Francis eat of it, but Brother Bernard of Quintavalle was called in to also get a portion of the unusual luxury.[1]

Jacopa de Settesoli's visit fell in the last week that Francis lived.[2] The Thursday following, which was the first of October, he collected the Brothers about him and blessed each one of them. With special love he placed his hand on the head of Bernard of Quintavalle. "Write," said he to Brother Leo, "that I, as well as I am able, wish and command that all Brothers in the whole Order shall honor Bernard, as if it were myself, for he was the first who came to me and gave his goods to the poor."[3]

Francis then gave a last sermon of admonition to the Brothers, pressed it upon them above all to be faithful to poverty, and — as a symbol thereof — to be true to poor little Portiuncula. "If they drive you out of one door, then

---

[1] *Spec. perf.*, cc. 112, 107. *Actus*, c. 18. Cel., *Trac. de mirac.*, VI, nn. 37–38. Bernard a Bessa in *Anal. Franc.*, III, p. 1687. Compare *Vita Bernardi*, ditto, p. 42, where Bernard is brought down from Assisi on this occasion.

[2] *Spec. perf.* (Sab.), p. 223.

[3] *Spec. perf.*, cc. 112, 107. *Actus*, c. 5 (*Fioretti*, c. 6), where Brother Elias is blessed by Francis with the left hand only, while Bernard is blessed with the right and is also made General of the Order. Compare *Vita Bernardi* in *Anal. Franc.*, III, p. 42. In Celano, *Vita prima* (II, c. VII, n. 108) Elias only receives the blessing; in *Vita sec.*, II, c. 162, Francis blesses all, *incipiens a vicario suo*.

go in the other," said he, "for here is God's house and the gate of Heaven!" He blessed finally with the whole of his overflowing heart, not only the absent Brethren but also all Brothers who should ever enter the Order — "I bless them," said he, "as much as I can — *and more than I can.*" Francis perhaps never said anything which better expresses the whole of his innermost nature, than this *plusquam possum.* The spirit which actuated him had never rested before it had done more than it could. And now at the end it gave him no rest. After he had blessed his disciples he had himself completely undressed and placed on the bare earth in the hut. Lying there he took from the guardian as a last alms the cowl, in which he was to die, and as this did not seem poor enough, he had a rag sewed to it. In the same way he received a pair of breeches, a rope, with a hat he wore to hide the scars which always showed on his temples. Thus he had held his faith with Lady Poverty to the last and could die without owning more upon this earth than he had owned when he came into it.[1]

Exhausted, Francis fell into a sleep, but early on Friday morning he awoke with great pains. The Brothers were constantly gathered about him, and Francis' love to them constantly sought some new outlet. Thinking it was still Thursday, the day on which the Lord held the Last Supper with his disciples, he had them bring a loaf of bread, he blessed it, broke it, and gave them all bits of it. "And bring me the Holy Scripture and read the Gospel of Maundy Thursday to me!" said he. "To-day is not Thursday," one told him. "I thought it was still Thursday!" he answered. The book was brought, and as the day dawned the words of the Holy Scriptures were read over Francis' death-bed — the words in which were summarized all his life and learning:

"Before the festival-day of the pasch, Jesus knowing that his hour was come, that he should pass out of this world to the Father: having loved his own who were in the world, he loved them unto the end. And when supper was done, (the devil having now put into the heart of Judas Iscariot, the son

---

[1] Cel., *Vita prima*, II, c. VII, nn. 106, 108; c. VIII, n. 109. *V. sec.*, II, c. 162, nn. 214-215. *Spec. perf.*, pp. 222 and 33. Bonav., XIV, nn. 3-4.

of Simon, to betray him,) knowing that the Father had given him all things into his hands, and that he came from God, and goeth to God: He riseth from supper, and layeth aside his garments, and having taken a towel girded himself. After that he putteth water into a basin, and began to wash the feet of the disciples, and to wipe them with the towel wherewith he was girded. He cometh, therefore, to Simon Peter, and Peter saith to him: Lord, dost thou wash my feet? Jesus answered and said to him: What I do, thou knowest not now, but thou shalt know hereafter. Peter saith to him: Thou shalt never wash my feet. Jesus answered him: If I wash thee not, thou shalt have no part with me. Simon Peter saith to him: Lord, not only my feet, but also my hands, and my head. Jesus saith to him: He that is washed, needeth not but to wash his feet, but is cleaned wholly. And you are clean, but not all. For he knew who he was that would betray him; therefore he said: You are not all clean. Then after he had washed their feet, and taken his garments, being sat down again, he said to them: Know you what I have done to you? You call me Master, and Lord; and you say well, for so I am. If then I, being *your* Lord and Master, have washed your feet; you also ought to wash one another's feet. For I have given you an example, that as I have done to you, so you do also." [1]

During the days Francis still lived, none of the Brothers left his bed-side. Again and again Angelo and Leo had to sing the Sun Song to him — again and again did the sick one say the last words: "Praised be thou, O Lord, for Sister Death!" Again he asked his guardian to have his clothes removed, when the last hour would come, and received permission to expire lying naked on the earth.

Friday passed and Saturday came (October 3, 1226). The physician came, and Francis greeted him with the question of when the portals to the everlasting life should be opened to him. He required of the Brothers that they should strew ashes over him — "soon I will be nothing but dust and ashes."

Towards evening he began to sing with unusual strength. It was no more the Sun Song, but the 141st Psalm of David,

[1] St. John xiii. 1-15. *Spec. perf.*, cap. 88. Cel., *Vita sec.*, II, c. 163 (d'Al.)

the one which in the Vulgate begins: *Voce mea ad Dominum clamavi.* As the October evening fell rapidly, and it grew dark in the little hut in the Portiuncula woods, Francis prayed in the deep stillness, among the disciples listening breathlessly:

"I cried to the Lord with my voice: with my voice I made supplication to the Lord.

"In his sight I pour out my prayer, and before him I declare my trouble:

"When my spirit failed me, then thou knewest my paths.

"In this way wherein I walked, they have hidden a snare for me.

"I looked on my right hand, and beheld: and there was no one that would know me.

"Flight hath failed me: and there is no one that hath regard to my soul.

"I cried to thee, O Lord; I said: Thou art my hope, my portion in the land of the living.

"Attend to my supplication: for I am brought very low.

"Deliver me from my persecutors; for they are stronger than I.

"Bring my soul out of prison, that I may praise thy name: the just wait for me, until thou reward me."

While Francis prayed it was quite dark in the little cell. And as his voice ceased all was still as death — a stillness which this voice was never more to break. Francis of Assisi had closed his lips for ever; he went into eternity singing.[1]

But as a last greeting to the departed singer of God at this moment, over and around the house there was a loud and sudden twittering — it was Francis' good friends the larks who said their last farewell.[2]

---

[1] "mortem cantando suscepit." Cel., *Vita sec.*, II, c. 162 (d'Al.).
[2] *Spec. perf.*, c. 113. Cel., *Trac. de miraculis*, IV, n. 32.

CHAPTER VIII

THE END

THE first who was admitted to see Francis' body was Jacopa. Weeping she fell upon the master's lifeless body and with burning tears flowing, kissed over and over again the wounds in the feet and hands of the dead saint. Together with the Brothers she watched through the night by the master's bier, and when Sunday morning dawned her resolve was taken — she would not leave Assisi, but would spend the rest of her life in the places where Francis had walked and worked. Like San Damiano her house in Assisi became a meeting place for the faithful disciples, and many alms went through her hands, to Brother Leo, Brother Giles or Brother Rufino. It is certainly more than a suspicion, when Sabatier says that she closed Brother Leo's eyes; he died full of years about 1274. She lies buried in the Franciscan church in Assisi; a fresco shows her in the habit of a tertiary and with the cowl woven for Francis over her arm; the inscription reads: *Hic requiescit Jacoba sancta nobilisque Romana*, "Here Jacoba rests, a holy and noble Roman."[1]

Early Sunday morning the people came from all sides to give the dead saint his first homage. The rumor of Francis' stigmata flew from mouth to mouth, and the influx of those wishing to see them was beyond computation. The clergy came in solemn procession down from Assisi to take the remains, and with olive boughs and lighted candles in their hands, with sound of trumpet and hymns of jubilee, the line reached up to the city. To fulfil the promise Francis had

---

[1] *Tract. de mirac.*, VI, n. 39. See also E. d'Alençon: *Frère Jacqueline* (Paris, 1899, with reproduction of the fresco), and Sabatier in *Spec. perf.*, p. 85, and pp. 273–277. For Jacoba and Brother Giles see *Anal. Franc.*, III, p. 102, *Actus*, c. 44.

made Clara, the road by San Damiano was taken, and with bitter grief and lamentation the Sisters here said their last farewell to their beloved guide and teacher.[1] Then the procession went to the church of San Giorgio, to the place where now is the church of Santa Chiara, and there the lifeless body of St. Francis was temporarily laid, until on May 25, 1230, it was removed to the beautiful church of St. Francis built by Brother Elias.

None of the old chroniclers tell us where Jacopa de Settesoli remained during this funeral procession. It is quite improbable that she as a woman followed in the procession of clericals, brothers and soldiers. We may believe that she stayed behind in Portiuncula. When the great procession with all its splendor and chantings had disappeared among the trees, she may have again stepped within the hut where Francis lived and breathed twenty-four years before. And the gruesome emptiness overcame her — the emptiness which every death leaves behind it, and how much more such a death! Only now could she fully realize what she had lost, and kneeling in the little Portiuncula chapel that was so dark and desolate to her, she thought with weeping of him whose body they had borne in triumph to Assisi, but who never again would call her "Brother Jacoba."

[1] See page 137.

APPENDIX

AUTHORITIES FOR THE LIFE OF SAINT FRANCIS OF ASSISI

AUTHORITIES FOR THE LIFE OF SAINT FRANCIS OF ASSISI

IN recent times there have been few sources of more vivid discussion in the learned world than the question of the true value of the authorities for the life of St. Francis of Assisi.

This discussion was aroused by the appearance in 1894 of Sabatier's *Vie de S. François d'Assise* and by his edition in 1898 of the work *Speculum perfectionis* with the bold sub-title, "The oldest legend of St. Francis, written by Brother Leo and now published for the first time." Without going too close to the limits of veracity one can say that the celebrated Frenchman had to give up nearly all the theories which he undertook to uphold in this work. But his errors have proved to be very fruitful, as they have led to new researches, and if one inquires who it is who above all others in most recent times has found new grounds for Franciscan researches, it is the name of Paul Sabatier that first and foremost will form itself upon the lips. Even a Columbus based his discoveries upon false theories, and if it should be the last result of the new movement in Franciscan studies, inspired by Sabatier, that the old modes of thought should be intrinsically fortified hereafter, tested as they have been by a sharp critic, they will be only stronger for the test.

In the following pages I shall seek to unravel the difficult question with which we are here concerned, while I pay strict regard to all the researches hitherto carried on by Sabatier and his school or by their opponents.

As the first and most authoritative source for the life of Francis of Assisi we may name

I — HIS WRITINGS

BROTHER FRANCIS was not only a preacher, but he also impressed the written word into his service. We have from his hand, besides the two or three *Rules of the Order* (*Tres Socii*, IX, 35), Admonitions, Letters, Psalms of Praise, and Prayers, nearly all in Latin. We know the names of several people with whom he corresponded: St. Clara, Sisters of her Order, Cardinal Hugolin, who afterwards was Pope under the name Gregory IX, Brother Elias of Cortona and St. Anthony of Padua.[1] We know also the name of his secretary; it was *Brother Leo*. Legend presents him in the eighteenth chapter of the *Fioretti* wandering with Francis on the road from Perugia to Santa Maria degli Angeli, and step by step Francis called out to him and ordered him to write what he was now saying—"Mark that accurately, Brother Leo, and *write that down*." This is what Brother Leo constantly did, and he thus became not only the secretary of Francis of Assisi, but also his biographer and one of the principal sources of our knowledge of the Umbrian founder of the Order.

The writings of Francis, whether they were in manuscript or put down with the pen of Brother Leo, whether they were, like most, in Latin or, like some, in Italian, are not all in existence. Thus the Florentine chronicler Mariano (d. 1527) speaks of "some Praise Songs in Italian to the Sisters of St. Clara"; we have them no more.[2] To make up for this and other losses the Irish Minorite, Luke Wadding, in his well-known edition of the works of St. Francis (Antwerp, 1623), injected a quantity of "Sayings, Conversations, Witticisms, Comparisons and Examples" which various legends had placed in the mouth of St. Francis, and which he now without further research brought forward in direct form as "Words of St. Francis." Down to the most recent time this principle has been more or less followed; the year 1904 first produced a real critical edition, due to the Franciscans in Quaracchi.

---

[1] *Acta Sanctorum*, Aug. II, p. 767. *Seraphicae Legislationis Textus originales* (Quaracchi, 1897), pp. 63, 276. Thomas of Celano, *Vita prima*, II, 5, *Vita secunda*, III, 99. *Tres Socii*, XVI, 67. *Speculum perfectionis*, Sabatier's ed., cap. 108, Lemmens' edition, cap. 18.

[2] *Opuscula S. P. Francisci Assisiensis* (Quaracchi, 1904), p. IX, n. 1. In the *Speculum perfectionis* (Sabatier's ed., Paris, 1898), cap. 70, are given "quædam sancta verba cum cantu," which Francis wrote "pro consolatione et ædificatione pauperum dominarum"; compare the same work, p. 291, for the researches which were organized to find them, and Sabatier: *Vie de S. François* (1894), p. 377; see also the Testament of St. Clara (*Acta SS.*, Aug. II, p. 747).

In this new edition, *Opuscula Sancti Patris Francisci Assisiensis* (Ad Claras Aquas, 1904, xvi and 209 pp.), are found only the works which the writers are justified in accepting. The principal source is a manuscript of the fourteenth century (MS. No. 338 in Assisi, described by Ehrle in *Archiv für Litteratur und Kirchen-Geschichte des Mittelalters*, Vol. I, pp. 484-485).[1]

The severity of the criticism to which all was subjected is shown by the fact that while Wadding in his collection had seventeen letters of St. Francis, the Quaracchi edition gives only six. Also the Rule of the Order of the Poor Clares and the Rule of the Third Order of St. Francis, which were formerly ascribed to St. Francis, are attributed to him no longer.

While I abandon the sequence in which the editors have arranged the authentic writings of St. Francis still in existence, I have divided them into *poetic* and *prose* works, and take up in the first group what I would call Francis of Assisi's

RELIGIOUS POEMS

Francis was by nature of a joyful spirit.

Thomas of Celano, speaking of the time before his conversion, says that Francis and his friends disturbed the citizens of Assisi at night with "drunken songs"[2]; the *Tres Socii* say that he was "addicted to joke and song." This delight in song did not leave him after his conversion. After having abandoned his paternal inheritance he wandered through the woods "singing the praise of the Lord"; as he begged the sons of his city in the marketplace of Assisi for stones to restore the church of San Damiano he did it singing; he went out with Brother Giles on his first mission trip with song. It was song that comforted him during his many long sicknesses, and he received the approach of death singing — *mortem cantando suscepit*, as Thomas of Celano wrote.[3]

His religious feelings broke forth easily. Often in his prose writings it is to be remarked how inspiration will suddenly seize the writer, and in the middle of a Rule of the Order one is aston-

---

[1] See also Sabatier: *Vie de S. François*, pp. 39-41 and p. 370, n. 1, where the manuscripts in question are given to about 1240, W. Götz in Brieger's "Zeitschrift für Kirchengeschichte," vol. XXII, p. 373, note 2, as well as Faloci in *Miscellanea Francescana*, VI, p. 45. The Quaracchi edition contains only the Latin works and therefore does not include the Sun Song.

[2] Cel., *V. sec.*, I, 3; *Tres Socii*, n. 2.

[3] Cel., *V. pr.*, I, 7; *Tres Socii*, nn. 21, 33. Cel., *V. sec.*, III, 66, 138. Cel., *V. pr.*, I, 8. Cel., *V. sec.*, III, 139.

ished to find a Song of Praise to the Almighty, a laud, as the technical expression eventually became. In the first of the Rules of the Order, preserved to us in Chap. XXI, Francis himself produces such a laud for the Brothers to sing, when and how they wished, and which began thus:

> Timete et honorate,
> laudete et benedicite,
> gratias agite et adorate
> Dominum Deum omnipotentem in trinitate et unitate. . . .

Another more complete laud is preserved for us in the last chapter of the same Rule,[1] and as independent poetical works we have from the hand of St. Francis of Assisi no less than four Praise Songs — three in Latin and one in Italian. The Italian is the celebrated Sun Song, the Latin ones are entitled *Laudes Domini*, *Laudes de virtutibus* and *Laudes Dei*.

1. The Sun Song or Song about Creatures (*Cantico di frate sole, laude delle creature*).

That this, the first-born work of the Italian school of poetry, is not a translation of a Latin text, but was really written by St. Francis in his mother tongue, is now proved by the old description of St. Francis' wanderings and doings in Rieti (*Libellus actuum b. Patris Francisci tempore quo fuit in civitate Reate et comitatu ejusdem*). This work seems to belong to the end of the fourteenth century; a copy of the one which is in the great convent library in Assisi is dated 1416. In it it is said explicitly that Francis "had written this Praise Song in the language of the country. . . . And because our Holy Father has composed it I have not ventured to change it."[2] The work *Speculum perfectionis*, which belongs to about the year 1300, contains the Sun Song in Chapter 120, the

---

[1] The 17th chapter also has a species of Lauds; they specially resemble the *Laudes Dei* named below.

In *Chronica XXIV generalium* it is told — which also belongs here — that Brother Rufino on Mt. Alverna *more solito*, "in his usual manner," gave Francis the greeting: *Laus et benedictio sit Domino Deo nostro* (*Anal. Franciscana*, III, p. 48).

Chap. XXI of the First Rule of the Order is to be found written side by side with the Sun Song, in a manuscript in S. Isidoro in Rome dating from the fourteenth century with the special endorsement *De laude et exhortatione, quam possunt omnes fratres facere*. (*Doc. antiq. Franc.*, Lemmens' ed., III, Quaracchi, 1902, p. 62.)

[2] MS. 679 in Assisi, is given in Marcellino da Civezza's and Teofilo Domenichelli's edition of the *Legenda trium sociorum*, Rome, 1899, pp. 208.

occasion of its composition is told in Chapter 100, and in Chapters 101 and 123 the reasons are given why it was afterward increased with some few strophes. Thomas of Celano knows Francis of Assisi's "song about creatures" and knows that he wrote it on his sick-bed.[1]

That the remaining Italian poems, which have long been ascribed to St. Francis (*In foco amor mi mise* and *Amor di caritade*) were not by him, but by Jacopone da Todi, was known to Pater Ireneo Affò a hundred years before the modern north European philologers knew it.[2]

2. *Laudes Domini*, "the praises of the Lord," a laud which consists (*a*) in a paraphrase of the Paternoster, (*b*) of a sort of part-song, made up in parts from the Apocalypse, from the Book of Daniel and from the literature of the Church. (*Te Deum*.) It is apparently this laud that Francis refers to when he, as Eccleston tells us, in a letter to the Brothers in France exhorted them to sing with jubilee the praises of the Divine Trinity with the words: "Let us praise the Father and the Son with the Holy Ghost."[3] In the *Speculum perfectionis* (cap. 82, ed. Sabatier) it is told that the Brothers in Portiuncula, as a punishment for having spoken superfluous words, had to recite the prayer "Our Father" with "The praises of the Lord," and in the same place it is said that Francis himself was very fond of reciting this prayer and always strenuously recommended it to the other Brothers. The rubric in the Assisi Manuscript No. 338 agrees with this. We are there told that Francis prescribed these *Laudes Domini*

---

[1] *Vita secunda*, III, 138: "Laudes de creaturis tunc quasdam composuit et eas utcumque ad Creatorem laudandum accendit." III, 139: "Invitabat omnes creaturas ad laudem Dei, et per verba quaedam, quae olim composuerat ipse eas ad divinum hortabatur amorem."

[2] Affò: In *cantici di S. Francesco*, Guastalla, 1777. In more recent times the Sun Song was studied by Böhmer ("Romanische Studien," Halle, 1871, H. I, p. 120), by Ozanam (*Les poètes franciscains*, 1882, p. 87 and p. 361), by Sabatier (*Vie de S. François*, pp. 349-353, *Speculum perfectionis*, pp. 277-283 and p. 198, n. 1), by Faloci-Pulignani (*Miscellanea Francescana*, II, 190, III, 3-6, IV, 87-88, VII, fasc. I). Della Giovanna has (in *Giornale storico di letteratura italiana*, vol. XXV, vol. XXIX, vol. XXXIII) questioned the authenticity of the Sun Song. On the other side, *Misc. Franc.*, VI, 43-50, and *Analecta Bollandiana*, XIV, p. 227. Götz (Briegers Zeitschrift, vol. XXII, pp. 561-563) regards the Sun Song "provisionally" as genuine.

Editions of the text of the Sun Song: Papini: *Storia di S. Francesco*, II, Foligno, 1827, p. 144; Cristofani: *Storia di S. Damiano*, Assisi, 1883; Faloci: *Misc. Franc.*, III, 3-6 (five variations): Sabatier: *Speculum perfectionis*, Paris, 1898, pp. 284-289 (four variations).

[3] *Analecta Franciscana*, I, p. 232.

"for all Canonical hours of the day or night and for the Hours of the Blessed Virgin Mary." [1]

As a sort of continuation of these lauds there usually appears a *Greeting to the Blessed Virgin*, which is given in the Quaracchi edition, p. 123. These must not be confused with:

3. *Laudes de virtutibus* or *Salutatio virtutum* (Quar. ed., pp. 20-21), whose authenticity is testified to by Thomas of Celano, who (*Vita secunda*, III, 119) tells us that Francis "In the Laud he composed concerning virtues speaks thus, 'Hail to thee, Queen Wisdom, God salutes thee, and thy Sister, the pure holy Simplicity.'" But this is a literal quotation from *Laudes de virtutibus*, which, with its invocations of the "Holy Lady Poverty," of "Lady Charity," "Sister Humility," and "Sister Obedience," bears so strong and genuine an imprint of Francis.

4. *Laudes Dei.* These lauds have a particular status because the original manuscript of one of them holds a place as one of the few autographs of St. Francis which have been preserved up to the present time.[2] It is written on the back of another autograph, namely, *Blessing to Brother Leo*, and the two autograph pieces are best treated in connection with each other.

According to Thomas of Celano (*Vita secunda*, II, 18; compare Bonav., *Legenda major*, cap. XI, n. 9) it came to pass in the year 1224 that Brother Leo, while he was on Mt. Alverna together with St. Francis, fell into a great but purely spiritual temptation. "And he desired inwardly to have a reminder of the word of the Lord written by the hand of St. Francis.... And one day St. Francis addresses him and says: 'Bring me paper and ink, for I want to write down the Word of God and his Praise which I have preserved in my heart.' At once there is brought to him what he asks for, and with his own hand he writes the praises of God (*laudes Dei*), together with the Word as he wished it and finally a blessing for the Brother, while he says, 'Take this paper with you and preserve it carefully until your death. By the same all your temptations flee.' The letter is preserved and afterwards worked miracles."

This was not the only time that Francis gave some lines to one of his disciples written by his own hand with the exhortation to

---

[1] The Franciscans still use in part this form — see my "Pilgrimsbogen," 1903, pp. 34-36.
[2] There are three: *Laudes Dei, Blessing of Brother Leo* and a letter to Brother Leo. See Faloci: *Gli Autografi di S. Francesco* in *Misc. Francescana*, VI (1895), pp. 32-39, and VII, p. 67.

preserve them. Thus he said in the end of the letter to Elias of Cortona: "Keep this writing with you, so that you can better comply with it."[1]

Whether Brother Elias followed this advice literally we do not know, but the humble Brother Leo — "God's little lamb," as the master called him — faithfully kept with him the blessing from the hand of St. Francis until his death, that finally occurred on November 14, 1271. The parchment so faithfully preserved by him was inherited by the Franciscan convent in Assisi (Sagro Convento), within whose walls Brother Leo ended his days.[2] There the autograph, somewhat faded, was smoothed out and framed; in a list of the relics of St. Francis made in 1348 there is named "a wooden frame with the blessing of Brother Leo," together with "Praise of the Creator written by St. Francis' own hand."[3] When Wadding was in Assisi in 1619, he was able, therefore, to copy the *Laudes Dei* for the use of his edition of the works of St. Francis after the original manuscript, as he himself states.[4]

In our days the old autograph is to be found in the sacristy of the celebrated convent chapel, enclosed in a beautiful silver reliquary dating from the seventeenth century. Behind the glass of the reliquary is seen the piece of parchment, 14 centimetres high and 10 centimetres wide (5.6 inches by 4 inches), with evident traces of being long kept folded. The first glance shows one that there are two different handwritings on the parchment. The larger, which is written with black ink, is from the hand of St. Francis; the smaller writing, which is in red ink (rubrics), is by Brother Leo.

The parchment has three things on it from the hand of St. Francis. The first is the *Blessing*, the next is the *Dedication* of the same, and the third is the *Subscription*, given in the form of a hieroglyph.

1. *The Blessing*. It reads:

>Benedicat tibi Dominus et custo
>diat te ostendat faciem
>suum tibi et misereatur tui
>convertat vultum suum ad te
>et det tibi pacem.

[1] *Opuscula*, Quaracchi ed., pp. 110, 106, 112, 114-115. Sabatier's *Collection d'études et de documents*, vol. II, p. 115.
[2] *Analecta Franciscana*, III, p. 65.
[3] The list is found in MS. No. 344 in the communal library in Assisi. *Misc. Franc.*, vol. I, pp. 141-150.
[4] Edition of 1623, p. 101.

This is the blessing of the Old Testament (Numbers vi. 24–26), as now given in Lutheran churches: "The Lord bless thee and keep thee. The Lord shew his face to thee, and have mercy on thee. The Lord turn his countenance to thee, and give thee peace!"

2. *The Dedication.*

>   Dominus bene
>   dicat
>   Leo te

"The Lord bless, Leo, thee." There is some particular significance in the way Brother Leo's name is put in between the verb of the sentence and its object. It is as if we saw Francis, lifting his eyes from the parchment, look with love upon his bowed-down friend and brother. "The Lord bless — Leo! — thee!"

3. *The Subscription.*

To understand this we must recollect the occasion on which the blessing was written down. It was on Mt. Alverna at the end of the month of September, 1224. On the festival of the Elevation of the Cross immediately before (September 14) St. Francis had received the stigmata. Now he signed as his signature, not his name, but a hieroglyph, a symbol whose meaning was the *Crucifixion*. The upright T is the prophet Ezekiel's letter *Thau* (Ez. ix. 4), which in the script of the Middle Ages was accepted as the sign of the *Cross*. And this Cross is shown standing on the Mount Golgotha — the very rough outline of the sketch — together with a skull, the inner figure resembling a fruit, which in so many of the Calvaries of the Middle Ages is shown under the foot of the Cross. A single modern interpreter,[1] perhaps too imaginative, has even claimed to find in the mountain of the sketch, not Golgotha, but La Verna, and in the jagged line thinks that he sees a crude attempt to reproduce the rugged profile of La Verna. The meaning of the sketch in any case is the same — an expression of the words of the Apostle, "I bear the marks of the wounds of the Lord Jesus on my body!"[2]

---

[1] M. Carmichael: *La Benedisione di S. Francesco* (Leghorn, 1900).

[2] As far as this interpretation is correct it must be referred to the time after the stigmatization and therefore to the last two years of St. Francis' life, as St. Bonaventure says in his Legend (IV, 9): "This sign" (i.e., of the Cross) "the saint held in an especially great honor, commanded in his sermons that it should be used, and subscribed it with his own hand in the small letters which he sent (in eis quas dirigebat litterulis manu propria subscribebat), exactly as if all his effort was to fulfil the words of the prophet and 'mark Thau upon the

THE BLESSING OF BROTHER LEO
Autograph of St. Francis

As already noted, and as every one who visits Assisi can see for himself, the little bit of parchment shows clear traces of having been long kept folded up. This indicates that Brother Leo observed his lord and master's command and kept the blessing with him until he died.

But besides this, in the long time he survived his spiritual father he preserved the valued memory of his journey to the heathen in not less than three notes, which are now the most important proofs of the genuineness of the document. Right over the little seal he has written thus: *Beatus Franciscus scripsit manu sua istam benedictionem mihi fratri Leoni,* "The blessed Francis wrote with his own hand this blessing for me, Brother Leo." Under the signature comes next: *Simili modo fecit istud signum thau cum capite manu sua,* "He also with his own hand made this sign thau with a head (skull)." Finally, the uppermost part of the parchment bears the most important of the three additions. What Brother Leo has written here is this: *Beatus Franciscus duobus annis ante mortem suam fecit quadragesimam in loco Alverne ad honorem beate Virginis Marie matris dei et beati Michaelis Archangeli a festo assumptionis sancte Marie virginis usque ad festum sancti michaelis septembris et facta est super eum manus domini propter visionem et allocutionem seraphim et impressionem stigmatum christi in corpore suo fecit has laudes ex alio latere cartule scriptas et manu sua scripsit gratias agens domino de beneficio sibi collato.*

In English: "Two years before his death the blessed Francis kept his fast in the locality of Alverna in honor of the Blessed Virgin Mary Mother of God, and of the holy Archangel Michael, from the feast of the Assumption of the Holy Virgin Mary up to the feast of St. Michael in September and the hand of the Lord came over him on account of the vision and allocution of the seraphim and of the impression of the stigmata of Christ upon his body he made these praises written upon the other side of the paper and giving thanks to the Lord for the benefit conferred on him wrote with his own hand."

Brother Leo certainly intended with this explicit note to have verified the genuineness of the blessing beyond any doubt. For

foreheads of the men that sigh and mourn,' in the present case those who were truly converted to Christ Jesus."

In Thomas of Celano, in this *Miracula beati Francisci* (first published in the *Analecta Bollandiana,* vol. XVIII) is found the following: "the sign 'Thau' was dear to him above all other signs, and with that alone he subscribed his letters (*missivas cartulas*) and marked the walls of his cell all over with it" (ditto, pp. 114-115).

many years the relic in Assisi was regarded as a document of high rank because it contains the observations of a contemporary and almost of an eye-witness of the stigmatization.

It happened at the end of the nineteenth century that the well-known church and art historian, F. X. Kraus, got possession of a poor facsimile of the parchment, and basing his conclusions thereon, claimed that it was a counterfeit, and that an examination of the signature on the document would go to show that the so-called blessing of St. Francis, at the earliest, can only be ascribed to the fifteenth century.

The first to oppose this attack — and which came from the Catholic side — was Paul Sabatier. As an answer to Kraus he sent to the editor of the journal in which the attack had been published a photograph of the document in dispute, and in order to obtain for himself an authoritative opinion the editor placed this photograph before three authorities on palæography, one being Wattenbach. In a report dated October 25, 1895, the unanimous opinion was expressed by the investigators that there is "no palæographic reason for denying that this manuscript may date from the time of St. Francis." The French *Société Nationale des Antiquaires* came to the same conclusion January 22, 1896. Later, Walter Götz placed a copy of the blessing of St. Francis before Professor Seeliger in Leipzig for his opinion; his answer was also favorable to the authenticity of the document.[1]

The blessing *may*, therefore, be real. The manuscript actually dates from the thirteenth century, but may we not think that we stand before a very old copy?

This new doubt emanated again from Kraus, who did not wish to give up his hypercritical standpoint. He declared that according to Thomas of Celano and to Brother Leo the *Laudes Dei* written by Francis should be found on the other side of the parchment. Now it happens that in Assisi the back of the blessing is carefully kept hidden — but why? Because the *laudes* spoken of are not to be found there!

This was easily answered. The silver back of the reliquary was simply removed, and there was seen — what Wadding had already seen in the seventeenth century — the perfectly recognizable *Laudes Dei*, although partly obliterated, because of the long time Brother Leo had carried the parchment with him.

[1] Kraus and Sabatier in "Theologische Literaturzeitung," Leipzig, 1895, pp. 404 and 627. The French palæographer, *Bulletin critique*, March 5, 1896. Seeliger in Brieger's "Zeitschrift für Kirchengeschichte," vol. XXII, p. 370.

As an example of St. Francis' Latin poetry this laud is given in the foot-note below, in the form reconstructed by Faloci (*Misc. Franc.*, VI, p. 38) with the help of Wadding's copy. The words which still can be read in the Assisi autograph are printed in italics.[1]

As early as the fifteenth century the laud was partly illegible, while even the oldest copies — such as Bartholomew of Pisa's or the one in Jacob Oddi's chronicle *La Franceschina* — do not give us the complete text. The text in the Quaracchi edition is a little different from that given below, taken from a manuscript of Assisi of the fourteenth century, which the editor suspects to have been a direct copy of the original.

In near relationship with Francis of Assisi's religious poetry must be placed the *Officium Passionis Domini* arranged by him — which in fact is made up of quotations from the Bible. Its genuineness is confirmed by reference to Thomas of Celano's Biography of St. Clara.[2]

Prose Writings

These embrace two classes — Letters and Rules of the Order.

Wadding gives seventeen letters from St. Francis in his edition. The Franciscans in Quaracchi have accepted only six. The eleven others are partly fragments or later copies of other, authentic letters, in part without any manuscript proofs, reconstructed by Wadding in Latin after old Spanish translations. One — the letter to Anthony of Padua — is excluded from the Quaracchi edition as doubtful. Sabatier regards it as a forgery, but on the other hand it is accepted both by Götz and Lempp.[3] Of one of the letters of which Wadding had only a Spanish translation, Sabatier

---

[1] Tu es sanctus dominus deus. Tu es deus deorum, qui solus facis mirabilia. Tu es fortis, *tu es magnus, tu es* altissimus. Tu es omnipotens, tu es *pater sancte rex celi* et terrae. Tu es *trinus et unus dominus deus* deorum. *Tu es bonum, omne bonum, summum* bonum, dominus deus *vivus et verus. Tu es caritas*, tu es sapientia, tu es *humilitas, tu es* patientia. Tu es pulchritudo, tu es *securitas*. Tu es quietas, *tu es gaudium*. Tu es spes *nostra, tu es justitia* . . . et *temperantia* . . . *tu es omnia divitia nostra ad sufficientiam.* . . . *Tu es mansuetudo* . . . tu es *protector, tu es custos et defensor.* . . . *Tu es refugium* nostrum et virtus. Tu es fides, spes et caritas nostra. Tu es magna dulcedo nostra. Tu es bonitas infinita, magnus et admirabilis dominus deus, omnipotens, pius et misericors et salvator.

[2] *A. SS.*, August II, p. 761.

[3] Sabatier, *Vie*, p. 322. Götz in "Zeitschr. f. Kirchengesch." (Gotha), vol. XXII, p. 529, Lempp in same, vol. XII, p. 425, n. 2, and pp. 438 et seq.

some few years ago found a Latin counterpart, but which differs considerably from Wadding's text.[1]

The different letters will be found described in the biography, where they belong; there also will be found the necessary critical elucidations.

The same applies to the Rules of the Order which have been preserved for us — the first called by Karl Müller the Rule of 1221, and the second approved in 1223 by Honorius III. In connection with the Rules of the Order the so-called *Admonitiones* (Admonitions) will also be treated, as well as the *Hermit-Rules* belonging with them, and the circular letter, "On Reverence for the Lord's Body."

The Rule of the Poor Clares and the Rule of the Third Order of St. Francis, such as we now know them, are no longer attributed by anybody to St. Francis; in the Rule of the Poor Clares we find, however, some few lines of his hand, remains of the *Forma vivendi* (Mode of life) he originally wrote for the Poor Clares and of his *Ultima voluntas* (Last charge) to them. These two will be spoken of in the proper place.

Finally, we have from the hand of Francis of Assisi a remarkable document, which can often be found referred to in this work — his *Testament*. This document is half of the regular character, half a sort of autobiography. Its genuineness has been disputed by Karl Hasse; he regards it as being "made up of real and known utterances of Francis, in confirmation of his Rule and of the Roman spirit." For Sabatier it is practically the reverse, "almost a revocation" of the same Rule. Götz regards it as so reliable a document "that all the other remains," according to him, "may be proved thereby."[2]

In reality the genuineness of the Testament is beyond all doubt. Not only that the descriptions and thoughts therein are so truly Franciscan and accord with all that we otherwise know of St. Francis, but, as Götz has remarked, the speech also bears everywhere the marks of having been written down from dictation, and is primitive and unpolished. Besides, a whole quantity of other criteria speak for its authenticity. Thomas of Celano and Julian of Speier give it three times separately. Gregory IX refers to it in his bull (*Quo elongati*) of September 28, 1230, twice and gives

---

[1] *Collection d'études*, etc., ed. Sabatier, vol. II, pp. 135 et seq.
[2] Hase: "Franz v. Assisi" (Leipzig, 1856), p. 136, n. 8. Sabatier: *Vie*, p. 316. Götz in Brieger's "Zeitschr. f. Kirchengesch.," vol. XXII (Gotha, 1901), p. 376.

it in indirect form. Finally, it is cited twice in the Three Brothers' Legend.[1]

Sabatier thinks that Francis wrote his Testament several times, and bases this conclusion on Cap. 87 of the *Speculum perfectionis*, where the sick saint has Brother Benedict of Prato called to him and "in three words" imparts his last will to him and to all the Brethren.[2] He also left to St. Clara and the Sisters of her Order testamentary notes.[3]

II — BIOGRAPHERS

THE list of the biographers of St. Francis, whom it is permissible to take as original sources, begins shortly after his death with Thomas of Celano and ends about the year 1400 with works of compilation such as Bartholomew of Pisa's *Conformitates* (1385) and the anonymous *Speculum vitae S. Francisci et sociorum ejus* (about 1445). I divide these biographers into four successive groups, each with its own definite chronological limits and also with its express character, and I will designate the following groups, named after the most prominent of the authors or books:

1. Thomas of Celano Group (about 1230).
2. Brother Leo Group (about 1245).
3. St. Bonaventure Group (about 1265).
4. Speculum Group (later than about 1320).[4]

---

[1] As an example I give this single comparison:
Celano, *Vita prima*, I, 7: sicut ipse in testamento suo loquitur, dicens: Quia cum essem in peccatis, nimis amarum mihi videbatur videre leprosos, et Dominus conduxit me inter illos, et feci misericordiam cum illis.
Testament: quia, cum essem in peccatis, nimis mihi videbatur amarum videre leprosos; et ipse Dominus conduxit me inter illos, et feci misericordiam cum illis. (Quaracchi ed., p. 76.)
See also Cel., *V. pr.*, I, 15 = Test. (Q. ed.) p. 79; I, 17 = pp. 77–78; Cel., *V. sec.*, III, 99 = pp. 78–79; Julian of Speier (*A. SS.*, Oct. II, p. 579, n. 182) = p. 80; *Quo elongati* (Sab., *Spec. perf.*, pp. 314–322) = p. 82, p. 80. *Tres Socii*, IV, 11 = Cel., *V. pr.*, I, 17; VIII, 26 = as quoted by Julian of Speier.

[2] The three words were: mutual charity — love of poverty — obedience to the Church.

[3] See his *Ultima voluntas* admitted into the Rule of the Clares. Compare the following place in St. Clara's testament: "plura scripta nobis tradidit, ne post mortem suam declinaremus a paupertate" (*A. SS.*, Aug. II, p. 767. *Seraph. legislationis textus originales*, Quaracchi, 1897, p. 276. Wadding, 1253, n. 5).

[4] As the first biographical work we may name the *Circular letter to all the Brothers*, sent out by Elias of Cortona immediately after Francis' death (Wadding, II, pp. 149–150; *A. SS.*, Oct. II, pp. 668–669).

1. THOMAS OF CELANO GROUP

I assign to this group first and foremost Thomas of Celano's *Vita prima*, next Julian of Speier's Legend, which later is quoted in the *Speculum historiale*, of the Dominican Vincent of Beauvais, finally the versified biography written by Brother Henry, with many shorter legends, especially for liturgical use.

(a) *Thomas of Celano's Vita prima.* Thomas of Celano, author of the celebrated Judgment Day Hymn *Dies iræ*, was born about 1200 and entered the Franciscan Order between 1213 and 1216. He was received into the Order by Francis himself, just at the time when St. Francis had decided to go to Morocco, but was prevented from carrying out that intention.[1] After the Pentecost Chapter of 1221 he went as a missionary to Germany, in 1222 was custodian in Mayence, later in Worms and in Cologne; in 1223 the German Provincial, Brother Cæsarius of Speier, installed him as his vicar, while he, Cæsarius, went to Italy; in 1227 he followed the new Provincial, Brother Albert of Pisa, to the General Chapter at Portiuncula. He spent the next year in Italy. His description of St. Francis' canonization in 1228 leads us to suspect that he himself was in attendance there. He received from Gregory IX the commission to prepare a biography of St. Francis and as early as February 25, 1229, was able to hand the complete work to the Pope.[2]

[1] On account of the uncertainty of this date we can only say that Celano's admission to the Order came within these limits. *Vita prima*, I, cap. 20: "Sed bonus Deus, cui mei et multorum ... placuit recordari, cum jam ivisset versus Hispaniam ... eum a coepto itinere revocavit. Revertente quoque ipso ad ecclesiam s. Mariae de Portiuncula, tempore non multo post quidam litterati viri ... ei gratissime adhæserunt." See *A. SS.*, Oct. II, p. 546, n. 6.

[2] For biographical notes on Thomas of Celano see Jordanus of Giano (*Anal. Franc.*, I, pp. 8, 11) and *Chronica anonyma* (*Anal. Franc.*, I, pp. 287, 289). In his preface to his biography of St. Francis he claims to write "jubente domino et glorioso papa Gregorio." One of the MSS. of the Legend (3817, National Library, Paris, fourteenth century) contains the following note: "Apud Perusium felix domnus papa Gregorius nonus secundo gloriosi pontificatus sui anno quinto kal. martii legendam hanc recepit, confirmavit et censuit fore tenendam." (*Catalogus codicum hagiographorum latinorum in Bibl. Nat. Parisiensi*, Brussels, 1889, I, p. 364.) Thomas of Celano's authorship is also testified to by Jordanus of Giano (1262): "Thoma de Celano, qui legendam sancti Francisci et primam et secundam postea conscripsit" (*Anal. Fran.*, I, p. 8), by Salimbene (1283, Parma ed., p. 60): "præcepit (fr. Crescentius) Thomae de Celano, qui primam legendam beati Francisci fecerat, ut iterum scriberet alium librum," by Bernard of Bessa, St. Bonaventure's secretary, who, in the introduction to his legend, says (about 1290): "beati Francisci vitam scripsit ... frater Thomas, jubente domino Gregorio papa" (*Anal. Fr.*, III, p. 666).

Thomas of Celano explains in the preface that he used two sources of information: his personal experiences and reliable witnesses, and that he always strictly followed the truth.[1] There is no reason to doubt this assertion of a serious man, and the modern attempts to represent him as a biassed writer and falsifier of history simply take away the ground which at one time seemed to have been conquered. To-day, as Götz has said, "Celano's *Vita prima* is the fixed point, from which the determination of the value of our sources must begin."[2]

When Thomas of Celano makes excuses in his preface for his "unpolished words," it is nothing but modesty. He is really what he himself calls himself, a *vir literatus*, a lettered man, who has perfect command of his style; one can turn over the pages of all literature without finding more captivating sketches of men and occurrences than in Celano, and his Latin is carried along by a constantly sustained, gently undulating rhythm. The faults which affect his style are the faults of the time; he does not always avoid, in spite of his attempts to do so, what he himself entitles

[1] "veritate semper prævia . . . quæ ex ipsius ore audivi, vel a fidelibus et probatis testibus intellexi . . . verbis licet imperitis studui explicare."

[2] Götz, Brieger's Zeitschrift, Vol. XXIV, p. 166. Attacking Thomas of Celano see Karl Müller: "*Die Anfänge des Minoritenordens*," pp. 181 et seq. Sabatier: *Speculum perfectionis*, pp. 98–199.; in part Minocchi: *La Legenda trium sociorum*, Florence, 1900, pp. 81–85. In support of Celano see Faloci in *Miscellanea Francescana*, VIII, pp. 140 et seq., Tilemann: "*Speculum perfectionis und Legenda trium sociorum*," Leipzig, 1902, pp. 23–33, and Götz. Sabatier also formerly gave Celano a high standing: "He makes an entirely direct impression of being honorable and true; if he is partial he does not wish to be so, and perhaps does not know it. . . . One feels at every instant restrained emotion, the heart of the writer overcome with the moral beauty of his hero." (*Vie de S. François*, 1894, pp. liv and lvi.)

But later Thomas of Celano became for Sabatier a real falsifier, who, to serve a bad cause, found every method good (see *Speculum perfectionis, Opuscules de critique historique*, III, p. 70, n. 1); now he has become the accomplice of Brother Elias of Cortona and of Cardinal Hugolin and consequently an enemy of the Franciscan ideal. Yes, Sabatier will in Celano's *Vita prima* only see an answer to Brother Leo's *Legenda antiquissima*, "the Mirror of Perfection," issued in 1227. As will be shown later, Brother Leo, in 1227, had issued no such work and the hypothesis falls to the ground. If Thomas had perhaps in his first legend, which was written long before the deposition of Elias of Cortona, looked favourably upon this remarkable and unfortunate man, so in his *Vita secunda*, written in 1247, he has given his better views their due expression. Far from being a malicious betrayer, Thomas reveals himself as a simple, almost naïve soul whose principal failure as a biographer is that of being too careful a stylist. His picture of St. Francis is essentially the same as we get from the *Legenda trium sociorum* and from the *Fioretti*. (Sabatier, *Vie de S. Fr.*, p. lvi, Götz, Vol. XXIV, pp. 179, 193.)

"verbal decorations," *verborum phalleras*, and on long-continued perusal his work may have a tiresome effect — somewhat in the same way as the writings of the highly rhetorical religious authors of the seventeenth century in France.[1]

(*b*) In perfect sequence to Thomas of Celano's *Vita prima* stands Julian of Speier's Legend. Before his entrance into the Order Julian was choirmaster with Louis VIII of France; besides the Legend he also composed in prose a *Nocturnale Sancti officium in littera et cantu*.[2] He made the acquaintance of Thomas of Celano in the General Chapter of 1227. According to Glassberger's Chronicle (*Anal. Franc.*, II, 46) Julian's Legend begins with the words *Ad hoc quorundam*. But these are precisely the first words in the prologue to the Bollandists' so-called "second biography" of St. Francis, which they had ascribed to John of Ceperano, Notary Apostolic under Gregory IX (see later).

Julian's work is thus preserved; his prose legend — which does not offer much that is new — as well as his rhymed Office, has in recent years been an object for deep studies.[3]

Julian of Speier died 1250.

[1] Celano's *Vita prima* was first published by the Bollandists in *Acta Sanctorum*, Oct. II (1768), then by Rinaldi, 1806, and by Amoni, 1880. A new edition of all Celano's works is due to Rev. Edouard d'Alençon, Historian of the Capuchins' Order.

As Thomas described St. Francis' canonization, July 16, 1228, but not the transfer of his relics to the church of St. Francis (Pentecost, 1230), it is natural to place the writing of the Legend between these two dates, especially as the above-named Paris manuscript declares, that Gregory IX, February 25, 1229, received the Legend and gave it his approval. From the summer of 1228 to March, 1229, the Papal Curia was part of the time in Perugia and part of the time in Assisi. Tilemann (in the work already referred to, p. 30) has cast some doubt upon the note in the Parisian manuscript.

[2] Bernard of Bessa, *Liber de laudibus b. Francisci*: "In Francia vero frater Julianus, scientia et sanctitate conspicuus, qui etiam nocturnale Sancti officium in littera et cantu posuit." (*Anal. Franc.*, III, p. 666.)

[3] Julian of Speier's Legend is found in a fragmentary state in the Bollandist's biography of St. Francis, *A. SS.*, Oct. II, pp. 548–727. A complete edition is based on new manuscripts in the *Analecta Bollandiana*, XXI (1902), pp. 160–202. As Julian describes the transfer of St. Francis' body to the church of St. Francis, 1230, but does not mention Brother Elias of Cortona as General — which he became in 1232 — the Legend was probably written in the interim. (See, however, *Anal. Boll.*, XXI, p. 156, in which its time of composition is placed three years later.)

Besides the prose legends we possess the rhymed Office (*historia* as it was called in the literary expression of the Middle Ages). See also J. E. Weis, *Julian von Speier* (München 1900) and "*Die Chorāle Julians von Speier zu den Reimoffizien des Franciskus- und Antoniusfestes . . . nach Handschriften herausgegeben*" (Munich, 1901).

(c) The legend in verse (*Vita metrica*) formerly was regarded as identical with Julian of Speier's rhymed Office or was ascribed to an Englishman named John Cantius. Edouard d'Alençon has lately (*Misc. Franc.*, IV, pp. 33-34) pointed out that the author of the *Vita metrica* is Master Henry of Pisa, the same of whom Salimbene so pleasantly writes that he "could write, draw with colors, which some call illuminating, write notes, compose very beautiful songs, both for instruments and voice. . . . He was my singing teacher in the time of Pope Gregory the Ninth. . . . Brother Henry wrote many melodies and many sequences. He wrote both text and melody to *Christe Deus, Christe meus, Christe rex et domine*, suggested by a maid-servant's song, who went through the cathedral in Pisa and sang: *E tu no cure de me; e no curaro de te!*"[1]

(d) *Liturgical Legends*. The short legends divided into the required nine lessons were used for the choral prayer. Thomas of Celano himself — and likewise at a later period Bonaventure — seemed to have extracted these from his long legend. Denifle found a second legend for liturgical use in a Dominican Book of Lessons in Toulouse; the nine lessons belonging to the Feast of St. Francis have since been published by d'Alençon. The most remarkable thing about them is perhaps that in the manuscript they are declared to be taken from a legend which begins with the words *Stella matutina*, but as Bernard of Bessa states (*Anal. Franc.*, III, p. 666), the legend of St. Francis beginning with the words *Quasi stella matutina* was composed by the Notary Apostolic John of Ceperano. And according to Celano's *Vita prima* (pub. in *Act. SS.*, Oct. II, 125) Gregory IX, for his discourse at the canonization of St. Francis, had chosen this portion of scripture for his text (Ecclesiasticus, Cap. 50, v. 7). It may well be thought that the Notary Apostolic had made up his legends about St. Francis as a sort of a replica of the Pope's address, and that we thus have the remains of it in the Book of Lessons from Toulouse. The contents otherwise compares with Celano's *Vita prima*.[2]

[1] Salimbene, Parma ed., p. 64. The poem was first published by Cristofani (Prato, 1882).
[2] Edouard d'Alençon: *Spicilegium Franciscanum. Legenda brevis Sancti Francisci nunc primum edita* (Romae, 1899).
Denifle in *Archiv für Litt. u. Kg.*, I (1885), p. 148.
For Thomas of Celano's *Legenda brevis*, see Papini, *Notizie sicure della morte . . . di S. Fr. d'A.* 2ª ed. (Foligno, 1824), pp. 239-243. It is preceded by a letter to "Brother Benedict" (of Arezzo? See Sabatier, *Collection*, Vol. II, p. xliv).

2. BROTHER LEO GROUP

Among the first disciples there is none who plays a more weighty or a more effectual rôle than Brother Leo for futurity's understanding of St. Francis.

He was, as already noted, his master's secretary, and also his confessor and most intimate confidant. In the last years of St. Francis' life, when God's Poor Little Man from Assisi drew back more and more into a contemplative life, it was Leo who was the connecting link between him and the surrounding world. He was not afraid to go to the master when approach was forbidden to all others.

It is therefore obvious that this favorite disciple has seen and heard much which others neither heard nor saw, and it also follows that Brother Leo wished to preserve these his reminiscences for after generations. It thus came about that he began to write down what the master had said or done — *tam de mandato sancti patris quam etiam de devotione praedicti fratris*, as Angelo Clareno (d. 1337) has rightly seen and said, "as much by command of the holy father as inspired by the personal devotion Brother Leo nourished for St. Francis."[1] For the space of a hundred years, down to the days of Hubert of Casale (about 1259-1338), Brother Leo's descriptions and the legends emanating directly or indirectly from him and his circle kept alive the holy fire from the first days of the Order in the hearts of the young.

The legends in which Brother Leo has a direct part are two: *Legenda trium sociorum* and Thomas of Celano's *Vita secunda*. The three compilations of a later date rest more or less on his observations: *Speculum perfectionis*, *Legenda antiqua*, and *Actus b. Francisci* ("Fioretti").[2]

As a companion piece to *Legenda trium sociorum* comes the legend whose author the Bollandists term the "Anonymous one from Perugia," and whom I have also assigned to this group.

a. *Legenda trium sociorum*, "*The Legend of the Three Brothers*"

Between Celano's first biography of St. Francis and the other legends dependent on it and the appearance of the group of writ-

---

[1] *Archiv für Litt. u. Kirchengesch.*, III, p. 168.

[2] Furthermore Brother Leo has written a biography of his friend Brother Giles (Salimbene, *Chronica*, p. 322) and took part in the writing of the Legend of St. Clara. See Cozza Luzi in *Bollettino della società umbra di storia patria*, Vol. I, pp. 417-426).

ings which have their origin in Brother Leo of Assisi and his friends there is an important occurrence: Brother *Elias of Cortona's* Generalship and abrupt fall.[1] Even those who hitherto had been adherents of this brilliant man, who was, however, a danger to the Order at last, could not avoid seeing what he bore on his shield, and that, if he had obtained permission to carry out his own ideas, there soon would have been an end of Franciscanism. Due to the influence of the recognition of this fact, so powerfully impressed by the Pope's anathema against Elias, it is that refuge was sought in a return to the spirit of olden times. At the General Chapter in Genoa, 1244, it was determined to invite all who had anything to tell about St. Francis to collect their recollections and send them in to the newly chosen General of the Order, Crescentius of Jesi.

As a consequence of this invitation there came two years later from the little convent of Greccio in the valley of Rieti a selection of such sketches, written down by three close friends of St. Francis; namely, Brother Leo and Brother Rufino, both of Assisi, together with Brother Angelo Tancredi from Rieti. A letter which accompanied these papers, addressed to Crescentius and dated August, 1246, named as additional collaborators in the work a number of the first Brothers of the Order, such as Brother Philip, the Clares' Visitator, Brother Illuminato from Rieti, Brother Masseo from Marignano, together with another otherwise unknown Brother John, who joined in the work because he had known intimately Brother Bernard of Quintavalle (d. 1242) and Brother Giles (Lat. *Egidius*) — the first two disciples who had joined St. Francis.

In the letter the authors expressed themselves in the following way on the scope of their work:

"We who, although unworthy of it, have lived for a long time along with St. Francis, have, with truth for our guide, wished to present to your Holiness" — i.e., Crescentius — "a selection of his many actions which we have either seen ourselves or have obtained through other Brothers, especially" (here follow the

---

[1] It will undoubtedly be of interest to have a list of the first Generals of the Order at hand. I therefore give them here:

Vicars (while St. Francis lived): Pietro dei Cattani, September 29, 1220–March 10, 1221, when he died. Elias of Cortona succeeded and was Vicar to June 16 (Pentecost), 1227. *Generals:* Johannes Parenti, June 16, 1227–1232; Elias of Cortona, 1232–1239; Albert of Pisa, 1239; Aymon of Faversham, 1240–1244; Crescentius of Jesi, 1244–1247; John of Parma, 1247–1257; St. Bonaventure, 1257–1274.

names. The original text, as one will see below, has the words *per alios sanctos fratres*, "through other Holy Brothers." The difficulty, which is due to the fact that Leo, Angelo and Rufino first speak of themselves and then of "other" holy Brothers, is solved perhaps best by taking *sanctos* as in apposition to *fratres* and to understand it thus: "through other Brothers; namely, the holy Brother Philip," etc. But if one was in doubt about the authenticity of the letter, I would affirm that this expression, "Brother Leo, Brother Rufino and Brother Angelo wrote it down," might make one suspect a falsifier, who unwittingly betrayed himself by having the authors of the Legend sign themselves for that which they were in the eyes of him, a writer of a later period: *sancti fratres*.[1])

"It is not sufficient for us" — thus the writers go on to say — "to tell of miracles alone, of which indeed holiness does not consist, but which can indicate its presence,[2] but we wish to show the holy way of living and pious regard and desires of our most holy father Francis, to the praise and glory of the highest God and to the edification of those who will follow after him. Which, however, we do not wish to write in the form of a legend, as there are already written legends of his life and the works of wonder which the Lord let him perform. But we have plucked the flowers in the meadow which seemed to us the fairest; we do not offer therefore a continuous story, for we have omitted much which in the above-named legends is written both truthfully and in good style; and if it meets your approval our little work can be added thereto. We believe, indeed, that if the honorable gentlemen who wrote the above-named legends had known what we now are about to tell, they would not have let it pass by, but would have desired to have written down at least a part thereof in their beautiful style, and thus handed it down to the memory of coming generations."[3]

[1] The word *sanctos* we may believe was inserted by a copyist. The Brothers themselves never gave the Legend the title *Legenda trium sociorum*, as it is now found in the manuscripts.

[2] This expression is from Thomas of Celano; *miracula, quae sanctitatem non faciunt, sed ostendunt*, he says in his *Vita prima*, I, p. 16.

[3] Reverendo in Christo patri fratri Crescentio, Dei gratia Generali ministro, frater Leo, frater Ruffinus et frater Angelus, olim socii, licet indigni, beatissimi patris Francisci, reverentiam in Domino debitam et devotam.

Cum de mandato proximi praeteriti capituli generalis et vestro teneantur fratres signa et prodigia beatissimi patris Francisci, quae scire vel reperire possunt, vestrae paternitati dirigere; visum est nobis, qui secum licet indigni fuimus diutius conversati, pauca de multis gestis ipsius, quae per nos vidimus,

This preface is found in all the fourteen manuscripts of the Legend which have been preserved for us, and of which the oldest belongs to the last quarter of the fourteenth century. There are also found five manuscripts of the Legend in Italian translations.

All these manuscripts present the highly impressive peculiarity that the writing, the Legend, which in all of them follows the preface, and which in nearly all of them is practically the same, does not seem on a little closer examination to answer to what we had a right to expect from this work according to the authors' own statements. In the preface the reader is promised, not a description of the life, but a collection of flowers; not a continuous relation like that of Thomas of Celano or of Julian of Speier, but various minor traits of the pious ways of St. Francis, and finally nothing we already knew from earlier works, but absolutely new things never before published — *de l'inédit*, as the French say. If Thomas of Celano had been St. Francis' Plato, the Brothers should now want to write a collection of *Memorabilia* in the spirit of Xenophon. Had the poet of *Dies iræ* been the great follower of Christ, John, they would have wished to write his *Logia*.

One had every right to expect all this from the Three Brothers' Legend — and what do we find there? Almost exactly the opposite! Of the eighteen chapters of the Legend the first eight concern themselves with the history of Francis' youth and con-

vel per alios sanctos fratres scire potuimus, et specialiter per fratrem Philippum visitatorem pauperum Dominarum, fratrem Illuminatum de Reate, fratrem Masseum de Marignano, et fratrem Joannem, socium venerabilis fratris Ægidii, qui plura de his habuit de eodem sancto fratre Ægidio et sanctae memoriae lratre Bernardo, primo socio beati Francisci, sanctitati vestrae, veritate praevia, intimare; non contenti narrare solum miracula, quae sanctitatem non faciunt, sed ostendunt, sed etiam sanctae conversationis eius insignia et pii beneplaciti voluntatem ostendere cupientes, ad laudem et gloriam summi Dei et dicti patris sanctissimi, atque aedificationem volentium vestigia eius imitari. Quae tamen per modum legendae non scribimus, cum dudum de vita sua et miraculis quae per eum Dominus operatus est, sint confectae legendae. Sed velut de amoeno prato quosdam flores, qui arbitrio nostro sunt pulchriores, excerpimus continuantem historiam non sequentes, sed multa seriose relinquentes, quae in praedictis legendis sunt posita tam veridico quam luculento sermone; quibus haec pauca, quae scribimus, poteritis facere inseri, si vestra discretio viderit esse iustum. Credimus enim, quod si venerab libus viris, qui praefatas confecerunt legendas haec nota fuissent, ea minime praeterissent, nisi saltem pro parte ipsa suo decorassent eloquio, et posteris ad memoriam reliquissent. Semper integre valeat vestra sancta paternitas in Domino Jesu Christo, in quo nos filios vestros devotos sanctitati vestrae recommendamus humiliter et devote. Data in loco Graecii, III idibus augusti, anno Domini MCCXLVI (*Acta SS.*, Oct. II, p. 723.)

version. The next four treat of the reception of the first eleven Brothers into the Order, the tribulations in the earliest days of the Order, and Innocent III's approval of the Rules. In the next two chapters is a sketch of the first convent and the way in which the Chapters of the Order were held. The fifteenth chapter tells of the death of the first Protector of the Order and the choice of a new one, the sixteenth of the Brothers' first departure on a European mission. Two concluding chapters — which, moreover, in one of the manuscripts are put into one — contain finally the description of Francis' death, of his stigmatization (in this inverted order) and canonization, and this brings the Legend of the Three Brothers to an end. It must be remarked that this text is almost the absolute reverse of the author's promise in the letter to Crescentius. The Brothers had wished to bring a collection of flowers — and here we stand before a legend which, if incomplete, is in good chronological sequence. They had wished to bring new material, and here, although with many characteristic additions and minor features, is told the same history of the merchant's son from Assisi, of his conversion and life with his first disciples, all which we already knew from Thomas of Celano and Julian of Speier. Here were missing finally the whole mass of little traits from St. Francis' inner life, all that which the author had promised under the name *sanctae conversationis eius insignia*, and which one could expect from those who, "although unworthy thereof," had been with him in his most sacred moments, in his most secret hours, who had followed him to the grotto at Fonte Colombo, where he with fast and prayer wrote the Rule of the Order, and who at his side had climbed up Mt. Alverna and had seen him come down therefrom, marked on hands and feet by the miracle of the Lord! Was this really all that the whole body of Francis' most trusted friends — Leo, Rufino, Angelo, Bernard, Philip, Illuminato, Masseo and Giles — could tell the world about their beloved master and glorified spiritual father? For that the two miserable chapters at the end could not pass for a fulfilment of the promises of the preface, and that they even did not originally belong to the Legend, is evident from the difference in style and their undoubted dependence on Bonaventure's book of 1263 on St. Francis. These two chapters were clearly enough only written as a makeshift — as one temporarily throws boards over a house that has not been sufficiently advanced in building to resist the coming of winter.

The Three Brothers' Legend, as it lies before us in manuscript, seems also to have been a fragment. But how could it have been that? Is it conceivable that the Brothers became weary of their work when half-finished, that they were tired, that they did not desire to finish the wreath of flowers in honor of St. Francis, which was to be woven around the Master's name a hundred years later by other hands, by him or by them who wrote *Fioretti?*

The matter stood thus undecided, when the Bollandist Suysken in 1768, in the second October section of the *Acta Sanctorum*, published the Three Brothers' Legend according to a manuscript in Louvain. The question stood as before — or rather it was not disposed of. All manuscripts contain the Legend in this form — who then could form any other conclusion than that we have here not only the authentic but also the complete work?

And yet there was one thing which pointed in the other direction. In Wadding, the celebrated Irish annalist who wrote in the first quarter of the seventeenth century, and also in the Florentine chronicler, Mariano (d. 1527), used by him, quotations from the Three Brothers' Legend occur several times, which are not found in the text published by the Bollandists. Suysken satisfies himself with the idea that Wadding may have quoted wrongly, but the thought also was in his mind that Wadding (or his source Mariano) might have known another *Legenda trium sociorum* than the only one which was now before him.[1]

In these quotations of Wadding it is remarkable that several of them seem to be so good that they would accord with a legend of the quality which would be expected from their hands after the Brothers' letter to Crescentius. There was, for example, a description of how St. Francis in his eagerness for poverty wanted to tear down a house with his own hands, which the citizens of Assisi during his absence had built for the use of the Brothers. There was another tale of how Francis, in the face of Cardinal Hugolin, refused to assent to the Brothers in his Order holding Church preferments. In a third place Wadding relates that Francis in Bologna, in the same way as at Portiuncula, commanded all the Brothers to desert the convent which was built for them. Finally, following always the Three Brothers' Legend, we are told how St. Francis in his last moments had greeted death with the words: "Be welcome, Sister Death."[2]

[1] Omnino oportet Waddingum habuisse Legendam, trium sociorum nomine (forte non recte) inscriptam, diversam a nostro; aut, quod verisimilius est, eosdem ab aliis perperam citatos legisse. *A. SS.*, Oct. II, p. 858, n. 238.

[2] Wadding, *Annales*, 1218, n. 10, 1219, n. 1-2, 1220, n. 15, 1224, n. 28. See also 1210, n. 49, and 1219, n. 3.

With these and many other similar extracts before our eyes it was impossible that one or another would not finally recollect those words in the letter of the Brothers from Greccio concerning St. Francis' devout conduct of life. Quotations in Wadding gave a brief commentary both on one or the other of these expressions, for what was Francis' "pious intentions," his *pii beneplaciti voluntas*, other than the adherence to the evangelical poverty, whose devoted lover he showed himself both during the occurrences in Bologna and the incidents at Portiuncula?

Led by such and similar indications it was that Paul Sabatier, in his study of the Bollandists' work on St. Francis, came to the conclusion that the Three Brothers' Legend as it exists in the manuscripts was really a fragment, a torso. In his *Vie de Saint François d'Assise* (Paris, 1894) he writes on page lxiii: "It is clear that the Three Brothers' Legend, as we now have it, is only a fragment of the original, which, without doubt, was put together, arranged, and much abridged by the authorities of the Order before it was put into circulation." And he remarks, too, that Crescentius of Jesi, to whom it was sent, was not the most zealous adherent of the intransigent Franciscanism, such as Leo and his friends upheld.

Sabatier was here — as so often — unjustly suspicious. The state of affairs was that the Legend's incompleteness was well known, and Sabatier had, moreover, the happy fortune in a late Franciscan work of compilation of nearly finding the missing part of the Three Brothers' Legend.

The question concerned the work written about 1445 and first issued in Venice, 1504, *Speculum vitae S. Francisci et sociorum ejus*. Out of this formless book Sabatier threw out a whole quantity of material of all sorts — chapters of St. Bonaventure, devout memoranda of St. Bernard of Clairvaux, a whole quantity of chapters which appeared to be the Latin text of the *Fioretti*, some Franciscan prayers, with much else. What was now left strongly recall in style and thought the Three Brothers' Legend. And what made him certain of his case was that in this heart of the Speculum there occurred no less than nineteen times an expression in which the authors constantly referred to themselves and which reads: *nos qui cum ipso fuimus*, "we who were with him." For was not this precisely the same which the Three Brothers in their letters to Crescentius had used to designate themselves — that it was they who, in spite of their unworthiness, had known St. Francis the longest and the best, *visum est nobis, qui secum licet indigni fuimus diutius conversati?* The coincidence of the two expressions was striking and convincing for Sabatier. There is found in the printed *Speculum vitae* (from Folio 8*b* to Folio 136*a*) undoubtedly a considerable portion of the missing pages of the Legend.[1]

Full of these thoughts, it next happened that Sabatier, in the Mazarin Library in Paris, found a manuscript, No. 1743, in which the very chapters which he himself separated from the *Speculum vitae* are found joined together under the title *Speculum perfectionis fratris minoris*, "Mirror of Perfection of The Friar Minor." How Sabatier was led by this discovery into new paths, how he, with a copyist's error in the dating of the manuscript as a starting point, developed a whole theory about the *Speculum perfectionis* as the oldest Franciscan legend, written in May, 1227, in Portiuncula by Brother Leo — to this we will refer later. In fact he was right, as far as he, in the Legends of the Speculum, saw the remains of the complete *Legenda trium sociorum*. And from this foundation the task of reproducing the Legend was also taken up by two Italians, students of St. Francis, the two Franciscans Marcellino da Civezza and Teofilo Domenichelli. Their work, which appeared in Rome, 1889,[2] had the following interesting history.

About the year 1855 Stanislao Melchiorri, then Annalist of the Franciscan Order, received a very old manuscript sent him as containing an Italian translation of the Legend of the Three Brothers. On comparing this translation with the Bollandists' edition of the original text (and with Rinaldi's edition of 1831), it appeared that the Italian legend in the first place did not have the last two chapters of these editions, and in the second place offered in their stead a whole quantity of highly important additions. Carried away as Melchiorri was in the prevalent view of the Legend, as only identical with the fragment contained in the manuscript, he regarded these additions as interpolations and edited them with a preface, in which he declared that the translator, in order to complete the Legend, had added to it a number of chapters, taken from Thomas of Celano, St. Bonaventure, Bartholomew of Pisa and others. But he could not maintain this theory of the origin of the individual portions.[3]

---

[1] Sabatier: *Vie de S. Fr.*, pp. lxx-lxxi.

[2] La Leggenda di S. Francesco, scritta da tre suoi compagni (*Legenda trium sociorum*) pubblicata per la prima volta nella vera sua integrità dai Padri Marcellino da Civezza e Teofilo Domenichelli dei Minori. Roma, MDCCCXCIX.

[3] The book appeared in 1856 in Recanati with the title, *Leggenda di S. Francesco d'Assisi scritta dalli suoi compagni che tutt'hora conversavano con lui*. In 1862 it was published in France with the less correct title, *Légende de S. François*

According to a note in the manuscript, the legend was written in the year 1557 by the oratorian, Muzio Achillei, after another much older manuscript.[1] Muzio is known in history as a disciple of St. Philip Neri and a friend of the church-historian Baronius, who often made use of his assistance.

The language from the chronological standpoint might be assigned to the same period as the *Fioretti;* Zambrini, who was misled by the editor's mistaken conception of the date of the work as being later than the day of Bartholomew of Pisa (1385), could not help finding "much of the simplicity of the fourteenth century therein."[2] In reality the language of the translation with its frequent Latinisms, its Latin use of the subjunctive after *quando* (where the Italian now has the indicative), bears the clear imprint of a century when the new language of the people had not freed itself from Latin influence.

And now it appeared, that with this translation as a basis, it was possible to attempt a reconstruction of the Latin Three Brothers' Legend in its integrity. The often servile fidelity of the translator, that led him to repeat the Latin text word for word, made the work easy. The majority of the work was — as was to be expected — to be found in the *Speculum perfectionis* brought to the light by Sabatier (the French scholar's edition of this work, 1898, gave great assistance). By a simple translation of the Italian legend into Latin, there appeared a whole quantity of chapters which either plainly agreed with the text in the *Speculum* or at any rate originated therefrom. Sixteen of the seventy-nine chapters of the Melchiorri legends were identical with Chapters I–XVI in the manuscript legend, fifty-seven agreed with chapters in the *Speculum perfectionis*, only six could have been derived from other sources, apparently from Thomas of Celano.

That the Three Brothers thus in minor part had copied one or several of the earlier biographies of St. Francis was not remarkable; they had done this and in a much greater degree in what I,

d'Assise par ses trois compagnons; manuscrit du XIIIe siècle publié pour la première fois (!) par M. l'abbé Symon de Latreiche. A second edition of this translation appeared in 1865 (Paris, Lethielleux).

[1] The notice reads:

Ad lectorem. Superiora hæc divi Francisci gesta e vetustiori quodam codice manu mea descripsi Mutius Achilleus (a) Sancto Severino, rogatu venerandi Patris Felicis . . . recentioris Ordinis Franciscanorum (quos Capuccinos appellant). Septemped. anno a Christi Salvatoris Nostri natalibus MDLXXVII, VIII Kal. ianuarii.

[2] sente molto della semplicità del trecento. (Zambrini: *Le opere volgari a stampa dei secoli XIII e XIV*. Ed. 4, Bologna, 1884, p. 563.)

hereafter, will call the first part of their legend (Capp. I-XVI). It is still more remarkable to see how completely the second part of the legend now found or rediscovered answered to what the Three Brothers had promised in the letter to Crescentius. Here they write in most characteristic detail what they and no other had seen and heard, here they over and over again repeat their *nos qui cum eo fuimus*, "we who were with him," here we have the light and perfume of the flowers from the oak woods of Umbria, from the loneliness of the valley of Rieti, from the cliffs of Mt. Alverna, as the Brothers had promised. A glance at the titles of the chapters was enough to show, that here were really found all those relations of St. Francis' "devout conduct of life" and "pious intentions," whose existence we had only been able to suspect hitherto through references of Mariano and Wadding.

All this, however, did not say that the attempts at reconstruction of da Civezza and Domenichelli should be regarded as completely successful. As Tilemann[1] has remarked, the reconstructed chapters were of a more meagre, more condensed, less freely descriptive character than the existing pieces in the *Speculum perfectionis*. One is tempted to lay the blame for this on the old Italian translator, whom we can suppose now and then to have lightened his work by condensing the narrations. What else was there to prevent one from inserting chapters from the *Speculum* in those places where the Italian text makes it evident that they belonged in the original legend?

A question still remains: How did it come about that the Three Brothers' Legend has thus been divided into two halves, of which the one invariably appears in all the manuscripts accompanied by the preface, which, in consequence of the division, so poorly suits it, while the other half portion has led, as it were, a subterranean existence and only in the most recent days has come out into the light? The answer to this question can be better given in connection with the treatment of Thomas of Celano's *Vita secunda*.

Here we can only refer to the fact that this work in more recent times, contemporaneous with the production of the Three Brothers' Legend in its full scope, has raised for itself critical and—it may as well be said—hypercritical voices, that desired to rob the beautiful old legend of all its value. It is especially the Bollandist, van Ortroy, who, with an incredible display of learning, has sought to

[1] Heinrich Tilemann: "*Speculum perfectionis und Legenda trium sociorum*," Leipsic, 1902, pp. 134-148.

show that the *Legenda trium sociorum* was a compilation in which such late authors as Bonaventure (1263) and Bernard of Bessa (about 1290) were utilized. The letter to Crescentius, according to van Ortroy, certainly does not belong where it now stands, but on the other hand belongs to Thomas of Celano's *Vita secunda*, which upon the whole should be the Three Brothers' Legend. This inexpressibly unreasonable hypothesis was powerfully advocated by Paul Sabatier, but has found an adversary in the present Annalist of the Franciscan Order, P. Leonard Lemmens. Another Catholic Franciscan researcher, S. Minocchi, sees in the *Legenda trium sociorum* the missing work of John of Ceperano. His legend begins, namely (see page 355), with the words *Quasi stella matutina*, and only one of the manuscripts of the Three Brothers' Legend has a prologue beginning with these words.[1] Other more recent researchers, such as Faloci-Pulignani, stand firmly on the old ground, that the first part is the whole of the legend, and this, although in the edition brought out by Faloci after a manuscript in Foligno of the Three Brothers' Legend, outside of the sixteen traditionally accepted chapters and the two unaccepted and added ones, there are still found two chapters of the second part of the legend, namely, one "of the Names of the twelve first Brothers" (Da Civezza-Domenichelli, Cap. XII) and one concerning the Portiuncula indulgence (Cap. XLIX, same work, in a slightly different form). Da Civezza and Domenichelli finally weaken their position by following Sabatier in his *Speculum* theories, so that they and their introduction to the Legend treat the Three Brothers' Legend of 1246 as little more than a copy of what Leo alone had already written in 1227. Even so conservative a critic as Götz, who on the whole is friendly to tradition, regards the authenticity of the Legend as impaired; but he does not deny that both in the *Legenda trium sociorum* as well as in the work of the nearly related anonymous writer from Perugia there is found valuable material, though, according to his view, material of the second rank.[2]

---

[1] *Præfulgidus ut lucifer et sicut stella matutina, imo quasi sol oriens* (MS. Vatic., 7339). *Quasi stella matutina* is not found here a single time, but always *sicut*. (See Da Civezza-Domenichelli, p. 4, n. 1. Tilemann, pp. 125-133.)

[2] Van Ortroy, *Analecta Bolland.*, XIX (1900), pp. 119-197; Sabatier, *Revue historique*, LXXV (1901); Minocchi, *Archivio storico ital.*, XXIV, pp. 249-362, and *Nuovi Studi* (1900), pp. 100 et seq.; Lemmens, *Documenta antiqua franc.*, I (Quaracchi, 1901), pp. 26-27; Faloci-Pulignani, *S. Francisci Legenda trium sociorum*, Fulginice (1898), et *La Leggenda*, etc., Rome, 1899 pp. 1-cxxxvi; Götz, Brieger's Zeitschr. f. Kgsch., XXV (1904), pp. 34, 36-37, 40.

b. *Anonymus Perusinus*

When the Bollandists in their time commenced their studies of the history of St. Francis, they had, among other things on which to exercise their judgment, a manuscript from Perugia, out of which they had formerly extracted a biography of the third disciple of St. Francis of Assisi, Brother Giles. (*Acta Sanctorum*, April 23.) In this manuscript there is now found also a biography of St. Francis, and as the Legend of Giles was undoubtedly a Work of Brother Leo,[1] Paplebroch believes that the legend of St. Francis may also be attributed to him.

In reality this legend offers numerous and close points of comparison with the *Legenda trium sociorum*. Even the title and preface remind us of this work; these are given here:

"Of the origin and doings of the Friars Minor who were the first in the Order and faithful friends (*socii*) of St. Francis.

"In order that the servants of the Lord may not be ignorant of the ways and the doctrine of holy men, by which it is possible to progress to God, so have I, who have seen their actions, heard their words and also been their disciple, related and compiled several of the doings of our most holy Brother Francis and of some of the other Brothers in the beginning of the Order."[2] These words indicate a disciple of the first disciples. Now we know that Brother Giles lived in the convent of Monte Ripido near Perugia until his death on April 23, 1261; was it therefore *unreasonable* to see in the author of the anonymous legend a young Brother who — like Ubertino of Casale in Greccio with John of Parma — sat early and late at the feet of the Franciscan veteran "and heard his word from his holiest mouth and looked into his angelic countenance"?[3] Thus already had many Brothers even from distant England sat in Portiuncula at the feet of the old Brother Leo and heard him tell of the perfect joy, and how he and St. Francis had

---
[1] Salimbene, *Chronica*, p. 322.
[2] De inceptione et actibus illorum fratrum minorum, qui fuerunt primi in religione et socii beati Francisci.
Quoniam servi Domini non debent ignorare viam et doctrinam sanctorum virorum . . . ideo ad honorem Domini et aedificationem legentium et audientium ego, qui acta eorum vidi, verba audivi, quorum etiam discipulus fui, aliqua de actibus beatissimi fratris nostri Francisci et aliquorum fratrum qui venerunt in principio religionis, narravi et compilavi, prout mens mea divinitus fuit docta.
Anonymus Perusinus is partly given in *Acta Sanctorum*, Oct. II, pp. 549–560, and completely by v. Ortroy in *Miscellanea Francescana* IX (1902), pp. 33–48.
[3] Ubertino of Casale, *Arbor vitae crucifixae* (Venice, 1485), lib. V, cap. III.

the same Breviary. The words they thus heard from the older Brothers were written down.[1] We possess still several of these collections, "Words of Brother Giles," "Words of Brother Leo," "Words of Conrad of Offida," and we later find similar notes among the sources of the *Speculum perfectionis*, in whose introduction we accordingly find the following: "This Work is compiled from what the friends of St. Francis wrote or had written in different convents."[2] There is certainly nothing to hinder us from seeing in *Anonymus Perusinus* (the anonymous writer of Perugia) a repetition of Brother Giles' recollections, and undoubtedly the work, when we omit the preface, can also be regarded as an extract from or, as Götz prefers, a sketch of, the Three Brothers' Legend. With his usual radicalism van Ortroy has thrown out the preface as a forgery intended to give authority to the work.[3] The anonymous writer did his work after 1290, for Bernard of Bessa's Legend is referred to in it. But Brother Giles died April 23, 1261.

c. *Thomas of Celano's Vita secunda*

In many manuscripts the *Legenda trium sociorum* is introduced by the following words: *Haec sunt quaedam scripta per tres socios beati Francisci*, "These are some things written by three companions of blessed Francis." Leo, Angelo and Rufino had sent their work to Crescentius of Jesi, as *scripta*, as written documents, not as legends. And now what use did he make of the incomparably valuable material that thus came into his hands? With the complete *Legenda trium sociorum* before one it is easy to answer this query. The three *Socii* had written in their preface, that "if the honored men who had written the foregoing legends had known these things, they would not have passed them by, but would have adorned them in their own beautiful style."[4] There

---

[1] Ista scripsit frater Garynus de Sedenefeld ab ore fratris Leonis. (Eccleston, *Anal. Fr.*, I, p. 245.) Supererant adhuc multi de sociis . . . de quibus ego vidi et ab ipsis audivi quae narro (Angelo Clareno, ca. 1245-1337, *Chron. Tribulationum*, quoted in *Spec. perf.*, ed. Sab., p. LXXIX, n. 1). Hanc historiam habuit frater Jacobus de Massa ab ore fratris Leonis (*Actus B. Francisci*, IX, 71). See also the interpolation between chapters 71 and 72 of *Spec. perfectionis* and *Actus b. Fr.*, cap. 65.
[2] Sabatier's ed., p. 250.
[3] Götz, vol. XXV, pp. 40-47. V. Ortroy, *Anal. Boll.*, XIX, p. 123.
[4] Si venerabilibus viris qui præfatas confecerunt legendas, hæc nota fuissent ea minime præterissent, quin . . . sua decorassent eloquio.

can be no doubt that they here were thinking of Thomas of Celano, whose diction they also in another place in the preface had characterized as "truth-inspiring as well as lucid." [1] And Crescentius followed this hint — he handed over to Thomas of Celano the Three Brothers' work for revision. The result of this was Celano's *Vita secunda*, which to all intents and purposes is the *Legenda trium sociorum* "decorated," i.e., improved in style. Even in the preface we can see how the Brothers' simple words concerning their relation to the manuscript appear in improved style and amplified sentences.[2] And Thomas of Celano regarded himself as the Three Brothers' interpreter to this degree, that the legend is not produced as one of his works — he is mentioned in the prologue only as the author of the later written legends — but as a work of the Brothers. It is they who, without naming themselves, are writing the preface in the plural number; to them Crescentius gave the commission that they, out of their long intercourse with St. Francis, should write down his *gesta* and *dicta*, his action and words: it is they who apologize for their low ability, being only ignorant men. At any rate their prologue closes with a real Celano-like touch, a flattering pun on the name of Crescentius of Jesi.[3]

That it was Brother Thomas of Celano who applied his pen to the work, is not only perfectly clear on the basis of these internal criticisms; it is shown by a series of proofs that we cannot reject. Thus we have in Salimbene, whose chronicle was written 1283-1284 and who had known both Bernard of Quintavalle and Brother Leo: (Crescentius) "ordered Brother Thomas of Celano, who had written the first legend of blessed Francis, that he should write another book, because many things had been found out about the blessed Francis which had not been written, and he wrote a very beautiful book, which he called *Memoriale beati Francisci in*

[1] Iam veridico quam luculento sermone.
[2] *Tres Socii* in preface: *Sanctæ conversationis ejus insignia et pii beneplaciti voluntatem ostendere cupientes.* While we read in the *Prologus* of Celano: Experimere intendimus et vigilanti studio declarare quæ sanctissimi patris tam in se quam in suis fuerit voluntas bona, beneplacens, et perfecta in omni exercitio disciplinæ cœlestis et summæ perfectionis studio.
[3] Placuit sanctæ universitati olim capituli generalis et vobis, reverendissime pater . . . parvitati nostrae injungere, ut gesta vel etiam dicta gloriosi patris nostri Francisci nos quibus ex assidua conversatione illius et mutua familiaritate plus ceteris diutinis experimentis innotuit ad consolationem præsentium et posterorum memoriam scriberemus. . . . Memoria nostra velut hominum rudium. . . . Ut ea quæ benedicta vestro judicio docto probantur, cum nomine vestro vere Crescentio crescant ubique. . . . *Prologus* to *Vita secunda*.

desiderio animae."[1] But the legend which under the name of *Vita secunda* is ascribed to Thomas of Celano begins as follows: *Incipit memoriale in desiderio animæ de gestis et verbis sanctissimi patris nostri Francisci.* (Amoni's edition, Rome, 1880, pp. 7 et seq.) Furthermore, Jordanus of Giano in the Chronicle, which he in 1262 as an old man dictated to Brother Balduin of Brandenburg in the convent in Halberstadt, expressly names Thomas of Celano as author both of a first and then of a second legend of St. Francis.[2] And in the work of Brother Arnold of Serrano, *Chronica XXIV generalium* (before 1369), as well as in Nicholas Glassberger's Chronicle (completed 1491), both of which are founded on important, now partly vanished, sources, this view is repeated.[3]

As a last addition to these proofs of Thomas of Celano's authorship or co-operation with the Brothers, who had best known St. Francis, we have the beautiful prayer with which the *Vita secunda* ends, and in which the Brothers (*socii*) invoked their sainted father and called down his blessing on

---

[1] Hic praecepit fratri Thomae de Celano, qui primam Legendam beati Francisci fecerat, ut iterum scriberet alium librum, eo quod multa inveniebantur de beato Francisco, quae scripta non erant. Et scripsit pulcherrimum librum, tam de miraculis quam de vita, quem appellavit: Memoriale beati Francisci in desiderio animae. *Salimbene*, Chronica, Parma, 1857, p. 60.

[2] et Thoma de Celano qui legendam sancti Francisci et primam, et secundam postea, conscripsit. Jordanus in *Analecta Franciscana*, vol. I, Quaracchi, 1887, p. 8.

[3] Frater Crescentius autem, Generalis Minister, praecepit universis fratribus, quod sibi in scriptis mitterent quidquid de vita et prodigiis sancti Francisci veraciter scirent. . . . Item, eius mandato inducti, frater Leo, confessor beati Francisci, frater Angelus et frater Rufinus, quondam socii reverendi Patris, multa, quæ de ipso Patre beato viderant et a fide dignis fratribus, videlicet Philippo Longo, Illuminato et Massæo de Marignano et a fratre Iohanne, socio sancti patris Ægidii, audierunt, per modum legendæ in scriptis redegerunt et eidem Generali transmiserunt. Alii etiam plurimi quæ noverant recollegerunt, et sic multa magnalia, quae Sanctus in diversis orbis partibus fecerat, fuerunt publicata. Et *postmodum* ex mandato eiusdem Generalis Ministri et generalis capituli compilavit frater Thomas de Ceperano (Celano) primum tractatum legendæ sancti Francisci, de vita scilicet et verbis et intentione eius circa ea quæ ad regulam pertinent; quæ dicitur Legenda Antiqua, quam dicto Generali et capitulo destinavit cum prologo qui incipit: "Placuit sanctæ universitati vestræ." Glassberger, *Anal. Franc.*, tom. II, pp. 68-69. As appears from the preceding page, note 3, the Preface of Celano's *Vita secunda* begins with the exact word cited by Glassberger. The *postmodum*, italicized by me, gives a good connection between the Document and Thomas of Celano's work. See also Bernard of Bessa (ca. 1290) in *Anal. Franc.*, III, 666, and *Chronica XXIV generalium*, *Anal. Franc.*, III, 276.

"this thy son who now and formerly wrote piously in thy honor," and who "together with us offers and dedicates to thee this little work."[1] Only Thomas of Celano can be seen in this reference. That the poet of *Dies irae* — as Sabatier, prejudiced against him, would have it — should have himself invented this prayer to give thereby to his work the most reliable possible character, this is — as Götz has said — to postulate a spiritual impossibility.[3] What should Thomas and the milder party represented by him, according to Sabatier, have gained thereby, since the *Vita secunda* in spite of all collaboration extols the true Franciscanism, the absolute ideals from the first days of the Order, just as strongly as does the *Legenda trium sociorum?*

The legend which Thomas of Celano sent to Crescentius and which therefore was written in the course of less than one year (August 12, 1246, date of the completion of the Three Brothers' Legend, July, 1247, date of Crescentius' removal from the generalship), consists of two parts, each with its prologue; the second part, which has the wider scope, is furthermore divided into two books.

We should now expect a clear parallelism between these two parts of Celano's new work and the two parts of the *Legenda trium sociorum*. The first part of Celano's biography of St. Francis answers with great exactitude to the first part of the Three Brothers' Legend (below is a comparison of these

---

[1] *Vita secunda*, III, 143; *Oratio sociorum:* Supplicamus etiam toto cordis affectu, benignissime pater, pro illo filio tuo, qui nunc et olim devotus tua scripsit praeconia. Hoc ipse opusculum . . . una nobiscum tibi offert et dedicat (Amoni's ed., p. 140).

[2] Sabatier in *Opuscules de crit. hist.*, III, p. 70, n. 1: "Avec une habilété que je me dispenserai de qualifier, Thomas de Celano parla de façon à suggérer à ses lecteurs l'idée, que la seconde vie avait été faite en collaboration avec les Socii."

[3] Götz in Briegers "Zeitschrift f. Kgsch." 1903, p. 178: "Mir will scheinen, die Möglichkeit dieses Betruges sich ausdenken, heisst sie verneinen. Es liegt eine seelische Unmöglichkeit vor, ganz abgesehen davon, dass ein Widerspruch gegen den Fälscher sich in der spätern Literatur vorfinden müsste auch wenn der erste Protest der Vergewaltigten (i.e. the *Socii*) uns veloren gegangen sein sollte." In note 2 on the same page Götz adds, that from Sabatier's standpoint it must seem very remarkable that such a consciencelesss falsifier, as Sabatier considers Thomas of Celano to be, should be held in such high esteem by his superiors and should always get new commissions for work, which he kept up to the end of his life; "so niedrig stehende Naturen pflegen sich auch mit ihren Freunden zu überwerfen."

accordances).[1] As regards the second part, the contents do not compare so closely.

Up to the most recent times it has been held that Thomas of Celano did not send to Crescentius more than the first part of his *Vita secunda*, and only wrote the two last and most important books at the request of Crescentius' successor, John of Parma.[2] This belief rests on a note in *Chronica XXIV generalium*, in which it[3] is said of this immediate successor of Crescentius, that he "repeatedly invited Brother Thomas of Celano to complete his

[1] *Tres Socii*		Chap. XVI-XVII *Vita sec.*, Celano
Prologue		Prologue
Chap.	I, n. 1, Chap. II, n. 4	Chap. I
"	II, 5-6	" II
"	III, 7-8	" III
"	III, 8-10	" IV
"	IV	" V
"	V, 13, VI, 16	" VI
"	VI, 16-20, VII, 23	" VII
"	VII, 24	" VIII
"	VII, 22	" IX
"	VIII, 27-28	" X
"	XII, 46, XIII, 54	" XI
"	XIII, 55-56	" XII-XIII
"	XIV, 59	" XIV
"	XVI and XV	" XVI-XVII

(Cap. XXXIII in the complete *Legenda trium sociorum*, ed. Da Civezza-Domenichelli, corresponds to Cap. XV in Celano and to Cap. 27 in *Spec. perfectionis*.)

For every one who with any degree of attention compares the chapters which correspond to each other, there can exist no doubt on which side the originality lies. As fresh and original as are the narrations in the *Legenda trium sociorum*, so are they stiff and involved in Thomas of Celano. Moreover, he abbreviates to such an extent that it is often impossible to understand what he is telling us, if we do not know it in advance. In one place we see him pass over a whole series of narrations of the first disciples (*Leg. trium sociorum*, Capp. IX-XI), saying that it would be too long to follow out each narration (*longum esset de singulis persequi. Vita sec.*, Cel., I, 10).

It is worthy of remark that Thomas of Celano's working up of the first part of the Three Brothers' Legend ceases with Cap. XVI; he did not know of the two chapters 17 and 18 added at a later period and which are found in the manuscripts. It is impossible to give the time of these editions more accurately than that it was before 1375 probably, and, as it is based upon St. Bonaventure's work on St. Francis, they come after 1263.

[2] Thus Sabatier, *Speculum perfectionis*, p. 125, and the editors of *Analecta Franciscana*, vol. II, p. 18.

[3] *Anal. Franc.*, III, 276.

biography of St. Francis, for he had only written about his conversation and sayings in his first treatise which he had composed by command of Brother Crescentius." As Thomas does not treat of Francis's *conversatio* and *verba* in the first, but does treat of them in the second part of the *Vita secunda*, it is perfectly clear that this cannot be the part of the biography which John of Parma asked him to write. Since van Ortroy's publication of a hitherto unknown treatise on St. Francis' miracles, which without doubt can be ascribed to Thomas of Celano, we also know thereby that this is the work John of Parma wished written to complete the *Vita secunda*.[1]

The fact that the division between the two parts of Celano's new work so accurately corresponds with the conclusion of the traditional Three Brothers' Legend seems to indicate that there was a division in this place in the very work sent out from the Convent in Greccio. In the first part of the manuscript the Three Brothers describe a period of time, of which it is certain that their scribe, Brother Leo, knew nothing from his own experiences; therefore they had to content themselves as best they could with Thomas of Celano's relation in the *Vita prima*, although certain parts, such for example as that treating of the Brothers' first missionary trips, are completely worked over *con amore*. But the part of their legend which corresponds to the first and third of Celano's *Vita secunda* was made up first and foremost out of their own remembrances of St. Francis, and the form became — as the *Speculum perfectionis* and the Melchiorri Legend show — completely different: no well arranged *history* but detached *stories*. If the first part reminds us of a regularly arranged legend,

---

[1] Published in *Analecta Bollandiana*, XVIII (1899), pp. 81-177; the manuscript was found in Marseilles.

Götz, "*Die Quellen zur Geschichte des hl. Franz. v. Assisi*," published in book form in Gotha, 1904, pp. 234 et seq., is inclined to ascribe the work to Julian of Speier. But as Julian always copied Celano, he must have had an exactly corresponding work of Thomas before him, and the notes in the *Chron. XXIV gen.* indicate this.

That the material for the whole of the *Vita secunda* was sent immediately by Crescentius to Thomas is to be seen in this, that he already in the first volume (chapter XV) treats of a source which in the *Legenda trium sociorum* was not be found in that part, but in the second half of the Legend. Sabatier therefore suspects unjustly (*Vie*, p. 76) that John of Parma had at first given Celano the rest of the Three Brothers' Legend for revision. Moreover, it was Sabatier who, before v. Ortroy, discovered in an Assisi MS. fragments of Celano's *Treatise on Miracles* (*Misc. Franc.*, 1894, pp. 40 et seq. Compare *Opuscules*, fasc. III, pp. 66-67).

the second part supplies precisely the flowers, the *flores* which the Brothers promised to pluck from the fields of their memory. It is likely that the second part of the Three Brothers' Legend originally or in very early manuscripts bore the title we know in some Franciscan manuscripts, now injured by fire: *Flores beati Francisci et sociorum ejus*.[1]

That the Three Brothers' Legend did thus consist of two parts is clearly indicated by a peculiarity we find in several of the manuscripts. In these manuscripts we find, namely, together with the *Legenda trium sociorum* and in close sequence thereto, sometimes the *Speculum perfectionis*, sometimes the *Actus beati Francisci et sociorum ejus*. These two compilations of the fourteenth century are exactly — as will show later — the substitutes of a later time for the second half of the Three Brothers' Legend, and *their presence in this place is an indication partly of the incompleteness of the traditional legend and partly of the character of the missing second portion*. In the Bollandists' Leonine manuscript of the Three Brothers' Legend, the *Speculum* and the *Actus* follow it; the same association occurs in the case of the manuscript N. 1743 of 1459, in the Mazarin Library, but with the *Legenda trium sociorum* between the *Speculum* and the *Actus*. In the same library the manuscript 989 of 1460 contains the *Tres socii, Speculum* and the *Actus*. Manuscript 343 of Liege of 1408 contains: *Tres socii, Actus, Admonitiones, Speculum*. Manuscript 1407 in the Riccardi Library in Florence contains first in Italian the traditional *Legenda trium sociorum* and *Lo specchio di perfectione*, and finally a quantity of St. Francis' letters and prayers, rules for hermits, *Admonitiones*, The Blessing of Brother Leo, with a whole lot of small pieces of the character of the *Fioretti*, the whole collected under the title *Incominciano alquanti fiori spirituali*. Also manuscript 2697 in the University Library in Bologna of about 1500 contains: (1) *Tre Compagni*, (2) *Specchio di perfectione*, (3) *Fiori spirituali*. (See the detailed description of these and many similar manuscripts in the introduction to Vols. I, II and IV of Sabatier's exhaustive *Collection d'études et de documents sur l'histoire réligieuse et littéraire du moyen âge*. Paris, 1898-1902.)

[1] See Papini: *Etruria Francescana* (Siena, 1797), pp. 162-163, quoted in Sabatier's *Collection d'études et de documents*, IV, pp. 30-31. One of these manuscripts was *in vulgari* and they cannot well have had anything else in them than the *Fioretti*, and we find in this book a part of the original Franciscan *Flores*. The question is first and foremost this: where was the title first used and what work did it originally indicate? And here it cannot be denied that the Three Brothers in 1246 used it for their own legend.

This theory of mine of the original division of the Three Brothers' Legend into two parts would, among other things, make it clear how Bartholomew of Pisa, who otherwise knew and cites a more complete *Legenda trium sociorum* than the traditional, is nevertheless (*Conform.*, Milano, 1510, fol. 181-182) able to quote Francis' prophecy about Cardinal Hugolin's elevation to the Papal throne, as being "almost at the end of the legend" (*quasi in fine legendæ*). This quotation agrees, namely, with the traditional fragmentary legend, in which the prophecy is certainly found in the last lines of the last chapter, and can only be brought into unison with the author's undoubted acquaintance with a completer *Legenda trium sociorum*, if we accept that he here by the word *legenda* has intended to indicate the first legendary or historic part of the work, which he distinguished from the *flores* (flowers) of its second division.[1]

I grant, moreover, that the Italian Three Brothers' Legend does not support this thesis. As this, namely, is contained in Muzio's copy, no division into two parts is to be found in it, but a whole quantity of the chapters I have designated as *flores* are found intercalated, partly between Chaps. XII and XIV of the first part of the Legend, partly between Chaps. XIV and XV-XVI of the same. But whether even the Muzio manuscript gives us an idea of the original contents of the Three Brothers' Legend or not, it does not necessarily follow that the division into the two parts should have been followed in it. In the Middle Ages they took the most extensive liberties in this respect.[2]

In any case in the second division (second and third book) of Celano's *Vita secunda*, we have to see an editing of the material the Brothers had sent to Crescentius, and which did not appear in the first book of the *Vita secunda*. But we shall go entirely wrong if we expect to find an actual written authority for every single chapter in Celano. We must not forget that Thomas not only drew from the notes of the Brothers, but also from their verbal descriptions; the prologue and concluding prayer show us that this co-operation existed, even if we are not in a position to say

---

[1] An indication of Bartholomew of Pisa's knowledge of a complete Three Brothers' Legend is in Da Civezza-Domenichelli, pp. 46-49. Tilemann, (same work, p. 69) on account of the contradiction whose explanation is attempted above, considers the quotations of Bartholomew of Pisa quite unavailable as proofs of the existence of a *Legenda trium sociorum* of greater scope than the traditional one.

[2] In this connection is it worthy of remark that Sabatier in the Muzio manuscript sees an intermediate work between the original and the traditional Three Brothers' Legend. (*Opuscules*, fasc. III, p. 70.)

how and under what forms. We have a right to expect a certain similarity with other works of the Brother Leo group, and such similarity is found, not only when we compare the *Vita secunda* with the Italian Three Brothers' Legend edited by Melchiorri, but also when we institute the comparison with the work that more than any other may be said to represent the tradition originating with Brother Leo and his circle, *Speculum perfectionis*. A whole quantity of chapters of both works are found introduced in Celano's *Vita secunda* — we may compare for instance the *Speculum*, 30-35, with the *Vita secunda*, sec. III, 31-34, or the complete Three Brothers' Legend, Caps. 30, 37, 38, with Caps. 37, 30, 32, in the same part of Celano's second biography.

There are not a few chapters in the *Vita secunda* that did not originate in the *Speculum perfectionis*, and there are also many without parallel texts in the Muzio-Melchiorri Legend. In consideration of the exact, almost servile parallelism with the *Legenda trium sociorum* in the first book of Celano's second biography, I would be obliged to accept the conclusion that *the personal co-operation between Thomas and the Three Brothers began first with the second book*, in whose prologue, exactly in the Brothers' spirit, Francis is conceived and represented as *speculum sanctitatis* and *imago perfectionis*. From now on there is less adherence to Celano's method of work. The dedication to Crescentius preceding the entire book may — like the Brothers' letter of 1246 to Crescentius — have been written last.[1]

[1] As an illustration of the relation between the Three Brothers' Legend, *Speculum perfectionis*, and Celano's *Vita secunda*, I append the following parallel:
Legenda trium sociorum
(Da Civezza-Melchiorri's ed.)

Cap. XIX. *Quomodo exivit cum fervore ad quemdam fratrem qui ibat cum eleemosynis laudando Deum.* Alio quoque tempore, beato Francisco existente apud Sanctam Mariam de Portiunculam, quidam frater, spiritualis valde, veniebat per stratam, revertens de Assisio pro eleemosyna, et ibat alta voce laudando Deum cum magna jucunditate. Quum autem appropinquasset ecclesiae beatae Mariae, beatus Franciscus audivit eum, qui cum maximo fervore et gaudio exivit ad eum, occurrens sibi in via, et cum magna laetitia osculans humerum ejus, ubi apportabat peram cum eleemosyna. Et accepit peram de humero ejus et sic apportavit ipsam in domum fratrum et coram fratribus dixit: "Sic volo quod frater meus vadat et revertatur cum eleemosyna laetus et gaudens et laudans Deum."

Speculum perfectionis (Cap. 25) has exactly the same text (as *pauper* for *frater* is only a copyist's error).

Celano's *Vita secunda*
(ed Amoni)

III, cap. XXII. *Qualiter osculatus fuit humerum eleemosynam portantis.* Alio tempore apud Portiunculam cum frater quidam rediret de Assisio cum

Celano's second biography seems thus to rest upon two separate foundations — partly upon the second part of the *Legenda trium sociorum*, partly upon more exact descriptions and statements from Leo, Angelo and Rufino.

As the *Speculum perfectionis*, which was written in 1318, contains much more of the material for Celano's second biography than the *Legenda trium sociorum* in the Muzio manuscript, we are apparently forced to believe that the original Three Brothers' Legend was less detailed than Brother Thomas' *Vita secunda*. But as there is undoubtedly an ancient text, the foundation for the relations in the *Speculum*, even when they are not found in the Italian *Legenda trium sociorum*, which ancient text concerns also the relations of Thomas of Celano, there is nothing else for us to suppose than *that the Brothers co-operating with Thomas brought to light more reminiscences of St. Francis than those they had put down in their own legend* — the same, which in part is preserved for us in the *Speculum perfectionis*.[1]

Whether the question can be answered, as to why in all the Latin manuscripts of the Three Brothers' Legend only half is preserved, is doubtful, in the face of all these researches.

There is no doubt that there is a sort of division in the legend itself, which is almost enough to give the first part of the work an independent character.

The legend's special value was due to the fact that it was written by the nearest friends of the departed founder of the Order, but Celano's second biography had the same pre-eminence and in addition bore an official stamp, as the Three Brothers' Legend must be looked upon as a predecessor from which Brother Thomas extracted the best parts.

This point of view explains well why the Three Brothers' Legend on the whole returned to the old form. But it does not explain how the second part of it has disappeared. Thomas of Celano had worked upon the whole legend — why did not the whole of it disappear?

eleemosyna, propinquus jam loco coepit in cantum prorumpere, et Dominum alta voce laudare. Quo audito, repente exilit sanctus, accurrit foras, et osculato fratris humero, sacculum suo imponit: Benedictus, inquit, sit frater meus, qui promptus vadit, humilis quaerit, gaudens revertitur.

[1] It is clear to the most superficial observation (see the foregoing remark) how Thomas abbreviated and adorned the simple explicit presentation which is preserved for us in the Three Brothers' Legend and in the *Speculum*. Also how the material is not reproduced word for word, but — as in the parallel just given — becomes a simple statement much improved in style.

The real reason must therefore be sought elsewhere. It lies in the appearance on the scene of a manuscript that in various ways crowded upon, even overshadowed all early biographies of St. Francis — the legend produced by St. Bonaventure as General of the Order.[1]

3. ST. BONAVENTURE GROUP

Bonaventure (John Fidanza) from Bagnorea had never personally known St. Francis. He was — this he tells in the prologue to his legend — when a little boy cured by a miracle of the great Saint.[2] He was born in 1221 and took Orders when seventeen years old, and therefore after Francis' death.

It was a General Chapter in Narbonne in 1260 which entrusted to Bonaventure the writing of a new legend of St. Francis so that — in the words of the Chapter's resolution — a "serious and correct presentation" can be given "of the many different legends" which now exist.[3]

Bonaventure undertook the commission, proposing "according to his ability to collect the words and actions of the Saint, as it were certain fragments in part dispersed, less they should perish by the death of those who had lived in the society of the servant of God." Like a good historian he then travelled to Assisi and there sought Francis' "still living familiar friends," "especially some who knew well how holy he was," who therefore claimed confidence before all others.[4] First and foremost he sought

---

[1] Editions of Celano's *Vita secunda*, Rome, 1806 (Rinaldi), and Rome, 1880 (Amoni).

It is clear to be seen, that Celano in his authorship always sought the same authorities. This is evident in the fact that we find in Celano's *Tractatus de miraculis*, written by order of John of Parma — concerning the presence of Jacopa de Septemsoliis at the deathbed of Francis — what is a perfect sequel to the present narration in the complete *Three Brothers' Legend* (Cap. LXXVIII), and *Speculum perfectionis* (Cap. 112). Even as the biographer of St. Clara, he worked in unison with Brother Leo.

[2] ea quam ad sanctum patrem habere teneor devotio . . . utpote qui per ipsius invocationem et merita in puerili aetate, sicut recenti memoria teneo, a mortis faucibus erutus, si praeconia laudis eius tacuero, timeo sceleris argui ut ingratus. (*Legenda major*, ed. Quaracchi, 1898, Prologus, 3).

[3] ut ablata varietate multarum legendarum ex diversis historiarum fragmentis, quae de s. Francisco circumferebantur, gravem et sinceram ipse concinnaret historiam. Wadding, 1260, n. 18.

[4] actus et verba quasi fragmenta quaedam partim neglecta, partimque dispersa, quamquam plene non possem, utcumque colligerem, ne, morientibus his, qui cum famulo Dei convixerant, deperirent . . . adiens locum originis

Brother Leo, with whom he had already corresponded, as he had to send reports to the General of the Order concerning the Clares in S. Damiano (after 1260 in St. Clara), whose visitator he was.[1] Next comes Brother Illuminato, who up to 1273 was Provincial of Umbria and who seems to have given Bonaventure much material (on the trip to the Orient in which he took part, and from the Rieti district, where he had his home). Furthermore, Bonaventure's work appears as a skilfully prepared compilation of all the preceding sources — Celano's *Vita prima*, which he used in Julian of Speier's adaptation, the first part of the Three Brothers' Legend, Celano's *Vita secunda* and *Treatise on Miracles*—finally he uses in one place an expression that reminds one of a relation in the later *Speculum perfectionis*.[2] There is little new in St. Bonaventure; most that is new consists of further adornments of the legends. Thus the Priest Silvester, in the vision which converts him, sees not only a cross issuing from the mouth of St. Francis, but sees also a dragon that surrounds the whole of Assisi, and which Francis puts to flight. Also the tale of the man in Assisi, who in Francis' youth honored him by spreading his cloak before him in the street, is found for the first time in Bonaventure.[3] In this and other new details we seem to hear the echo of all the more or less fabulous and numerous tales about St. Francis, which went from mouth to mouth in the market-place in Assisi, or were told by the firesides in the evening when they were entertaining each other with stories.

Thode in his well-known book has undertaken to collect together these new incidents in Bonaventure's legend.[4] Here we must observe that St. Bonaventure — as the editors of *Analecta Fran-*

conversationis et transitus viri sancti, cum familiaribus eius adhuc superviventibus collationem . . . habui diligentem, et maxime cum quibusdam, qui sanctitatis eius et conscii fuerunt et sectatores praecipui, quibus . . . fides est indubitabilis adhibenda. (Prolog. 3-4.)

[1] Intelligens semper, dilectae in Domino filiae, per carissimum nostrum fratrem Leonem, quondam socium sancti patris, quomodo velut sponsae regis aeterni servire Christo pauperi crucifixo in omni puritate studeatis. . . . (Letter of October, 1259, to the Clares in S. Damiano, in Bonaventure's *Opera omnia*, Quaracchi, 1898, VIII, p. 473).

[2] See the comparison with Da Civezza-Domenichelli, p. 186, note a. Sabatier's assertion (*Spec. perf.*, pp. 130 et seq.), that Bonaventure used the *Speculum* throughout his work, is refuted by Tilemann (loc. cit., p. 74).

[3] *Legenda major*, III, 6; I, 1.

[4] H. Thode: "*Frans v. Assisi und die Anfänge der Kunst der Renaissance in Italien*," Berlin, 1885, p. 535. See also Götz: "*Quellen*," Gotha, 1904, pp. 243-257: Tilemann, loc. cit., pp. 72-76.

ciscana say in one place — referring to the whole of this question of origin, "for the sake of peace, somewhat modified it,"[1] in other words that he modified the too severe development of the original Franciscan ideals, as it is found both in Celano and in the *Legenda trium sociorum*. And here we have the reason for the condemnation of the last named legend.

After Bonaventure had finished his biography he laid it before the Chapter of the Order in Pisa in 1263, and they were so pleased with his work *that they resolved to destroy all the other legends of St. Francis*. As Tilemann has said: "they canonized the General's Legend and proscribed all others."

This momentous resolution reads as follows:

"The General Chapter commands likewise in the name of obedience, that all legends that have been written about St. Francis shall be destroyed, and where they are found outside the Order, the Brothers will seek to dispose of them, because the legend which was written by the General is made up of what he heard from their mouths, who were with St. Francis nearly all the time and knew everything with certainty. . . ."[2]

The decree disposed of all earlier legends, but especially of the two in which this ideal, dangerous to the preservation of peace, was most definitely announced — Celano's *Vita secunda* and the *second part of the Three Brothers' Legend*. Thomas of Celano's work was somewhat protected by the name of its author — he was indeed the Order's first official historian and, after the canonization of St. Clara in 1255 by Pope Alexander IV, had received the commission to write also her legend. Nevertheless there are only two manuscripts of his "Second Biography." And for Leo's, Rufino's and Angelo's "Wreath of Flowers" no pity was felt, and with dutiful zeal, following the order of the General Chapter, the Brothers scattered them before the winds. Only the first half

---

[1] Ut paci consulat, aliquatenus mitius procedit S. Bonaventura (*Anal. Fr.*, II, p. 22).

[2] Item praecipit capitulum generale per obedientiam, quod omnes legendae de beato Francisco olim factae deleantur et ubi inveniri poterunt extra ordinem, ipsas fratres studeant amovere, cum illa legenda, quae facta est per generalem, sit compilata, prout ipse habuit ab ore illorum, qui cum beato Francisco quasi semper fuerunt et cuncta certitudinaliter sciverint et probata ibi sint posita diligenter. (Rinaldi's edition of Celano, Rome, 1806, p. XI.) Also Angelo Clareno (d. ca. 1337) knew that "quae scripta erant in legenda prima, novâ editâ a fratre Bonaventura, deleta et destructa sunt, ipso jubente." (*Chronica septem tribulationum*, in "Archiv für Litt. u. Kgsch." II, p. 56.) Compare Wadding, 1260, n. 18.

was in some cases spared, as well as Celano's *Vita prima* for the sake of its less significant character, and yet of the *Vita prima* there are only seven manuscripts preserved and of the condemned Three Brothers' Legend only eighteen manuscripts, while for the use of the new Quaracchi edition of Bonaventure's work no less than one hundred and seventy-nine manuscripts were at hand.

To the same group as St. Bonaventure's legend is naturally attributed the work *De laudibus Sancti Francisci*, written by his secretary, Bernard of Bessa, about 1290. After having decreed the destruction of all the earlier legends, the highest authorities of the Order seemed to have realized a too radical treatment of the old remains, and in 1277 the Chapter of the Order in Padua invited new researches for the collection of all memoirs of St. Francis still in existence.[1] Bernard of Bessa seems to have accepted this invitation; in any case his work is later than 1277, because he (*Anal. Franc.*, III, p. 682) refers to John Peckham as Archbishop of Canterbury, a dignity to which this Franciscan was first raised in 1279.[2]

The fact is that Bernard of Bessa's manuscript presents little that is new; he is, like his teacher and master, a compiler. In the prologue he names as his sources Celano's first biography, John of Ceperano, Julian of Speier and "Brother Bonaventure, General of the Order, formerly a distinguished teacher of theology in Paris, then Cardinal in the Holy Roman Church and Bishop of Albano." But neither the *Vita secunda* nor the Three Brothers' Legend is named, which, with the decree of 1263 in mind, seems very natural, although Bernard used them so much.[3] Tilemann clearly saw that this silence about the *Legenda trium sociorum* was an argument for the incompleteness of the traditional legend; Bernard says nothing of it, nor of Celano's *Vita secunda*, because both works contain things that were not well looked upon by the peace-loving majority. Sabatier suspects that Bernard in his functions as secretary to Bonaventure had access to the condemned legends.[4] On the other hand, Bernard did not need to have extracted his story of the visit of Jacopa of Settesoli to the deathbed of Francis from the yet unwritten *Speculum;* it is to be found both in Thomas of Celano's Treatise on Miracles and

---

[1] *Anal. Boll.*, XIX, 133.
[2] Eubel: *Hierarchia cath. medii aevi*, p. 169.
[3] Parallel places cited by Tilemann, pp. 79–80.
[4] *Speculum perfectionis*, p. CXXXIV.

probably also was in the complete form of the Three Brothers' Legend.[1]

4. SPECULUM GROUP

After 1263 we hear little said of the Three Brothers' Legend; the *Chronica XXIV generalium* a hundred years later mentions it again and quotes the letter to Crescentius.[2] But until 1271 the man was still living who was, so to say, the living reproduction of the Three Brothers' Legend; namely, Brother Leo. In spite of all prohibitions, memories of his beloved lord and master's life still bloomed in his aged heart, and when the young Brothers from near and far visited him in his cell at Portiuncula, his mouth overflowed with what filled his heart, and he told them *multa magnalia*, many great things about St. Francis. Sometimes he criticized the official legend and declared that things went altogether different from its descriptions. And both his relations and his criticism were remembered by the young men and written down for edification and for later discussion. Thus Brother Leo came in contact with all the best among the Order: Brother Conrad of Offida (d. 1300), Brother Salimbene, Brother Peter of Tewkesbury (Provincial of England), Brother Francis of Fabriano (d. 1322), Brother Angelo Clareno (entered the Order a little after 1260).[3]

---

[1] Da Civezza and Domenichelli's Legends, cap. LXXVIII.
Bernard of Bessa's work appears in the *Analecta Franciscana*, III, pp. 666–692, and by F. Hilarin Felder, Rome, 1897.

[2] *Anal. Franc.*, III, p. 262.

[3] parum ante mortem fratris Leonis apparuit (fratri Ioanni) sanctus Franciscus dicens, ut, assumpto fratre Corrado, pergeret ad fratrem Leonem, qui tunc in sancta Maria de Portiuncula morabatur, et ab ipso inquireret de verbis et vita sua, scilicet sancti patris Francisci. Quod cum fecisset, ambo multa magnalia de beato Francisco ab ipso fratre Leone audiverunt. (*Anal. Franc.*, III, p. 428.)
Sicut dixit mihi frater Leo socius suus (Salimbene, *Chronica*, p. 75).
Sed et frater Leo, socius sancti Francisci, dixit fratri Petro, ministro Angliae, quod apparitio seraphim facta fuit sancto Francisco in quodam raptu contemplationis, et satis evidentius, quam scribebatur in vita sua. . . . Ista scripsit frater Garynus de Sedenefeld ab ore fratris Leonis. (Eccleston, *Anal. Franc.* I, p. 245. See *Anal. Franc.*, III, p. 646.)
Wadding (1267, n. 5) quotes the following from Francis Venimbemi of Fabriano: De supradicto fratre Petro Cathanii, quod fuit generalis minister, habetur ex dictis fratris Leonis, unius de sociis sancti Francisci, quem scilicet fratrem Leonem ego vidi et eius scripta legi, quae recollegit de dictis et vita sanctissimi patris nostri Francisci.
Finally Angelo Clareno in his *Chronica septem tribulationum* (quoted in Sabatier's edition of *Spec. perf.*, p. 89, n. 1) says: Supererant adhuc multi de sociis . . . de quibus ego vidi et ab ipsis audivi quae narro, qui ex

And when the young men had departed and Brother Leo was again alone in his poor little cell, whose whitewashed walls always seemed to him to be shining with bright sunlight, then the old Franciscan sat down at his work-table and began to write just as in the old days when St. Francis dictated. Memory after memory came upon him, one sheet of parchment was written full after another in his beautiful clear handwriting, and when twilight came and the clouds grew gold in the evening over Perugia's distant towers, then Brother Leo rolled up his parchments and carried them down the road, which under the olive trees passes along Assisi's wall out to St. Clara's convent. Thither he had already brought one of his dearest treasures, the Breviary St. Francis had used; now his reminiscences of the great departed one were to be entrusted to the guardianship of the Sisters. Little by little they thus collected a considerable collection of anecdotes, in part identical with the older writings from the time when he collaborated with Thomas of Celano; but we may well believe that many a new page was inserted in this book of reminiscences. During such quiet hours at the writing table were written also the "Leaves of Memory," as they may be called, which Leo, like his master, was wont to give or to send to his disciples, and by which he impressed them with the Franciscan ideals.[1]

In these *rotuli* or *schedulæ*, "rolls or schedules," of Brother Leo

toto corde revelata eorum patri fideliter et pure servare satagebant. It follows from the words quoted, that Clareno here and foremost is thinking of Brother Leo; for it is exactly he who knew what had been revealed to Francis at Fonte Colombo and on Mt. Alverna and preserved it all in his heart.

[1] quod sequitur a sancto fratre Conrado predicto et viva voce audivit a sancto fratre Leone. . . . Et hoc ipsum in quibusdam *rotulis* manu sua conscriptis, quos commendavit in monasterio sanctae Clarae custodiendis ad futurorum memoriam dicitur contineri. In illis autem multa scripsit, sicut ex ore patris audiverat. (Ubertino of Casale, in his work, written 1305, *Arbor vitae crucifixae*, Venice 1485, fol. 222a1. *Rotulus*, according to Ducange = scheda, carta in speciem rotulae, seu rotae, convoluta. Brother Leo's documents are also called *schedulae*, i.e., schedules. Both titles seem to indicate pieces without connection with each other. St. Francis' Breviary in the convent of Santa Chiara in Assisi has on its first page a note written by the hand of Brother Leo. It runs thus: frater Angelus et frater Leo supplicant sicut possunt dominae Benedictae abbatissae pauperum dominarum monasterii sanctae Clarae . . . ut in memoria et devotione sancti patris librum istum in quo multoties legit dictus pater semper conservent in monasterio sanctae Clarae. (Quoted in Sabatier's *Spec. perf.*, p. 175, n. 2.)

Brother Leo's schedule to Brother Conrad of Offida is found interpolated between Chapters 71 and 72 in the *Speculum perfectionis*, and in another form the *Actus b. Francisci*, cap. 65. Compare *Anal. Franc.*, III, p. 70.

is found the matter for the three works which complete the circle of the Franciscan legends; namely, *Speculum perfectionis*, *Legenda antiqua* and *Actus beati Francisci et sociorum ejus* (*Fioretti*).

a. *Speculum perfectionis*

As already mentioned, Paul Sabatier, in his search for the missing portion of the *Three Brothers' Legend* in the late Franciscan compilation, *Speculum beati Francisci et sociorum ejus* (printed 1504), found a series of chapters which offer the most striking likeness to the legends of Leo, Angelo and Rufino, and whose authors — for there appeared to be several — in not less than seventeen places declare that they had been Francis' nearest friends and companions, *nos, qui cum eo fuimus* — an expression which strikingly reminds us of the words in the Brothers' letter to Crescentius: *visum est nobis, qui secum licet indigni fuimus diutius conversati*. Sabatier was just on the point of concluding that he here stood face to face with the missing *Three Brothers' Legend* when in a manuscript in the Mazarin Library in Paris (No. 1743) he found these chapters from the *Speculum beati Francisci* as a distinct division with the title *Speculum perfectionis* and, what completely overcame him, with the following ending: "Here ends the Friars' Minor mirror of perfection. . . . All praise, all glory be to God the Father and Son and Holy Ghost. Honor and thanks to the most glorious Virgin Mary and to his Holy Martyr Kunera, exaltation and veneration to his most Holy Servant Francis, Amen. Done in the most holy place of St. Mary of Portiuncula and finished May 11, in the year of the Lord 1227."[1]

What should at once have made Sabatier doubtful about this date was the reference immediately preceding it to the German Saint Kunera, who especially was honored in the district of Utrecht, but to whom it was hardly probable that an Italian legend writer in the year 1227 should give a place of honor, immediately after the Blessed Virgin and before Francis himself. But the text of the manuscript contains a whole quantity of things

---

[1] Explicit speculum perfectionis fratris minoris, scilicet beati Francisci, in quo scilicet vocationis et professionis suae perfectionem potest sufficientissime speculari. Omnis laus, omnis gloria sit Deo patri et filio et spiritui sancto. Honor et gratiarum actio gloriosissimae virgini Mariae, eiusque sanctae Martyri Kunerae, magnificentia et exaltatio beatissimo servo suo Francisco. Amen. Actum in sacro sancto loco sanctae Mariae de Portiuncula et completum V° ydus May, anno domini M°CC°XXVIII°. (*Spec. perf.*, ed. Sabatier, p. 246.) The year 1228 in the Florentine reckoning of time used in the above corresponds to our 1227.

which tell against so early an authorship. For example, in speaking of Cardinal Hugolin it says "who afterwards became Pope." In 1227 the expression should have been: "who has just become Pope," for Gregory IX (Hugolin) reigned from March 12, 1227, to August 21, 1241. But the clause named above is applied to Hugolin's name not less than four times (Capp. 21, 23, 43, 65) and always in the same words. Also in the commencement of Chapter 107 we are told of the death of St. Bernard of Quintavalle. But this first successor to St. Francis was alive in 1242, as Salimbene visited him in this year in the convent in Siena.[1] Sabatier decided that these statements were later inserts, and published his work in 1898, as "the oldest legend of St. Francis, written by brother Leo."[2]

Sabatier's edition follows the text of the Mazarin manuscript, with the exception of one point, and this is very important; namely, the beginning. The Mazarin manuscript begins with the following introduction, fatal to Sabatier's thesis of the early authorship of the manuscript: "Here begins the mirror of perfection of the Friars Minor; namely, of St. Francis." *This work is compiled as a legend of various old relations, which the nearest friends of St. Francis wrote or had written in various convents.*[3] Sabatier on his own responsibility omitted this introduction and replaced it with another, which he took from a Vatican manuscript, of the *Legenda antiqua*, which, even if akin to it, was a work of different character and whose introduction was the following: "Here begins the mirror of perfection of the Friars Minor; namely, of St. Francis," which the text immediately follows. In 1227, the year after the death of St. Francis, it is evident that they could not speak of "old relations" written in various convents by St. Francis' nearest disciples; if, therefore, the date of the work was correct, this unsuitable introduction must be taken away from it.[4]

[1] Vidi enim et primum, scilicet fratrem Bernardum de Quintavalle, cum quo in conventu Senensi una chyeme habitavi. Et fuit intimus meus amicus et mihi et aliis juvenibus de beato Francisco multa magnalia referebat (*Chronica*, p. 11).
Salimbene entered the Order in 1238.
[2] . . . Legenda antiquissima auctore fratre Leone.
[3] Italics mine. The Latin text is as below:
Istud opus compilatum est per modum legendae ex quibusdam antiquis quae in diversis locis scripserunt et scribi fecerunt socii beati Francisci.
Loci, "Places," was the oldest designation of the Franciscan convents.
[4] See Sabatier's text, p. 1. On page 252 in his book he adds the Incipit to the legend, which was improperly removed, but explains that he has not accepted it, because it "serait en contradiction manifeste avec tout le contenu de l'ouvrage,

The appearance of Sabatier's edition of the *Speculum* excited active interest among students of Franciscan history, and a whole quantity of treatises appeared for and against him.[1] Among other things the didactic character of the work was appealed to as an argument against its early date; for such works, in which the legend's individual elements, as is the case in the *Speculum*, are arranged under heads of virtues — "Of his complete poverty," "Of his charity to his neighbor," "Of his complete humility, obedience," etc. — as a rule appear only after long perfecting of the legend.

But Sabatier meanwhile held vigorously to his assumed discovery and would not give up even after Minocchi of the convent library in Ognissanti, Florence, produced a new manuscript of the *Speculum perfectionis* which both in introduction and text compared perfectly with the Mazarin manuscript, but at the end, in place of 1227, was dated 1318. The early dating in Sabatier's manuscript was due, therefore, as van Ortroy had already suspected, to a copyist's error, and a glance at the two dates as they are found in their manuscripts will show that such an error could easily take place.[2] Now the reference in the introduction to the compilatory character of the work, and the invocation of the German saint at the end, became intelligible; the *Speculum* was a compilation written in Portiuncula in 1318, and Sabatier's manuscript was a copy of it made in a Dutch convent. In 1318 the Franciscan Order had a number of Dutch and Belgian convents, and a Brother in one of them in the end of the legend had

car l'unité de plan, de style et de pensée se revéle dans toutes les parties de cette legende." Such arguments based on "unity of style" are always very attractive and this one has its attractions also. But it gives no right whatever to remove a part of the legend that is found in all manuscripts because it does not accord with an individual's conception of the character of the work. Sabatier, in his *Collection d'études*, II, p. 148, n. 3, has given a further defence of his method of treatment.

[1] In Götz, "*Quellen*," p. 148, n. 2, is given a sketch of the most important of these.

[2] In *Anal. Boll.*, XIX, pp. 59-60, v. Ortroy gives the following convincing comparison of the Explicit in the two manuscripts explaining the true bearings of the case:

Mas. Bibl., 1743	Ognissanti-Manuscript
Explicit speculum perfectionis . . . Actum in sacro sancto loco sanctae Mariae de Portiuncula et completum V°ydus may anno Domini M°CC°-XXVIII°.	Explicit Speculum perfectionis . . . Actum in sacrosancto loco sanctae Mariae de Portiuncula et completum V idus maii M°CCC°XVIII.

It is easy to see how the date MCCCXVIII by the putting of an X for a C became MCCXXVIII.

injected his invocation of the patron saint of the locality. This accords with the fact that the manuscript, before it reached the Mazarin Library in Paris, according to a notice on its first page, had belonged to a convent in Namur.[1]

But although, as Götz has said,[2] it can no more be disputed that the *Speculum perfectionis* as we now possess it is a compilation of the year 1318, it is by no means to be denied that, as Sabatier affirms, it really originated with Brother Leo. It was not written by him in its present shape, *but it is founded on material he left after him;* namely, upon his "schedules," his *schedulæ* or *rotuli*.

The existence of these schedules was not forgotten in the half century which, in 1318, had passed since the death of Brother Leo. In the course of time they were read and examined by a whole quantity of men, who ranked among the best in the Order, and in the battle of the Franciscan ideals which these men waged, "Brother Leo's Schedules" and what they contained were always the last and most weighty argument.

The first who thus appealed to Brother Leo was Peter John Olivi, who died March 14, 1298. In his "Explanation of the Rule of the Order" he quotes a story that now is found in the fourth chapter of the *Speculum perfectionis* and which he says he read in "Brother Leo's Schedules."[3]

The next in series is Angelo Clareno (about 1245-1337). He joined the Franciscan Order a little after 1260 and, as has been already said, knew several of Francis' disciples, whose communications he used for his *Historia septem tribulationum*.[4] In this chronicle he now names, as the four biographers of St. Francis, John (of Ceperano), Thomas of Celano, Bonaventure and "the man of wonderful simplicity and holiness, Brother Leo, St. Francis' intimate friend."[5] With this last as authority (*ut scribit frater Leo*) he produces three passages, which are now found in the *Speculum perfectionis*. Remembering the decree of

---

[1] Ista legenda b. Francisci patris seraphici est fratrum cruciferorum Namurcensium. (Tilemann, loc. cit. 95.)

[2] Götz: "*Quellen*," p. 149. Compare Tilemann, pp. 111-113, and H. Bœhmer: "*Analekten zur Geschichte des Franciscus von Assisi*" (Tübingen u. Leipzig, 1904), p. 68.

[3] Unde et in cedulis fratris Leonis, quas de his, quae de patre nostro tamquam ejus singularis socius viderat et audierat, conscripsit, legitur . . . (*Firmamentum trium ordinum*, Venice, 1513, f. 123, quoted by Sabatier in his edition of *Spec. perf.*, p. 246, n. 1. Tilemann, p. 83).

[4] Tilemann, p. 117.

[5] vir miræ simplicitatis et sanctitatis frater Leo (Quoted by Sabatier, *Spec. perf.*, p. 138).

1260 we are at liberty to believe that he — as Tilemann and Sabatier would have it — here gives us the complete *Legenda trium sociorum*.[1] This is quite probable, because Mariano (d. 1527), whom Wadding quotes, seems also to have known it, and because the Italian Three Brothers' Legend, published by Melchiorri, dates at the earliest from the fourteenth century. If he did not get his knowledge from the legend, it must have come from Brother Leo's *rotuli*.

The principal witness for the existence of Brother Leo's schedules is Ubertius or Hubert of Casale (1259–ca. 1338). This contender for original Franciscanism was living in the year 1305 on Mt. Alverna, and there in the course of seven months wrote his great work, *Arbor vitæ crucifixæ*, completed the Michælmas Eve of the same year.[2]

Hubert himself had not known the "ancient Brothers," *antiqui fratres*, now the accepted designation of the last of the original disciples, but through Brother Conrad of Offida (d. 1306) heard much of what Brother Leo, Brother Masseo and others had told about St. Francis. In his youth he had been in Greccio, and in this little mountain convent, that hangs on the cliffs like a swallow's nest, he had sat at the feet of John of Parma, "looked into his angelic face" and heard him tell about Francis and about the great departed ones, who had lived and written in his cloister — Leo, Angelo, Rufino. John of Parma died March 19 or 20, 1289, and Hubert's residence with him was four years before his death. The impression from the early years of his youth could never be weakened, and the holy fire, which the great Franciscan from Parma had lit, was nourished through Hubert's friendship with Conrad of Offida and his narrations.[3]

In the fifth book, third chapter, of *Arbor vitæ* Hubert gives a whole quantity of quotations of the words of St. Francis which Brother Leo had written down with his own hand and which were preserved in St. Clara's convent in Assisi. "Unfortunately," Hubert adds, "I hear that these notes, at any rate in part, cannot

---

[1] *Spec. perf.*, p. 140, n. 1. Tilemann, p. 87.

[2] *Arbor vitæ crucifixæ Jesu*, Venice, 1485, fol. 2b2: terminavi in vigilia Michaelis Archangeli anni presentis MCCCV a felicissimo ortu veri solis Jesu. A mei vero vili conversione anno XXXII ... septem mensium tempore duravit huius libri tractatus.

[3] (Hubert on his relations with John of Parma): Nam et ego tunc juvenis ... quarto anno ante eius felicem transitum expressum verbum audivi ab eius ore santissimo, intuens in eius angelicam faciem. (*Arbor vitæ*, fol. 210b.) Compare Salimbene, p. 317.

be found there any more and may even be entirely lost."[1] The passages Hubert thus produces are now found in *Speculum perfectionis*, capp. 1, 2, 26, 3, 71, 73, 4, 11.

That these places in Leo's schedules were also in part derived from the Three Brothers' Legend follows from what Hubert says, that "Brother Bonaventure deliberately omitted using them in his legend"; accordingly he had them before him for use, but he seemed to think it was proper to pass them by.[2]

That this does not need to be the very *Speculum perfectionis* which Hubert alludes to (as Sabatier would have it), Lemmens has proved by publishing from a manuscript of the fourteenth century in S. Isidore in Rome two small pieces written by Brother Leo with the titles: "Book concerning St. Francis' design with his Rule" and "Words which Brother Leo wrote," and in which the places quoted by Hubert are to be found.[3]

Six years after having written the *Arbor vitæ* Hubert of Casale stood before the Curia in Avignon to answer the complaints which the advocates of the slack direction of the Order, Raimond of Fronsac and Bonagratia of Bergamo, had made against him and the other *fratres spirituales*. Again it was — outside of the Franciscan Rule and St. Francis' Testament — Brother Leo's narrations to which Hubert appealed when he showed that the strict interpretation of the spiritual Brothers was based upon the very words of Francis, "which was solemnly written by the holy man, Leo, his companion, both by the command of the holy father, as well as from devotion of the said Brother, and which are found in the book which is kept in the library of the Friars of Assisi and in those rolls *which I have with me*, written by the hand of the same Brother Leo."[4]

[1] quod sequitur a sancto fratre Conrado praedicto et vivâ voce audivit a sancto fratre Leone, qui praesens erat... Et hoc ipsum in quibusdam rotulis manu sua conscripsit, quos commendavit in monasterio sancte Clare custodiendos... cum multo dolore audivi illos rotulos fuisse distractos et forsitan perditos, maxime quosdam ex eis (fol. 222a).

[2] quae industria frater Bonaventura omisit et noluit in legenda publice scriberi, maxime quia aliqua erant ibi in quibus etiam ex tunc deviatio regulae publice monstrabatur (*Arbor vitæ*, loc. cit.).

[3] *Documenta antiqua franciscana*, ed. Fr. Leonardus Lemmens. I. *Scripta fratris Leonis* (Quaracchi 1901). Even if Götz ("*Quellen*," p. 153, n. 1) is correct in his view, that we have not Brother Leo's writings in their original form, we nevertheless can, by the help of Lemmens' manuscript, form a conception of what Brother Leo's "schedules" were.

[4] sua verba expressa, quæ per sanctum virum Leonem eius socium tam de mandato sancti patris quam etiam de devotione praedicti fratris fuerunt solemniter conscripta in libro, qui habetur in armario fratrum de Assisio, et in rotulis

The attempt has been made to make Hubert contradict himself, by noting that he in 1311 declared that he possessed the writings of Brother Leo and then wrote in 1305 that they were partly lost. But, as Götz has suggested in answer to this attack, there is nothing unreasonable in supposing that Hubert's complaint in *Arbor vitæ* can very well have brought about a new collection of Leo's *rotuli*, and it is reasonable that he himself took interest in the affair and got the papers into his own hands in order to secure them from destruction.[1]

That the compilation of the *Speculum perfectionis* in 1318 has some kind of connection with these efforts of Hubert follows almost of itself. The relations within the Franciscan Order were such that a resurrection of the spirit of the first days of the Order was badly needed. In the years 1317-1318 "the zealous ones" were hard pressed; April 27, 1317, John XXII called them anew to a reckoning in Avignon, in spite of Hubert's assertions and explanations six years before. The "zealous ones" did not succeed in winning the Pope to their side; in October of the same year he declared himself against them. Other Papal announcements of this time were directed against them or against the related, but heretical, *Fraticelli*. It was then that Angelo Clareno wrote his letter of defence to the Pope to free the Brethren of the strict observance from all false accusations. *And at the same time there was issued from Portiuncula as illustrative of the requirements of the Franciscan Rule in the matters of poverty, obedience, humility, etc., this collection of incidents of the Life of St. Francis, which explained his relation to all these virtues, and in which the Friars Minor of the fourteenth century could see themselves as in a looking-glass.*[2]

In this work we have not only Brother Leo's *schedulæ*, but also all that Brother Bernard, Brother Masseo and the other "old Brothers" had told in the various convents and which had been written down and preserved.

ejus, quos apud me habeo, manu ejusdem fratris Leonis conscriptis. (Hubert's *Declaratio*, cited by Sabatier, *Spec. perf.*, p. 150.)

In the catalogue of 1381 of the convent library in the Sacro Convento in Assisi, there is named a *Liber dictorum beati Francisci in papiro et sine postibus, cuius principium est*: Quid faciet homo in omni temptatione, *finis vero:* Oratio, saepe est premittenda insidias. Like so many manuscripta of this kind in the above library, this book cannot be found. (Da Civezza-Dominichelli, p. XCVII, n. 1.)

[1] Götz, "*Quellen*," p. 152.
[2] Tilemann, loc. cit., pp. 112-113.

b. *Legenda antiqua*

The years following directly after the appearance of the *Speculum perfectionis* brought better times for the ideal party within the Order. Gonzalvo of Balboa, who was General from 1303 to 1316, and Michael of Cesena (1316–1328) both desired to restore the old spirit; and to bring this about the last named, in spite of the decree of 1263, used to have read at meal-times, even in the great Franciscan convent at Avignon, a legend which was designated as "the old legend," and which therefore was not Bonaventure's new one. That he risked something in doing so he very well knew, and he therefore had it announced that he had only brought forward this legend to show that even it, without any criticism of Bonaventure, was "true, useful, authentic and good."[1]

Under the title *Legenda antiqua* several manuscripts have been preserved in reasonable accordance with each other, the most important in the library of the Vatican. In the preface to this manuscript we are told that although "Herr Mester Bonaventura's" work is beautiful and good, yet there are several things, both notable and useful, omitted therefrom, such as Francis' zeal for poverty, for humility, for charity, for the exact observance of the Rule, of which a part can be read in the "old legend" of which Bonaventure has copied a great part, and long passages word for word, and a part is found in "true words of the friends of St. Francis, which are put into writing by experienced men in the Order." The writer says that he knew both "the old legend" and the "true words" from his student days in Avignon when the General had the old legend read at meal-times; to this he adds in the present manuscript other references to a book which belonged to "our honorable father and lord, Brother Frederick, Archbishop of Riga, a very learned man of our Order," together with a treatise on St. Francis' and his faithful disciples' lives and actions.[2]

---

[1] (Quædam vero sumpta et reparata sunt de) legenda veteri ipsius sancti quam et generalis minister me præsente et aliquoties legente fecit sibi et fratribus legi ad mensam in Avinione ad ostendendum eam esse veram, utilem et autenticam atque bonam. (*Legenda antiqua.* Sabatier, *Collection*, I, pp. 152–161, and Tilemann, pp. 120–121.) Compiler's preface to the *Legenda antiqua*, Vatican MS. No. 4354. The MS. contains in almost unbroken sequence 57 chapters of *Speculum perfectionis*, along with a quantity of other material, especially *Actus* (*Fioretti*).

[2] plura tamen valde notabilia et utilia, zelum caritatis, humilitatis et paupertatis, necnon circa praedictorum et regulæ totius observationem, intentionem et voluntatem ipsius sancti experimentia, tam in legenda veteri, de qua

A Franciscan from the provinces about the Baltic Sea, who had studied in Avignon under Michael of Cesena, and who later had access to a book about St. Francis in possession of the Archbishop Frederick of Riga, therefore was the author of this compilation. He refers to various authorities, which it is not always easy to distinguish from one another. In referring to the "veritable words of St. Francis' friends," which are "put into manuscript by reliable men in our Order," it seems clear that he was thinking of the *Speculum perfectionis*, which at this time had just been brought out; therefore he has, also, the expressions *zelum caritatis, humilitatis et paupertatis* as titles for the different sections of the *Speculum*. It is also the *Speculum* which treats of Francis' zeal for an exact observance of the Rule.

On the other hand, it is not very clear what kind of an "old legend" it is of which Bonaventure has copied much, but has also left out much of the most important character. Sabatier holds that this is the *Speculum perfectionis*, but Bonaventure used nothing of this (see page 379, n. 2). It is more reasonable, as Tilemann does, to consider it a complete *Three Brothers' Legend*.[1] Of this Bonaventure used much and left out more — something which Hubert of Casale complained about. This must be the book which Michael of Cesena, while General, used to have read at meal-times in Avignon.

From Bishop Frederick's book the compilers have only taken a few miracles, although of rare and impressive nature (*rara et ardua*); on the other hand, the writings of St. Francis' friends seem to be a more important source in which his and their lives and actions are told of. This collection, in connection with which

---

idem fr. Bonaventura saepius longas orationes et passus de verbo ad verbum in suam legendam posuit, quam etiam ex dictis veridicis sanctorum sociorum b. Francisci per viros probatos ordinis redactis in scriptis, quorum sociorum vita sancta . . . ipsorum dicta et testimonia credibilia reddit, in imis cum essem studens in Avinione reperi, quorum aliqua . . . collegi et inferius annotavi.

Posui autem primo rara et ardua facta seu miracula patris nostri quæ in legenda nova, ut praedicitur, non habentur; quorum quædam in libro reverendi patris et domini fratris Friderici archiepiscopi Rigensis, ordinis nostri studiosissimi viri. . . . Quædam vero sumpta et reparata sunt de legenda veteri ipsius sancti quam et generalis minister me praesente et aliquoties legente fecit sibi et fratribus legi ad mensam in Avinione. . . . Nonnulla vero sumpta de scriptis sanctorum sancti praedicti sociorum, vitam sancti et gesta, sociorumque sanctorum ejus experimentia. . . . Demum etiam quaedam de sancto Antonio rara scripsi et de sancto fratre Johanne de Alvernia. . . . (Printed in Sabatier and Tilemann, as above.)

[1] Sabatier, *Spec. perf.*, p. 153, n. 1. Tilemann, p. 123.

the author of the preface gives some narrations about St. Anthony of Padua and about Brother John of Mt. Alverna, reveals itself thereby as identical with the *Actus b. Francisci et sociorum ejus;* that is to say, with the ancient text of the *Fioretti,* of whose chapters so very many are devoted to St. Anthony and the ecstatic Brother from Alverna.

The compilers entitled all this material *Legenda antiqua,* under the impression of a certain concordance, both with each other and with the "old legends" read in Avignon. As the Franciscan Frederick Baron was Archbishop of Riga from 1304 till his death in 1340,[1] it must have been written during this period. As the *Speculum perfectionis* is quoted in it, the authorship of the work must be later than 1318. As the Pope in 1328 removed Michael of Cesena, and the preface shows no knowledge of this punishment of the bold churchman, we have to concede that the collection belongs between 1318 and 1328.

c. *Actus beati Francisci et sociorium ejus*
("*Fioretti*")

This manuscript is older than the *Legenda antiqua,* the compiler of which has adopted a great part of it and cites it as one of his sources. It appears in many manuscripts united and even mixed in with the *Speculum perfectionis;* possibly it can be regarded in part as the remains of the narrations, unavailable for the last named work, that are told by "the ancient Brothers."

The core of the *Actus* is the group of tales which relate to Brother Bernard, Brother Masseo, Brother Rufino, Brother Silvester, St. Clara and Brother Leo; undoubtedly this part of the work had its origin in the real Franciscan tradition, of whose richness we may form an idea when we remember that tales such as those about Brother Leo, who said the Breviary with St. Francis and always answered wrongly, or such as those about the perfect joy, were here first put into writing.[2]

On this foundation a series of chapters about other prominent Franciscans were subsequently erected; Brother Conrad of

[1] Sabatier, *Collection,* I, p. 158, n. 1; IV, p. 17, n. 1. Eubel: *Hierarchia cath.,* p. 442.

[2] The origin of one chapter is explained by Brother Leo in the work itself, the proof coming through a succession of witnesses. See close of chapter 9: Hanc historiam habuit frater Jacobus de Massa ab ore fratris Leonis et frater Hugolinus de monte Sancta Mariae ab ore dicti fratris Jacobi, et ego qui scripsi ab ore fratris Hugolini viri per omnia fide digni. (*Actus,* ed. Sabatier, p. 39.)

Offida, Brother Giles, Brother John of La Verna (d. 1322) here play a prominent rôle. Sabatier believes that he can indicate Brother Hugolin of Monte Giorgio as the author of this portion, of whom we know nothing else than that he was called by Celestin V to fill the Bishop's throne in Teramo in the Abruzzi, while Boniface VIII, on December 12, 1295, cancelled this selection.[1] Sometimes Brother Hugolin seemed to appear as the author of the work; thus in Chap. LXIX, 21, "and all these things Brother John himself told me, Hugolin." In other places, as in the end of Chap. IX, Hugolin was referred to by the author as the original source, as a link in the chain, which by Brother Jacob of Massa leads back to Brother Leo.[2] The whole question is, however, of secondary importance; the principal thing is that in the *Actus* — of which the *Fioretti* is the Italian translation or development — we have a series of Franciscan traditions collected with diligence, of which many never strayed far from the convent in Greccio, where Leo, Angelo, and Rufino two generations earlier plucked their *flores*.

From the first Franciscan centuries many works could be named which in any case have a certain degree of value as sources, such as the manuscript *Actus b. Francisci in valle Reatina*, improperly ascribed to Angelo Tancredi, and of which some pages are printed in Sabatier's edition of the *Speculum perfectionis*, pp. 256 et al.; Brother Francesco Bartholi's book on the Portiuncula Indulgence of about 1335, published by Sabatier in the second volume of his *Collection d'études*, Paris, 1900; finally *Commercium beati Francisci cum domina paupertate* (perhaps written in 1227 by John of Parma, edited by Alvisi, Citta di Castello, 1894, and by d'Alençon, Rome, 1900), a work which has significance, since Dante evidently derived from it the principal idea for his celebrated lines about St. Francis in the eleventh Canto of *Il Paradiso*.

Moreover, after the publication of the *Speculum* and the *Actus*, there came a time of compilation, of combination and even confusion. If it is a question of titles, they are mixed together, and thus the great work of Brother Fabian of Hungary appears as *Speculum vitæ beati Francisci et sociorum ejus*, written in the last half of the fourteenth century and published in Venice in 1504, and many times since then in more or less changed and impaired forms, eventually (Cologne, 1623) as *Antiquitates franciscanae*, "written by Brothers Fabian, Hugolin, and other Friars Minor

[1] *Actus*, ed. Sabatier, p. 20.
[2] The best editions of the Italian *Fioretti* are those of Caesari (Verona, 1822), and of Fornaciari (Florence, 1902, Collezione Diamante).

contemporaneous with the divine Francis"[1] (!) The author tells about himself, that he visited Mt. Alverna in the year 1343. Probably he is identical with the Brother Fabian from Hungary who in 1330 and 1337 was Inquisitor in Hungary and Bosnia.[2]

A working over of all the important material, which little by little accumulated, is what we have in Bartholomew of Pisa's *Conformitates*, that series of parallels between Christ and Francis which are carried out with such great acuteness and comprehensive scope of learning. Bartholomew of Pisa's work, which was begun in 1385 and was received at the Chapter of the Order in Pisa August 2, 1399, with thanks and praise, is founded on the most exact knowledge of the sources of information, combined with a critical sense of their values. "Of this thing or of that thing," one can thus see him declare, "I have not found anything in authentic sources, but on the other hand they are shown in pictures and inscriptions in several places. My Brother Bonaventure does not tell this in his legend, his reason being unknown to me, because it is partly told by Bernard of Bessa and partly confirmed by a document witnessed by a notary public."[3] This comparative and discursive method of progress we usually find in Bartholomew of Pisa, and his method is a predecessor of modern methods.

III — OTHER SOURCES

a. *Histories of the Order*

I. *Jordanus of Giano's Chronicle* of the Franciscan arrival in Germany. It begins with Francis's conversion in 1207 and ends 1238. Brother Jordanus himself tells how he, "in the year of the Lord 1262, after the Chapter in Halberstadt, remained in the same convent where the Chapter was held" and there dictated his book to Brother Balduin of Brandenburg.[4] While Jordanus' Chronicle

---

[1] auctoribus ff. Fabiano et Hugolino et aliis minoribus Divo Francisco coaevis, castigatore autem et emendatore R. P. Philippo Bosquierio. . . . Coloniae, MDCXXIII.

[2] *Analecta Franciscana*, III, pp. 9-10.

[3] De isto in loco authentico non reperi, sed depictum et scriptum in pluribus locis inveni. Sed de nullo praefatorum dominus fr. Bonaventura facit mentionem, et quid fuerit in causa ignoro: cum tamen de primo dictus Bernardus Bessa facit mentionem, et secundum de scriptura publica notarii reperi Florentiae transscriptum. (*Conformitates*, 1510, p. 149a.)

[4] Anno ergo Domini MCCLXII post . . . capitulum Halberstadense . . . in loco capituli remanentes, me narrante et fratre Baldawino scribente . . . qui et sponte et a frate Bartholomaeo, tunc ministro Saxoniae, jussus se obtulit ab scribendum. (*Anal. Franciscana*, I, p. 1.)

is considered by several, such as Carl Müller and van Ortroy, as an authority of the first rank from the point of view of chronology, it is proper to remember that Jordanus himself, on the first page of his book, remarks that he now is an old man, and therefore can easily make an error in one or the other of his dates.[1]

Jordanus' Chronicle was first published by G. Voigt (*Memorabilia des Minoriten Jord. v. Giano*" in "Abhandlungen der sächs. Gesellschaft der Wissenschaften," philos.-hist. Klasse, 1870); later, after a Berlin manuscript in *Analecta Franciscana*, I (Quaracchi, 1885). A new and complete edition is announced (1905) by H. Boehmer as the second volume of Sabatier's *Opuscules*.

II. The first volume of the *Analecta Franciscana* contains Brother *Thomas Eccleston's Chronicle* of the Brothers' coming to England, including the period 1224 to 1250, written 1264 to 1274. The first edition is by Brewer in *Rer. brit. script.: Monumenta Franciscana*, I (London, 1858), and Howlett, same, Vol. II (London, 1882).

III. *Salimbene's Chronicle.* Brother Salimbene degli Adami of Parma — or, as he at home and among friends was called, Omnebonum, "All good" — was born on October 9, 1221, and entered the Franciscan Order in 1238. He knew Brother Bernard of Quintavalle, with whom he spent a winter in the convent in Siena, and from whose lips he and the other young men heard many great things about St. Francis; he also knew Brother Leo, who told him that St. Francis after his death looked exactly like one who had been crucified and taken down from the Cross, as well as the last Brothers whom St. Francis received into the Order, and whom Salimbene met in a hermitage near Città di Castello (presumably Monte Casale).[2] His Chronicle, written 1282-1287, covers the years 1167-1287; the edition published at Parma in 1857 is incomplete and contains only the period 1212-1287. See Em. Michael, *Salimbene und seine Chronik* (Innsbruck, 1889).

IV. *Catalogue of the first twenty-four Generals of the Order.* Originally written about 1297, continued later up to 1305. It was

[1] Super annorum vero numero sicubi per oblivionem, utpote jam senex et debilis, ut homo erravi, veniam postulo ab lectore (*ibid.*, p. 2).

[2] sicut dixit mihi frater Leo socius suus ... in morte videbatur recte sicut unus crucifixus de cruce depositus. (*Chronica*, p. 75.) A sociis vero et a familia dicebar Omnibonum. ... Cumque de Marchia Anconitana irem ad habitandum in Tusciam et transirem per Civitatem de Castello, inveni in heremo quendam nobilem fratrem antiquum ... qui IIII filios milites habebat in sæculo. Hic fuit ultimus frater, quem b. Franciscus et induit et recepit ad ordinem, ut retulit mihi. ... Vidi etiam et primum sc. fr. Bernardum de Quintavalle, cum quo in conventu Senensi uno hyeme habitavi ... et mihi et aliis juvenibus de beato Francisco multa magnalia referebat (*Chronica*, p. 11).

already published in 1504 in the *Speculum vitae*, then in the third volume of *Analecta Franciscana*, by Ehrle in "Zeitschcr. f. kath. Theologie,"VII (Innsbruck, 1883), p. 338, and in P. Hilarin Felder's edition of Bernard of Bessa (Rome, 1897).

V. The *Chronicles of the (first) twenty-four Generals of the Order*. The author of this work, of which a great part of the material is taken from the *Actus b. Francisci*, was a Franciscan from the Province of Aquitania, because this province was the only one the names of whose Generals he knew. Wadding (1373, n. 24; 1374, n. 16) believes that the author might be that Brother Arnold of Serrano of whom Bartholomew of Pisa (*Conformitates*, I, fructus XI) tells us that he "wrote out all he could find about the blessed Francis." Gregory XI sent this Brother Arnold to Spain to reform the convents of the Minorites and Clares in Castile. As a consequence of the Civil War many Brothers and Sisters of this country were driven out of their convents and wandered about, while at the same time in many convents "irregular customs and abuses" had been introduced (*irregulares consuetudines et deformitates*).

Chronica XXIV generalium, which is its Latin title, was written in its essential parts before 1369. Under headings 1327 and 1360 the author expresses his wishes for the canonization of the pious royal pair Elzéar and Delphina, which took place in 1369. The Chronicle begins by relating the history of St. Francis and the earlier Brothers, and is continued down to 1374. Its author had the best sources for his work; thus we can recognize material from Celano's two biographies, from the traditional Three Brothers' Legend, from St. Bonaventure and Bernard of Bessa. It is doubtful if Brother Arnold used Salimbene and Eccleston; on the other hand he has taken much from *Speculum vitae, Legenda antiqua* (as these are now extant in the Vatican, Manuscript 4354) and from the *Actus* (*Fioretti*), and from Hubert of Casale. He has furthermore drawn upon a collection, *Dicta fratris Leonis* ("Sayings of Brother Leo"), from a now lost *Chronicon breve*, that is ascribed to Brother Pilgrim of Bologna,[1] and finally used verbal tradition. His work was used a great deal by Mariano of Florence, Marcus of Lisbon, Rudolf of Tossignano and Wadding. It is published in *Analecta Franciscana*, III (Quaracchi, 1897).

VI. *John of Komorowo's Chronicle* is especially devoted to the Order's Polish province, was written about 1512, and comes down

[1] See Sbaralea: *Supplementum ad Scriptores trium ordinum*, p. 579, and Denifle in "Archiv f. Litt. u. Kgsch.," I, p. 145.

to 1503. It is published by Zeissberg in *Archiv. f. osterr. Gesch.*, Bd. 49 (1872). Brother John died in 1536 and wrote the year before his death a *Memoriale ordinis fratrum minorum*, published, 1886, by Liske and Lorkiewicz. See Eubel in *Historisches Jahrbuch*, 1889, pp. 383 ff., 570 ff.

VII. *Glassberger's Chronicle.* Nicholas Glassberger entered the Franciscan Order in the year 1472 and for some time was confessor for the Clares in Nuremberg. He was a very diligent writer, who among other things copied with his own hand the *Chronica XXIV generalium*, together with the Three Brothers' Legend; a Tyrolean manuscript of this work from his hand contains the following concluding note: "The eve of the Vigil of Christmas in the year of the Lord 1491 ends for me, Brother Nicholas Glassberger, in great cold and discomfort, owing to the nature of the weather."[1] In 1498 he published Brother Louis of Prussia's *Trilogium animae*, and in 1508 he was progressing with the writing of his Chronicle. He had for his authorities the Chronicle of the twenty-four Generals, the Three Brothers' Legend and Bartholomew of Pisa; the Friars' establishment in Germany he described after Giordano of Giano; finally he quotes also Brother Jacob Oddi's Italian Chronicle of the fifteenth century.[2]

Glassberger's Chronicle is published in the *Analecta Franciscana*, II (Quaracchi, 1887). See Eubel in *Hist. Jahrbuch*, 1899, pp. 376 et seq.

VIII. *Writings of Angelo Clareno.* This celebrated leader of the "Zealous" among the Brothers (*i zelanti*) was also called Peter of Fossombrone. He entered the convent in Cingole and from 1265 joined the zelanti in Mark Ancona. Of the first disciples he knew Brother Angelo of Rieti, Brother Giles, Brother Leo (see page; 382, n. 3), and the Brother John, otherwise unknown, who is

---

[1] Explicit in provigilia nativitatis Dni, 1491, per me fratrem Nicolaum Glassberger in magno frigore et incommoditate juxta temporis qualitatem. (*Anal. Franc.*, II, p. 5.)

[2] Giacomo da Oddi from Perugia was guardian in Portiuncula convent about 1485 and in 1474 wrote his *Specchio dell' Ordine minore*, usually called *la Franceschina*. The original manuscript is now in Communal Library in Perugia and formerly belonged to the Franciscan convent of Monte Ripido near Perugi. When in the chronicle of the Convent of the Clares of Monte Luce for the year 1574, under the date of February 5, it is said of this book, that it *fu gia composto da un reverendo padre chiamato fra Edigio da Perugia*, there is undoubtedly a confusion with the writings, which are due to the celebrated disciple of St. Francis of this name. (Aegidio in English is Giles.) *La Franceschina* contains much material of interest by some third writer. See *Miscellanea Francescana*, VI, 37; LV, 87, 127, 146-150.

mentioned in the prologue to the *Three Brothers' Legend*.[1] He died June 15, 1339, in Santa Maria de Aspro, near the city of Marsico in south Italy. Of him Sabatier says: "We see in him the revival of a true Franciscan, one of those men who, while entirely desirous of being submissive sons of the Church, could not resign themselves to permitting the ideal which they had embraced to disappear in the realm of imagination. They often came near to heresy; in their words against the bad priests and unworthy pontiffs there is a bitterness which the sectaries of the sixteenth century would not exceed. . . . And yet Protestantism would do wrong in seeking their ancestors among these. No, they wished to die, as they had lived, in the communion of this Church, which they loved with a heroic passion, the same with which certain former French noblemen, even in 1793, loved France, and poured out their blood for it, although it was governed by the Jacobins."

As the essence of the doctrine of Angelo Clareno's spiritual doctrines, Sabatier quotes the following beautiful words in one of his letters: *Totum igitur studium esse debet quod unum inseparabiliter simus per Franciscum in Christo*, "Our whole desire should be that we are inseparably one in Christ through Francis," and Sabatier ends his description of him thus:

"Clareno and his friends were of those violent souls who would assail the kingdom of heaven. Thus when, at the end of the frivolities and sterile preoccupations of the every-day world, we find ourselves face to face with these men, we are at once humbled and uplifted, for we find suddenly, hidden in human hearts, hitherto unexpected powers and unknown melody controlled by them."[2]

Angelo Clareno's writings fall into three groups:

(1) *Epistola excusatoria*, an apology for his and his friends' reform movement, presented to Pope John XXII in the year 1317. It is published by Ehrle (*Archiv f. Litt. u. Kirchengesch.*, I, pp. 521 ff.).

(2) "Letter-book" (*Liber epistolarum beati Angeli de Clareno*). The Augustinian hermit Simon of Cassia (according to Ossinger, *Biblioth. Augustiniana*, p. 214; d. February 2, 1340) brought out a collection of letters of his friend and teacher Angelo. It is, however, uncertain that this collection is quite identical with those in two manuscripts still in existence. Part of the letters were written from Avignon (1311-1318), part from the vicinity of Rome (1318- ca. 1336), some finally from S. Maria de Aspro. A selection of the letters is given by Ehrle (*Archiv* I, pp. 543-569).

[1] Ehrle, "Archiv" II, p. 279. Sabatier: *Vie de S. François* (1894), p. CV.
[2] Sabatier: *Vie de S. Fr.* (1894), *Introduction*, pp. CII–CIII.

400   AUTHORITIES

(3) *Historia septem tribulationum ordinis minorum.* "History of the seven tribulations of the Minorite Order." The seven tribulations which according to Clareno descended upon the Order of St. Francis are (1) The Vicariate of Elias of Cortona, (2) his Generalship, (3) the Generalship of Crescentius of Jesi, (4) the Generalship of Bonaventure, (5) the persecutions of the strict Franciscans between 1274 and 1304 (from the council of Lyons to the death of the Inquisitor, Thomas d'Aversas), (6) the persecutions between 1308 and 1323 (the time of the appearance of the *Speculum perfectionis*), finally (7) the Pontificate of John XXII.

"The history of the seven tribulations" occupied in its writing a long series of years, the earliest section about 1314, the latest about 1330. It is incompletely given by Ehrle (*Archiv* II, pp. 108-163 and 249-336). A complete edition was prepared by Felice Tocco for Sabatier's *Collection d'études et de documents*.[1]

b. *Authorities outside of the Order*

1. *Papal bulls and other Instruments* of diplomatic or judicial character. To this belong the bulls of Honorius III and Gregory IX, and letters in favor of the Franciscan Order, in Sbaralea's *Bullarium. franciscanum* continued by Eubel, and in Pressuti's and Auvray's new edition of Registers of Honorius III and Gregory IX. Here belongs Hugolin's Register published by Levi in *Fonti per la Storia dell' Italia;* here too is best assigned the Count

---

[1] See Ehrle's various treatments of the Vienna Council. ("Archiv" II, 353-416 and III, 1-195), of Petrus Johannes Olivi ("Archiv" III, 409-552), of Fraticelli and Spirituales ("Archiv" I, 158-164, II, 653-669, III, 533 et seq., IV, 1-200.) Ehrle's edition of the oldest constitutions of the Franciscan Order is also important ("Archiv" VI, 1-138). It contains the resolutions of the General Chapters from before 1316, after older printed works and after 16 different manuscripts.

The following may be counted among the histories of the Order:

Mariano of Florence's *Chronicle*, which goes down to 1486. This exists only in manuscript and was used by Wadding. Mariano died 1527. Notes on his life and work have been collected by Sabatier in the second volume of his *Collection d'études*, pp. 137-146.

Mark of Lisbon's *Chronicle*, written in Spanish about 1550. The author died about 1580. It came out in Salamanca, 1626; in German translation, Munich, 1720.

Rudolph of Tossignano's *Historia Seraphicæ religionis* (Venice, 1586).

The work of the General of the Order, Gonzaga, entitled *De origine seraphicæ religionis* (Rome, 1587. Venice, 1603), with a description of all the Franciscan convents.

Henricus Sedulius: *Historia Seraphica* (Antwerp, 1613).

of Chiusi's Letter of Donation of La Verna, issued July 9, 1274, and reprinted by Sbaralea in *Bull. Franc.*, IV, p. 156.

2. Jacob of Vitry's Letters and his description of St. Francis and the Franciscans in the second book of *Historia occidentalis*. Of the letters, one was written in Genoa, October, 1216, the second in the Holy Land, in the end of August, 1220, after personal intercourse with St. Francis before Damietta 1219. They are therefore authorities of the very highest value. The *Historia occidentalis*, according to the preface, was begun about 1220 and was probably completed before the return from the Holy Land in 1227.

The first letter is published in *Nouvelles mémoires de l'academie de Bruxelles*, XXIII, pp. 29-33, and in better shape in Brieger's "Zeitschr. f. Kirchengesch.," XIV, pp. 101-106. The second letter is given in Bongar's *Gesta Dei per francos* (1611, pp. 1047 f.). *Historia occidentalis* was printed in Douai in 1597. The letters, together with the corresponding chapters of the *Hist. occ.*, are to be found in Boehmer's *Analekten*, pp. 94-106.

Jacob of Vitry was Canon in Oignies in northern France, afterwards was Bishop of Acre in the Holy Land, and after his return was Cardinal Bishop of Frascati. He died in 1244.

3. Thomas of Spalato's (and not, as Boehmer, *Analekten*, p. lxi, erroneously writes it, Spoleto) *Testimony* about St. Francis' preaching in Bologna in 1220. Printed in Sigonius, *De episcopis Bononiensibus* (Bologna, 1586), in *Monum. Germ. Scriptores* (XXX, p. 580), in Wadding, 1220, n. 8, and in *Acta Sanctorum* (Oct. II, p. 842).

4. Finally, a series of contemporaneous authors, who in their writings accord St. Francis a more or less explicit description, such as the Dominican *Vincent of Beauvais* (d. 1264) in the 30th and 31st books of his *Speculum historiale*; his fellow Dominican *Jacob of Varaggio* in "The Golden Legend"; *St. Anthony of Florence* in the third part (Tit. 24, cap. 7) of his chronicle; *Pietro dei Nadali* (d. shortly before 1406) in his *Catalogus sanctorum;* the Abbot *Albert of Stade* in his Annals; the unreliable *Matthew of Paris* in his *Historia major*, etc.

c. *Modern Works*

1. The series of modern authors on the subject of St. Francis begins with the Irish Franciscan, Luke Wadding. This zealous investigator and indefatigable worker treats in his *Annales Minorum* (8 vols., Rome, 1625) the whole of the history of St. Francis, together with the history of the Order up to 1540. His work has

only one defect, but which was not his fault — outside of St. Bonaventure he only knew the oldest biographers through Bartholomew of Pisa, Mariano of Florence and Marcus of Lisbon. It is the decree of 1263 which this late biographer of St. Francis had to suffer for.

Candide Chalippe's well known and much read book on St. Francis (1728) is based entirely upon Wadding's Annals.

2. It is the Bollandists, first Stilling and after his death Suysken, to whom honor is due for having again brought forward a part of the old biographies. In the second October volume of the *Acta Sanctorum*, published 1768, Celano's *Vita prima* and the traditional fragment of the *Three Brothers' Legend* are printed for the first time, together with a whole series of fragments of Julian of Speier and the *Anonymous of Perugia*. In a detailed commentary and a comprehensive collection of *Analecta*, still further material is collected. Carl Hase's biography of St. Francis of 1856 is entirely based on this material.

3. The third development in the field of Franciscan research is due to an Italian Franciscan, Nicolo Papini, in his two works, characterized by a sharply critical spirit, *Notizie sicure sopra s. Francesco* (Florence, 1822, and Foligno, 1824), together with *Storia de S. Francesco, opera critica* (2 volumes, Foligno, 1825). Since 1806 the world was in possession not only of Thomas of Celano's first biography, but also of his *Vita secunda*, and Papini now built up his book with these two works as foundation. And that he did not use biographies later than the time of Celano — even the *Fioretti* is among those omitted — is only what was to be expected; those who originate a new principle are always inclined to carry it too far. Papini's error in this respect is richly made up for by Ozanam (*Les poètes franciscains d'Italie*, Paris, 1852), by Chaving de Malan (*Vie de S. François d'Assise*, Paris, 1841), by Leon Le Monnier (*Histoire de S. François d'Assise*, Paris, 1889).

4. The most recent studies on Franciscan research came under the names of Karl Müller (*Die Anfänge des Minoritenordens under Bussbruderschaften*, Freiburg, 1885), Henry Thode (*Der hl. Frans von Assisi und die Anfänge der Kunst der Renaissance in Italien*, Berlin, 1885, new edition, 1904), and Paul Sabatier (*Vie de S. François d'Assise*, Paris, 1894, 32d edition, 1904). Sabatier must again and again be extolled as the one to whom the renaissance of interest in St. Francis and his Order is essentially due. All that has been written since his work appeared — by Lempp, van Ortroy, Lemmens, Mandonnet, Minocchi, Götz, Tilemann, Boeh-

mer, Felder, Gustav Schnurer — is to be regarded as a continuation of Sabatier or as refutation of him. Even the author of the present book stands in such a relation to Paul Sabatier, and recognizes it here with deference and thankfulness.

Conditions which I could not control prevented me from writing this book at one time. A space of a year intervened between the writing of the first portion (the first two books and the appendix) and the remainder. As the work was only printed long after much of the text was written, it was inevitable in these days, so rich in Franciscan literature, that more than one new work should have been published. The attentive reader will have felt this trouble in reading the appendix. In order in some degree to compensate for this imperfection, a summary is here given of the last contributions to this line of research.

First and foremost, Boehmer's "Analekten zur Geschichte des Franciscus von Assisi" is to be named. In the text of my book it is often used and cited. It contains not only (like the Quaracchi edition) the unquestioned real Latin writings of Francis of Assisi, but also the uncertain ones, the fragments as well as the Sun Song. There is also given the most important of the testimony concerning the Rules of the Order, the stigmatization, and the parts of the work of Jacques de Vitry, so important in the history of the Order. Finally, it gives a review of the literature about St. Francis, with an exact and comprehensive index to the history of St. Francis and of his Order from 1182 to 1340.

The latter is open to few criticisms. It is undoubtedly incorrect to state, as on page 128, that the *Regula prima* in its existing form was submitted to the Pentecost Chapter of May 30, 1221. Jordanus of Giano says, clearly enough, that this Rule came into existence after this Chapter. Boehmer in his Introduction, p. xxxix, written apparently at a later period, seems clear on this point. Could he have been unable to correct it in the index? — Again he is certainly wrong, when he places St. Francis' last stay in San Damiano (*Spec. perf.*, c. 100) in October, 1224. Francis left La Verna only on September 30 of the same year. He then travelled in slow progress to Città di Castello, where he remained an entire month. In snowy weather he thus crossed the Apennines, at the earliest about the first of November — see page 305 of this book. But the climate of Assisi in the month of November is such that one could not sleep in a wattle hut, as Francis did during the residence in question at San Damiano. Therefore it must be assigned to the next summer (1225), and what the *Speculum* tells in chapter 101 of the dispute between the Podestà and the Bishop, which Francis stopped by having the Sun Song chanted, undoubtedly did not take place in the fall of 1224, but between May and September, 1226. Francis then lay sick in the Bishop's palace, and the reconciliation took place then and there. The account of this in the *Speculum* naturally falls into chapters 122–123, which Boehmer rightly assigns to the period in question.

Next referring to the oldest biographies, thanks to the Vicar-General of the Order, Rev. Edouard d'Alençon, we now possess an excellent edition of all the works of Thomas of Celano, the biographer of St. Francis: *Vita prima, Vita secunda, Tractatus de miraculis,* the short legend for liturgical use, together with the two sequences composed by Thomas — *Sanctitatis nova signa* and *Fregit victor virtualis.* In the *Vita secunda* d'Alençon has removed the third part of the work introduced by Amoni, and has put in the original third portion (Amoni's pars II and III — pars II in d'Alençon. Where I in this work have used d'Alençon's edition, I have always noted it. Moreover, a table in d'Alençon makes it easy to find quotations taken from Amoni). The large and beautifully printed book was published by Desclée, Lefebvre et Cie. in Rome, and bears the title *S. Francisci Assisiensis Vita et miracula, additis opusculis liturgicis, auctore Fr. Thoma de Celano* (lxxxvii + 481 pp.).

The work of the Englishman, Rosedale, published in 1904, *St. Francis of Assisi, according to Brother Thomas of Celano* (London, Dent and Co., xxxiv + 174 pp.), can only be regarded as an unsuccessful attempt to get first to the mill with one's grain. Rosedale made good use of d'Alençon's guidance, but his edition cannot be designated by a milder word than a hasty and perfunctory performance. He has had the curious idea of first printing one MS. (from Assisi) and then the other (from Marseilles), instead of comparing the two manuscripts of the *Vita secunda* and so producing a critical text. As the two relations are thus given in succession, the whole produces a very bewildering effect. It is done in very good style, but is full of printer's errors (on the title page of *Vita secunda,* for instance, we read "*de Assisii*"). D'Alençon has pointed out a quantity of wrong readings in the *Prolegomena* to his own edition (pp. lxxii–lxxv).

In his well-known collection so often cited in this book, *Opuscules de Critique* (I, pp. 69 et seq.), Paul Sabatier, following the

Liegnitz MS. of the *Legenda antiqua*, calls attention to seven chapters, which according to his views are the remains of the original Three Brothers' Legend (*Legenda vetus*, see page 391 of this book). Meanwhile van Ortroy has found the same chapters in Angelo Clareno's *Commentaries on the Rules of the Order* just as they are found in a manuscript of the fourteenth century in S. Isidoro in Rome (*Anal. Boll.*, XXX, pp. 441 et seq.). Clareno's commentary, where the chapters, according to van Ortroy, belong, is to appear in Sabatier's *Opuscules*.

Even if the learned Bollandist is right in his contention, the contents of the chapters in question may very well have their origin in the old Three Brothers' Legend. Moreover, the conviction is formed more and more that the various names of the original Franciscan writers are of little weight. It appears clear that there are really only three original sources for the biography of St. Francis of Assisi:

(1) Francis' writings.
(2) Thomas of Celano's *Vita prima*.
(3) All that directly or indirectly can be referred back to Brother Leo and his friends. From Brother Leo's *rotuli* and the other *scripta fratrum antiquorum* originate (a) the Greccio collection from 1246 = the original Three Brothers' Legend (*Legenda vetus*); (b) Celano's *Vita secunda*, with portions of the Treatise on Miracles (§32 = *Spec.* 113; §§37-38 = *Spec.* 112); (c) *Speculum perfectionis*, *Actus* (*Fioretti*), *Legenda antiqua*, and the other collections from the fourteenth century down to the *Speculum vitae* of about 1250.

One of these numerous compilations, perhaps based upon Angelo Clareno's work referred to above, is also the Italian *Leggenda antica* given by Salvatore Minocchi under the impressive title *Nuova fonte biographica* (Florence, 1905, xxxii + 184 pp.). As Golubvich remarks (*Luce e amore*, II, Florence, 1905, pp. 255-264), the term "*Legenda antiqua*" in the older Franciscan speech was often the designation of one or another legend that was older than Bonaventure's biography and was of "Leonine" origin. Thomas of Celano's *Vita secunda* is often designated by this name, which, all things considered, can only be a wrong designation.

The order of the Chapter-meeting of 1263 (see p. 380), in compliance with which all the legends which were older than Bonaventure's were to be destroyed, was only known through a quotation of Rinaldi's from a lost manuscript from Gubbio. The ominous decree has now been again found by A. G. Little in an

Oxford MS. (*English Historical Review*, XIII, pp. 704-708), and by v. Ortroy (*Anal. Boll.*, XVIII, p. 174) in a Vatican MS. of the thirteenth century which had belonged to Queen Christina.

Salimbene's chronicle was published by Holder-Egger in *Mon. Germ.*; the first part appeared in Vol. XXXII. Felice Tocco is preparing in Sabatier's *Collection d'études* an edition of Angelo Clareno's *Chronica septem tribulationum*, and in Sabatier's *Opuscules* there is to appear a new and complete edition of Jordanus of Giano by H. Boehmer. In Suttini's *Bolletino critico* (Florence, 1905, pp. 45-47) Little has published a hitherto unknown source for the *Chronica XXIV generalium*, namely, Brother Pilgrim of Bologna's Chronicle (see p. 397).

One could be tempted to regard Nino Tamassia's work, *S. Franciscus d'Assisi e la sua leggenda* (Padua and Verona, 1906, XI + 216 pp.), as a contribution characterized by great learning. The author is professor of the History of Law and of Church Law in the University of Padua, and his work testifies to a wide-spread knowledge of works on the ancient Church and Middle Ages. He here works on the principle that every part of the legend of St. Francis, to which parallels can be found in earlier hagiography, necessarily are plagiarisms therefrom. For Tamassia the whole Franciscus legend resolves itself into a mosaic of reminiscences and quotations. When Thomas of Celano begins his relation with the simple words *Vir erat in civitate Assisii*, the learned professor sees at once a quotation from Gregory the Great's biography by Benedict of Nurcia, which very naturally begins with the words *Fuit vir!* "It is a pure illusion," Tamassia therefore declares, "when modern Franciscan researchers try to find any remains of historical truth in Celano's writings." Both this author's *Vita prima* and *Vita secunda* are works with a purpose, arranged by Brother Thomas by Gregory's orders to change the heretic and Valdensian Francis to a saint after the best orthodox patterns. Add to this that Tamassia as well as v. Ortroy regard the *Legenda trium sociorum* as an unreliable and late work of compilation, and there is certainly nothing more for them to say. Not unjustly has a critic of Tamassia's book (in *Etudes franc.*, XV, pp. 481 et seq.) put the ironic question: *S. François a-t-il jamais existé?*

It is pleasant to turn from this flight into the extremes of hypercriticism to the observations on the questions of the authorities for the life of St. Francis which Henry Thode has brought together in the new edition of "*Franz von Assisi und die Anfänge der Kunst der Renaissance in Italien*" (Berlin, 1904, pp. 586-609).

Not without justifiable pride does Thode remark that it was precisely his book, published originally in 1885, which established a basis for all modern Franciscan literature; a work in whose tracks C. Mandachs follows closely in writing on St. Anthony of Padua. He adheres strongly to the thesis, that in the question of the sources of the biography of St. Francis after twenty years' indefatigable research all the essentials are in the older works (p. 609). Now as always the principal sources are Celano's *Vita prima* and *Vita secunda*, in which last Thode sees the undoubtedly real *Legenda trium sociorum*, that of Leo, Angelo, Rufino and the others, including Thomas, a composite biography of Francis. "*Alles wissenswethe bezuglich des Heiligen und der Auffassung, die seine Junge von ihm hatten, ist in den einzigen wahren Quellen, den beiden Viten des Thomas zu finden*" (p. 599).

I concede that Thode here goes farther in opposition to Sabatier than I can follow him. For example, it is not clear to me that the natural and naïve style of the relations in the *Speculum* is to be taken as a proof of their late origin (pp. 600–601). Even Sabatier does not claim that the *Speculum* was written in 1227. But I do not see that Thode has proved it impossible that Leo's *rotuli* in their original simple style even in 1318 lay before this man or those men who collected and published the *Speculum perfectionis*, and were piously preserved in their original form. Neither has Thode proved that the *Legenda vetus*, which was read at the table in Avignon under Michael of Cesena (p. 391) is identical with the *Speculum perfectionis*, although on his page 604 et seq. he upholds this view. The untenability of his hypothesis becomes at once clear when we examine it in the light of the explicit utterance in the prologue to the *Legenda antiqua* on the subject of the "old legend" — that it, namely, (1) was used by Bonaventure and (2) is inserted in *Leg. antiqua*. None of this applies to the *Speculum perfectionis*. Bonaventure has not inserted it, for the simple reason that it was not in existence in his time. And the *Legenda antiqua* certainly quotes the *Speculum*, but from a source widely different from the *Legenda vetus*. The two cannot be identified, and it seems for the present most reasonable — as on my page 392 — that the "old legend" read in Avignon is to be understood as having been the original *Legenda trium sociorum*.

In his commendable zeal to establish Thomas of Celano's throne in safety against the attacks of Sabatier, Thode goes too far to the other side. The *Speculum* will always hold its place in the first rank among the biographies of St. Francis. It is therefore a pity that Thode — like Lemmens — in the traditional (incomplete) Three Brothers' Legend can only see a pure compilation — arranged to form an introduction to the *Speculum perfectionis*. So far no one — not even v. Ortroy — has shown the sources of characteristic minor traits from the childhood of Francis given in this work and nowhere else. And until this proof is produced all credit remains here, as Thode says, "with the old" sources.

Finally, a few words must be said of Karl Hampe's article in "Hist. Zeitschr.," 1906, "*Die wundmale des hl. Franz von Assisi*." I cannot go into all this writer's subtilties — such as, that the seraph who appeared to Francis at La Verna cannot have floated in the air, because one authority states that the angel showed himself standing on a stone (p. 399). When an angel does reveal himself, he may well overcome first one and then another thing; but to Hampe it appears that his view is finely adapted to show the contradictions existing in the sources of information.

There are not many such solid arguments in Hampe's article, but it is written in the suspicious style affected in certain modern circles. Nothing is insisted on and nothing is denied, but by a series of indirect suggestions, general suspicions and indefinite circumlocutions, the reader is brought into the narcosis of doubt and uncertainty aimed at by the author. When two testimonies of the stigmatization, for example, two mutually independent documents say exactly the same, then he assumes that one of them has been adapted to fit the other's appearance (p. 398). This is an easy way to get rid of an inconvenient witness.

It is significant that Hampe — in spite of all this — does not at all deny Francis' stigmatization. The stigmata existed in Francis' last year, that is certain (p. 390). Hampe only denies (1) that they had the appearance given in this book; for example, according to him they can only have been "vernarbte Locher, in deren Risse sich der Schmutz gesetzt hat, i.e., inflamed openings, in whose cracks dirt had accumulated (p. 391); (2) that Francis received the stigmata on La Verna in September, 1224.

As principal proof for these denials Hampe cites the letter of Elias of Cortona to Gregory and the French Brothers written immediately after Francis' death. (Appendix to this book, p. 351, note 4.) It reads thus (see Boehmer, p. 91):

"Non diu ante mortem frater et pater noster apparuit crucifixus, quinque plagas, quae vera sunt stigmata Christi, portans in corpore suo: nam manus ejus et pedes quasi puncturas clavorum habuerant ex utraque parte confixas, reservantes cicatrices et clavorum nigredinem ostendentes. Latus vero ejus lanceatum apparuit et saepe sanguinem evaporavit." Hence Hampe believes that (1) Francis received the stigmata shortly before his death (*non diu*), not two years before; (2) the stigmata did not project like nails, but were only black (*clavorum nigredinem ostendentes*). The answer to this is:

(1) Hampe places too much stress on the expression *non diu* written by Elias without regard to later critical historians. Elias had been in the Order sixteen years when he wrote this, and had a certain right to use the expression "not long" for a lapse of two years. But what would Hampe say to it, when Thomas of Celano describes a lapse of seventeen years by the words *paulo post*? This is the case in the *Vita secunda* I, VI, 11, where it is said of Francis' prayer in San Damiano: "Ab ea igitur hora liquefacta est anima ejus, ut dilectus ei locutus est. Patuit *paulo post* amor cordis per vulnera corporis."[1] And in her Rule St. Clara writes: "*paulo post conversionem ipsius*" (i.e. Francisci) "una cum sororibus meis obedientiam voluntarie sibi promisi" (*Textus originales*, p. 62). When the expression *paulo post* in Clara's diction can indicate five years, in that of Thomas of Celano seventeen years, then Elias can also by *non diu* have indicated two years. As far as the reckoning of time went, none of these old writers apparently weighed their expressions on a bullion-balance.

Finally, with regard to (2) the following is to be said. Hampe lays much stress on the fact that Elias speaks of the stigmata only as "clavorum nigredinem ostendentes," whereas Celano says in *Vita prima* (II, c. 3; Boehmer, p. 93), "manus et pedes ejus in ipso medio clavis confixi videbantur." This seems to him a developing of the legend.

My view is that the expression "clavorum nigredinem" is only to be taken as a flower of rhetoric. In those days, if a fine expression was sought for, one would not say, for example, "per densas silvas," but "per densitatem silvarum," analogous to the ways of certain French symbolists in our own times. In like manner one would not say "clavos nigros," but more elegantly "clavorum nigredinem." *Hinc illa dissertatio.*[2]

[1] I am indebted to Rev. Michael Bihl for this valuable indication.
[2] I must state here, that Monsignor Dr. N. Paulus, who formerly ("Der Katholik," 1899, I, pp. 97 et seq.) has defended the theory of the origin of the Portiuncula Indulgence from St. Francis himself, in an article in the "Kölnische Zeitung" for July 26, 1906, essentially places himself upon the same standpoint as P. A. Kirsch. ("That Honorius III did not grant the Portiuncula Indulgence, Kirsch has convincingly shown".)

The Wolf of Gubbio

The legend of the Wolf of Gubbio in the *Fioretti* is as follows: A savage wolf terrorized the inhabitants of Gubbio. It kept itself in the environs, and no one dared to go out there alone, no matter if he was armed. St. Francis went out to see the wolf and to tame it by his influence. He found it in its haunts, addressed it as Brother Wolf, told it how bad had been its life, told it that if it would cease its attacks it would be supported, and thus subdued it. For two years thereafter, we are told, the wolf went through the town of Gubbio from house to house and was fed by the inhabitants, and then died. — Translator's Note.

INDEX

INDEX

ABRUZZI, the, 265.
Abstainers, the Third Order, 241.
ABU JACOB, the Miramolin, 199.
ACCURSIUS, celebrated Lawyer of Bologna, bequeaths his villa *La Richardina* to the Order, 228; sent to Morocco, 1219, 197.
ADAM OF MARSH, B., opposed to ELIAS of CORTONA, 239.
ADJUTO, B., sent to Morocco, 1219, 197.
Admonitions, summary of, 214–217.
ÆGIDIUS, B. See GILES, B.
AGNELLO OF PISA, B., *Custos* in Paris, 239; leader of English mission of 1224, 239.
AGNOLO, B., 158.
Albernio, hermitage of, near Siena, 319.
ALBERT, the beggar, 52; meets ST. FRANCIS in Pisa, 146.
ALBIGENSES, 87.
Alviano, the swallows of, 151.
ALEXANDER III and the care of lepers, 33; gives VALDES permission to preach, 88.
Angel plays for ST. FRANCIS, 295, 317.
"Angel's Bread," 274.
ANGELA OF FOLIGNO, 73.
ANGELO, brother of ST. FRANCIS persecutes him, 52.
ANGELO CLARENO, B., his strict observance, n., 272.
ANGELO TANCREDI, B., characterized by ST. FRANCIS, 282; humiliated, 158; living with Cardinal BRANCALEONE, 259; and LEO with the dying saint, 324; ST. FRANCIS' calls to him, 76; test of his humility and obedience, 158.
ANGELUS meets ST. FRANCIS in Pisa, 146.
ANTONIN OF FLORENCE, ST., 27.
Apulia, ST. FRANCIS' futile trip to, 22–24.
Ascoli, ST. FRANCIS preaches in, 153.
Assisi, its history, 8–9, 10, 18, 19, 22, 86–87, 99, 129; peace with Perugia, November, 1203, 20; blessed by ST. FRANCIS when dying, 329; doors in, closed to Brothers, 81; PTOLEMY'S Aisision, 8; stable in, birthplace of ST. FRANCIS, 10.
AYMON OF FAVERSHAM, B., 228; at Bologna, 228; favors the book-learned as officers of the Order, 239.

BARBAROSSA, 18.
BARBARUS, B., 76.
BARBARUS, in Cyprus, 202.
BARNABAS, on German missions of 1220 or 1221, 210.
BARTHOLI, FRANCESCO, and the Portiuncula indulgence, 170.
BARTHOLOMEW OF PISA, analogies between OUR LORD and ST. FRANCIS, 9.
BENEDICT OF AREZZO, B., goes as a missionary to Greece, 1219, 196; the Portiuncula indulgence, 169.
BENEDICT OF PRATO, B., says mass for ST. FRANCIS, 288; writes ST. FRANCIS' blessing on the Order, 321.
Benedictines on Monte Subasio, owners of Portiuncula, 105.
BENEDICTINE Sisters of St. Pauls and ST. CLARA, 127.
BERARDO, B., leader of the missionaries in Seville, 199; sent to Morocco, 1219, 197.
BERNARD OF BESSA, B., n., 62; testifies to HUGOLIN'S friendship for ST. FRANCIS in difficulties of 1221, 207; uses title of Third Order, and describes it, 244.
BERNARD OF QUINTAVALLE, B., his abstraction in God, 106–107; characterized by ST. FRANCIS, 282; in Florence, 70; gives all to the poor and is converted, April 16, 1209, 62, 65; prays for divine guidance in the church of ST. NICOLO, Assisi, 64; sometimes acts as leader on trip to Rome, 1210, 84; preaches in Bologna, 1212, 227; settled at Bologna, 1213, 227; tests ST. FRANCIS' sincerity, 63; ST. FRANCIS' special commendation of, 330; his last days, 280.
BERNARD OF VIGILANZIO, 76.

INDEX

BERNHARD PRIMUS, 91.
Birds, sermon to the, 149-150; welcome the Friars to Mount Alverna, 292.
BOEHMER describes his letters, 267.
BOEHMER and MÜLLER and the Rule of 1221, 221-222.
BOLOGNA and BERNARD OF QUINTAVALLE, 227; centre of opposition to ST. FRANCIS, 227; and the learned Franciscans, 227-228; ST. FRANCIS preaches in, 234-235.
BONA DONNA, wife of LUCHESIO, 241.
BONIZIO, B., at Fonte Colombo with ST. FRANCIS and Brother LEO to finish the Rule, 252.
BRIENNE, JOHN OF, 151; WALTER OF, 151.
"BROTHER ASS," 148.
"Brother Francis' Plant," 122.
"Brother Giles' Wisdom," 109.
"BROTHER JACOBA," 152.
Brothers not to take more than three mouthfuls when at strange tables, 272.

CÆSARIUS OF SPEIER, B., a collaborator in the writing of ST. FRANCIS' circular letters, 271; first German in the Order, 201; leader of German mission of 1220 or 1221, 210; helps ST. FRANCIS in writing the Rule of 1221, 213, 221; returns from Germany, June 11, 1223, 271; and ST. FRANCIS' Work, 223-225.
Camaldolites of Monte Subasio, give San Domiano to the Clares, 129.
Camaldolites and Portiuncula, 105.
Canterbury, the Friars in, 239.
Carceri, the original convent at, 218.
CATHARI, 87-88, 153-154.
CATTANI, ORLANDO DEI, 161-162.
CATTANI, PIETRO DEI, B., prays for divine guidance in the Church of St. Niccolo, Assisi, 63, 64.
Chapter of Mats (1220 or 1221), 209, 210; of Michaelmas, 1219, 205; Pentecost, of May 14, 1217, 182; Pentecost, of 1218, 194-196; Pentecost, of May 26, 1219, 196, 236; Pentecost, of 1220 or 1221 (of Mats), 209-210; Pentecost, of 1221, 200, 201, 239; Pentecost, of 1221 at Portiuncula, 206; Pentecost, of 1224, 267, 269, 270.
Chapters or Chapter Meetings, 176, 178.
Cheerfulness, 54, 220, 289.

CHIARAMONTI, CARDINAL NICHOLAS, 164.
CHRISTIAN, ARCHBISHOP OF MAYENCE, 18.
CLARES follow Rule of ST. BENEDICT after 1219, 189; GREGORY IX tries to modify the Rule of Poverty, 190; Poverty, the core of Observances of ST. DAMIEN, 189; privilege of poverty ratified by INNOCENT III, 1215, 185; rigidity of rule makes CARDINAL HUGOLIN weep, 189; Severe Cloister of, 189.
CONSTANCE OF SICILY, 21.
Convents, the first Franciscan, 218.
COPPOLI, JACOPO and the Portiuncula indulgence, 170.
CRECENTIUS OF JESI, B., at Bologna, 228.
Cross in San Damiano, voice of, 1207, 297.
Crucigers, 77.

Damietta, siege of, beginning May, 1218, 203-204; fight before, on July 29, 1219, 203; attack on by crusaders repulsed, July 31, 1219, 203; great defeat of crusaders, August 29, 1219, 203; falls, November 5, 1220, 204.
DANTE at the Franciscan convent, 155.
DAVID OF DINANT, 87.
Despair, temptation of, 266.
Disciple, the first, 62.
Disciples, first four, 67; first seven, 67; persecution of early, 69-70; taken for thieves, 70.
Dominicans and learning, 230; Dominicans' Rule for the Franciscans, 231.
DOM PEDRO, Infanta of Portugal, 199; Infanta of Portugal at head of the MIRAMOLIN'S army, 199; missionaries put in his care by the MIRAMOLIN, 199.
Donato, story of, n., 124.
DURAND OF HUESCA, 84; adheres to church, 88; authorized to preach, 83.

EGIDIO, B. See GILES, B.
ELECTUS, B., goes as a missionary to Tunis, 1219, 196; a martyr in Tunis, 1219, 197.
ELIAS BOMBARONE, B. See ELIAS OF CORTONA, B.
ELIAS OF CORTONA, B., n., 27, 227; opposed to the "Portiuncula men," 169; placed over Province of Holy Land, 183; ST. FRANCIS in opposi-

tion, 226-227; and his party said to have attempted to invalidate the Rule and substitute the Dominicans' Rule, 231; and the Final Rule, 248; visits ST. FRANCIS at Fonte Colombo to plead for a gentler Rule, 252-253; loses the Rule, 253; begs ST. FRANCIS to have his eyes treated, 316; ST. FRANCIS transported to Assisi by him, 321.
England, Franciscans go there, September 10, 1224, 239.
Eremi and *ritiri*, 72.
Erimitorium of the Franciscans, 218.

FAVORINO DEI SCIFI, 122, 124.
FIUMI family of Sterpeto, 122.
FLORENCE, ST. ANTONIN OF, 27.
Fonte Colombo, the interview at, 252-253; the original convent at, 218; ST. FRANCIS with Brothers LEO and BONIZIO at, 252-253.
FRANCIS OF FABRIANO, b. 1251, d. 1322, 171; obtains the Portiuncula indulgence, 171; his reminiscences, 171; visits Assisi in 1268, 172.
FRANGIPANI family, 152.
FREDERICK BARBAROSSA, 18.
FREDERICK II, 21; and San Damiano, 135-136.
Friars Minor, origin of title, 100-101.
FRU PICA, 41, 44-45.

GEORGE, Houses of ST., 32.
Germany, mission of 1220 or of 1221 to, 210-212.
GIACOMA. See JACOPA.
Giorgio, church of S., 64.
GILES, B., n., 67, after the death of ST. FRANCIS, 238; and the beggar woman, 66-67; his biography written by Brother LEO, 107; and book learning, 236-237; "Brother Giles' Wisdom," 109; is called a hypocrite, 107-108; carries water and helps the cook in Santi Quattro Coronati, 108; characterized by ST. FRANCIS, 282; choice of life, 145; comments on ST. FRANCIS' preaching, 67; his conversion, April 23, 1209, 65-66; his devotion to Poverty and Chastity, 237-238; and the Doctor of Theology, 138; earns his food while a guest with CARDINAL NICHOLAS, 109; his employment in Ancona, 107; episodes in life of, 107-109; an extensive traveller, 107; faithful to his first love, 239; in Florence, 70; gives his rich cloak to a beggar woman, 66-67; goes as a missionary to Tunis, 1219, 196; imitates playing the violin, 109, 238; instances of his Franciscan goodness, 108-109; interrogates ST. BONAVENTURE, 238; "Knight of the Round Table," 67, 107; life in the convent at Perugia, 109; living with CARDINAL CHIARAMONTI, 259; his occupations, 108; opposes new tendency to learning and study, 236-237; "Paris, thou ruinest ST. FRANCIS' Order," 238; prays to find ST. FRANCIS, 66; rejects too large a payment for wood, 108; his remarks to the two Cardinals, 109; says that a priest cannot lie, 108; sells water in Brindisi, 107; sent out of Tunis by force, 1219, 197; stops a doctor of theology preaching in San Damiano, 138; his sonnet to chastity, n., 110; traits illustrating his views of doing and study, 237-238; his death, April 22, 1262, 239.
GOZZOLI, BENEZZO, 9-10.
GRATIAN, B., and ST. ANTHONY OF PADUA, 212.
Greccio, the Christmas at, 1223, 260-262.
GREGORY OF NAPLES, B., vicar of the Order, 205.
GREGORY IX, 181 (see also HUGOLIN); grants indulgence to church of ST. FRANCIS in Assisi, 166, 167, 168; protector of the Third Order, 243; and Rule of the Clares, 190; and ST. CLARA, 133; and ST. CLARA'S poverty, 136-137; tries to modify the Rule of Poverty of the Poor Clares, 190; withdraws his prohibition of preaching by Franciscans in San Damiano, 133.
GUBBIO, the hospital in, 50; JOHN OF, 9; ST. FRANCIS' friend in, 49; wolf of, 100, 235, 410.
GUELFUCCI, BONA, 125.
GUIDO, BISHOP OF ASSISI, 1204, n., 31, 45, 76; probably confessor of ST. FRANCIS, 31; his law suits, 78; objects to the begging, 77; poverty of ST. FRANCIS, 76-78; receives the Brothers in Rome, 1210, 84; and ST. FRANCIS' early preaching, 98.
GUIDO OF FLORENCE, his alms refused, 71.
GUIDO VAGNOTELLI, B., enters the Order, 145.

HENRY VI, 18, 21.
HONORIUS II and the Portiuncula Indulgence, 167.
HONORIUS III, authorizes mass for the Friars Minor, December, 1224, 288; Bull of 1220, 207; defines the Dominicans, 187; goes to Rieti, 1225, 316; leaves Rome, April, 1225, 316; letter of commendation for the missionaries (June 11, 1219), 196; his letter about Poor Clares to CARDINAL HUGOLIN, August 27, 1218, 185-186; on December 16, 1221, orders the Bishop of Rimini to protect the Third Order in Faenza, 243; protector of the Third Order, 243; ratifies Rule, November 29, 1223, 226.
HUBERT OF CASALE and ANGELA OF FOLIGNO, 171.
HUGOLIN, CARDINAL, 165, 180, 181-182; assists ST. FRANCIS in drawing up Rule of Third Order, 244; in Bologna, 1221, 243; became POPE GREGORY IX in 1227, 136, 181; Bishop of Ostia and Velletri, May, 1206, 181; chooses Rule of the Benedictines for the Poor Clares, 187; defends the cause of the church against Markwald, 1188, 181; co-operation with ST. FRANCIS on the final Rule, 247; establishes Order of Poor Clares, 1217-1219, 185-186; first visit of, to Friars Minor and how they impressed him, 164-165; forbids ST. FRANCIS going to France, 1217, 184; founds a convent for the Franciscans in Viterbo, 181; founds a convent, San Cosmiato, for the Poor Clares in Rome, 181; founds convents in Lombardy and Tuscany, 181-182; founds a poor-house with church in Anagni and gives it over to Hospital Brothers, 181; says that he helped to write the Rule and to obtain its ratification, 257; instances of his influence and correcting the final Rule, 247; intermediator between ELIAS OF CORTONA and ST. FRANCIS, 226; Papal Chaplain of St. Eustachio, 1198, 181; Papal Legate in Tuscany to preach a crusade and allay disputes between the republics, 183; at Pentecost Chapter of 1218 as protector of Order, 194; and the Rule of the Order of Clares, 186-187; and ST. FRANCIS and the final Rule, 247-248;

ST. FRANCIS' Spiritual Father, 184; secured for side of ST. FRANCIS' adversaries (about 1223), 231; his view as to Rule differed from ST. FRANCIS', 248; washes beggar's feet, who complains, 195; weakens the Rule, 247-248, 251; weeps at rigidity of Rule of Poor Clares, 189; and Humiliations of the Friars, 158.

Idiota, 228.
ILLUMINATO in the Holy Land with ST. FRANCIS, 1219, 204.
Indulgence granted Church of St. Francis in Assisi, 166, 167, 168; example of early ones, 166-167; and the Lateran Council of 1215, 166; old methods of granting, 166; the Portiuncula, 166-174.
Indulgentia de Terra Sancta, 166.
INNOCENT III, 11, 31; afraid to enter Assisi, 86-87; blesses ST. FRANCIS' mission to the Saracens, 152; his dream, n., 85; driven from Rome, 86; and the Clares, 130-131; insulted, 85-86; journey of homage through Umbria, 87; rebellious era of, 87.
INNOCENT IV in Assisi, 1253, 139; in Perugia, 1252, 138; and Poor Clares, 189; visits the dying ST. CLARA, 138-139.
IRSLINGEN, CONRAD OF, 18, 86.

JACOPA DE SETTESOLI, b. about 1190, 152, 257-258; in Assisi, 334; epitaph in the Franciscan church in Assisi, 334; her lamb given her by ST. FRANCIS, 257; meets ST. FRANCIS, 1212, 152; prepares almond cream for him, 257; her first son Giovanni, born 1210, 152; her second son Gratiano, born 1217, 152; visit to the dying saint, 330; a widow in 1217, 257.
JACQUELINE. See JACOPA.
JACQUES DE VITRY, his description of the Friars Minor, 163-164; chapter meetings, 214; in St. Jean d'Acre, tells of Franciscans, 1219, 203.
JOHN, MORICO and SABBATINO, BB., early disciples, 67.
JOHN OF PARMA, 192; at Bologna, 228.
JOHANNES PARENTI, B., 228; enters the Order, 145.
JOHN OF PIANO CARPINO on German Mission of 1220 or 1221, 210.
JOHN OF SAN COSTANZO, 76.
JOHN OF ST. PAUL, CARDINAL, be-

INDEX

friends the Brothers in Rome, 1210, 84-85; interviews Pope about St. Francis, 90.
John, The Simple, B., his conversion, 115-117; copies St. Francis in all things, 117.
John of Brienne, 151.
John Capella, B. (of the hat), 67; tries to establish a new order of lepers, 1219, 205.
John Colombini, his wife converted, 241.
John of Giano, B., and the German mission of 1220 or 1221, 210.
John of Gubbio, 9.
John de Laudibus, B., characterized by St. Francis, 282-283.
John Vellita, Messer, helps St. Francis with the Christmas celebration at Greccio, 1223, 261.
Jordanus of Giano, B., his account of the German mission of 1220 or 1221, 211; describes his own character, 240; describes St. Francis' dislike of compulsion, 226; does not know what a convent is, 211, 218.
Julian, St., 32.
Juniper, B., or Ginepro, 106, 111-112; anecdotes of, 106, 111-115; characterized by St. Francis, 282; cooks a huge meal that is uneatable, 113-114; his "flaming sparks of words," 115; "news from God," 115, 139; and the pig's foot, 112-113; and St. Clara, 115; and the Seesaw, 114-115; gives his superior hot porridge at night, 114; his way of giving lessons, 114.

Ketteler, Bishop of Mayence, and the poor family, 277.
Knights of Lazarus, 32.
"Knight of the Round Table," 67, 107.

Larks, their last farewell to the Saint, 333.
Lateran Council of 1215 and Indulgences, 166; its Interdiction of New Orders, 187; and religious orders, 83; said to have accepted Dominicans and Friars Minor, 187.
La Verna, gift of, 162, 168; at the present day, 293.
Lauds, 69, 222-225.
Laymen, as preachers, 83.
Lazarus, Knights of, 32.
Lent, 1211, 147.

Leo, B., 106; and angels with the dying saint, 324; the Blessing of Brother, 303-304; characterized by St. Francis, 282; describes St. Francis failing in health, 251-252; he intrudes on St. Francis' solitude, 295-296; opens the Book of Gospels for St. Francis' guidance, 294; the Portiuncula indulgence, 170; the prayer with St. Francis, 117-119; St. Francis prays with him, 287; St. Francis attendant in his last weeks of life, 293, 295; with St. Francis and Brother Bonizio at Fonte Colombo to finish the Rule, 252; St. Francis describes the perfect happiness to him, 119-121; with St. Francis on La Verna, 295-297; says part-prayers with St. Francis, 117-119; says mass for St. Francis, 288; and the Stigmata, 301-302; his story about the attempted invalidation of the Rule, 231; his vision of Francis defending his Order, 230; his eyes possibly closed by Jacopa de Settesoli, 334; died about 1274, 334.
Leo IX, St., 32.
Leonard, B., his thoughts read by St. Francis, 284.
Leper and Martyrius, 32.
Lepers in Middle Ages, 32.
Liberius, Pope, 105.
Luchesio of Poggibonsi, 241-242; his new life, 241; his wife Bona Donna, 241; and wife died April 28, 1260, 241.
Lucidus, B., characterized by St. Francis, 283.
Lucius III and Valdenses in 1184, 88.

Mariano of Florence, his character of Pietro di Bernardone, 45; describes the preparing of the Rule of the Third Order, 247.
Mark Ancona, Friars' early days in, 68.
Markwald, 21.
Martyrs of Morocco, 200; of Seville, their bodies enshrined in Coimbra by Queen Urraca, 200; news of their deaths at the Pentecost chapter of 1221, 200-201.
Martyrius and the leper, 32.
Masseo, B., of Marignano, 74, 97, 106; anecdotes of, 106, 110, 111; and Brother Rufino, 281; characterized by St. Francis, 282; his cheerfulness, 111; exercised in hu-

28

mility by ST. FRANCIS, 111; goes to seek advice for ST. FRANCIS from SILVESTER and ST. CLARA, 149; his praying, 111; ST. FRANCIS makes him find the road they are to take, 110; his success as a beggar, 110; testimony as to Portiuncula indulgence, 169-170.
Mats, Chapter of the, 209.
MATTHEW OF NARNI, B., 201, 205.
MAYENCE, ARCHB. CHRISTIAN OF, 18.
Middle Ages, Church of the, 85-86.
Minerva, temple of, in Assisi, 129.
Mission journey of 1217, 236; to Tunis, 197-200; to Germany, 210.
Missions, great Franciscan, began 1217, 182-183, 192-193, 220.
Missionaries, their experiences in Germany, 1217, 192; the first, 68-70; ill-treated, 68-70; in Seville irrepressible, 199; in Seville martyred, 200; six go to Morocco, 1219, 196; start for their provinces, 1217, 192.
MONALDO, uncle of ST. CLARA and ST. AGNES attempts to recover ST. AGNES by force, 128-129.
Monism, the struggle for, 88-89.
Montefalco, 10.
Montefeltro, Festival at castle of, 159-162.
Monte Paolo, hermitage of, 212.
Monte Subasio, 48, 77-105.
Monticelli, ST. AGNES and the Rule for, 190.
MORICO, SABATINO and JOHN, BB., early disciples, 67.
Morocco, ST. FRANCIS' journey to, 163.
Mount Alverna, the original convent at, 218; taking possession of, 291.
Mutual love of the Brothers, 82.

Nature, ST. FRANCIS' relations to, 309-312.
Neo-Manichees, 87.
NICHOLAS, Cardinal, and Giles, 109.
NICHOLAS IV, Pope, a Franciscan, his letter of May 14, 1284, 171.
NICHOLAS OF PEPOLI, professor in the University of Bologna, 228; takes up the Franciscan mission in Bologna, 146.
Niccolo, Church of S., 64.
Ninety brothers volunteer for the German mission, 210.
NOTTIANO, n., 117.
Novitiate established 1220, 155; of one year required by Bull of HONORIUS III, 207.

Obedience, perfect, defined by ST. FRANCIS, 285-286; to the Rule first, 248.
Observances of St. Damian, 189-190.
Order to be reorganized, 1221, 207.
ORLANDO DEI CATTANI, 161-162; glad as Friars take possession, 1224, of La Verna, 292; verbal gift of La Verna, 168.
Ortis, life in, 96; the rest at, 96-97.
ORTLIEB OF STRASSBURGH, 87.
ORTOLANA, 122, 124.
Orvieto, faction in, 86.
Ostia, CARDINAL HUGOLIN of, 165; also see HUGOLIN.
OTTO OF AQUASPARTA and the Portiuncula indulgence, 170.
OTTO, Brother, sent to Morocco, 1219, 197.
OTTO OF BRUNSWICK, FRANCIS' message to, passing through valley of Spoleto, September, 1209, 82-83.
Over-sanctification, 62.
Oxford, the Friars established there, November, 1224, 239.

PACIFICUS, B., does not play for ST. FRANCIS for fear of making a disturbance, 317; returns to French mission, 1219, 236; goes as a missionary to France, 1209, 196; and the Sun Song, 313-314; the vision of, 279.
PADUA, ST. ANTHONY OF, 212.
Papal commendation of May 29, 1220, 236.
Papal sanction refused Dominicans and Friars Minor, 187.
PARENTI, JOHANNES, 145-146, 228.
Paris, the Order in, 236.
PAUL OF PHERME, 124.
PAULINUS OF NOLA, 152.
PEPOLI, NICOLO DE, 146, 228.
Penitential Brothers, the Third Order, their life, 242.
"Penitents from Assisi," 81.
Perugians, danger of their capturing ST. FRANCIS in his last illness, 321.
PETER, B., sent to Morocco, 1219, 197.
PETER JOHN OLIVI, b. 1248; d. 1298, upholds authenticity of the Portiuncula indulgence, 172.
PETER OF STACIA, opposes ST. FRANCIS and opens a House of Study in Bologna. 226, 228, 230-231.
PETER VALDES, permission to preach given him by ALEXANDER III in 1179.

PHILIPP LUNGO, 76.
PHILIP, Brother, superior of the Clares, seeks bull of excommunication to protect them, 205.
PIETRO DEI CATTANI, 227, 228, 276; sails with Crusaders, 1219, 202; d. March 10, 1221, 208.
PIETRO DI BERNARDONE, 40-41, 43; captures and imprisons his son, 44; tries the civil law against his son, 45.
PEREGRINE of Fallerone, B., conversion of, n., 235.
Poenitentium Collegia, 242.
Poggio Bustone, cave near, 72.
"Poor of Christ," 106.
"Poor men from Lyons," 87.
Portiuncula, 33; ST. FRANCIS weeps at, 42; ST. FRANCIS begins its restoration, 54; called Santa Maria degli Angeli, St. Mary of the Angels, 54; ST. MATTHEW'S mass in, 56; the first four Friars in, 67; ST. FRANCIS' sermon to the first six disciples in the forest near, 68-69; its origin and name, 105; owned by Benedictines, 105, 57b; at the present time, 105; and the Cameldolites, 105; abandoned, 1075, 105; ancient picture in, 105; visions at, 168; "God's house and the gate of Heaven," 331; legend of Fru Pica in, 105; life of the Friars in, 105-106; a vision of, 121; new brothers received at, about 1214, 163; Brothers invested with the habit there, 175; meetings at, on specified dates, 175-176; the original convent at, 218; its Rule, 219-220; ST. FRANCIS at, 1224, 306.
Portiuncula indulgence, authenticity upheld by PETER JOHN OLIVI in a pamphlet, 172; first known late in the thirteenth century, 172; HERIBERT HOLZAPFEL and the, 173-174; legends of, 167-168; not mentioned in the *Speculum Perfectionis*, 174; the stricter party upholds it, 170-171; testimony of October 31, 1277, 169, 170, 172; theory of, 172-173.
Poverty, evangelical, 91-92; impaired by PETER STACIA, 231; of older Orders, 92; ST. CLARA'S privilege of, 190-191; ST. FRANCIS' new conception of, 92.
Preaching, early, 67-68; by laymen, 83.
Priest, first, in the Order, 65.

"Prisons" on Monte Subasio, 77.
Provinces, division of, 1223, n., 227; or mission-districts, 176, 182.

RAINER, Prior of St. Michael, 203.
RAYNALD, Cardinal, later Pope ALEXANDER IV, visits San Damiano, 138.
RAYNER OF AREZZO and the Portiuncula indulgence, 169.
Regula Prima, 214, 220-225.
RENAN, ERNEST, and Franciscanism, 121.
Restoration of Roman Senate, 1143, 86.
RICERIUS, Brother, 102-103.
RICETIUS from Muccia, B., conversion of, n., 235.
Rieti, valley of, 71-72, 265; ST. FRANCIS' journey to, 316-317.
Ritiri and *eremi*, 72, 218.
Rivo Torto, life of early disciples there, 77-81, 82, 97, 101.
Robbers on Monte Casale converted, 156-157.
ROBERT OF ARBRISSEL, 89.
ROGER OF TODI, B., characterized by ST. FRANCIS, 283.
RUFINO, B., 106, 158; his abstraction in prayer, 111; characterized by ST. FRANCIS, 282; choice of life, 145; humiliation of, 158; his origin, 111; and MASSEO, 281; and ST. CLARA, 125; and ST. FRANCIS, 281-282; sanctified while living, 282; temptations, 280-282; test of his humility and obedience, 158.
RUFINUS, SAINT, 9.
Rule, additions to the fundamental, 222; the first, 77-80, 213-214; the final, fears excited about, 252; for Hermitages, 219; HUGOLIN'S cooperation with ST. FRANCIS in final, 247; of the Clares, 189; Clares', approved by Pope, 130-131; to be obeyed *litteraliter*, 248; for Portiuncula, special, 219-220; ratification of early, 94; the, reduced in strictness, 251-252; of Rivo Torto, 220, 222; of San Damiano, 185; of Third Order, First, lost, 244; of 1210, 219; of 1221, material for, 221; final, accepted November 29, 1222, 234; much abbreviated as accepted by the Pentecost chapter of 1223, 125, 254-256; ratified by HONORIUS III, November 29, 1223, 226; of 1228, for Third Order, discovered by SABATIER, 244-246.

INDEX

SABBATINO, 67

ST. AGNES, 123; becomes a nun, 128; her uncle Monaldo attempts to remove her from the convent by violence, 128-129; her visit to the dying ST. CLARA, 139; and the Rule of the Order of Clares, 190.

ST. ANTHONY OF PADUA in Forli, about 1222, 212, 234; leaves Bologna, 1224, to go to Montpellier, 234; permission given him to teach theology, 233-234.

ST. BRIDGET on forgiveness of ST. FRANCIS' sins, n., 75.

ST. CLARA, her family and family tree, 122, 125; authorities for her biography, 122-123; FAVORINI SCIFI, Count of Sasso Rosso, her father, 122; ORTOLANA FIUMI of Sterpeto, her mother, 122; her four sisters and brother, 122-123; origin of name of CLARA, 123; ORTOLANA'S pilgrimages, 123; first suitor when fifteen years old, 124; hears ST. FRANCIS preach in San Rufino and in San Giorgio, Assisi, in Lent, 1212, 124-125; ST. FRANCIS becomes her spiritual guide, 125; ST. FRANCIS' advice to her, 125; RUFINO and SILVESTER, BB., assist her, 125; leaves the world, Palm Sunday, March 18, 1212, 126; BONA GUELFUCCI accompanies her when she visits ST. FRANCIS and when she leaves her home, 125, 127; the flight from home, 126; reception by the Franciscans in Santa Maria degli Angeli after her flight from home, 126; BISHOP GUIDO carries an olive branch to her on Palm Sunday, 1212, 126; puts on the habit, 127; taken to Benedictine Sisters of St. Pauls, Isola Romanesca, 127-128; transferred to convent of Sant' Angelo in Panso, 128; the Camaldolites of Monte Subasio give San Damiano for the Clares, 129; her sister BEATRICE and mother ORTOLANA join ST. CLARA, 129; a forma vivendi written for the Clares by ST. FRANCIS, 130; INNOCENT III approves the Rule of the Clares, 130; Abbess of San Damiano, 1215, 130; the privilegium paupertatis, 130-131; life of the sisters in San Damiano, 130; GREGORY IX withdraws his prohibition of preaching by Franciscans in San Damiano, 133; ST. CLARA and another sister get answer in prayer for guidance of ST. FRANCIS, 149; GREGORY IX's vain attempts to dissuade her from poverty, 136-137; INNOCENT IV, 138-139; INNOCENT IV ratifies the privilege of poverty two days before her death, 190, 191; her final Rule and privilege of poverty, 140-141; CARDINAL RAYNALD gives her the sacrament, 138; INNOCENT IV visits her when dying, 139; ST. AGNES, her sister, visits her when dying, 139; Brothers LEO, ANGELO, and JUNIPER visit her when dying, 139; JUNIPER'S "news from GOD," 139; her dying ejaculations, 139; washing the Sisters' feet, 131; cares for sick in San Damiano, 131; her industry and humility, 131, 132; her religious life and devotion to prayer and meditation, 131-132; the feast with the Franciscans in Santa Maria degli Angeli, 134-135; provides a wattle hut for ST. FRANCIS, 308; ST. FRANCIS recites the Miserere in San Damiano, 133; ST. FRANCIS withdraws from visiting San Damiano, 133; ST. FRANCIS says farewell to her and her Sisters, summer, 1225, 316; death message of ST. FRANCIS to her and the Sisters, 137; her last sight of ST. FRANCIS, 137; protects San Damiano from FREDERIC II's soldiers, 135-136; her garden, 140-141; her death in her sixtieth year, 137; the Blessed Virgin at her death-bed, 140; soul taken to heaven, 140.

ST. CYRIL, 105.

St. Denis, Friars in, 236.

ST. DOMINIC first meets ST. FRANCIS in Rome about 1217, 194; and the Lateran Council of 1217, 187; at the Pentecost Chapter of 1218, 187; proposes to ST. FRANCIS to join the two Orders, winter of 1220-1221, 194; his second meeting with ST. FRANCIS, 195.

ST. FRANCIS OF ASSISI. Biography: Origin and family, 8-9; Fru Pica and Portiuncula, 105; birth and baptism (September 26?) 1182, 8-11; stable in Assisi his birthplace, 10; baptized JOHN, changed to FRANCIS by his father, 11; business, skill in, 12; extravagance, 15; French and Latin, knowledge of, 12,

30–31; imprisonment of 1202–1203, 19–20; his illness, 1204, 3–7; feels that his youth is gone, 6; starts for the war, 23; returns, 24; the last festival, 1205, 25–26; vision at Spoleto, 24; again visited by the Lord, 1205, 25; a distinguished person his friend after his conversion, 27; gives church goods to poor priests, 29; goes to Rome about 1205, 30; throws a handful of coins into the Apostles tomb at Rome, 30; begging at St. Peter's Rome, 30–31; lepers, natural abhorrence of, 33–34; the voice from the Cross, 1207, 38; sells horse and cloth from his father's store for the benefit of St. Damiano, 39; starts to repair St. Damiano's chapel, 38–39; the cave near San Damiano, 40; he enters Assisi, April, 1207, followed by a mob, 43; BERNARDONE'S rage on his son's return from the cave near San Damiano, 44; confinement in *carcer* by father, 44; BERNARDONE attempts to use the law against his son, 45; refuses to appear in his father's lawsuit, 45; trial before the Bishop of Assisi, 45–47; disowns his father, 46; forsakes the world, April, 1207, 47; the first cowl, 47; robbers on Monte Subasio, 48–49; ANGELO, his brother, persecutes him, 52; ALBERT, the beggar, as his father, 52; a public beggar, 51–52; begging oil for the sanctuary camp, 53; St. Matthew's mass, 1209, opens the messagebook in S. Nicolo, Assisi, as a guide to action, 64; Mark Ancona and Rieti, trip to, 1209, 67; the forgiveness of his sins in the cave at Poggio Bustone, 74; probably pacified troubles in Assisi, 1210, 99; starts for Rome, summer, 1210, 84; Rome decides as to whether his order is orthodox,, 1210, 88; interviews with POPE INNOCENT III, 1210, 90–91; INNOCENT III's dream, 1210, 92–93; INNOCENT III accepts him, 1210, 94; return from Rome, 1210, 95–97; passes Lent of 1211 on an Island, 147; missionary journey of, 1211–1212, 145–146; pacifies troubles in Perugia, 1211–1212, 145; third journey to Rome, 1212, 151; INNOCENT III blesses his mission to the Saracens, 152; unsuccessful start for the Orient, 1212, 153; a stowaway on a ship to Italy, 1212, 153; stranded in a ship upon the coast of Slavonia, 1212, 153; spends winter 1212–1213 in Sarteano near Chiusi, 147; visit to Rome, 1213, 151; founds a church, 1213, 54; at Sasso Feltrio, 1213, 159; journey of 1213 to Romagna, 159; travels through Spain to go to Morocco but falls sick about 1213–1214, 163; he helps renovate Santa Maria del Vescovado in Assisi, 1216, 54; relations with Cardinals, 1216, 214; apprehensions as to his reception at the Pentecost Chapter of 1217, 182; preaches extensive missions at the Pentecost Chapter of 1217, 182; visits Rome probably in winter 1217–1218, 193; interview with the new Pope, HONORIUS III, probably 1217–1218, 195; preaches to the Brothers at the Pentecost Chapter of 1218, 195; preaches to the Brothers and to the Morocco missionaries at the Pentecost meeting of 1219, 197–198; appoints MATTHEW OF NARNI his vicar in Portiuncula, 1219, 201; starts for the Holy Land with PIETRO DEI CATTANI, 1219, 201, 202; lands at St. Jean d'Arc, July, 1219, 202; meets Saracen CONRAD, 1219, 203–204; bad news from Italy brought to him in the Holy Land, 1219, 205; returns from Holy Land, 1219, with several Brothers, 206; seeks HUGOLIN on return from Holy Land, 1219, 206; has Egyptian eye sickness, 208; resigns as Head of the Order, St. Michael's day, 1220, 208; asks for missionaries for Germany at the Chapter of Mats (1220 or 1221), 210; German mission of 1220 or 1221, twelve priests and thirteen laybrothers go on, 210; sermon in Bologna, August 15, 1222, 234–235; fails in health after the Pentecost Chapter of 1223, 251–252; his last visit to Rome, 1223, 257; goes North from Rome, 1223, 260; the crib and sermon at Greccio, Christmas, 1223, 261–262; Poggio Bustone, advent near, 1223 or 1224, 273; letter to the Brethren at the Pentecost Chapter of 1224, 269–270; meets ORLANDO DEI CATTANI, 1224, 292–293; fasting in 1224, 291; his health improves, 1224, 291; the final retreat before death, 293; cures a woman of hysterics, 1224, 305; returns to Portiuncula late in 1224, 306; the night on the Appennines, November, 1224, 305; trip to La Verna, 1224, 292; begs for the stigmata, 298-299; stigmatization, September 14, 1224, 298-300; leaves Mount Alverna, September 30, 1224, 304; his eye-sickness worse, 1225, 308; leaves San Damiano, summer, 1225, 316; journey to Rieti, 1225, 316-317; physician's efforts to cure his eyes, 318; dropsy attacks him, 321; in Siena, 1225, 319; at Celle, 1225, 321; leaves Rieti for hermitage of St. Eleutherio, winter, 1225, 318; his last will, 316; crowds come to see him at San Fabiano, 317; hot cauterizing irons cause no pain, 318; appeases dispute between the Podesta and Bishop of Assisi, 1226, 322-323; refuses to say the last farewell to the Poor Clares, 324; apologizes for trouble he occasions the Brethren in his last hours, 328; his last view of Assisi before entering the gate to die there, 329; he blesses Assisi when dying, 329; he is carried to Portiuncula, 329; his last blessing of the Order, 331; he wishes to die in utter poverty, 331; his death October 3, 1226, 333; the funeral procession, 334.

The Friars: BERNARD OF QUINTAVALLE tests his sincerity, 63; hides his holiness from BERNARD OF QUINTAVALLE, 63; Knights of the Round Table, 67, 233; calls on ANGELO TANCREDI to join the Order, 76; "et sint minores," origin of Friars Minor, 100; the hungry Brother, he eats with him, 103; warns Brothers against excessive mortifications, 103; his kindness to Brothers, 103-104; he gathers grapes for a sick Brother, 104; Brother MASSEO begging gets more than ST. FRANCIS, 110; exercises Brother MASSEO in humility, 111; he makes Brother MASSEO find what city they are to go to, 110; the newer generation of Franciscans staid with him, 110; "I wish we had a whole grove of such juniper trees," 111; imitated by Brother JOHN, the simple, 117; saying part-prayers with Brother LEO, 117-119; describes the perfect happiness to Brother LEO, 119-121; meets ANGELUS and ALBERT in Pisa, 146; goes out to preach with Brothers MASSEO and ANGELO, 149; Brother MASSEO sent to seek advice as to hermit life, 149; seeks advice as to hermit life from Brother SILVESTER and ST. CLARA, 149; SILVESTER gets answer in prayer for guidance of ST. FRANCIS, 149; Verse King, the, 154; he humiliates RUFINO and AGNOLO, 158; promises paradise to AGNOLO, 158; forbids Brothers to seek written privileges from the CURIA, 168; said to have applied for Portiuncula indulgence with Brother MASSEO, 167; wishes to have Brothers with him, 175; attachment to ELIAS OF CORTONA, 183; "My Brothers are *minores*, let them not become *majores*," 194; ELIAS OF CORTONA, vicar of the Order, 208; "The Brother" his title, 210; wishes Brothers to carry copies of his admonitions with them, 221; his and CÆSARIUS OF SPEIER'S work, 223-225; opponents led by ELIAS OF CORTONA, 226-227; PETER STACIA and his house of study, 230-231; permission to teach theology given to ST. ANTHONY OF PADUA, 233-234; ELIAS and the Final Rule, 248; sinning Brothers, 249-251; assisted by CÆSARIUS OF SPEIER in writing his circular letters, 271; letter to Brother LEO, 271; Brother BERNARD OF QUINTAVALLE 280; sends Brother MASSEO to help Brother RUFINO, 281-282; he characterizes different Brothers, 282-283; blesses the Spanish Friars, 283; reads the thoughts of Brother LEONARD, 284; makes Brother BERNARD stamp upon his mouth, 285; Brother ELIAS begs him to have his eyes treated, 316; has his blessing of the Order written down by Brother BENEDICT, 321; asks Brothers ANGELO and LEO to be with him as he is dying, 324; "I bless them as much as I can, and more than I can," 331; asks the Brothers to strew ashes over him, 332; Brothers sing the Sun-Song, 332.

Association Outside the Order: HUGOLIN, CARDINAL, comes to his aid, 180; sees the future Pope in CARDINAL HUGOLIN, 181; meets CAR-

DINAL HUGOLIN in Florence, 1217, 183; CARDINAL HUGOLIN his spiritual father, 183–184; casts himself at HUGOLIN'S feet and begs him to be the protector of the Brotherhood, 184; asks Pope to appoint CARDINAL HUGOLIN protector of the Order, 193–194; part he took with HUGOLIN in the Rule of the Third Order, 244–247; begs his bread when CARDINAL HUGOLIN'S guest, 259; JOHN OF COLONNA, his advocate at Rome, 92; describes his plans to CARDINAL JOHN of St. Paul, 90; ST. DOMINIC'S admiration for him, 194; ST. DOMINIC, meetings of, 194–195; meets JACOPA DE SETTESOLI in Rome, 1212, 152; Almond cream prepared for him by Brother JACOBA, 257; visits Brother JACOBA, 257; gives a tame lamb to Brother JACOBA, 258; last visit of JACOPA DE SETTESOLI, 330.

Sermons, Prayers and Writings: an early laud, 69; his prayer of the Cross, 69; his description of life in the early days of the Order, 78; he writes a *forma vivendi* for the Clares, 130; begins to prepare a New Rule about 1221, with CÆSARIUS OF SPEIER, 208; his way of writing his Rule, 217–218; on pious living in a hermitage, 218–219; defends his Rule, 231–232; at Fonte Colombo to finish the Rule of the Order, 252; appeals to and is answered by the Lord at Fonte Colombo as to the Rule, 253; works on new writings to supplement the Rule as approved, 265; his letters described by BOEHMER, 267; last writings, 267, 269–272; the dying sinner described, 268–269; letter of 1223 to Brother LEO, 276–272; ideal general of the Order, 274; composes the Sun Song, 309–313; describes the Franciscan convent, 320; sends ST. CLARA his last blessing in writing, 324; his Testament, 325–328; his prayer before the crucifix in San Damiano, 38; his early sermons, 67–68; sermon to the first six disciples, 68–69; preaches in Cathedral of Assisi, 98; would not preach in San Damiano, 133–134; preaching to the birds, 149–150; preaching at Montefeltro, 159; preaches in Ascoli and wins thirty recruits for the Brotherhood, 153;

his quality of preaching, 154–155; preaching and admonitions at Chapter meetings, 176, 177–178; preaches to crusaders, 203; before the Soldan, 204; preaches at the Chapter of Mats, 209–210; his admonitions, 214–217; effect of his sermons in Bologna, 234–235.

Nature and Animals: the swallows in Alviano, 151, 240; his feeling for lambs, 257–258; his tame lamb at Portiuncula, 258; birds welcome him to Mount Alverna, 292; his love of nature, 309–313; love of animals and birds, 311; the sheep near Siena, 312; the fish of Lake Rieti, 312; fire, 312; the sun, 312; the wild rabbit at Greccio, 312; the pheasant, 312; the hare of Lake Thrasimene, 312; the cicada, 312; larks, their last farewell, 333.

St. Germain des Prés and the Friars, 236.
ST. GREGORY, 152.
ST. MICHAEL, ST. FRANCIS' devotion to, 291.
St. Pauls, Benedictine sisters of, and ST. CLARA, 127.
St. Peter, ST. FRANCIS starts to repair it, 53.
SALVATOR VITALIS' *Paradisus Seraphicus*, 105.
Salzburg Brothers and CÆSARIUS OF SPEIER, 211–212.
SANCIA, sister of KING ALFONSO gives Friars Minor a chapel in Alenquer, Portugal, 198.
San Damiano, its Byzantine crucifix, 37; care of sick in, 131; the cave near, 40; closure in, about 1219, 133; its present aspect, 140–141; a gift to the Clares from the Camaldolites, 129; rebuilding of, 50–51; ST. FRANCIS' first days there, 40; ST. FRANCIS leaves it, summer, 1225, 316; ST. FRANCIS sells horse and cloth from his father's store for its benefit, 39; ST. FRANCIS supplies money for oil for its sanctuary lamp, 39; special Rule for, 185; the voice from the crucifix, 38.
San Fabiano, vintage of the priest of, 316–317.
San Rufino, church of, 62–63.
San Salvatore degli Pareti, 77.
San Severino cloister, 154.
Sant' Angelo of Panso, ST. CLARA and, 128.

INDEX

Santa Maria degli Angeli, in Assisi, St. CLARA received into religion there, 134-135; the name of Portiuncula, 54.
Santa Maria della Rocca, 49, 156.
Santa Maria del Vescovado restored, 1216, 54.
Seminary in Paris, 236.
Septizonium of Septimus Severus, 152.
Sermon to the birds, the, 149-150.
Seville, preaching in, 199.
SILVESTER, B., choice of life, 145; complains of price paid him for stone for S. Damiano, 65; conversion, 65; his dream, 97-98; dream of St. FRANCIS, 298; longed to be alone, 106; "no one can serve two masters," 65; and St. CLARA, 123.
Sinner, the dying, described by St. FRANCIS, 268-269.
Sinning Brothers, how to treat, 249-250.
Speculum perfectionis written 1318, 174.
STEPHEN, the lay-brother, 205.
Sun Song, the, 313-315; additional verses of the, 322, 323.

Terni, Bishop of, and St. FRANCIS, 147.
Testament of St. FRANCIS, 325-328.
Third Order described by BERNARD A BESSA, 244; foundation of the, 240-246; need of, 179; origin, 240-242.
THOMAS OF CELANO, B., 70; the additions to the Rule, 215; describes St. FRANCIS and his prayers, 286; enters the Order about 1214, 163; goes on the German mission, 1220 or 1221, 210; his picture of the life at Rivo Torto, 101; and St. FRANCIS' early preaching, 98; St. FRANCIS'

first biographer, 12; and the twenty-eight admonitions, 217; his view of acquaintance of St. FRANCIS and CARDINAL HUGOLIN, 183.
THOMAS OF SPALATO, his account of St. FRANCIS' preaching in Bologna, 234-235.
TODI, JACOPONE DE, 238.
Tunis, mission to, 197.
Tusculum, Bishop of, and GILES, 109.

Universities founded in the thirteenth century, 230.
URRACA, QUEEN OF PORTUGAL, gives the Friars Minor a convent near Coimbra, 198-199; the Morocco Martyrs, 200.
URSLINGEN, WERNER OF, 100.

VAGNOTELLI, GUIDO, 145.
VALDES, PETER, 87-88; his authorization to preach, 83; St. FRANCIS, 89.
Velletri, CARDINAL HUGOLIN, bishop of, 180.
VICTORINUS, ST., 9.
Viri literati, 155-156.
VITALE, B., falls sick in Arragon, 1219, 198.

Washing of feet at Pentecost Chapter of 1218, 194-195.
Washing the impatient leper, 306-307.
WADDING'S story of the swineherd, 145-146.
WALTER III OF BRIENNE, 22.
WERNER OF URSLINGEN, 100.
WILLIAM, the first English friar, 152.
Wolf of Gubbio, 235, 410.

ZACHARIAS joins the Order, 151-152.

INDEX TO APPENDIX

Actus beati Francisci (Fioretti), 356.
Actus beati Francisci et Sociorum ejus, 383-384, 393-395.
Actus beati Francisci in Valle Reatina, 394.
AFFO, PATER IRENEO, 343.
ALBERT OF PISA, B., 352.
ALBERT OF STUDE, his annals, 401.
ALVISI, editor of *Commercium beati Francisci*..., 394.
"Ancient Brothers," the, *antiqui fratres*, 388.
ANGELO CLARENO, B., and Brother LEO's work, 356; his chronicle, 387; his letter of defence to Pope JOHN XXII, 390, 399; names the four biographers of ST. FRANCIS, 387; and the Three Brothers' legend, 387-388; his writings, 398-400.
ANGELO TANCREDI, B., 394.
Annales Minorum, 401-402.
Anonymus Perusinus (Anonymous Perugian), 367-368.
Antiquitates franciscanae, 394-395.
ARNOLD OF SERRANO, B., possibly author of the chronicles of the twenty-four generals..., 397; and GREGORY XI, 397; and the *Vita Secunda*, 370.
Arbor vitæ crucifixæ of HUBERT OF CASALE, 388.
Author of the *Legenda Antiqua* anonymous, 392.

BALDWIN OF BRANDENBURGH, 395.
BARTHOLOMEW OF PISA, his *Conformitates*, 351, 395; text of the laud written for LEO, 349; and the *Vita Secunda*, 375.
BERNARD OF BESSA, author of *De laudibus S. Francisci*, 381; a compiler, 381; ST. BONAVENTURE's secretary, 381.
Biographers, 351-395.
BOLLANDISTS' "Second biography of ST. FRANCIS," 354.
BOEHMER, *Analekten zur Geschichte* etc., 403-404.
Book of Lessons from Toulouse, 355.

CÆSARIUS OF SPEIER, B., 352.
Catalogue of the first twenty-four generals of the Order, 396-397.
Catalogus sanctorum, 401.
CANTIUS, JOHN, 355.
CIVEZZA MARCELLINO DA, B., 363.
Chapter of Geneva, 1244, 357; of Narbonne, 1260, 378; of Padua, 1277, invited new researches for the life of ST. FRANCIS, 381; of Pisa, 1263, and the destruction of the early legends, 380-381.
CHIUSI's Letter of Donation, 401.
Chronica XXIV generalium, 382, 397.
Chronicles of the (first) twenty-four generals of the Order, 397.
Chronicon breve.
Civezza's, da, reconstruction of the Three Brothers' Legend, 365.
Collaborators in the Three Brothers' Legend, 357.
Collections of "Words" of the early Friars, 368.
Commercium beati Francisci cum domina paupertate, 394.
Conformitates, 395.
CONRAD OF OFFIDA, B., 393-394; friend and informant of HUBERT OF CASALE, 388; and JOHN OF PARMA, 388.
CRESCENTIUS OF JESI, 357; and the *Vita Secunda*, 368-369.

D'ALENÇON, EDOUARD, and the *Vita Metrica*, 355; his editorial work, 394, 404.
DANTE and the *Commercium beati Francisci*..., 394.
De laudibus Sancti Francisci, 381.
Destruction of the early legends, 380-381.
Dicta fratris Leonis, 397.
Die Wundmale des hl. Franz von Assisi, 408.
DOMENICHELLI, TEOFILO, B., 363; his reconstruction of the Three Brothers' Legend, 365.

ECCLESTON, THOMAS, B., and his chronicle, 343, 396.

EHRLE, 344; ANGELO OF CLARENO'S *Historia septem tribulationum*, etc., 399, 400.
ELIAS OF CORTONA, 345; his letter to GREGORY and the French Brothers, 408-409.
Epistola excusatoria of ANGELO CLARENO, 399.
EUBEL and GLASSBERGER'S Chronicle, 398; and JOHN OF KOMOROWO'S Works, 398.

FABIAN OF HUNGARY, B., his *Speculum vitæ beati Francisci et sociorum ejus*, 394-395.
FALOCI-PULIGNANI'S text of the laud written for LEO, n., 349; the Three Brothers' Legend, 366.
Fioretti, the translation or development of the *Actus beati Francisci* ..., 394.
FRANCESCO BARTHOLI, B., on the Portiuncula Indulgence, 394.
Francisco d'Assisi e la sua legenda, 406.
Frans von Assisi und die Anfänge der Kunst der Renaissance in Italien, 406-408.

Gesta Dei per francos, 401.
GILES, B., 394; at Monte Ripido, 367; his death, 368.
GLASSBERGER'S Chronicle, 398; and JULIAN OF SPEIER'S Legend, 354.
GONZALVO OF BALBOA, general of the Order, 391.
GÖTZ accepts ST. FRANCIS' letter to ST. ANTHONY OF PADUA, 349; and *Anonymus Perusinus*, 368; and HUBERT OF CASALE, 390; and the *Speculum beati Francisci* ..., 387; and the *Vita prima*, 353; and the *Vita secunda*, 371.
GREGORY IX orders THOMAS OF CELANO to write a life of ST. FRANCIS, 352; the Testament, 350-351; and Brother ARNOLD OF SERRANO, 397.
Gubbio, the wolf of, 410.

HENRY OF PISA, author of the *Vita metrica*, 355; SALIMBENE, 355.
Historia occidentalis, 401; *septem tribulationum ordinis minorum*, 400.
Histories of the Order, 395-400.
HUBERT OF CASALE, Avignon, 388-390.
HUGOLIN OF MONTE GIORGO, B., 394.
HUGOLIN'S Register, 400.

ILLUMINATO, B., and ST. BONAVENTURE'S Legend, 379.

JACOB OF MASSA, B., 394.
JACOB ODDI, B., n., 398.
JACOB OF VARAGGIO and his Golden Legend, 401.
JACOPONE DA TODI, 343.
JOHN XXII and the "Zealous" division of the Order, 390.
JOHN OF CEPERANO, 354-355.
JOHN OF KOMOROWO, his chronicle, 397-398; his *Memoriale ordinis fratium minorum*, 398.
JOHN OF PARMA, B., and CONRAD OF OFFIDA, B., 388; possibly author of *commercium beati Francisci* ..., 394; and the *Vita secunda*, 372-373.
JOHN PECKHAM, B., Archbishop of Canterbury, 381.
JOHN OF LA VERNA, B., 394.
JORDANUS OF GIANO'S, B., Chronicle, 370, 395-396.
JULIAN OF SPEIER, B., biographical notes of, 354; his legend, 354; his rhymed Office, 354-355.

KARL HAMPE, his criticism and interpretation of ELIAS OF CORTONA'S letter to GREGORY and the French Brothers, 409; *Die Wundmale des hl. Frans von Assisi*, 408.
KARL HASE'S biography of ST. FRANCIS, 402.

Legenda Antiqua, 356, 391-393.
Legenda trium sociorum, 356-366.
Legend by the Anonymous Perugian, 367-368.
LEMMENS' publication of S. ISIDORE M.S. of pieces by Brother LEO, 389; and the Three Brothers' Legend, 366.
LEO, B., his associations, 382-383; his Leaves of Memory, 383; his relation to the *Speculum perfectionis*, *Legenda antiqua* and *Actus*, 383-384; his schedules or rolls, 383, 387; his work, 356.
Letter to CRESCENCIUS accompanying the Three Brothers' Legend, text and discussion, 357-358.
Liber epistolarum beati Angeli de Clareno, 399.
LITTLE, A. G., and the decree of destruction of legends, 405-406.
Liturgical Legends, 355.

INDEX 427

MALAN, CHAVING DE, his *Vie de S. François d'Assise*, 402.
MANDACHS, C., 407.
MARIANO, the Florentine Chronicler, 340; and the Three Brothers' Legend, 361.
MATTHEW OF PARIS, his *Historia major*, 401.
Memoriale ordinis fratrum minorum, 398.
MICHAEL OF CESENA, General of the Order, 391, 393; ordered the "Old Legend" to be read aloud in convents, 391.
MICHAEL EM., on Salimbene's Chronicle, 396.
MINOCHI, SALVATORE, his *Nuova fonte biographica*, 405; his MS., of the *Speculum beati Francisci* . . ., 386.
MONNIER, LE, and LEON, *Histoire de S. François d'Assise*, 402.
MÜLLER, CARL, *Die Anfänge des Minoritenordens* . . ., 402; and JORDANUS OF GIANO's Chronicle, 397.
MUZIO ACHILLEI and the Three Brothers' Legend, 364.

NICOLO PAPINI, 402.
Notizie sicure sopra s. Francesco, PAPINI'S, 402.

ODDI'S, JACOB, Italian Chronicle, 398.
Officium passionis Domini, 349.
OZANAM, his *Les poètes Franciscains d'Italie*, 402.

Papal Bulls as sources for the Life of ST. FRANCIS, 400.
PAPEBROCK and the Anonymous Perugian, 367.
PETER JOHN OLIVI, B., and Brother LEO, 387.
PIETRO DE NADELI, his *Catalogus Sanctorum*, 401.
PILGRIM OF BOLOGNA, B., 397.

QUARACCHI edition of ST. FRANCIS' writings, 340-341.

ROSEDALE, FRANCIS OF ASSISI, according to, 404-405.

SABATIER, PAUL, and the *Actus beati Francisci* . . ., 394; and *Angelo* CLARENO, 399; and BERNARD OF BESSA, 381; his edition of the *Speculum perfectionis*, 364; and the

MAZARIN M.S., of the *Speculum beati Francisci* . . ., 363, 384-387; his rôle in Franciscan research, 339; and the *Speculum Vitæ S: Francisci*, 362-363; his theories, 339; and the Three Brothers' Legend, 362, 384-387; *Vie de S. François d'Assise*, 402; the *Vita secunda*, 371.
ST. ANTHONY OF FLORENCE, 401.
ST. BONAVENTURE's amplification of, early legends, 379; his book of 1263 and the Three Brothers' Legend, 360; date of birth, 378; history and origin of his Legend, 378-381.
ST. FRANCIS OF ASSISI and BENEDICT OF PRATO, 351; blessing of Brother LEO, described with the text, 344, 345-349; *Forma vivendi* of the Clares, 350; GÖTZ, WALTER, and the blessing of Brother LEO, 348; GÖTZ and the Testament, 350; GÖTZ and the Three Brothers' Legend, 366; greeting to the Blessed Virgin, 344; HASSE, CARL, and the Testament, 350; JULIAN OF SPEIER and the Testament, 350; KRAUS, F. X., and the Blessing of Brother LEO, 348; *Laudes Domini*, 343, 344; *Laudes de Virtutibus*, 344; LEMPP accepts ST. FRANCIS' letter to ST. ANTHONY OF PADUA, 349; LEO's, B., note, 347; LEO preserves ST. FRANCIS' writing, 345; LEO, his secretary, 340; minor Italian songs not authentic, 343; ODDI, JACOB, his text of the laud written for LEO, 349; praise songs or lauds, 342; both preacher and writer, 340; prose writings, 349-351; Rules of the Orders, 350; SABATIER, PAUL, and the Blessing of Brother LEO, 348; SABATIER and ST. FRANCIS' letters, 349-350; SABATIER and the Testament, 350, 351; SABATIER, his view of ST. FRANCIS' letter to ST. ANTHONY OF PADUA, 349; ST. CLARA and the Clares, testamentary notes for, 351; *Salutatio virtutum*, 344; song about creatures, 342-343; "Sun Song," the, 342-343; the Testament, 350-351; "The three Words," n., 351; THOMAS OF CELANO and the Testament, 350; *Ultima Voluntas* to the Clares, 350; WADDING, 1619, sees the "Blessing of Brother LEO," 345; "Words of St. Francis," 340; his writings, 340.
SALIMBENE'S, B., chronicle, 396; and

Lightning Source UK Ltd.
Milton Keynes UK
25 March 2011
169889UK00001B/18/P